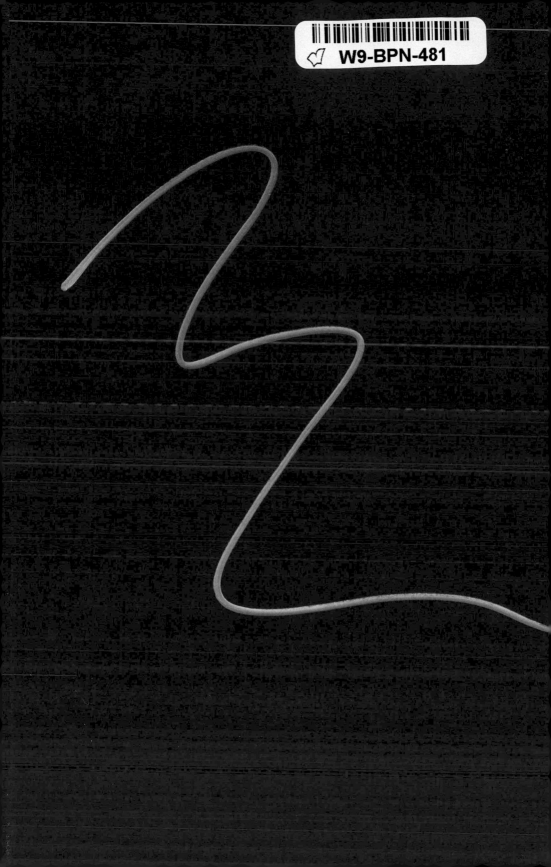

FEMOCRATIC ADMINISTRATION

Gender, Governance, and Democracy in Ontario

Femocratic Administration

Gender, Governance, and Democracy in Ontario

TAMMY FINDLAY

UNIVERSITY OF TORONTO PRESS
Toronto   Buffalo   London

ISBN 978-1-4426-4896-8

Printed on acid-free, 100% post-consumer recycled paper
with vegetable-based inks.

Publication cataloguing information is available from Library and
Archives Canada.

University of Toronto Press acknowledges the financial assistance to its
publishing program of the Canada Council for the Arts and the
Ontario Arts Council, an agency of the Government of Ontario.

 Canada Council **Conseil des Arts**
for the Arts **du Canada**

 ONTARIO ARTS COUNCIL
CONSEIL DES ARTS DE L'ONTARIO
an Ontario government agency
un organisme du gouvernement de l'Ontario

University of Toronto Press acknowledges the financial support of the
Government of Canada through the Canada Book Fund for its
publishing activities.

Contents

Acknowledgments vii

Abbreviations ix

Introduction: Gender, Governance, and Democracy in Ontario 3

1 A Feminist Political Economy of Representation 23

2 Gender Regimes of Public Administration 62

3 Experiments with State Feminism in the Weberian
Gender Regime 105

4 Gendered Governance and the New Public
Management Regime 146

Conclusion: Building a Femocratic Administration 186

Notes 217

Bibliography 243

Index 271

Acknowledgments

This book began as a PhD dissertation at York University, where many people helped to bring this project to fruition. I would like to thank my doctoral supervisor Barbara Cameron for her incredible insight, patience, generosity, and mentorship. My internal and external committee members, Greg Albo, Ann Porter, Meg Luxton, Wenona Giles, and Pauline Rankin, also provided invaluable feedback, advice, and encouragement. Many friends provided academic and personal support during my time at York. I am especially grateful to Kimberly Earles, Maya Eichler, Dan Irving, and Hepzibah Muñoz-Martinez.

My professors at Huron University College, David Blair, Neil Bradford, and Paul Nesbitt-Larking, sparked my interest in political science as an undergraduate student. In fact, my first introduction to the world of femocrats was in a course paper I wrote for Dr Bradford many years ago. Later, when I returned to Huron as a sessional lecturer, I also got the chance to know them as wonderful colleagues, alongside those "across the road" in Women's Studies and Feminist Research at Western University, as well as at Trent University and the Labour College of Canada.

From 2008 to 2010, I held a post-doctoral research fellowship at the Human Early Learning Partnership (HELP) at the University of British Columbia, where I developed and revised this manuscript. I have been wholly enriched by working with the interdisciplinary team at HELP, especially my supervisor Paul Kershaw and childcare policy researcher and advocate extraordinaire Lynell Anderson. At HELP, I also had the immense opportunity to learn from the late Clyde Hertzman, an international leader in early childhood development, social justice, and community engagement.

Driven by a commitment to social change and the advancement of women, Mount Saint Vincent University (MSVU) has provided the ideal place to complete this book. I have found a welcoming, collegial, and multidisciplinary home in Political and Canadian Studies at MSVU, as well as in Public Policy Studies, Women's Studies, Cultural Studies, and the Alexa McDonough Institute for Women, Gender and Social Justice.

I owe much of my intellectual and political development to the amazing feminist activists and troublemakers that I've been able to collaborate with across Canada, including the Feminist Political Economy Reading Group and Network; the Graduate Political Science Student's Association (GPSSA) Women's Caucus; the CUPE 3903 TIWI Caucus; Western's Caucus on Women's Issues; the Women's Advisory Committee for the City of Vancouver; the Child Care Advocacy Association of Canada; the Canadian Centre for Policy Alternatives Nova Scotia; the Canadian Political Science Association (CPSA) Women's Caucus; the Canadian Research Institute for the Advancement of Women; the Halifax-Dartmouth & District Labour Council; and the Women's Action Alliance for Change Nova Scotia. They are true innovators of democratic theory and practice.

Critical financial assistance for study, research, and travel throughout this process was provided by the York Faculty of Graduate Studies; CUPE 3903; the York Graduate Student's Association; the York GPSSA; CUPE 3908 at Trent; the CPSA; the Association for Women's Rights in Development (AWID); the Ontario Graduate Scholarship; the Social Sciences and Humanities Research Council of Canada; the Human Early Learning Partnership; the International Collaboration on Complex Interventions; and the MSVU Aid to Scholarly Publications and Community Connections Grants.

Of course, this project would not have been possible without the participation of those who shared their valuable time and experiences with me candidly in the interviews. I truly appreciate their stories, analysis, and dedication to public service, and take full responsibility for the interpretation of results.

Daniel Quinlan, the Law and Politics Editor at the University of Toronto Press, kindly guided me through this journey with perseverance and enthusiasm, making it a pleasure to work with him. And the anonymous reviewers, who provided a carefully engaged reading of the manuscript, are owed considerable credit for fostering a greatly enhanced final product.

Finally, and most of all, thank you to my family – to my Mom and Dad, Judy and John Findlay, my sister Elisha, and Larry, Connie, Nicole, and Carol – for their love, understanding, and inspiration, and for often providing a much-needed distraction!

Mom and Dad, this book is dedicated to you, in honour of your lifetime of hard work and struggle.

Abbreviations

ACTEW	A Commitment to Training and Education for Women
ADM	Assistant Deputy Minister
CACSW	Canadian Advisory Council on the Status of Women
COMSOC	Ministry of Community and Social Services
CSF	Conseil du statut de la femme
DAWN	Disabled Women's Network
FI	Feminist Institutionalism
FPE	Feminist Political Economy
FPT	Federal-Provincial-Territorial
GBA	Gender-based Analysis
GLC	Greater London Council
IPR	Institutionalization of Power Relations
KWS	Keynesian Welfare State
NAC	National Action Committee on the Status of Women
NDP	New Democratic Party
NGO	Non-governmental Organization
NPM	New Public Management
OACWI	Ontario Advisory Council on Women's Issues
OPS	Ontario Public Service
OTAB	Ontario Training and Adjustment Board
OWD	Ontario Women's Directorate
PC	Progressive Conservative
POS	Political Opportunity Structure
RCSW	Royal Commission on the Status of Women
RRD	Race Relations Directorate
SUFA	Social Union Framework Agreement
SWC	Status of Women Canada
UI/EI	Unemployment Insurance/Employment Insurance

FEMOCRATIC ADMINISTRATION

Gender, Governance, and
Democracy in Ontario

Introduction: Gender, Governance, and Democracy in Ontario

Is that the state's business? Maybe it isn't. How does the state deal with power relations? (Interview 2).

What exactly *is* the state's business? For some, its "business" is taken literally, to transplant a corporate model into the public sector. In fact, since the 1980s, the idea that states should be more business-like has come to dominate political discourse. But for others, the state is not a business. Instead, the state's "business," or its responsibility, is much more profound: states are responsible for governance. And governance is about democracy, representation, citizenship, equality, and justice. So dealing with power relations *is* the state's business – it is *the* business. Which leaves us with the more difficult question: *How* does the state deal with power relations, and probably more importantly, how *should* the state deal with power relations? *Femocratic Administration* is my answer to this question.

What Is Femocratic Administration and Why Do We Need It?

The pressing need for the state to address unequal relations of power is evident all around us. The wage gap for women in Canada is still 71 per cent; 55.6 per cent for racialized women. Poverty is feminized and racialized. Women are more likely to be concentrated in precarious work, and constitute seven out of ten part-time workers. The labour market continues to be marked by sex segregation, with 67 per cent of women in female-dominated fields, and is segmented along racial lines, or "colour-coded" (Block and Galabuzi 2011). Unpaid domestic work persists as a gendered domain. Shocking rates of violence against women remain largely unchanged. Women's representation as members of legislatures and cabinets is stubbornly stalled at below 30 per cent in all but two provinces (women make up 36.4% of British Columbia's legislature and 32.8% in Quebec), and female cabinet ministers are often streamed into traditional portfolios or "pink collar ghettoes." And as already documented from previous iterations of austerity politics, new cuts to social assistance, disability and child benefits, health care, and education, and loss of public sector jobs, will disproportionately harm marginalized communities including women, Aboriginal peoples, racialized groups, and people with disabilities (Ontario Common Front 2012; Ferrao 2010; Block and Galabuzi 2011; Canadian Women's Foundation 2013).

With its commitment to fundamental social, economic, and political change, feminism provides us with valuable tools for understanding power relations. For many feminists, the pursuit of change has meant a particular interest in democracy and representation in the process of governance. Strangely, though, public administration has figured quite inconspicuously within feminist theory and practice. This book argues that state administration is crucial to the feminist transformational project.

For its part, public administration has remained largely unaffected by feminist analysis. In her challenge to the field, Stivers (1993) observed that "public administration theory appeared to be innocent of a feminist theoretical perspective" (viii).[1] Twenty years later, the same can be said of much of the mainstream literature, despite efforts by Stivers (1993), and others including Phillips, Little, and Goodine (1997), Agócs (1997), Bacchi (1999), Hutchinson and Mann (2004, 2006), and D'Agostino and Levine (2011) to introduce gender to public administration. Even efforts within critical public administration and democratic administration to challenge governance as usual rarely apply a gender lens. It is imperative that a serious engagement with feminism take place within the fields of public and democratic administration, which femocratic administration demands.

Democratic administration entails a reconfiguration of the relationship between state and society. It emerged as a critique of traditional Weberian bureaucracy based on hierarchy, secrecy, expertise, and neutrality. It is also a reply to neoliberalism, positing that only more democratic and participatory governance can challenge the growing inequality and polarization in Canada. As Isabella Bakker notes, one of the main threats of neoliberalism and globalization is that "such a sweeping homogenization and privileging of market forces over democratically organized decision making obscures the historically specific form of the state in different countries" (1999, 50). Thus, not only is democratic administration intended to challenge the forces of globalization and neoliberalism, it seeks to do so in a way that is suited to national specificities.[2]

There are many competing understandings and definitions of globalization. Most agree that it involves heightened interaction across national borders through some combination of free trade, regional trading blocs, capital mobility, international production networks, transnational corporations, international financial institutions (IFIs), international migration, and cultural diffusion (Yeates 1999; Brodie 1995a; Panitch 1994; McBride 2001; Cohen and McBride 2003; Evans, McBride, and Shields 2000).

The root of most disagreements is generally not what the signifiers of globalization are, but how one conceptualizes the role of the nation state within it (Yeates 1999).[3] I take up the perspective that globalization does not involve the superseding of states by transnational corporations and transnational governance structures. Instead, like those such as Brodie, Panitch, and McBride, I see globalization as a conscious pursuit by states, including (or especially) the Canadian state. My definition, strongly influenced by Cohen and McBride (2003), explicitly links globalization with neoliberalism. For them, "globalization represents a uniform system of thought and practice, based on a 'consensus' originating in Washington, that all nations and all people within nations throughout the world should root their decisions and actions in one type of [neoliberal] economic system" (1). Burke, Mooers, and Shields (2000) also stress that globalization is an "ideological process" of advancing a neoliberal policy agenda (15). Therefore, I define globalization as *the attempt at universalizing the norms and values of neoliberalism worldwide*. So what, then, is neoliberalism?

Neoliberalism is a repackaged version of classic liberalism[4] (Brodie 1995a; McBride 2001), which seeks to limit the state's reach into (and therefore democratic control over) the market,[5] and to prioritize individual over collective forms of action (McBride 2001, 14). While neoliberals purport to advance politically neutral values, the inherently political nature of neoliberalism is clear in its policy preferences. These preferences include lowering taxes, cutting social spending, privatization, deregulation, downsizing, contracting out, weakening the power of labour unions, monetarism (low inflation and debt/deficit reduction), and free trade and capital flows. Many of these aspects are integral to the neoliberal governance model, the New Public Management, which is a main focus of this project. They all have one thing in common: their propensity for advantaging the powerful, and disadvantaging the already marginalized, due to their race, gender, class, (dis)ability, or sexual orientation. In this way, neoliberalism is much more than a collection of policy preferences, it is about a very particular set of power relations and a restructuring of social forces. This book contributes to a vast and growing body of work that exposes neoliberalism as a fundamentally political, and destructive, project, which, at its base, is about the undermining of democracy and that sees democratization of the state as the only path to take us beyond neoliberalism.

Democratic administration will help to create the conditions needed in Canada for a socially just alternative to global capitalism. Just as Leo Panitch and Sam Gindin (2000) refer to "concrete utopias" (2), Judy Rebick emphasizes the need for clear alternatives on the Left (2000; Rebick and Roach 1996) and democratic administration begins to provide some. This means, among other things, that public sector workers have closer contact with citizens and social movement organizations (Findlay 1995); that positions are elected whenever possible (Panitch 1993) and representative of the full diversity of Canadian citizens in terms of race, gender, class, sexuality, nationality, and ability;[6] that the use of referenda on major policy decisions (such as free trade) is encouraged (Rebick and Roach 1996; Rebick 2000); that our electoral system more effectively reflects the democratic will of citizens (Rebick 2000);[7] and that a decentralization of power and a levelling of hierarchies is pursued (Albo 1993; Ferguson 1984).

Femocratic administration expands on democratic administration, making explicit the ways in which the state, and democracy, are gendered and racialized. It is also heavily influenced by the Australian femocrat experiment where the bureaucracy, through a complex web of women's policy machinery, has been a main strategic focus of feminist politics.[8] The term "femocrat" originated in Australia to address "those feminists who took on women's policy positions in the bureaucracy" (Sawer 1990, xv) and can also describe feminists elsewhere in the public service. The term has since gained currency in other places outside of Australia, including Canada.

However, the label "femocrat" often carries with it a derogatory connotation. In Australia, it has been used as a synonym for "career feminism" (Kaplan 1996) or "sell-out" (Eisenstein 1990). This is partly a reflection of the uncomfortable place that femocrats inhabit within feminism and feminist theory, and the fear of co-optation that is associated with integrating women into the bureaucracy. It is also a conservative denunciation of the perceived policy influence of "special interests" (Chappell 2002). In response to both, some femocrats, and feminist observers, have reclaimed the label and "have imbued the term with a more positive meaning" (ibid., 84). Nonetheless, some prefer the terms "state feminist" and "state feminism." For instance, Rankin and Vickers (2001) and Mazur and Stetson (1995) use these as a replacement for "femocrat." Because they have basically the same meaning,[9] I use the term femocrat and state feminist interchangeably, although clearly, my principal concept, "femocratic administration" is a hybrid of femocrat and democratic administration.

Femocrats are usually located in bureaucracies that are charged with responsibility for women's equality and women's policy issues. These bureaucracies have been given a variety of names. Malloy (2003) refers to "special policy agencies," but I have avoided his terminology, because it conjures up negative undertones associated with the neoliberal discourse of "special interests." Commonly, such bureaucracies are called women's policy machinery, or women's policy agencies. While I do use these labels, I prefer "women's structure of representation," which is drawn from Rianne Mahon's (1977) unequal structure of representation, discussed in later chapters, and is used in Sue Findlay's work on gender and bureaucracy in Canada. This concept is useful in highlighting the contradictory reality that women have been incorporated into state structures in ways that simultaneously challenge and reinforce inequality. "Women's structure of representation" corresponds with my view of the state, as the institutionalization of power relations, developed throughout the book.

Femocratic administration is an incomplete, but growing project, as feminist scholars have been building a body of literature and a movement. There are a number of areas in which attention has been focused in Canada. Alexandra Dobrowolsky (2000) argues that "the input of femocrats (i.e., feminists within the bureaucracy) is a significant, if underacknowledged, aspect of the women's movement in this country" (9). Sue Findlay charts this territory by analysing and problematizing the experiences of feminists working in women's policy machinery (federal, provincial, and municipal) in Canada and their interactions with the women's movement. Others are beginning to explore this terrain as well (Alboim 1997; Findlay 1997, 1993a, 1993b, 1988, 1987; Gabriel 1996; Geller-Schwartz 1995; Lavigne 1997; O'Neil and Sutherland 1997; M. Randall 1988; Teghtsoonian 2000; Vickers 1997b; Chappell 2002).[10] Work is also being done around the need for reinstating federal funding of women's groups to strengthen these "inside/outside" ties (Rebick and Roach 1996; Rebick 2000). Efforts have been aimed at pushing for feminist policy analysis and for gendering budgets (Bakker 1998, 1996a, 1996b; Bakker and Elson 1998; Teghtsoonian 2000; United Nations 2000). Feminist concern around representation is beginning to filter into calls for a more representative bureaucracy (Agócs 2012; Vickers 1997a, 1997b; Ferguson 1984; S. Findlay 1993a, 1987; Gabriel 1996). Of particular interest is the work that has been done to show how current public bureaucracies and structures of representation are organized in defiance of "intersectionality" (the idea that citizens have overlapping experiences of class, race, gender, sexual orientation, ability, nationality, and age) (Gabriel 1996; Findlay 1993a, 1993b). Finally, the onslaught of neoliberal "restructuring" of the public sector, including downsizing, privatization, and managerialism has been problematized for its devastating impact on women's labour (both paid and unpaid) and their working conditions (Armstrong 1996; Armstrong and Connelly 1997; Bakker 1998, 1996a, 1996b; Bakker and Elson 1998; Brodie 1995a, 1996; Cohen 1997; Evans and Wekerle 1997; Rebick and Roach 1996; Rebick 2000). More work of this sort needs to be done to create a truly femocratic administration, and this book seeks to contribute to the dialogue.

Feminist democratization, or feminist social transformation, is a wide-ranging project aimed at the institutions of the state, market, family, and civil society. It incorporates socialist, feminist, and anti-racist influences, which seek to combine procedural democracy based on participatory, inclusive, representative, accountable, and less hierarchical decision-making, with substantive outcomes of equality and justice. The primary focus of feminist democratization is on those who are excluded from, or marginalized within, our current political, social, and economic structures and processes, and on eliminating these systemic inequalities. My project on femocratic administration, a subset of feminist democratization, addresses only one part of this larger program, through the democratization of public administration.

The democratization of state administration involves the transformation of the internal structures, processes, and cultures of the state, as well as the relationship between the state and society. This entails fundamental changes to the Weberian principles of bureaucracy: hierarchy, compartmentalization, and neutrality. It also requires that the public (individuals and groups) are able to actively participate in political decision-making not only in periodic elections, but also as an ongoing practice of citizenship.

This is what distinguishes femocratic administration from representative democracy. Femocratic administration, while concerned with women's relationship to bureaucracy (a largely neglected area of research), also explores how an integrative feminist project of democratization would link the state (the bureaucracy, electoral and constitutional politics) to non-state forms (the women's movement and other social movements, communities). It sees representation much more broadly than just electoral politics. It also moves beyond representation as simply numerical, superficial, passive, and paternalistic, to a substantive conception of representation that focuses on actively mobilizing and seeking public participation, and valuing alternative knowledges. State feminists, or "femocrats," have an important role to play in advancing this project.

The Argument: State Feminism and Transformational Politics

The period under review (1985–2000) is particularly interesting. Beginning in the late 1980s and early 1990s, there appeared to be a growing consensus around the idea of transforming public administration, as it was embraced by both the left and the right of the political spectrum (Sossin 1999). This convergence revolves around several key elements of bureaucratic reform, including the need for accountability, empowerment, flattened hierarchies, and decentralization (Osborne and Gaebler 1993; Sossin 1999). In response, many have pointed to the substantial difference between social democratic and neoliberal efforts at restructuring the bureaucracy, with the former emphasizing citizenship and equality, and the latter prioritizing consumer choice and efficiency (Albo 1993; Shields and Evans 1998; Sossin 1999). The Ontario case study further highlights these differences by illustrating the greater possibilities for women's representation and democratization that exist within a citizenship and equality paradigm over one based on consumers and efficiency. I demonstrate that neoliberalism, particularly in the form of the New Public Management (NPM), has undermined gender democracy at both the procedural and the substantial level. Yet returning to the traditional model of public administration is not the answer. My central argument is that, since neither gender regime (Weberian or

NPM) has sufficiently advanced procedural and substantive democracy for women in Ontario, an alternative regime should be explored in the form of femocratic administration.

I would like to stress here that my purpose is not to explain why these changes occur from one gender regime to another. Though certainly an important question, my goal is different. I am interested in the procedural and substantive outcomes of these governance models, and the possibilities for reorganizing state institutions in ways that move women's representation and public policy forward.

A pivotal conceptual framework used in this piece is procedural and substantive democracy. Without using these specific terms, C.B. Macpherson advanced procedural and substantive notions of democracy in *The Real World of Democracy*, where he distinguishes between liberal and non-liberal dimensions of democracy. In outlining the particularities of liberal democracies, or democracies within capitalist systems, Macpherson (1965) points out that the capitalist market economy pre-dated democracy (competitive elections, universal franchise, freedom of speech, press, and association) and so democratic freedoms were fused onto an already functioning liberal capitalist system. The result is a system in which equal individual freedoms or political rights (procedural democracy) are exercised within a capitalist economy where social inequalities are inherent. In contrast, in non-liberal democracies, without a capitalist economic system, social equality (substantive democracy), as in "the classic notion of democracy as an equal human society" (Macpherson 1965, 33), exists, but in the absence of formal democratic rights and freedoms (18, 22). For Macpherson, it is possible for both ends and means to be democratic, something that is now referred to, as procedural and substantive democracy.

Procedural and substantive democracy (or equality) are common concepts in feminist legal scholarship, where, like Macpherson, feminists have emphasized the disjuncture between them. Even though procedural equality posits that equality results from same treatment, in reality, it became more and more clear that this frequently is not the case. For instance, Comack (1999) problematizes the law's focus on "equality before the law," or treating everyone the same, because it requires "abstracting people from their social contexts or locations" (23). Therefore, feminists began to argue that to achieve substantive equality, or equal outcomes, it is sometimes necessary to treat some groups differently (Porter 2003, 195). As Fudge and Cossman (2002) note, "feminists demanded that rather than ignoring the patterns of social inequality that shaped men's and women's roles and responsibilities, law and social policy should actively compensate women for the legacy of historical discrimination" (405).

The weaknesses of a procedural notion of equality were revealed in a now infamous case in Canada, *Bliss*, 1978. Strict adherence to a notion of procedural equality resulted in a decision that found that an Unemployment Insurance (UI) provision denying benefits to a pregnant woman was not discriminatory because the rule was based on pregnancy, not sex.[11] In other words, the same rule applies to women and men equally, regardless of circumstance. Feminist legal theorists responded to *Bliss*, and similar cases, by pressing for a *substantive* notion of equality. Substantive equality assumes that a uniform process is not enough, and may in fact lead to greater inequality. Active measures are necessary to provide for equality of results. Considering the *Bliss* case again, feminists argued that, because only women can become pregnant, a disqualification from UI benefits based on pregnancy is de facto discrimination against women. Substantive equality then, concerns itself not only with an equal process, but with equal results as well. This is true in the legal realm and in democracy more generally.

However, there is a tendency in "progressive" circles to treat procedural democracy as an inadequate replacement for "real" substantive democracy, and therefore to see both as distinct entities. It is true that procedural democracy, also called formal democracy, has been problematically applied without attentiveness to difference, but Macpherson's idea that the process of decision-making matters must remain central to democracy, especially in the current political context. I take procedural democracy in a broad sense to refer not only to elections, voting, freedom of expression, association, and the press, and so on, but also to a wider range of structures and processes necessary for democratic citizenship, representation, and participation. For instance, Weberian bureaucracy is designed around a strictly procedural notion of equality. Weber (1997) celebrated "the dominance of a spirit of formalistic impersonality, '*Sine ira et studio*,' without hatred or passion, and hence without affection or enthusiasm. The dominant norms are concepts of straightforward duty without regard to personal considerations. Everyone is subject to formal equality of treatment" (340). As Maley (2011) maintains, "bureaucracy treats those who are socially and economically unequal as equals" (44), thus perpetuating inequality.

I maintain that neoliberalism is an attack on both procedural *and* substantive democracy, which is equally problematic for each on their own, and also because they are interrelated and mutually reinforcing. My project explicitly links the transformation of democratic processes with the achievement of substantive democratic results, by showing that there is a correspondence between the quality of the process and substance of state feminism in Ontario in the two case studies described below.

The distinction between procedural and substantive democracy shapes my use of the term gender democracy. Democracy unmodified is not enough because democracy is not gender-neutral. In her book *Engendering Democracy*, Anne Phillips (1991) reminds us that, "with the odd exception, the entire debate on democracy has proceeded for centuries as if women were not there, or it has, with Rousseau, only acknowledged us to show us our place" (2). Gender, in concert with class, race, ability, and sexual orientation, determines one's ability to participate in the process of democratic decision-making, and to enjoy its results. Wyckoff-Wheeler (n.d.) defines gender democracy as

> an equal chance to achieve personal fulfillment and to be active in the development and transformation of society, inter alia, to achieve gender democracy. Gender democracy refers to a way of organising society, in which the individual participation of all citizens is respected and encouraged, and no one is excluded from full participation because of sex.

She is concerned with both equality of opportunity between women and men, and with equality of outcomes. My particular interest is whether, or how, "femocrats," or state feminists, can advance gender democracy or, more broadly, feminist democratization.

This is part of my larger point that despite both analyses of globalization and some feminists who have questioned the strategic importance of the state, the state matters. It is undoubtedly true, as Taylor and Rupp (2008) submit, that "to understand the shifting organizational forms, tactical repertoires, collective identities, and venues of women's movements requires a broader, less state-centred conceptualisation of power that recognizes that gender inequality has multiple sources, both symbolic and material" (xv). But the state continues to be a vital target for feminist action, as state administration matters for public policy and projects of social transformation, specifically for women. As Sue Findlay stresses, state administration is where policy is made and implemented (1995). Not only does the state (national and sub-national) and state administration matter, but democratizing state administration is a crucial part of the larger project of feminist democratization, because, as Stivers (1993) shows, "administrators have power" (2). We need to focus attention on how to democratize the state, including sub-national states, and in particular, on how to advance gender democracy. As one element of such a project, "femocratic administration" needs to be a central focus of the women's movement in Canada.

This project is situated within larger debates about the place of the state within globalization and responses in the form of theories of democratic administration. Writers such as Albo, Panitch, Langille (1993), and Sossin (1999) have pointed to the need for greater citizen participation in the policy process. Unfortunately, authors in this area have largely ignored the particular situation of women in the bureaucracy. While the importance of feminists in the bureaucracy has been a common thread, notably in Australian feminist scholarship (Sawer 1990, 1994; Eisenstein 1996; Yeatman 1990; and Franzway et al. 1989), little research has examined parallel structures of representation in Canada (Rankin and Vickers 2001; Findlay 1988), and even less has done so at the provincial level in Ontario. Feminists have extensively studied the relationship between women and the state and some have considered the bureaucracy expressly (Allen 1990; V. Randall 1988; M. Randall 1988; MacKinnon 1989; Brodie 1995a; Vickers 1997a and 1997b; Pringle and Watson 1992; Sawer 1990, 1994; Eisenstein 1996; Yeatman; 1990 Franzway et al. 1989; and Chappell 2002). I apply these feminist theories of the state to the actual experiences of women in the Ontario bureaucracy in an effort to formulate a more accurate picture of the relationship between theory and practice and to inform democratic administration. This study, then, attempts to fill in these gaps by applying ideas about democratic administration and Australian state feminism to the Ontario case. It explores theoretical and practical questions within political science, Canadian politics, public policy and administration, and women and politics. In particular, it draws upon feminist and non-feminist state theories, and explores their practical implications for the prospect of democratization in Ontario. As such, it brings together currently divergent streams in democratic administration, and in gender and public policy.

This book considers the promise of state feminism to the project of democratic administration and the challenges posed to gender democracy by both traditional Weberian organization and neoliberal public management, or the NPM. It argues that we must challenge the gender regimes of Weberian and NPM governance in pursuit of femocratic administration.

The Case Study: The Ontario Women's Directorate

The Ontario Women's Directorate (OWD) case study demonstrates both that the state matters for women and that the democratization of state administration matters for women. It reinforces the importance of the national (and sub-national) state to feminist social transformation and the significance of the role of women's structures of representation. Through an examination of the OWD under three governments over two distinct periods of governance and gender regimes – Weberian social democratic and neoliberal NPM – the case studies provide lessons on both the limitations of, and the potential for, state feminism as a strategy for democratization. Overall, it is intended to get at what exactly gender democracy, or a "femocratic administration," would entail.

The study reinforces the importance of examining the ways in which the state's administrative processes reinforce unequal power relations. This is made clear with both the social democratic and the neoliberal period. But what is also evident is that the former, a more participatory state, which advanced elements of femocratic administration, resulted in a considerably more open relationship with the community and substantive policy results for women. In making the particular substantive point, I use policy outcomes, through women's labour market policy, which was chosen for several reasons. The first is for practical reasons, because, for most of its lifetime, the OWD has focused on two key policy areas: women's economic independence and violence against women. Within women's economic independence, the OWD has mainly been involved with labour market issues. Second, there are now several comparisons of the New Democratic Party (NDP) and the Progressive Conservatives (PCs) on labour market policy (Bradford 2003; Haddow and Klassen 2004; Klassen 2000), but gender is not central to them. Finally, the example of women's labour market policy clearly demonstrates the link between the tremendous changes in policy process and substance over time in Ontario. In making this choice to highlight labour market policy, but not violence against women, I am erring on the side of a more detailed case study. This does not discount the value of comparisons across policy areas and/or jurisdictions.[12] But my objective is to compare procedural and substantive democracy in governance regimes over time, in one location.

I compare the differences in women's experiences with the governments of David Peterson's Liberals and Bob Rae's New Democrats with Mike Harris's Progressive Conservative government and demonstrate that while there are clear limitations for women working within public bureaucracies, lessons about democracy can be learned from studying these cases. Certain state forms and governance approaches provide women in the bureaucracy with greater opportunity for policy influence and participation than others. There were central differences between the social democratic period (Liberal/NDP governments) and the neoliberal period (Progressive Conservative government) with respect to their approach to femocrats and the representation of women within the state bureaucracy, with the social democratic coming much closer to the femocratic administration project I am proposing. These regimes also diverged in terms of their resulting policies for women, specifically, labour market policy. These findings broaden the scope of democratic administration to include gender, and add to the feminist discussion of women's relationship to the state, providing important insight about democratization of the state, and of the bureaucracy.

This project, then, is less about party politics than it is about different regimes of governance, including gender regimes. The Liberal and NDP governments were still operating within the social democratic framework of the late Keynesian welfare state, with its accompanying ideas about representation and equality, while the shift to a neoliberal state form is clear with the election of the Harris Tories (and in subsequent Ontario governments). These regimes represent distinct social projects and visions that transcend political parties and partisan politics. This meshes with Rankin's (1996) study of sub-national women's movements, which also found that party ideology was not necessarily a determining factor.

Although not linked explicitly to the notion of gender regimes that I elaborate in subsequent chapters, Outshoorn and Kantola's conclusions also provide support for my related arguments. While much of the literature emphasizes political parties as a central determinant of state feminist achievement, Outshoorn and Kantola (2007a) stress the relative uniformity of experience for women's policy agencies, regardless of political party.[13] They observe that "in general most countries encountered a rise of neoliberal ideas, with the emphasis on the market, privatization, efficiency and innovation. Reforming the welfare state and the introduction of principles from the New Public Management was an issue in all the countries (save perhaps Germany and Spain)" (ibid., 268).

The concept of gender regime stems from feminist critiques of the comparative welfare state literature. Such critiques point out that welfare state typologies, such as that of Esping-Andersen, ignore the different ways that gender relations are structured within regimes, and that within the varieties of welfare states, there are varieties of gender regulation based on diverse cultures, norms, ideas, policies, and institutions. Sainsbury (1999) defines a gender (policy) regime as "the rules and norms about gender relations, allocating tasks and rights to the two sexes. A gender policy regime entails a logic based on the rules and norms about gender relations that influences the construction of policies" (5).

There are ongoing debates about how to define a gender regime, and about which combination of factors to consider.[14] R.W. Connell (2002), for instance, distinguishes between the concepts of *gender regime* and *gender order*. She uses gender regime to refer to "a regular set of arrangements about gender" within a particular institution, such as a school, or a workplace and gender order to the broader patterns of gender relations in society (53). For my purposes here, the main point is that the gender regime literature shares a general focus on welfare state policy and the particular way that state mediation of production and reproduction (broadly defined) is gendered in a given context (Connell 2002; Sainsbury 1999; O'Connor 1993). As a result, gender regimes can be said to exist in all institutions, including those of public administration, but differ in character across space and time. Some gender regimes are more attuned to gender democracy than others.

Methodology

My research method was based on a combination of qualitative approaches in order to bridge the study of globalization and the state, gender and globalization, democratic administration, feminist state theory, gender and bureaucracy, state feminism in Canada and Australia, gender and federalism, gender and restructuring, and the New Public Management. I analysed primary publications and documents produced by the OWD and archival records from the Directorate, some accessed after an access to information request through the Archives of Ontario.

The other primary research was derived from nineteen interviews with both present and former feminist public servants working in, or having a close connection to, the OWD. I started with a very experienced staff member at the OWD. From there, interviewees were found mainly using the snow-ball technique. Those interviewed included staff from positions ranging from administrative support to policy staff to assistant deputy ministers (ADMs) (who acted as the head of the Directorate) to cabinet ministers. Three ADMs were interviewed, two from the Liberal period, and one from the NDP period. In addition, two former cabinet ministers, one NDP (Marion Boyd) and one PC (Dianne Cunningham) were interviewed. Two members of women's community groups involved in women's labour market policy were interviewed. In other cases, OWD staff had previously been involved in the women's movement, or became involved after leaving the Directorate.

Given the research focus on women's labour market training, for at least part of their time at the OWD, most of the staff I interviewed worked in a policy analyst role in the social and economic policy unit, although in some cases, interviews were conducted with staff who had been involved with the violence-against-women unit. Many acted as managers of their unit for at least part of their time at the Directorate. Most have since left the OWD. Some are no longer in government. Others have positions elsewhere in the Ontario public service. At the time of interviewing, a few remained at the OWD. These open-ended interviews were conducted between 2003 and 2005. Most of the participants wished to remain anonymous, which is reflected throughout the chapters. The only exceptions were the two cabinet ministers, and one former staff member, Judy Wolfe.

My research approach was influenced by feminist methodology. Generally, feminist methods involve recognition on the part of the researcher that methodologies are political, and that power relations exist between the researcher and the researched (Roberts 1990; Harding 1991; Wolf 1996; Reinhartz 1992). It is usually assumed that the former is more powerful than the latter. With my project, which relied heavily on elite interviews with government officials, this was clearly not the case. But the interviewing process involved raising feminist questions to these officials, and analysing their responses from a feminist perspective. Feminist methodology is about both *process* and *purpose*. I had a clear political purpose in mind with this research: a feminist approach to the democratization of the state.

I also incorporated feminist principles of narrative method, relying on the participant's own words to describe their experiences whenever possible. In order to limit some of the reliability risks of the narrative method, arguments are based on corroborating and recurring interview responses, and are often reinforced through the archival materials or secondary literature. When there are significant disagreements between interview participants, these are discussed in the text.

Theoretical Framework

This method is indicative of the political economy framework employed, which I discuss further in chapter 1. Although this is contested, I believe that the dominant approach to feminist political science in Canada tends to be institutionalism or neo-institutionalism. Neo-institutionalism, according to Chappell (2002), "is interested in examining the way institutional arrangements shape political behaviour," and the ways that institutions within a given system interact with each other (8). As Chappell indicates, in order for feminists to employ neo-institutionalism, they must correct for its failure to "take into account the gendered nature of institutions" (9), but she sees this as possible.

There is certainly a neo-institutionalist orientation in the literature on state feminism, which is generally concerned with how women negotiate institutional barriers and possibly try to bend the rigid rules of bureaucracies, but engages in little fundamental questioning of the structures and processes of public administration. For instance, in two comparative studies of Canada and Australia, both Malloy (2003) and Chappell (2002) highlight femocrats' lack of autonomy from the women's movement in Canada (as opposed to in Australia) as one of the main obstacles to state feminist success. For Malloy (2003), the inability of state feminists in the OWD to maintain an optimal distance from the women's movement hampered its effectiveness. In Chappell's case, she lays out two measures of femocrat success – their level of autonomy from the feminist movement and their location in the bureaucracy. She sees the former as a particular weakness of state feminism in Canada. In contrast, as will be seen, distancing state institutions from popular control is not the goal of feminist political economy. It seeks a more radical restructuring of state institutions, society, and the relations between them.

It is also common in neo-institutionalism to focus on the relationship between institutions and ideas.[15] The feminist political economy approach that I am using certainly agrees that institutions and ideas are important. Where it departs from neo-institutionalism is in its emphasis on how not only political behaviour, but also institutions themselves, are shaped by power relations, and how social forces bring about change within such a context. Armstrong and Connelly (1999) provide that for political economy, the "focus is most often the structures and relations that create, reflect and sustain class, race, gender and other inequalities, although ideas and discourse also play central roles" (1). For *feminist* political economists, social forces, reflect, to use Porter's words, "multiple strands of determination" or multiple oppressions (2003, 13), such as gender, race, ethnicity, class, and sexuality, and are key to understanding the contradictory process and substance of struggles with, and within, various state institutions.

Political economy also differs from institutionalism in its understanding of the relationships within and between states. In their approach to intergovernmental relations, Simeon and Robinson (1990) are influenced by political economy. They see federalism as resulting from the configuration of political forces, the mobilization of popular movements, and political conflict and cooperation,[16] and others have built on this perspective. For instance, Graefe (2003) suggests that "one needs to start from social forces, and consider how their struggles are mediated and transmitted through intergovernmental relations and institutions" (27).[17] Cameron (2006) also situates federalism within a structure of power relations – both class and gender. As seen in the following chapter, Cameron's feminist political economy approach sees political institutions, including federalism, as both determining and being determined by "the balance of power" and the contradictions between production and social reproduction inherent in capitalism (47). Such political economies of federalism are crucial to understanding governance at the sub-national level and they establish the context for democratization from which femocratic administration will emerge.

Gender, Governance, and Democracy in Ontario

I make the case for femocratic administration in five chapters. Chapter 1 indicates that feminist interactions with the administrative state pose questions for feminist approaches to the state. In response to some feminist reluctance to theorize the state, feminist institutionalism has been developing a rich body of work on gender and institutions, but it incorporates few of the tools of feminist political economy. I argue that both feminist institutionalism and feminist political economy would benefit from an active exchange of ideas and that the concept of gender regime provides the space to debate and analyse women's representation in public administration. Throughout the book, I draw from the insights of both feminist institutionalism and feminist political economy.

In chapter 2, I move from feminist analyses of the state more generally to feminist critiques of bureaucracy specifically. I examine public administration in two governance paradigms in Canada, Weberianism and the NPM. The chapter begins by reviewing the central components of Weberian administration: hierarchy, compartmentalization, and neutrality, and outlines the ways in which feminists have problematized these organizational forms as based on gendered values, principles, and relations. It then traces the rise in dominance of the NPM, a neoliberal governance approach that came to challenge Weberianism over the 1980s and 1990s. Bringing with it its own set of gendered processes, the NPM revolves around downsizing, privatization, and managerialism. Therefore, I argue that while Weberianism and the NPM are based on different governance models, they both rely on gendered versions of representation and democracy and exemplify gender regimes of public administration. I argue that an alternative, transformative public administration must focus on state feminism, representation, and democracy, and return to this point in the concluding chapter.

After laying out the broad strokes of the Weberian and NPM gender regimes, I shift to the case study. In chapter 3, the first decade of the Ontario Women's Directorate (OWD) is assessed. I examine the experiences of femocrats in Ontario with the three central elements of the Weberian gender regime: hierarchy, compartmentalization, and neutrality. I stress that we can get a glimpse into the ways state feminism fits into the project of democratic administration, and how it might work to challenge oppressive forms of organization and create an alternative gender regime of public administration. Procedural and substantive democratic lessons (using the example of women's labour market policy) can be learned from a period where experiments with state feminism, and within the wider public sector, occurred within the context of heightened attention to participation and equity. In the end, though, it is clear from the Ontario case that these Weberian forms of organization pose considerable challenges for state feminism, and complicate the optimism that democratic administration has about the public sector's potential for transformation.

Chapter 4 analyses the administrative change brought into Ontario by Mike Harris's "Commonsense Revolution." It interrogates the restructuring of the bureaucracy, based on the neoliberal governance principles of the NPM and its espousal of downsizing, privatization and managerialism. Using the state restructuring in Ontario from the mid-1990s onward, and its impact on women's structures of representation (the Ontario Women's Directorate) and resulting policies (women's labour market policy) as a case study, I argue that gender democracy has been undermined by the NPM regime, both procedurally and substantively (in policy terms), making the need for democratization all the more pressing.

I conclude by reiterating the continued importance of state admini-stration for feminist critique, but also for imagining responses to neo-liberalism. Informed by democratic administration, some feminist state theory, and state feminist practice, I explore feminist democ-ratization, or "femocratic administration." I propose that feminist bureaucratic restructuring, representative bureaucracy, and demo-cratic administration are central components of femocratic admini-stration and to bringing together gender, governance, and democracy.

1 A Feminist Political Economy of Representation

One of the most important feminist interventions into the discipline of political science has been to expand our definition of the "political" beyond the institutions of the state to include other political terrain, including non-governmental actors (NGOs) and social movements, and those relations previously considered to be private, such as the family. The success in demonstrating that "the personal is political," while essential in pushing the borders of political science, is fraught with feminist ambivalence about the state. Some feminists suggest that we turn our attention away from the state and focus instead on other spaces of struggle. Judith Allen (1990) even asks, "Does feminism need a theory of the state," and responds in the negative. In other feminist circles, there has been a revival in the analysis of state institutions. This chapter is based on the view that feminist intellectual and political engagements with the state continue to be strategically important for democracy or, as Armstrong and Connelly (1999) put it: "Gender, states and theory matter" (21). But which tools and approaches are best employed?

The relationship between gender and institutions has long been an interest of feminist political scientists seeking to understand how power and inequality are produced and reproduced through governmental and non-governmental structures and processes. Recently, feminist institutionalism (FI) has provided most of the thinking on gender and institutions, especially state institutions. While Driscoll and Krook (2009) claim that few feminists frame their research in relation to institutionalism, I believe that institutionalism is the dominant frame in feminist political science and policy studies.

In this chapter, I argue that FI has made some valuable contributions to the literature on gender, representation, and state feminism. However, it suffers from a lack of serious attention paid to feminist political economy (FPE). For its part, FPE has said very little about the workings of state institutions and policy machinery. Thus, I seek to initiate a dialogue between FI and FPE that can inform a developing feminist political economy of representation. I begin by outlining the main ideas, strengths, and weaknesses of FI. Then, I point to some key insights that can be taken from FPE. Finally, I suggest that the concept of gender regime, which incorporates the assets of both FI and FPE, is most useful for analysing women's representation in public administration and for moving towards femocratic administration.

Feminist Institutionalism

There has been growing attention to exploring FI as an analytical framework. In 2006, an international collaboration called the Feminist Institutionalist International Network (FIIN) was launched (Lovenduski 2011), followed by a June 2009 edition of the *Politics & Gender* journal dedicated to FI, and a new edited volume published in 2011 entitled *Gender, Politics and Institutions: Towards a Feminist Institutionalism* (Krook and Mackay 2011). The goal is to "integrate gender and neo-institutionalist perspectives" (1).

What Is FI?

According to Kenny, the "basic premise of new institutionalism is that institutions do 'matter'" (Kenny 2007, 92). Institutions matter because they are "the rules that structure political and social life. They are configurations of ideas and interests which are expressed as the "formal rules, compliance procedures and standard operating practices that structure relationships between individuals in various units of the polity and the economy" (Lovenduski 2011, viii).

Chappell (2002) argues that feminist scholarship on the state has been preoccupied with ideology and diverging feminist views of the state as explanatory factors, and she would like to bring "a stronger institutional focus to bear on feminist political science" (6). Therefore, some have looked to new institutionalism or neo-institutionalism for bringing about an "institutional turn in feminist political science" (Krook and Mackay 2011, 2) aimed at bridging feminism and new institutionalism (Kenny 2007).

There are theoretical and methodological divisions within neo-institutionalism, so there are at least four different forms of institutionalism with which feminists are engaging: rational choice, sociological, discursive, and historical (Krook and Mackay 2011; Mackay and Waylen 2009; Lovenduski 2011). Feminists disagree about whether all of these are equally promising, with some preferring a synthesis (Krook and Mackay 2011), but many showing an affinity for the historical variant (Lovenduski 2011; Waylen 2011).[1]

Very briefly, rational choice focuses on the behaviour of micro-level actors to explain the origins and outcomes of institutions at the macro level. Institutions are evaluated in terms of the incentives created for cooperation or competition. Some feminists are particularly sceptical of the assumptions and individualistic orientation of rational choice orientation.[2]

Sociological institutionalism is associated with organizational theory and is primarily concerned with critiquing the institutions and processes of Weberian bureaucracy. It moves between the micro and macro levels and challenges notions of institutional rationality and efficiency by uncovering the myths, cultural norms, symbols, interests, and social context that work to legitimize institutions (Mackay et al. 2009).

Discursive institutionalism spans the micro to the macro level. It is fixated on the influence of ideas and discourses on actors, institutions, and power relations. Kulawik (2009) sees discursive institutionalism as a bringing together of historical institutionalism and discourse analysis.[3]

Finally, historical institutionalism is based on the assumption that "the role of actors within a political system can be understood only by investigating, over time, the nature of the institutions within that system" (Chappell 2002, 8). Some of the central features of a historical institutionalist approach are that it disaggregates the state, takes a broad definition of political institutions, studies the interaction between institutions, and takes an "embedded and dynamic view of state" (ibid.). Waylen (2011) posits that historical institutionalism is best able to advance our understanding of structure and agency, and to explain why change occurs. For Chappell one of its main strengths is its ability to comprehend social behaviour by examining institutions over time (Chappell 2002, 8). Smith adds that historical institutionalism views "state institutions, as well as state policies, as potentially independent variables that structure political conflict and shape the mobilization of social forces" (Smith 1999, 14).

Notwithstanding these variations, together they form a distinct neo-institutionalist approach (Krook and Mackay 2011), and there are certain characteristics of neo-institutionalism that some feminist scholars have found especially useful. They have appreciated the expansive definition of institutions, the focus on the ways institutions shape political behaviour, and the importance of comparing institutions across time and place (Chappell 2002; Lovenduski 2011). The concept of path dependency, from historical institutionalism, has resonated with many feminist political scientists, interested in how initial choices about policy affect future ones (Chappell 2002; Krook and Mackay 2011) and how policy legacies affect policy change for women (Smith 1999). Drawing from Thelen's notions of institutional layering and conversion, Kenny (2007) maintains that path dependency allows for

> a historical, rather than a functional, answer for questions of institutional origins and change, suggesting that the forces that sustain an institution over time may be very different from the founding coalitions behind the institution's original creation. As such, they highlight the "unintended consequences and inefficiencies" of existing institutions … In contrast to traditional power-distributional perspectives which see institutions as straightforward reflections of the interests and preferences of the powerful, Thelen argues that institutional creation and change occur in specific historical contexts marked by multiple shifting interests and alliances. As a result, institutions designed to serve a particular set of interests often end up "carrying" other interests. Institutions frequently outlive their founding coalitions and can be transformed through political reconfigurations and realignments, as well as through the incorporation of new groups whose inclusion was unanticipated at the time of institutional creation. (93)

She points to several ways in which neo-institutionalism and feminist political science share a number of common preoccupations. Both share an understanding that seemingly neutral institutional processes and practices are in fact embedded in hidden norms and values, privileging certain groups over others. Both are centrally concerned with explanations of institutional creation, continuity, resistance, and change. Both emphasize the *historicity* of power relations, opening up the possibility of institutional resistance and power reversals. If institutional power relations are deeply historical and constantly evolving, then they are susceptible to agency, change, and transformation (Kenny 2007, 95). Nevertheless, feminists have stressed that neo-institutionalism, as it currently stands, is inadequate, as it does not account for the gendered nature of institutions (Lovenduski 2011; Kenny 2007). Neo-institutionalism does not analyse "the ways in which political institutions reflect, structure and reinforce gendered patterns of power" (Kenny 2007, 91).

Neo-institutionalism has as much, if not more, to learn from feminist political science, which demonstrates that institutions are not neutral – they have a "normative element" (Lovenduski 2011, viii). For Waylen (2011), "an HI [historical institutionalist] approach combined with feminist ideas and concerns can help answer important questions by combining the analysis of actors, particularly key actors in insider and outsider alliances, with their institutional contexts in ways that are mindful of institutional legacies, as well as institutional change and the importance of ideas and framing" (253). Therefore, FI is about bringing a gender lens to bear on neo-institutionalism, and in doing so, makes some significant contributions.

Contributions

FI poses a challenge to mainstream political science and public policy studies and raises some questions with which good social science research must contend. Krook and Mackay (2011) outline some of the starting queries for feminist institutionalists:

> How are formal structures and informal "rules of the game" gendered? How do political institutions affect the daily lives of women and men, respectively? By what processes and mechanisms are such institutions produced, both reflecting and reproducing social systems, including gendered power relations? How do institutions constrain actors, ideas, and interests? Finally, what is the gendered potential for institutional innovation, reform, and change in pursuit of gender justice, and what are its limits? (1)

Sawer and Vickers (2010) also highlight the need to ask "how such political architecture has affected women's citizenship and whether women were active in its design" (17).

Tackling these issues is vital to exposing the gender insensitivity of neo-institutionalism. In general, neo-institutionalism lacks a gender analysis of power, discourse, and interests (Grace 2011; Mackay et al. 2009). Mackay et al. (2009) see FI as a way to "remedy some of the difficulties associated with certain other institutionalisms, such as an overemphasis on a narrow conception of the "rational" actor and on formal institutions and practices" (254). Overall, as Chappell puts it, FI can "'undo the taken-for-grantedness' of institutions, to show how much of what is presented as 'neutral' is in fact gendered" (Chappell 2002, 11).

For instance, FI has problematized the concept of path dependency, showing how policy change is a gendered process, with "gendered legacies," and distinct obstacles to *feminist* policy change (Mackay 2011, 187; Grace 2011). Feminist institutionalists have sought a "middle notion of path dependence" (Waylen 2011, 151) that can capture the real constraints for women in the policy process, while also leaving room for agency. Kenny (2011) points out that "gender norms and gender relations are particularly 'sticky' institutional legacies with which to contend, but also that gender – at both the symbolic level as well as the level of day-to-day interaction – is primarily a means through which institutional reform and innovation can be resisted" (40).

FI establishes some foundational premises from which to examine institutions, the foremost being that all institutions are gendered. As Grace (2011) explains, "A gendered institution means that gender is present in the 'processes, practices, images and ideologies, and distributions of power' within that site" (99). Vickers provides that even though it may take multiple forms, "all states are patriarchies characterized by institutionalized male rule" (Vickers 1997a, 120–1). Kenny goes on to say:

> Not only are gender relations seen to be "institutional," but these relations are embedded in particular political institutions, constraining and shaping social interaction. While institutionalised gender relations are not fixed – they are dynamic, fluid and dependent on situation and context – institutions in general are marked as "masculine," shaping institutional structures, practices and processes. (Kenny 2007, 96)

Grace concludes that "just as HI [historical institutionalism] makes the case that institutions matter, FI makes a stronger case that they matter quite differently for women" (Grace 2011, 111).

These insights contribute not only to neo-institutionalism, but also to feminism. As noted earlier, some feminist approaches have downplayed the need to theorize the state (Allen 1990), raising tactical concerns (Brodie 1995a). In answering Skocpol's call to "bring the state back in," FI is redirecting attention to "institutions as a major determining variable shaping feminist strategies" (Chappell 2002, 8). With FI primarily, though not exclusively, focused on formal institutions, research at the micro and meso levels of the state has proliferated (Driscoll and Krook 2009), and has emphasized variations across and within states (Krook and Mackay 2011).

One of the consequences of this shift has been to generate new thinking about change and agency. This is fitting for FI, which is characterized by a normative commitment to social change for women. Citing Thelen, Driscoll and Krook (2009) submit that "understanding institutional evolution and change lies in specifying more precisely the reproduction and feedback mechanisms on which particular institutions rest ... for it is there that we will find clues as to the particular external processes that can produce political opening and change" (241).

Mackay (2011) insists that "institutions are not just a constraint but also may act as strategic resources" and "may be regendered" (185–6). Likewise, Chappell (2002) highlights "how gender norms influence the political opportunity and constraint structures faced by feminists, and ... illustrates when and how feminists can unsettle the entrenched norms in order to use institutions for their own ends" (11). Waylen (2011) identifies agents of change as "insurrectionaries" (outsiders) and "subversives" (insiders) (150). FI has clearly made a positive impact on neo-institutionalism and feminism by pushing both to reconsider how they view state institutions. Yet there are some shortcomings in FI.

Weaknesses

Here, I will outline three weaknesses in the FI approach: its analysis of power, its conceptualization of change and agency,[4] and its insular point of reference.

One of the strengths of FI, its attention to what is happening at the micro and meso levels of institutions, is also one of its weaknesses. Stemming from neo-institutionalism, FI shares its aversion to social theory. As Smith (2008) explains, "Precisely because historical institutionalism focuses on the mid-range level, it does not have a theory of history or an over-all theory of social power" (21). Therefore, Graefe (2007) posits,

  although historical institutionalism may look at institutions as products of struggle, it generally cannot theorize that struggle since it does not come down on a particular theory of society, be it a pluralist one or one structured by social relations such as gender or class. It seeks to ground explanation and determination in a limited range of political (and occasionally

collective bargaining) institutions, and thus consciously sidelines consideration of the contribution of deeper economic and social structures (to
say nothing of agency) to policy variation in time and space ... Its failure
to engage with structure limits its ability to embed policy within context,
a drawback which becomes especially noticeable when institutionalism is
compared to political economy approaches. (33)

This reluctance to examine wider structures of power is especially
problematic for understanding marginalized social relations, including
gender.

Early feminist work saw the cause of gender inequality in macro
terms, as systemic and structural, through the lens of patriarchal states
and institutionalized male power (Barrett 1980; Burstyn 1983; Ferguson 1984; MacKinnon 1989). For FI, this was too deterministic and
monolithic, failing to distinguish between different types of state institutions (Krook and Mackay 2011). While bringing valuable nuance to
some feminist interpretations, FI scholars have also oversimplified this
structural analysis. For instance, Chappell (2002) rejects conspiratorial
notions of patriarchal institutions, which she associates with radical and
socialist feminism. Citing those such as MacKinnon, Ferguson, Eisenstein, and Brown, she stresses that the state does not always operate to
oppress women, is not inherently patriarchal, and does not represent
"only male interests" (11). The problem is that none of them really make
such crude claims. They actually emphasize struggle and contradictions
(Burstyn 1983; Barrett 1980; Brown 1995; Ferguson 1984; MacKinnon
1989). In fact, they would likely agree with Chappell's (2002) own conclusion that we should "see the individual institutions that comprise it
[the state] as 'culturally marked as masculine' and as operating largely
as the institutionalization of the power of men" (11).[5]

Where they might differ is that they demand a more comprehensive theory of "the power of men" and the mechanisms by which it
becomes and remains institutionalized. This does not rule out the reality that there will be differences within and across states,[6] but it does
require a theory about how power operates at the societal, structural
level. Having aligned with neo-institutionalism, FI is relinquishing a
central feature of feminist political science – the desire to comprehend
how power functions.[7] Consequently, much of FI work errs on the side
of description over analysis. It does not attempt to answer the "why"
question, and is actually ontologically disinclined to do so. For Knuttila
(1987), the fundamental weaknesses of most state theorizing, feminist

or otherwise, is the inability to explain *why* states do what they do, and FI opts not to even try.

Take, for example, some of the FI research on federalism and multilevel governance. Much of it outlines the advantages and disadvantages for women, and demonstrates that the ways in which power is divided between levels, or scales of government, is gendered. Grace (2011) provides that in Canada

the principles upon which federalism was established at Confederation in 1867 have had a lasting impact on the way in which federal and provincial governments have responded to women's policy objectives … The division of powers also set in place normative ideas that women's issues were best left to the local jurisdiction, which became further institutionalized during welfare state development. (99–100)

But this does not tell us *why* and *how* these ideas became dominant – what were the relations of power that put them into place? Sawer and Vickers (2010) do stipulate that federations and their constitutional division of powers were created before women had political rights, which is a partial answer. Yet an explanation, such as that from Cameron, elaborated below, goes much further in teasing out the role of national identity and social reproduction. Alas, this work has had little impact on FI. Brennan (2010) also shows that in Australia the constitution reflected the public/private divide.

As another case in point, Chappell (2002) introduces the interesting concept of the "logic of appropriateness" (11) to draw attention to the ways in which value systems and gender norms are attached to institutions and limit what is possible. Citing Chappell, Mackay et al. (2009) indicate that "her analysis of the 'logic of appropriateness' that underlies the norm of bureaucratic neutrality demonstrates that it is profoundly gendered. Indeed, using evidence from Australia, Canada and the UK, she argues that the more embedded and enforced the norm of neutrality is, the harder it will be for feminists to advance 'biased' claims of gender equality" (259).

It will be echoed in the case study that such expectations about neutrality are certainly an obstacle for state feminists. However, is this "logic" merely a set of ideas? Whose ideas are they? How did they become dominant? Many feminist institutionalists reject theorists such as MacKinnon and Ferguson who use patriarchy as a theoretical frame. Yet when MacKinnon (1989) notes that "rationality is measured

by point-of-viewlessness" (162), she is drawing attention to the crucial point made by femocrats, that their knowledge is considered not
to be "expertise," but rather ideology, and that this process of value-
making does not occur outside of social relations. Surely a central factor in defining which policy actors and options are "appropriate" is
capitalism and the relations of production and social reproduction. In a
capitalist economy, the range of "acceptable" policies is limited (Graefe
2007), and unequal gender relations demands "theorizing the agency of
female actors as bounded" (Mackay 2011, 190).

This leads to the second concern I have with FI – the way it conceptualizes the relationship between state institutions and society in
terms of change and agency. Neo-institutionalism and FI are responses
to society-centred perspectives such as pluralism and neo-Marxism.
Smith (2008) holds that these approaches "assumed that the state's
actions were driven by social forces, that state decisions reflected the
power of the dominant forces in society, and that political institutions
played almost no independent role in shaping policy and political outcomes" (20). In contrast, neo-institutionalism highlights "the independent causal power of states and state institutions" (Smith 2008, 21). FI
also attributes significant autonomy to institutions. Krook and Mackay
(2011) submit that "to say that an institution is gendered means that
constructions of masculinity and femininity are intertwined in the
daily culture or 'logic' of political institutions, rather than 'existing out
in society or fixed within individuals which they then bring whole to
the institution'" (6). Here, institutions can drive change independently
from society.

Portraying state institutions as having minds of their own, and
distinct personalities, attributes too much autonomy to the state,
and sets the state outside of the society in which it exists. Eschewing
society-centric stances, some feminist institutionalists go too far in the
other direction, where social forces are tangential. Consider that Lovenduski (2011) identifies the focal point of FI to be the action "between and
within" state institutions (viii). What happens on the outside gets left out.

Again, some of the FI literature on federalism and multilevel governance is indicative. As noted above, there is a growing strand of work
that asks whether federalism and multilevel governance (MLG) are
good or bad for women (Findlay 2011). One line of FI thinking views
MLG pessimistically as a major obstacle to feminist progress. Because
in many federations women had little to no influence over the constitutional division of powers, and constitutions are difficult to change

(Sawer and Vickers 2010, 4), MLG is said to stall progressive policy change. Grace (2011) shows how federalism has allowed for "blame avoidance" in Canadian childcare policy. This, combined with the exclusionary, closed-door style of intergovernmental relations in jurisdictions like Canada, creates significant difficulties for women's activism (Sawer and Vickers 2010; Grace 2011).

Yet this can lead to an over-emphasis on MLG as the *cause* of the challenges for feminist advocacy. Grace (2011) considers federalism to be a chief limitation for feminist policy, since "federal government elites have often been preoccupied with responding to provincial concerns to the detriment of including policy communities and alternative policy prescriptions" (101). Undoubtedly an accurate observation, this nonetheless assumes things would be different in the absence of federalism, which is doubtful in Canada's liberal, residual welfare regime. Gray (2010) warns that MLG should not be viewed in isolation from political party conflicts and powerful interests (Gray 2010, 24). Similarly, Chappell (2002) quotes an insight from Graham White that "the most marginalised will be as marginal in a federal system as they are anywhere else" (168). This does not mean that MLG is irrelevant, but that it should be placed in the larger social, political, and economic context.

It also portrays MLG in rather static terms. Research from Australia reveals that "women have contested the division of responsibilities between the federal and State governments in a number of policy areas and actively attempted to reshape the contours of policy responsibility" (Brennan 2010, 37). Also, Chappell cautions that "similar political architecture in different countries does not necessarily produce the same opportunity structures" (Gray 2010, 27). For example, a centralization of power can happen in both federal and unitary systems, and federalism can allow for both progressive and regressive policy innovation (Gray 2010, 23). Therefore, institutions are not the defining issue; it is power relations.

In order to develop a thorough feminist understanding of MLG, the analysis must reach beyond neo-institutionalism and the fixation on institutions over the systems of power relations in which they are embedded. This calls into question the institutionalist orientation that is reluctant to point to the balance of social forces as an explanation. It also makes for awkward treatments of agency.

Neo-institutionalism is weak in dealing with agency (Lovenduski 2011), so FI continues to grapple with this question, and in the process seems to be oscillating between ascribing too little and too much.

In order to understand impediments to women's movement activity, many feminist institutionalists supplement neo-institutionalism with the additional tool of political opportunity structure (POS) (Chappell 2002). POS draws from barriers research, and holds that "the nature of the political architecture affects how women organise to advance gender claims and where they focus their attention" (Sawer and Vickers 2010, 10). However, POS has been criticized for being reactive (Vickers 1997a), portraying the women's movement as merely responding to external constraints rather creating opportunities (Mackay 2008). When Chappell (2002) puts forward that "what neoinstitutionalism offers, is a framework that highlights the independent effect that *the pattern of interaction between various institutions within a given policy* can have on the behaviour of social actors" (8), there is a one-way relationship, with limited space for social actors to influence institutions or to change political opportunities.

In her book *Feminists and Party Politics*, Lisa Young traces women's electoral activity in Canada and the United States and the extent to which the women's movements in the United States and Canada[8] have been able to influence party politics in the two countries. Her approach fits comfortably within FI. The emphasis, due to her political opportunity structure approach, is on how institutional configurations "discourage or encourage movement behaviours" (Young 2000, 12).[9] The main question then becomes, how can women work within the existing institutions, rather than how these institutions might be transformed or democratized.

Thus, in response to the rigidity and confinement of path dependency and political opportunity structure, some have sought to accentuate women's agency. Chappell uses a more flexible version of POS, which she describes as being "interested in how political actors can both take advantage of existing opportunities and create new ones" (Chappell 2002, 9). Others have also tried to shed a more optimistic light on women's political options, with Sawer and Vickers (2010) stressing "the institutional choices available to women in the world of politics" (3). In the process, FI swings to the other extreme, towards choice inflation.

Let us return once again to federalism and MLG as a case in point. Unlike the pessimists above, some feminist institutionalists are quite optimistic about the political opportunities provided by MLG, highlighting the democratic benefits of devolution, the "subsidiarity principle" and local governance, the multiple entry points for social movements, and the potential for policy experimentation at local, subnational, national, and international levels (Sawer and Vickers 2010).

If one government is unsympathetic to a citizenship claim, it is argued, women in MLG systems have a second resort and political leverage (Gray 2010; Chappell 2002; Brennan 2010). Some even maintain that MLG permits a form of "dual citizenship," "double-democracy," "federalism advantage," or "forum shopping" (Sawer and Vickers 2010, 5; Gray 2010, 21; Vickers 2011, 129).

In her work on the non-profit sector, Brock (2010) has distinguished between descriptive and normative classifications of the relationship between the state and civil society. The optimists above present a description of the options available to feminist activists in their interaction with states, but offer little judgment about whether these options are adequate, or what specific configuration of institutions would be more desirable for women's equality. The optimists remain committed to a neo-institutionalist approach that fails to account for the gendered democratic deficits across institutions at all levels of government. Smith (2010) maintains that

> traditional approaches to the study of political institutions can be used to provide foundational insights into the dynamics of change for social movements based on gender or sexual orientation. However, these approaches do not assist us in understanding how institutions themselves are gendered in the sense of how institutions specifically encode gender relations; rather they treat institutions as mechanisms and tools with which activists must contend. (109)

Feminist institutionalism certainly works to uncover the ways in which institutions are gendered, but those institutions continue to be treated largely as given – "as mechanisms and tools" that women's movements have at their disposal. With MLG, there is a political shopping mall in which to browse and choose.

At its base, this assumes that at least one level of government is democratic, or even more democratic than the other. The idea is that feminists can shop around the political marketplace until they find a political party or environment that fits best. The problem with this approach is that it emphasizes quantity over quality, when "local or regional government may be weaker in federal systems" (Sawer and Vickers 2010, 5). And it is quite possible to have a system where neither government is particularly democratic, or open to progressive change. Having inadequate spaces of representation replicated at multiple scales of governance is especially pertinent in this period of state restructuring, when it is difficult to distinguish between governments according to their receptiveness to feminist claims. What if none of the political parties or climates available is particularly open to feminist public policy? This, in fact, more accurately captures the situation under neoliberal globalization, and in Canada, where NPM dominates federal and provincial governance.

Forum shopping treats collective organizing as simply a tactical "choice" or "rational" political calculation (Mahon et al. 2007) and requires that feminists in Canada abandon their national project based on fundamental values of universal citizenship (Sawer and Vickers 2010). There is an immense difference between a national childcare system and thirteen separate childcare regimes. Sawer and Vickers (2010) also expose the gender-blindness in the notion that MLG "offers citizens the right of choice and exit," noting women's lack of mobility (7). In addition, forum shopping requires substantial resources, is not always easy, and in Canada has reaped few rewards (Mahon and Collier 2010; Brennan 2010; Sawer and Vickers 2010).[10]

Here, the rational choice influence is evident. Rational actors make calculated decisions in the absence of structural limits. The options often seem to be unlimited, with Sawer and Grey (2008) noting that "activists have selected a particular repertoire of contention" (5). There is little reflection on how "the wide range of strategies open to these activists" (Chappell 2002, 7), or repertoires, are greatly circumscribed by neoliberal restructuring, downsizing, and decentralization (Sawer and Vickers 2010). Hence, irrespective of their location at different ends of the agency spectrum, the MLG pessimists and optimists share in their need for greater consideration of social forces and power relations.

This might be remedied through a diversification of influences. FI has not cast its intellectual net very widely. This insularity has meant that feminist institutionalists have rarely explored or engaged with other perspectives that have been integral to feminist political science. There are only a few exceptions, where some have turned to poststructuralist and queer theory (Kenny 2007; Mackay et al. 2009; Smith 2008, 2010). And there has been little dialogue between FI and FPE. FI seems to operate largely as though FPE doesn't even exist. Because, as Krook and Mackay (2011) point out, "innovative conceptual tools and approaches ... are needed in order to address the considerable challenges posed by the turn to institutions," it makes sense to widen the range of theoretical influences. If FI is willing to draw from rational choice, which many see as very unfriendly to feminism (Kenny and Mackay 2009), then why not give FPE a chance?

Feminist Political Economy

I want to be clear that my goal is not a synthesis of FI and FPE. What I am simply suggesting is that an active exchange of ideas between FI and FPE would be fruitful. This would certainly enhance FI, but FPE would also benefit from this dialogue. FPE has provided very little analysis of questions of state institutions, governance, and representation. In turning its attention to these issues, it can build on the strengths of FI, while also addressing its weaknesses. In this section, I will begin with a short description of FPE, and will then identify what I believe are the central theoretical and conceptual contributions of FPE: structural inequality; social reproduction; intersectionality; and multiscaler analysis that can be applied to the study of state institutions and representation.

What Is FPE?

In their article "Gender at Work: Canadian Feminist Political Economy since 1988," Maroney and Luxton (1997) refer to political economy as "a holistic theory, on the one hand, and a framework for radical action, on the other hand" (86). In other words, political economy is both a theory and a practice. The critical Canadian political economy tradition has examined the interaction of economic, social, cultural, and political forces and the distribution of social power between classes, making links between broad social change and public policy (Graefe 2007). It foregrounds "how the organization of the economy affects the shape of policy-making and policy outcomes, and suggests that variation in policies across space and time may result from differences between economies and the organization of economic actors" (Graefe 2007, 21). It posits that the political and the economic are not separate and that private relations affect the public (Graefe 2007).

Feminist political economy (FPE) builds on this foundation. It is also heavily influenced by socialist feminism, and draws from liberalism as well (Luxton 2006, 13). It has also integrated some of the tools of post-structuralism, including discourse analysis (Graefe 2007), and is increasingly informed by anti-racist and post-colonial theory. It considers "the historical intersection of gender, class, race/ethnicity, colonialism, state, politics, ideology, sexuality, and identity." Viewing the state as "a contested terrain," FPE asks the question, "How is a gender order ... organized by the state, and how can women organize against their subordination?" (Maroney and Luxton 1997 87). Unlike some strands of

FI, which have largely dispensed with society-driven approaches, FPE does not see the state as outside of social relations.

Voices from within FI have identified the need for theory building, and for progressing beyond description to analysis (Mackay 2011; Krook and Mackay 2011). This is where FPE can be constructive. Structural inequality, social reproduction, multiscaler analysis, and intersectionality are underused resources that can be directed towards gendering institutions and understanding governance.

Structural Inequality: Power, Agency, and States

The fundamental difference between FI and FPE is their theorization of power, agency, and states. In much of feminist political science and feminist theory, inequalities in power are seen as structural. However, Kulawik (2009) points out that in neo-institutionalism, "research designs start from real-world puzzles and are problem-driven, rather than aiming at a general theory" (263). Likewise, Mackay (2011) says that the "goal is not to generate broadly generalizable theories, but instead to identify mechanisms that have explanatory purchase across different settings" (193). According to Kenny and Mackay (2009),

> while new institutionalists acknowledge that some groups are privileged over others, they are often criticized for underplaying the importance of power relations, and power is still a relatively slippery concept in the new institutionalist literature ... Historical institutionalism is frequently criticized for its overly conservative view of institutional power relations, emphasizing the power that past decisions hold for future developments. (275)

In her defence of HI, Waylen (2009) insists that it "does accommodate notions of inequality of power and resources between actors. Institutions have distributional effects. They reflect, reproduce, and magnify particular patterns of power. Moreover, political arrangements and policy feedbacks actively facilitate the empowerment of certain groups, and these factors will impact on actors' goals and strategies" (248). Kenny and Mackay (2009) are not entirely satisfied with these "distributional models [of power, which] are less likely to employ Foucauldian concepts of power as dispersed and constitutive" (275–6). Interestingly, they do not consider political economy approaches to power.

In so far as "historical institutionalists emphasize the importance of the overarching context" (Waylen 2009, 248), they probably hold the closest affinity to FPE. However, Graefe (2007) notes that even though historical institutionalism does emphasize the importance of context and power relations, it does so without regard for structure. This distinguishes it from political economy, where inequality is structural in character, and there is a hierarchy of social forces. From this view, "although they provide points of leverage for subordinate actors to exercise power through the state, the overall mix of institutions and projects within the state nevertheless favour the exercise of power by the relatively dominant" (Graefe 2007, 28). Thus, when Kenny (2007) refers to the "continuity of the power of the powerful" (92), this sounds much more compatible with FPE than FI.

Structural inequality captures the enduring nature of hierarchies of power and challenges pluralist understandings of competing interests (Graefe 2007). Without viewing gender inequality as structural, FI risks falling into a pluralism that refuses to prioritize any explanatory factor. If, as Lovenduski (2011) says, "feminist institutionalists recognize that political explanation is about ideas, interests, and institutions, which are intertwined" (ix), what drives the various emphases on these factors? Or, when Waylen (2009) stresses the role of actors in bringing about change, how is the relative power of these actors accounted for?

Furthermore, structural inequality leads us to fixate on the *consequences* of institutional arrangements for power relations. In her discussion of comparative political science, Vickers (1997a) indicates that "its frameworks for comparing usually focus on the characteristics of political systems rather than on the consequences of different kinds of systems for people's lives" (120). Feminist variants of institutionalism go part of the way to correcting this, but not nearly far enough. As said above, they err much more on the descriptive side of Brock's (2010) typology than the normative. For example, Chappell (2002) explains that Australian bureaucracy is more open to advocacy than in Canada, and that the Charter makes the litigation strategy more open to advocates in Canada. This describes well the respective institutional openings in the system, but provides no evaluation of the political and economic implications for marginalized groups.

Viewing power and inequality as structural does not mean that institutions are static and unchangeable. In FPE, conflict is central to understanding power and change, as "political economy stresses how rule is constantly negotiated" (Graefe 2007, 25), and "public policies act as resources and constraints, both in identity and interest construction and in the contestation of social relations. Policies can be seen as institutionalized compromises between social forces" (Graefe 2007, 26). In contrast, Kenny and Mackay (2009) maintain that neo-institutionalism bypasses conflict and contestation. Discussing sociological institutionalism, Mackay et al. (2009) underscore its "'curiously bloodless' account ... [that] misses the power clashes and contestation among actors with competing interests" (260). This can be seen in Grace's (2011) treatment of intergovernmental relations in Canada, where she refers to "the complex architecture of Canadian federalism which presents to feminist policy advocates a wide stretch of government to navigate (federal, provincial, territorial, and sometimes municipal), and hence a broad array of political elites to persuade" (97). Assuming that feminist policy success is likely once the obstacles to persuasion can be overcome overlooks the ways in which social conflicts are mediated through intergovernmental relations in Canada. Federalism is not just an institutional arrangement to traverse; it is an expression of power relations (Findlay 2008). Therefore, FPE has a different standpoint on how change occurs and on the agency of social forces.

Mackay et al. (2009) hold that theorizing power and agency is integral to feminist analysis. FPE stresses the contradictory nature of political action. Rather than highlighting institutional inflexibility as the cause of path dependency, for FPE, agency is constricted primarily by the balance of social forces. It recognizes that change is possible, and necessary, while at the same time maintaining a realistic estimation of agency in which the weakness of movements is seen as a key explanatory factor (Graefe 2007). The concern with how institutions structure social relations does not discard agency. How political actors, including women, mobilize, organize, influence, and create change is vital. Porter (2003) elaborates that

> the forms restructuring takes involve a complex relationship between the multiple forces and sites of oppression, resistance, and efforts to bring about change ... It is important to consider further the role of the *state* not only in shaping the form that restructuring has taken but also in responding to pressures to address various concerns – including gender and other equity demands – and in helping shape restructuring in ways that can build on or attenuate various inequalities. (19)

New state forms, such as femocratic administration, can play an important role in supporting and re-mobilizing the women's movement.

Interestingly, despite the prominence it gives to structural constraints, FPE sets its sights on radical and transformative change. In this sense, it draws from the traditions of socialist and radical feminism. Radical feminist Kathy Ferguson (1984) focused on "identifying the power structures of bureaucratic capitalist society as a primary source of oppression of women and men, and advocating the elimination of such structures rather than their amelioration" (ix). In comparison, the goals of FI remain quite limited, settling on seizing "appropriate," and "promising" opportunities within the confines of existing institutions (Chappell 2002; Kulawik 2009). These differences can be traced to competing perspectives on the state.

It is not enough to just to bring the state back in. What is more important is *how* the state is understood and analysed. We need to theorize the state (Graefe 2007). FPE has not yet plotted a clear course, but certainly moves us in the right direction. FPE operates simultaneously at two levels. First, it seeks to understand, and explain, the relationship between the state, the market, and the family, often referred to as the state-market-family nexus.[11] At the same time, it explores the possibilities for political action that emerge, and are created, out of this nexus. FPE, then, furthers our understanding of the relationship between theory and practice in reference to the state.

R.W. Connell is an Australian feminist theorist. She sees the state as a component of the overall structure of power relations. Echoing Eisenstein, Connell (1990) refers to the state as the "institutionalization of power relations" (520). More specifically, "gender is a collective phenomenon, an aspect of social institutions as well as external to the state. Put another way, the state as an institution is part of a wider social structure of gender relations" (509). While being mindful of the critiques of the gender blindness of Marxist state theory,[12] Connell draws upon Poulantzas, because we cannot ignore that states (at least those of concern here) are of the liberal democratic variety, requiring an analysis of capitalism, colonialism, and imperialism (Connell 1990). The state plays an often active role in creating and reproducing women's inequality, and while not *inherently* patriarchal, "the state is *historically* patriarchal, patriarchal as a matter of concrete social practices" (ibid., 535).[13] Nevertheless, Connell argues that a view of the state as simply patriarchal is also not enough. States vary over time and place, and are not passive instruments. States actively pursue agendas (i.e., globalization), mobilize interests, and construct identities (i.e., "welfare mothers").

Furthermore, Connell, while taking up some of his ideas on state process, departs from Foucault, and post-structuralism, with a political economy approach. She stresses "the process of internal coordination that gives state apparatuses a degree of coherence in practice" (1990, 509–10). She elaborates on the state's coherent activities:

> Through laws and administrative arrangements the state sets limits to the use of personal violence, protects property (and thus unequal economic resources), criminalizes stigmatized sexuality, embodies masculinized hierarchy, and organizes collective violence in policing, prisons and war. In certain circumstances the state also allows or even invites the counter-mobilization of power. (520)

For example, in the OWD study, it will be shown that there are clearly problematic discourses around neutrality and the representation of diversity, but one cannot understand, and attempt to alter these discourses, without considering the context of power relations in which they operate.

In their essay "'Visible Minority' Women: A Creation of the Canadian State," Carty and Brand (1993) also show that states pursue active strategies, including creating "conflicts which did not exist before or which were on the way to being resolved" (175). For example, the Canadian state's creation of the category of "visible minority" led to the situation where "women were actually consumed with state-generated conflicts, the major one being ... the question of who are 'visible minority'; or whether the question of accent was important enough to determine minority status" (ibid.).

In Canada, FPE has focused mainly in the areas of law and public policy. In their edited volume *Privatization, Law, and the Challenge to Feminism*, Fudge and Cossman (2002) outline an FPE approach to the law and the state. For them, law works to legitimate and shape power relations and dominant ideologies, it regulates social relations, it produces ruling discourses that shape social life, and it acts as a coercive force. Law works at all levels of life, from international agreements to the labour market and the family. States actively participate in the restructuring of the relationships between citizens, as well as its own relationship with them. This does not mean that the law has not been used to advance the interests of marginalized groups, but that on balance, legal norms, methods, institutions, and actors tend to support dominant ideologies of "property, liberty, the minimal state, and the rule of law" (34). Therefore, simply changing, or educating, the personnel within legal institutions will not fundamentally alter the gendered legal system.

This approach to the state can also be seen in FPE analysis of public policy. Graefe (2007) explains that in political economy, the state is not an actor or set of institutions, it is a space of struggle and the "state does not act: rather, social forces act through the state" (27).

In this process, social forces act on an unequal terrain, and states cannot be assumed to be neutral or as acting in the public or common interest (Graefe 2007). The result is that "public policies affect the relative power of actors in reproducing social relations, but they also institutionalize social relations ... Policies serve as institutionalized compromises" (Graefe 2007, 26). "Without denying the role of institutions, of knowledge, or of learning, it [political economy] insists that policy making be seen as an act of power, and not simply as a technical exercise of sorting and evaluating policy options" (ibid., 35).

FPE in Canada is much less developed when it comes to representation. Nevertheless, the Australian literature can provide guidance. Hester Eisenstein (1996) is a former Australian "femocrat" and sees her experience "as a moment of lived political theory" (xvi). Her conception of the state combines aspects of neo-Marxist, socialist feminist, post-structuralist, and post-colonial perspectives. She sees the state as patriarchal, capitalist, and racist (xix), but leaves room for agency. Borrowing from Poulantzas, Eisenstein stresses the legitimation function of the state, to move away from views of the state as merely instruments of capital, or patriarchy (xvii). According to Eisenstein, the Australian state, or more precisely, the bureaucracy, "was an arena in which male power and privilege were institutionalized" (207). Strategically, Eisenstein notes that ignoring the state is problematic, because it does not take seriously women's concrete policy gains. She describes the struggles of Australian femocrats who were well aware of the limitations of the state, of bureaucratic constraints and culture, and of the threat of co-optation, but, nonetheless, did develop counter-strategies and had a positive effect on women's material lives. Eisenstein argues that since women rely on the state, for both jobs and services, abstract debates about engagement versus disengagement, reform versus revolution, are not very helpful. However, she acknowledges that certain groups of women have definitely not had equal access to the femocrat strategy, or to its spoils.

Due to the shortcomings of the femocrat strategy, and her focus on institutionalized power, Eisenstein (1996) is careful not to focus all of her attention on the state. Rather, she emphasizes the relationship between those working "without" and "within." She places a lot of attention on the need for mobilization outside of the state. Eisenstein argues that while women cannot avoid the state, integrating women into the state is not enough, and that sustained pressure from, and alliances with, an organized women's movement, feminists in the labour movement, and political parties is necessary. This became one of the major weaknesses of women's strategizing in Australia, especially after the rise of neoliberalism (1996). Maillé (1997) makes a similar point about the importance of the Quebec women's movement in bringing about progressive policies for women. Dobrowolsky (2000) also notes how inside/outside ties have been essential in women's constitutional struggles in Canada.

Sue Findlay's work is an exception to the largely FI interest in representation in Canada. For Findlay (1995), women's representation within the state is about more than just numbers (or formal equality); it is about the ways in which power is institutionalized in the state, or "the ruling interests that are embedded in representative institutions" (11). Influenced by the work of Mahon, Findlay (1995) sees institutions such as Status of Women Canada as an "unequal structure of representation" that reflects powerful interests in society and dominant sources and forms of knowledge production. Graefe (2007) also shows that less powerful groups are more likely to be located "at the periphery of policy networks and in bodies at the periphery of the state" (28).

Findlay's work is particularly relevant to my project in understanding the location of women's structures of representation within the overall power structure of the state, and the ways in which unequal gender relations are institutionalized inside the state. There is no doubt that women's policy machinery, such as the OWD, occupies a subordinate position in the state's administrative structure, and that marginalized groups remain so inside the state. Where I depart from Sue Findlay is that, for her, representation and participation are counter-posed: "Democracy and representation are at odds" (1995, 28). Findlay (1995) identifies representation and participation as two distinct strategic streams that emerged in the 1960s. Representation then became institutionalized in the federal bureaucracy in the 1970s. She concludes that representation has worked in the last three decades to limit community participation in the democratic process and contain their interests in the policy and management processes of representative institutions (432). Representation, therefore, exists at the expense of participation.

While it is true that women's policy structures were institutionalized in a way that prioritized representation over participation, this does not mean that the two are *necessarily* in conflict. Even in Ferguson's (1984) rather pessimistic treatment of bureaucracy, she sees the possibility "to de-bureaucratize in favor of more participatory organizational forms" (6). In contrast with Findlay, I argue, over the next few chapters, that representation need not be in opposition to participation. The two can be mutually supporting. Women's structures of representation and state feminists can, in fact, facilitate democratic participation, and work towards transforming the state. Plus, participation from movements outside the state can empower feminist representatives and enhance their democratic legitimacy within the power structure of the state.

Social Reproduction

A feminist political economy of representation can provide a distinctive perspective on power, agency, and states because of its analysis of structural inequality. Central to this analysis is the concept of social reproduction, which can be traced back to early feminist theory. McIntosh (1978) argued that "the state plays a part in the oppression of women through its support for a specific form of household: the family household dependent largely upon a male wage and upon female domestic servicing" (256). Through this process, the state ensures that the household reproduces labour power through women's unpaid work, and also takes on some of these "family" responsibilities itself because the family is inadequate in fully meeting this task (1978). In maintaining women's economic dependence on men, the state has also positioned married women as a reserve army of cheap labour, and reinforced women's dependence through public policies such as social security and unemployment insurance, disability benefits, tax breaks for married men, protective labour laws for women and children, and pro-natal policies (McIntosh 1978). Such interrogations of the relationship between the state, market, and family provided the foundation for modern conceptions of social reproduction.

Bezanson and Luxton (2006) define social reproduction as

> the processes involved in maintaining and reproducing people, specifically the labouring population, and their labour power on a daily and generational basis ... Embedded in a feminist political economy framework, social reproduction offers a basis for understanding how various institutions (such as the state, the market, the family/household, and the third sector) interact and balance power so that the work involved in the daily and generational production and maintenance of people is completed. (3)

For Bezanson and Luxton (2006), social reproduction involves the care of people, as well as the transfer of knowledge, social values, cultural practices, and identities. Responsibility for social reproduction shifts over time, and is redistributed differently within the "state-market-family/household-third sector nexus," thereby restructuring the gender order (ibid., 5). FPE is concerned with the impact of various configurations of responsibility on social relations. For instance, state involvement in social reproduction has the effect of supporting families, and women in particular, yet at the same time acting as a form of social control and surveillance (Bezanson and Luxton 2006).

Social reproduction also figures prominently in Fudge and Cossman's (2002) framework. They posit that in a capitalist society, there is a contradictory relationship between production, including waged work, and social reproduction, the work (paid and unpaid) that must be done to maintain the working population. States are involved in mediating the contradictions between production and social reproduction, and in the process, states regulate the gender order (which they define as a particular sexual division of labour and gender discourse). This is echoed in Graefe's (2007) discussion of policy compromises aimed at stabilizing the social order. But these authors note that gender orders are not static. They vary according to the extent to which social reproduction is organized by the market, households, or the state, leaving space for political agency. Further, while the restructuring of the gender order complicates feminist struggle, the contradictions also create new forms of opposition and alternative conceptions of citizenship (Fudge and Cossman 2002).

While Bezanson and Luxton and Fudge and Cossman operate at a fairly high level of abstraction, Porter (2003) uses an FPE approach to study the welfare state more specifically. Porter also analyses the relationship between production and social reproduction, in terms of the work-state-family nexus. She puts forth a dynamic view of the nexus, and production and social reproduction, as both structuring, and being structured by, social relations, while also emphasizing women's agency as political actors. She highlights the significance of pressure outside of the state, as well as the divisions within the state for FPE. Porter proposes "a model for policy analysis; with a framework that can shed light on how particular policies came about, the constraints faced by various groups as they attempt to influence policy directions, and the possibilities for and limitations on new forms of restructuring" (2003, 14). These FPE perspectives offer alternative accounts of state variation, policy change (or preservation), and women's agency that hinge on social reproduction.

If we turn back to Grace's (2011) study of federalism and social policy in Canada, she found that "the federal government's commitment to developing a national child-care framework ... was cast in terms of reconciling work and family and promoting healthy child development rather than women's economic independence or women's equality" (103). To explain why this is the case, Grace points to the "institutional landscape" of intergovernmental relations situated within a neoliberal and social investment discourse (Grace 2011, 111). Social reproduction as an analytic device could enhance this approach by locating institutional arrangements, policy choices, and discourses within the power relations of the state/market/family, as seen below in Cameron's work.

Unfortunately, examinations of social reproduction and state institutions are relatively rare at this point. As mentioned earlier, the FPE literature is underdeveloped in a number of areas. In particular, work is scarce that examines representation and governance through the dynamic of social reproduction. This is a clearly a place for future research and for expanding the influence of FPE, and where this study aims to make an impact. Another contribution that FPE can make to institutional learning is to introduce a multiscaler analysis to the discussion.

Multiscaler Analysis

Recently, multilevel governance has been a popular fascination in FI, but Mahon et al. (2007) distinguish between the concepts of multilevel governance and multiscalerity. They explain that multilevel governance is heavily influenced by rational choice theory, where the self-interest of actors is the primary driver. The language of "levels" denotes a hierarchical view of the relations between governments, and a stubborn "methodological nationalism" (41). Alternatively, a multiscaler approach combines macro political economy with a relational understanding of space and place, taken from geography. The political economy of scale addresses "the way that social actors construct, contest, and negotiate larger societal arrangements at particular scales" (59). In particular, "scale theorists are interested in how interscaler rule regimes operate to reinforce (or counteract) class and gender inequality" (53). Scale is a social relation.

Like the multiscaler approach, FPE is attuned to the interaction between the micro, meso, and macro scales. Given the widespread use of the political opportunity structure in FI, that approach is oriented towards certain kinds of micro and meso institutions (Driscoll and Krook 2009), such as legislatures, political parties, bureaucracies, constitutions, and federalism. These are unquestionably important, and deserve more scrutiny from FPE. Where FPE distinguishes itself is in its attention to the meso level of the family, household, and labour market. FPE also excels at the macro scale, paying close attention to colonialism, globalization, restructuring, and the institutions of global governance (i.e., the World Bank, IMF, NAFTA, EU).

There has been greater awareness of globalization within FI. In 2007, Haussman and Sauer released *Gendering the State in the Age of Globalization: Women's Movements and State Feminism in Postindustrial Democracies*, with the central question, in an era of globalization, "Is there a place for state feminism in these changing times?" They tackle fourteen comparative national studies, across four continents (Asia, Australia, Europe, and North America), each based on issues related to the restructuring of government such as budget cuts, downsizing, decentralization, and marketization (Haussman and Sauer 2007a). The authors identify the paradoxical reality that increases in women's formal representation in the policy process over the 1980s and 1990s has occurred alongside the decline of gender-sensitivity in public policy. They aim to understand the impact of the women's movement and femocrats on policy changes under restructuring by considering factors such as policy outcomes, policy discourse, and the relationship between the movement and femocrats.

Their project looks at policy areas that do not immediately or obviously appear to be gendered, and which were identified as priority agenda items in their respective countries. Three patterns of restructuring emerge through the research: downsizing, expansion of state powers, and constitutional reorganization. Resource mobilization and political opportunity structure are used to analyse these trends, and they find that state feminists had little involvement in these debates (Haussman and Sauer 2007a).

The research on the impact of globalization and restructuring on state feminism is further developed in an edited volume by Outshoorn and Kantola (2007b), *Changing State Feminism*. Another comparative endeavour, the book traces women's policy agencies in twelve industrialized democratic nations in an effort to evaluate how the agencies have fared under changing political environments. Unlike Lovenduski et al. and Haussman and Sauer, their interest is less in the institutional factors related to "success" than in the overall political context in which state feminism operates.

One of the compelling contributions of the Outshoorn and Kantola text is the development of multilevel governance as a significant consideration in the changing political landscape for state feminism or women's policy agencies. Namely, shifting governance to the supra-national level (i.e., UN or EU) and sub-national level (i.e., regional or municipal governments) presents both opportunities and challenges for state feminism (Kantola and Outshoorn 2007). The UN and the EU have provided new openings for feminist policy influence and leverage, but have also been met with government foot-dragging and assertions of national sovereignty. Similarly, in some places, decentralization has multiplied and expanded the reach of women's policy agencies, while in other places it has created disparities and capacity problems (Outshoorn and Kantola 2007b). Both of these mesh with my contention that, in the end, what is significant about the scale of governance is the underlying power relations that matter most for gender democracy.

This recent literature has certainly developed the field of state feminist analysis significantly. However, there are still some research gaps. FPE provides a critical lens through which to analyse the literature on representation, state feminism, and the politics of scale, which is not built on a very strong theoretical foundation. Since most of these studies are heavily neo-institutionalist, the women's movement and state feminism tend to be abstracted from wider political and economic processes, which are often inadequately considered. Globalization and restructuring are theorized as new institutional (re)formations. But the re-scaling of governance, as has occurred under decentralization, or as Mahon et al. call it, "downscaling," is much more than an institutional shuffle. Scale is integral to social conflicts in Canada (Graefe 2007, 27), such as regional and class cleavages (Brodie 1990, 1995b; Mahon et al. 2007) as federalism has filtered and framed class and gender relations. The political economy of scale is about "the power-laden and contested nature of inter-scaler arrangements" (Mahon et al. 2007, 53). Globalization has brought a fundamental political and economic transformation of states, markets and families, or the gender order.

Cameron (2006) has shown that in Canada, social reproduction, or "the recreation of the population ... from one generation to the next" (45), is central to understanding the gendered underpinnings of federalism.

The constitutional division of powers reflects the prevailing assumptions of the gender order at the time of Canadian confederation, based on the public/private divide. Chappell also refers to Helen Irving's observation about federalism in the Australian context, who says that "for the most part, the domestic and familial – the sphere which constituted the greatest sources of interest to women activists – is left to state jurisdiction, often meaning in this period, to the private sphere. The nation, it might seem, is public and male, and the state the sphere of the female" (Chappell 2002, 162). For women's movements, such as in "English" Canada, that have a distinct preference for national social policy and standards (over the "patchwork"), this presents a significant challenge (Sawer and Vickers 2010).

Contrary to those who emphasize institutional factors, and the political opportunity structure, political economists see the politics of scale as a reflection of social forces.[14] Thus, multiscalerity is neither an opportunity nor an obstacle, but a reflection of social and political power at any given time and place, and is a tool with which to understand these relations (Findlay 2008). To complete the FPE toolkit, let us turn to intersectionality.

Intersectionality

Intersectionality is an innovation of post-colonial and anti-racist feminism. It has also begun to integrate elements of queer theory and critical disability studies. Intersectionality locates inequality within multiple and overlapping forms of oppression, social relations, and systems of power, including capitalism, colonialism, patriarchy, racism, heterosexism, and ableism.

Anti-racist/post-colonial[15] feminism offers both a critique of the state and of common feminist theories of it. Carty and Brand (1993) explicitly draw attention to the ways in which the state produces and reproduces not only unequal gender and class, but also race relations. They begin their essay with the following statement: "The Canadian state does not relate to all people(s) equally, and as far as it relates to women at all, it tends to treat Native, South Asian, Black, Chinese and other non-white groups of women as quantitatively aberrant and qualitatively homogeneous" (169).

Bannerji adds that the "state and the 'visible minorities' (the non-white people living in Canada) have a complex relationship with each other. There is a fundamental unease with how our difference is construed and constructed by the state, how our otherness in relation to Canada is projected and objectified" (Bannerji 1996, 105). Armstrong and Connelly (1999) also point out that the state is contradictory not only in the sense that it can mitigate and reinforce women's inequality, but also that it can advance the interests of some women and not others. Feminist state theorizing, therefore, must account for the different relationships that women of colour have with the state, providing a significant challenge to FPE.

Many Aboriginal women have introduced serious critiques of many feminist approaches to the state and public policy. One of the key feminist interventions into public policy has been around issues of violence against women. The "traditional" feminist critique has been centrally targeted at the public/private dichotomy, which, it has been argued, constructs violence against women as a private concern, and justifies non-intervention by the state into the realm of the family. For MacKinnon (1989), one of the main indicators of the patriarchal state is its refusal to intervene in cases of violence against women, and McIntosh (1978) makes a comparable observation.

But all do not share in the desire for the state to intervene in cases of intimate violence, particularly when it involves the criminal justice system. Many commentators have argued for a more nuanced view of the state, stressing that levels of state intervention and regulation, as well as the desire for it, differ by race, class, sexual orientation, and ability.[16] Feminists

> have generally not noted the ways in which different families may be more or less immune to state intervention. Aboriginal families have been particularly susceptible to state intervention in the child welfare arena, for example. Conversely, the state has often been all too willing to avoid intervening where housing and other services are required by Aboriginal peoples. This contradiction emphasizes the highly selective nature of action/inaction on the part of the state. (Koshan 1997, 96)

Public policy interventions have been based on dominant feminist understandings of gender violence, and on the demand for state intervention into the "private" sphere. The policy in Canada on automatic charging and prosecution "results in survivors' forced engagement with the criminal justice system via police and prosecution policy directives" (Koshan 1997, 100). Numerous studies have shown that this policy discourages women from marginalized groups from reporting violence.[17]

Similarly, FPE focuses heavily on the shift from a Keynesian gender order based on the male-breadwinner model to a neoliberal gender order based on a dual earner model of the family (Fudge and Cossman 2002). Some, such as Porter (2003), have integrated critiques from women of colour and anti-racist feminists reminding that the male-breadwinner model was not universal. As seen in the introductory chapter, her framework includes

> numerous variables – labour markets, unpaid work in the home, family work/life patterns, race and ethnicity, political struggles, gender ideologies, juridical norms, state policies … as part of a dynamic whole in which there are "multiple strands of determination" and complex processes of interaction and change. (13)

She goes on to say that "race, class, gender, sexuality, and other axes of domination constitute mutually constructing systems of oppression, manifested through a variety of institutions including schools, housing, and government bodies" (18).

Overall, even though most feminist political economists are aware that the male-breadwinner model acts as an ideal type at the policy level, some of the detail within the models gets lost in broad comparisons between the Keynesian and neoliberal gender orders. Thus, it is not always evident that feminist political economists have fully accounted for the reality that many families of colour (and working-class families) have never experienced production and social reproduction in the same way as white, middle-class families. In this way, Dua provides a very useful intervention into FPE. She demonstrates that the construction of the nuclear family cannot be considered outside of racism and nation building, and the exclusion of families of colour from the male-breadwinner model. Yet at the same time, Dua stresses the centrality of the nuclear family/male-breadwinner model to racialized and marginalized groups – acting to scrutinize and regulate their lives (Dua 1999).

Millbank (1997) also problematizes feminist treatments of the public/private dichotomy, but from the perspective of lesbians and their encounters with the law. As just seen, feminists have generally traced women's oppression to the public/private dichotomy, in which women are too often relegated to the latter, and denied access to the former. While the realm of the "private" has been shown to be a dangerous place for many women, Millbank (1997) argues that "the absence of any space conceived by the law as 'private' where lesbians, or at least lesbian mothers, are concerned" (281) signals the need for a more complex feminist theorization of the private, and of the right to privacy.[18]

She takes lesbian mothers' experiences with child custody cases as an example. In these cases, where women are inappropriately asked about the intimate details of their sex lives, and are pathologized, and constructed as dangerous (Millbank 1997), privacy takes on a different meaning. The "best interests of the child" doctrine, in addition to acting as a justification for blatant invasions of privacy, opens the door to a plethora of judicial biases and mythical assumptions, and in the end trumps any claim to a right of privacy that lesbian mothers might make (Millbank 1997). Such work challenges "traditional" feminist theorizing, as well as practical public policy prescriptions.

By now, knowledge of the interaction of race and sexuality with the state's most coercive elements is fairly well developed; much more must be done to understand these relationships with other sections of the state.[19] And there is still much to be learned from feminist interrogation of the state and about the dangers of failing to take into account women's differing experiences of family.[20] We saw above that postcolonial/anti-racist feminists have introduced a more nuanced view of production and social reproduction – specifically the male-breadwinner model and the sexual division of labour, arguing that neither describes the realities of most women of colour, who have always worked outside the home, often in the homes of white, middle-class women, and have not been positioned the same way in the sexual division of labour, often performing difficult, physical labour.[21] In addition, the male-breadwinner model, assuming as it does a heterosexual family, does not describe queer experiences with family.[22]

Intersectionality is beginning to be taken up more broadly in feminist research and in FPE in particular. It does not appear to have had the same effect on FI. Kenny (2007) is concerned that "while historical institutionalists acknowledge that some groups are privileged over others, little attention is paid to major social divisions such as gender, race or class" (96), and Kenny and Mackay believe "there are still significant limitations to new institutionalist conceptions of power, which continue to pay little or no attention to major social divisions such as gender and race" (Kenny and Mackay 2009, 275). So far, the feminist interventions into neo-institutionalism have introduced a gender analysis more than an intersectional one.

FPE's focus on structural inequality discussed earlier also makes it more compatible with an intersectional analysis. In the 2013 issue of *Signs* dedicated to the theme of intersectionality, Cho, Crenshaw, and McCall (2013) are careful to specify that their approach emphasizes political and structural inequalities," pointing to "the explicit references to structures that appear in much of the early work" and seeking an analysis of power that can discern "which differences make a difference" (797–8). In the same journal, reflecting on her groundbreaking work in intersectional theory, Mohanty (2013) describes her systemic understanding of power.

Together, structural inequality, social reproduction, multiscaler analysis, and intersectionality, make FPE an indispensible framework for understanding social inequality and state institutions. Still, with some notable exceptions,[23] it must be reiterated that FPE has engaged very little with the central research questions of FI. In this final section, I suggest that the gender regime literature provides FI and FPE with a conversational juncture in which issues of governance, representation, and democracy can be deliberated.

Gender Regimes

Despite their differences, FI and FPE also have commonalities. For one, they both struggle to have more influence in their wider fields and face hostility, or at least indifference, to feminist analysis. The feminist interest in neo-institutionalism (NI) has not been reciprocated. NI has made little progress in integrating a gender analysis (Kenny and Mackay 2009). FPE has faced similar resistance within political economy circles. Each challenges its respective roots, as they also belong to the family of feminist political science,[24] which "is explicitly concerned with recognizing how institutions reproduce gendered power relations, but perhaps more importantly, with how these institutions can be challenged and reformed" (Krook and Mackay 2011). FI and FPE coalesce around centring the institutionalization of power relations and how to achieve change.

For this reason, both have turned to, and helped to shape, the gender regime literature. Gender regime theory highlights the "ways in which institutions reflect, reinforce, and structure unequal gendered power relations in wider society" (Krook and Mackay 2011, 6). The state is important for feminists to study because it is a key site where the unequal power relations (including gender, but also class, race, sexuality, and ability) in society are institutionalized. Through the "institutionalization of power relations," social inequality is reflected, and reproduced by, and within, the state, and becomes embedded within state institutions and policies. This entails not simply that social inequalities are mirrored in the state, but that the state takes an active role in structuring and restructuring them. As Rankin (1996) shows, this can include sub-national states acting as "organizers and disorganizers of women's interests" (83). As such, the transformation of social relations cannot be achieved without also transforming the institutions that mediate and structure those relations.

Conceptualizing the state as the institutionalization of power relations (IPR) allows us to determine how various forms of oppression are interconnected at the level of the state, and at different levels of the state. It places the state *within* rather than *outside* of society and social relations. As Connell (1990) puts it, "The state ... is only part of a wider structure of gender relations" or is "one of the principal substructures of the gender order" (520), and of the social order generally. This avoids the pitfalls of some other approaches to the state. Knuttila (1987) identifies instrumentalism and functionalism as the two major flaws in state theory, concluding that "an adequate theory of the state must help to provide answers to the 'why' questions. Why does the state undertake certain actions?" (137). IPR asks not why, but rather, why not? Why would the state, which is embedded in a capitalist, gendered, racialized, colonial, heteronormative society, *not* reproduce these relations?

This does not preclude the internal struggles inside and between state institutions that are stressed in gender regime theory. This is key to my study of the OWD, which shows the importance of women's struggles both inside and outside the state, and to the feminist political economy approach more generally. As Krook and Mackay (2011) maintain, "reciprocal relationships" of cause and effect are always at play (7). FI and FPE agree that feminists must account for variation within and between states, or across space and time (Connell 1990, 521–2). Porter makes the point that struggles outside, and within, states are important to policy outcomes. Within states, gender relations differ by sector – the legislature, the bureaucracy, the judiciary, the military, police, social services, clerical, etc. – or what Connell calls the "gender structuring of state apparatus" (ibid., 524). Likewise, Melanie Randall (1988) adds that "not only is the state itself a site of struggle among social groups, but there is often conflict and contradiction between the actions and policies of the various levels, branches and agencies of the state" (14). Contextual or national differences are significant.

Surely distinctions must be made between women's relationships to previous Keynesian welfare states and current neoliberal states, for example. This will be seen in the case of the OWD, where different gender regimes mattered to women's representation and policy results.

FPE uses the concept of the "gender order" to refer to the particular form that gender relations and discourse take in a given time and place. A relatively stable, or institutionalized, gender order is eventually challenged by shifting social relations, which brings about a new gender order (Fudge and Cossman 2002). Feminists have also adapted Esping-Andersen's welfare state typologies to show that distinct gender regimes exist along the liberal, corporatist, and social democratic spectrum, and that states differ in their regulation of gender relations.[25]

This is why, historically, the Canadian state has been simultaneously a target of critique and a significant focus for advancing feminist projects. Canadian feminists have made both representational and social citizenship claims on the state, or claims for both procedural and substantive democracy. While such claims have certainly not always been adequately addressed, feminists have made significant progress in transforming law and public policy. The centrality of the state for feminist theory and practice must be recognized and the theoretical and practical links must be made clear. FI and FPE concur on this point.

There is also consensus on the explicitly political and normative nature of feminist institutional critique. Kenny and Mackay (2009) explain that "feminist political science has as a central feature a transformative agenda. That is to say that feminist political science is explicitly concerned not only with recognizing how institutions reproduce gendered power distributions but also with how these institutions can be changed" (276). Melanie Randall (1988) also insists that "the feminist concern with the state must ultimately lead to the question of our political strategy," and "although fraught with complexity and contradiction, we cannot afford to ignore the state in our theoretical or practical work" (14–15). For Connell (1990), too, theory must have practical applications: "The point of a theory of the state is a better capacity to make appraisals of political strategy" (509). She links theory and practice in this way: "Though the state is patriarchal, progressive gender politics cannot avoid it. The character of the state as the central institutionalization of power, and its historical trajectory in the regulation and constitution of gender relations, make it unavoidably a major arena for challenges to patriarchy" (ibid., 535). Theory should tell us "not whether feminism will deal with the state, but how, on what terms, with what tactics, toward what goals" (531). Gender regimes provide a framework for answering these questions and FPE can enrich this work.

I take from FPE not only the focus on structural constraints, but also on women's agency and struggle. For FPE, the gender order (including the relations of production and social reproduction) is contradictory, and in flux. This creates pressures to re-regulate the gender order, and find spaces for new forms of social organization. Within the wider gender order, there is also room for variations in gender regimes. In identifying such variations, feminists have emphasized the relationship among policy, women's mobilization, and structures of representation as important considerations that have generally been left out of mainstream welfare regime research. A combination of factors, including party and electoral politics, unions, corporatist structures, and state feminism go into the making of a gender regime (Sainsbury 1999).

Party politics and corporatist structures have received much more attention, but the case studies of the Weberian and New Public Management (NPM) models discussed in subsequent chapters indicate that the ways in which representation and democracy are conceptualized within regimes of public administration merit further exploration. This is especially relevant given feminist interest in both the substance and the process of policymaking.

I consider variations in gender regimes to be critical to an FPE approach to state institutions. Because, as seen earlier, Sue Findlay's analysis is largely focused on the Weberian regime of bureaucratic organization, it provides a limited view of representation. She is correct that representation, as integrated into the Weberian regime, was problematic. However, even these liberal forms of representation are under attack, and are seen as a threat to the neoliberal governance paradigm, the NPM. This speaks to the importance of an FPE approach, focused not only on critique, but also on investigating potential political openings within regimes.

FPE also introduces social reproduction to the gender regime scholarship. Mahon (2005) demonstrates that path-breaking can happen, and that there are internal conflicts, contradictions, and "alternative logics" within regimes that can reorganize social reproduction. This distinguishes FPE from FI in that changes in states over time are explained as primarily social, rather than institutional, processes. As a case in point, feminist political economist Sylvia Walby "conceptualizes gender regimes as societal, and theorizes change occurring when transnational, socioeconomic forces precipitate crises and institutional restructuring results" (Vickers 2011, 132).

My approach differs from FI in that it sees social reproduction as central to both the ways in which state institutions, including public administration, are structured, and to women's access to democracy and representation. Different gender regimes, and specifically gender regimes of public administration, provide alternative constructions of representation and democracy. Even though social reproduction has been central to FPE examinations of institutions of welfare state regimes, and to social and family policy, little has been written about the relationship among social reproduction, democracy, and representation. I submit that the state/market/family nexus can be as useful to understanding representative institutions as it has been for redistributive ones.

In reference to state administration, Sue Findlay shows that there is a hierarchical ordering of administrative institutions, or an "unequal structure of representation," drawing from Mahon. Mahon (1977) argues that the organization of state institutions represents the economic power structure, with the department of finance at the apex. For her, the federal bureaucracy is ordered based on the dominant class fractions. However, due to Mahon's neo-Marxist approach, power relations are viewed in a limited way – in reference to the relations of production. When one considers those at the top of the power structure (Finance, International Trade, Industry), in relation to things like Health, Immigration, and Women's Issues, it is not only about class fractions, but also indicates a valuing of production over social reproduction, and reinscribes the public/private divide. Bashevkin and McIvor have made comparable observations about other political institutions such as political parties and the allocation of cabinet portfolios.

Within departments and agencies, the public/private, production/social reproduction dichotomy is also reproduced. Elaborated more in the next chapter, Sue Findlay (1995) draws attention to sexual division of labour inside the state, between managers and other personnel (17). Even after twenty-five years of federal employment-equity policy, marginalized groups continue to be underrepresented in upper management and concentrated in clerical and temporary positions.[26] Likewise, in chapter 3, I will discuss how the governing principles of Weberian organization, such as neutrality, expertise, and categorization, are premised on the profoundly gendered ideology of the public/private divide, and how neoliberal public administration is reconfiguring the public and private.

In addition to the structuring of state administration, the gendered division of labour associated with social reproduction affects women's ability to participate democratically. When Anne Phillips (1991) speaks of "engendering democracy," she is pointing to the gendered inequality of opportunity that affects women's ability to participate in democratic processes. Women's primary responsibility for social reproduction, in addition to their paid work, means that women have less time to engage directly in decision-making and the policy process. This has become more pronounced as the shifting gender order brings more women into the paid labour force, and has increased their work in the spheres of both production and social reproduction. Therefore, policies aimed at re-balancing work and family are essential not only to substantive, but also to procedural democracy. In concert with such policies, a rethinking of the relationship between representation and participation is in order. Representation should account for women's lived realities, which interfere with their ability to participate. The goal of representation, then, should be to supplement, and facilitate, the participation of marginalized citizens – to move towards a feminist democratization.

Where it departs even more sharply from FI, an FPE perspective on political practice, including one relying on state feminism, must demonstrate a generous degree of state scepticism. Carty and Brand (1993) submit that

> because the state in capitalist society, by virtue of its goals and interests, does not operate within the interests of the working class – to which most immigrant and visible minority women belong – the limitations of any state-formed organization with a mandate to do so must be recognized and questioned. More important, whether such organizations perceive their limitations, and if so how they do, ought to be examined. (170)

Likewise, Melanie Randall (1988) advocates a form of feminist practice that has a realistic view of state power, and takes democracy as its starting point:

> In the short run it is perhaps most urgent that as feminists we collectively analyze our experiences of women who have chosen to work inside the various agencies of the state, their accountability to the women's movement, the constraints and contradictions which inevitably shape these experiences, and the openings and possibilities for shaping policy and making decisions about the use of state power and resources which may, or may not emerge. (15)

Engaging with the state, therefore, is only a first step in transforming it, since, in the end, as Eisenstein (1996) reminds us, "it is social movements, not governments that seek democratization and access" (213). The state is thus a crucial site of political struggle (Fudge and Cossman 2002; Maroney and Luxton 1997).

In terms of strategy, Connell (1990) advocates the democratization of state structures, which means moving beyond representation to more participatory forms of politics (536). This falls in line with Eisenstein's support for strengthening links between feminists inside and outside of the state, funding for social movement groups,[27] and gender-based budgeting (1993).[28] It also coincides with many of the recommendations by Judy Rebick in her book *Imagine Democracy* around electoral and campaign finance reform and participatory democracy.

Susan Phillips (1993) refers to *democratic governance*, while others use the term *democratic administration* (Albo, Panitch, and Langille 1993), but both signal a definition of democracy that goes beyond representative democracy in electoral politics, to representation and participation in the policy process for groups and citizens. Owing to the "fundamental inequality of society,"

> the task of creating a more participatory and democratic government might involve several interrelated steps: 1) expansions of mechanisms for citizen participation that provide realistic opportunities for large segments of society to participate; 2) extension of a regime for regulating fairness in representation which both regulates the privileged and assists the disadvantaged; 3) provision of open access to information; and 4) development of the capacity for self-management of policies by groups and communities. (Phillips 1993, 12–13)

The underlying feminist analysis in Phillips's recommendations is made more explicit by others.

Jill Bystydzienski and Joti Sekhon (1999) explore the "theoretical and practical implications of the connection between women's community-based movements and democratization. They define democratization as "a process by which the voices of ordinary people can find increasing organized expression in the institutions of their society" (9), and see the participation of grassroots movements, specifically grassroots women's organizations, as essential to the project of democratization. They maintain that "though not all grassroots organizations are necessarily participatory and progressive, many have emerged as a significant part of efforts to create and expand spaces for democratic decision-making" (10). Feminist engagement with the state must not be simply an end in itself, or an encounter with pre-existing structures; it can be a conscious, active, transformative process.

As seen above, Sue Findlay distinguishes between representation and transformation, and argues that "without an understanding of the limits of representation – of the particular way that democracy has been liberalized and embedded in the very forms of representation for which we have struggled long and hard – democratization is impossible" (Findlay 1993a, 162). I agree with Findlay that transformation involves moving beyond representation that simply categorizes interests and identities, towards transferring power to the people and making states accountable (Findlay 1993a, 163).[29] But I also assert that transforming representation, not abandoning it, must be a central goal of democratizing gender regimes and that state feminism can advance this project. Incidentally, the extensive FI literature on state feminism and representation can be a valuable resource for FPE.

Conclusion

A genuine dialogue between FI and FPE is long overdue. FI has broken new ground in the study of gender and institutions. This work is indispensible to constructing an FPE perspective that takes representation, governance, and democracy into account. FPE provides FI with fresh analytical tools to employ on state institutions: structural inequality, social reproduction, multiscaler analysis, and intersectionality. While not aiming for synthesis, there is a constructive discussion to be had, and the gender regime literature offers a hospitable meeting place.

This project is one attempt at growing the conversation in order to extend the stretch of FPE beyond its traditional foci. I believe this provides the best path to feminist democratization. For FPE, feminist interactions with the state are not simply reactive. Instead, they take radical social change as their ultimate objective, of which femocratic administration is part. I will now turn to developing this point in more detail in the next chapter.

2 Gender Regimes of Public Administration

In response to globalization and neoliberalism, many are looking to supra-national scales of governance. Others are arguing that we need to focus our attention on the democratization of the state, and state administration, and I locate myself within this perspective. However, as just seen in chapter 1, the state and democracy are complicated by considerations of gender, and notwithstanding ongoing ambivalence about the state, feminists have made some important contributions to the study of state institutions and public administration. This chapter examines public administration as it has developed in Canada, through two dominant governance models: the Weberian and the New Public Management (NPM). I argue that despite key differences between them, both result in a gender regime of public administration that involves only limited forms of representation and democracy. Therefore, alternative governance approaches must be explored.

The chapter begins by reviewing traditional bureaucratic organization and the feminist critiques of the main elements of Weberian administration: hierarchy, compartmentalization, and neutrality, which are said to be counter to feminist values and principles. I also explore some of the ways in which pressure from the inside and outside brought change to this regime. I then consider the period of the 1980s and 1990s, in which neoliberal bureaucratic restructuring, or the NPM, challenged Weberian organization, but not its gendered consequences. I briefly canvas some of the main features of the NPM: downsizing, privatization, and managerialism, and the feminist literature that identifies the gendered nature of neoliberalism and the NPM in particular. Finally, I suggest that we can move beyond both models with a transformative public administration focused on state feminism, representation, and democracy.

Feminist Critiques of Weberian Bureaucracy

Max Weber identified several key elements of an "ideal" bureaucracy, and modern bureaucracies, including in Canada, came to be organized around such characteristics as: hiring based on merit, rationality, technical training, tenure, professionalization, standard operating procedures, hierarchy, specialization, division of labour (or compartmentalization), secrecy, neutrality, and expertise (Weber 1994, 1997, 1999; Albo 1993; Sossin 1999). While Weberian organization was designed to promote fairness and efficiency, feminists have problematized many of its aspects due to their gendered consequences. In this section, hierarchy, compartmentalization, and neutrality will be elaborated in detail. These elements are central to the model of representation, and related gender regime, on which Weberian bureaucracy rests.

Hierarchy, Power, and Compartmentalization

For Weber, archetypal bureaucracies are organized hierarchically, and divided into discreet functions. Hierarchy is intended to provide a clear line of command, and is therefore linked to accountability. In a parliamentary system, as in Canada, ministerial responsibility places final answerability in the hands of an elected official, or a cabinet minister. In this way, representative democracy is the foundation for hierarchies in public bureaucracies. While considered by many to make the system democratic, this form of organization is quite problematic, particularly for feminism. Hierarchical organization is in fundamental opposition to feminist ideals that seek to end relations of subordination and unequal power.

From a radical feminist perspective, Ferguson makes such a case about the bureaucracy. She refers to it as an "organizational caste system" that involves "learning to play the role of the subordinate in social relations" (Ferguson 1984, 85, 92). She believes that "bureaucracy is the routinization of domination" in which "bureaucratic power creates an arena where the 'feminization' of subordinates is encouraged" (Ferguson 1984, 17, 98). Franzway et al. (1989) have traced the "bureaucratization of feminism" in Australia, saying: "Bureaucratization suggests adaptation to Weberian principles and regulated impersonal structures. These appear contradictory to feminism's own organisational ideals which are antipathetical to hierarchy, rules and authority, and problematic for the multifaceted and subjective nature of feminist issues" (143). Sawer (1990) reminds us that feminist bureaucrats, or "femocrats," "are caught up in a system still fundamentally based on hierarchy and secrecy" (252), and so entrance into the bureaucracy requires the renunciation of feminist principles and conformity to oppressive structures.

Hierarchy marks not only the relationship between bureaucrats, but between bureaucratic departments as well. As noted in the previous chapter, the bureaucracy parallels the hierarchies that exist outside the state. In exploring the relative autonomy of the state, Mahon (1977) has referred to the bureaucracy as an "unequal structure of representation" that reflects the inequalities in society (167). While the state's "organs and branches 'represent' the various social forces," dominant branches reflect dominant power (ibid., 170–1). Recall from chapter 1 that Mahon stresses the importance of the Department of Finance (175). O'Neil and Sutherland (1997) also mention "the invisible hierarchy of cabinet ministers as a ranking founded on whether the portfolios deal with macroeconomic and typically masculine endeavors as opposed to areas that are extensions of domestic capacity" (201). Similarly, Ferguson (1984) adds that "as both a structure and a process, bureaucracy must be located within its social context; in our society, that is a context in which social relations between classes, races, and sexes are fundamentally unequal" (7).

Therefore, the value placed on hierarchy is not simply a set of "rational" ideas; it is a way of organizing, and ordering, social relations.[1] This ordering of social relations entails a replication of the public/private divide, where, as noted in the previous chapter, state institutions are structured around the relations of production and social reproduction. From her experience as a former femocrat, Sue Findlay (1995) draws attention to "the way that the state bureaucracy was grounded in a sexual division of labour, how class and gender intersected in the hierarchies to shape the workforce in the federal bureaucracy, how this hierarchy limited the access of women to policy positions and the influence of those who were appointed as policy advisors" (39). She specifically notes the resistance of male managers to increasing the numbers of women in mid and upper management. Agócs (2012) also notes that the

> culture and structure of the public service, like corporate bureaucracies, were imbued with policies, practices and meanings that perpetuated inequality regimes. For example, women and minorities were clustered in lower ranks of the hierarchy in clerical job ghettos, and in specialized program areas such as "women's issues," immigration, and services to Aboriginal peoples. (4)

To explain this division of labour, Stivers (1993) cites Kanter's conclusion that "women and men constitute separate organizational classes, with women (in general) rewarded for routine services and men for rational decision making and leadership" (68). This is because "capitalism's structural necessity for surplus workers supports patterns in which women are disproportionately restricted to low-level, often part-time, organizational positions" and where the routine tasks performed to a great degree resemble housework (69, 73).

Stivers (1993) holds that public administration is predicated on the maintenance of the public/private divide, "grounded in an historical understanding of the public sphere as a male preserve, distinct from the domestic realm" (4). The administrative state "can only go on as it does because women bear a lopsided share of the burden of domestic functions without which life would simply not be possible" (5). The contemporary public service is still organized around the idea that there is someone at home; thus the continued lack of career advancement for women (25–6).

There is no question that, historically, the sexual division of labour was fundamental to the way the Canadian public service was staffed. Until 1955, women working in the public service were forced to resign if they got married (Felice 1998), which established a particular structuring of social relations in the bureaucracy. The male-breadwinner model was a central organizing principle of Canadian bureaucracy, in addition to it being structured into public policy itself.[2] We also saw in chapter 1 that those bureaucratic departments most closely associated with the relations of production are located at the centre of the state's power structure, while those associated with social reproduction are marginalized. A feminist political economy analysis of bureaucracy stresses the state's location within the wider system of power relations, so that administrative norms and procedures are expressions of social inequality.

Some feminists, then, take issue with both intradepartmental and interdepartmental hierarchies, and emphasize that bureaucratic organization mirrors the unequal relations of power in society. It is for this reason that Franzway et al. (1989) have referred to the state as the "institutionalisation of power relations" (35). Weber (1994) himself concluded that "where the bureaucratization of administration has been completely carried through, a form of power relation is established that is practically unshatterable" (228). These power relations constitute a particular gender regime, as well as institutionalizing inequalities of class, race, sexuality, and ability.

Weberianism emerged alongside capitalism, industrialization, and scientific management (Weber 1997). It shares with the Fordist and Taylorist models of production a focus on standard rules and specialization. Public bureaucracies mirror the organization of capitalist firms (Maley 2011, 36). In fact, Weber saw public bureaucracy as "just like a factory" (Weber 1999, 110; Maley 2011, 47) and as similar in organization whether for-profit or non-profit, corporation, church, military, or government (Weber 1997). Weber saw bureaucracy and capitalism as mutually dependent (ibid.). Stivers (1993) adds that as state administration developed, it strived to be more "businesslike" and masculine, by distancing itself from its roots in "women's benevolent work" (8, 118).

Weber's vision of bureaucracy, based on fixed jurisdictions and a strict division of tasks has also been challenged by feminists who have demonstrated that women's lived experiences do not fit neatly into compartments. The bureaucracy is organized into areas such as "Health," "Welfare," "Environment," "Immigration," and "Finance." Unfortunately for feminists, so-called women's issues do not fit easily into separate, artificial compartments. Women's policy goals often overlap into many areas.

When Christina Gabriel studied the Ontario Women's Directorate (OWD) and the Race Relations Directorate (RRD) (within the Ministry of Citizenship), she found that women's intersectionality was not recognized through these forms of representation, as "racism and sexism were ... largely conceptualized as separate and distinct" (Gabriel 1996, 185). The problem was that "women of colour ... often fall between the mandates of those advocacy offices promoting gender and racial equality" (191). Similarly, Tobin (1990) observed that in Britain's Greater London Council (GLC), "formal support for gay rights often ended up coming from either the Women's Committee which encompassed lesbianism within its remit or from the Ethnic Minorities Unit which employed gay rights workers" (60). The Women's Committee could not account for the existence of a lesbian who is also a woman of colour and a worker. The Ethnic Minorities Unit took for granted a unity of interest between lesbians and gay men (Tobin 1990). In neither case was there any room for women with disabilities, a situation analogous to that outlined by Sue Findlay. Findlay (1993a) gives an example from the municipal administration of the Mayor's Committee on Community and Race Relations and the Interdepartmental Action Committee on People with Disabilities. The operation of the two separate entities demonstrated to Findlay that categorization is obviously not a solution that "makes sense" for the representation of "women with special needs." Their lived realities visibly challenge the separation of race, gender, abilities – and obscure class differences ... "Women" is a highly differentiated category that can be defined only in terms of the interrelationships of class, race, gender, abilities, and sexual orientation in the everyday lives of women. (159–60)

Attempts at remedying impasses of this sort were resisted. Findlay (1987) recalls that femocrats in Canada "were discouraged from co-operating with feminists in other departments to address issues that cut across departmental lines" (47). In her work on gender and public policy, Burt (1993) has also criticized the lack of coordination between various government departments.

Again, it is evident that unequal relations of power are maintained in the bureaucracy through a gender regime of representation. The regime also stems from liberalism, where the world is viewed through the public/ private divide, and where policy can be broken into neat compartments, such as "work" and "family." The Weberian regime of representation reflects the paradigm of liberal pluralism in another way, where self-contained, individual actors compete for influence in the policy process. Such a model of representation, based as it is on individualism, prevents the expression of multiple and overlapping interests and identities, and impedes the collective action needed to empower marginalized groups. The importance placed on neutrality in the bureaucracy also serves to silence community voices and to maintain the power of dominant social forces. The next section will examine this reality.

Neutrality, Relations with the "Outside," and the Construction of Expertise

Historically, bureaucracies in Canada (and elsewhere) were staffed by partisan appointment or patronage. Over time, through popular struggles for democratic accountability (Albo 1993), this approach to public administration was rejected in favour of the Westminster model. This model rests on the principle of ministerial accountability, where bureaucrats are ultimately responsible to elected ministers, and to Parliament. Aucoin (2000) explains that in a Westminster model of government like Canada's, "good government," provided by bureaucracies, "is best secured through a professional, nonpartisan public service," based on the principle of political neutrality (23, 25). Therefore, "partisan ideology was replaced by public policy technocracy" (Aucoin 2000, 31). Weber (1997) thought that governance was best served by separating administration from politics, generally called the politics-administration dichotomy. In this ideal, politicians make value judgments based on the impartial, objective advice of bureaucrats: "The politics-administration dichotomy assumes a public service with an obligation to render advice that addresses the merits of government policy preferences or proposals against the broader public interest, whether requested or not: it must fearlessly 'speak truth to power'" (Aucoin 2000, 43).

While it was the result of democratic demands for responsible government over elitism, this vision of public administration actually serves to reinforce anti-democratic tendencies by substituting direct popular control with control by political parties (Albo 1993, 20).[3] Sossin (1993) also argues that the dichotomy between politics and administration, the foundation of Weberian bureaucracy, is based on an irrational detachment of the former from the latter (379). Sossin explains that Weberian bureaucracy values "impartial, independent, and technical expertise" based on "rational" decision-making (376). In this model, "rationality means the capacity to give 'good reasons,'" and thus ignores the reality that everyone does not have an equal ability to give "good reasons" (374). A number of factors, including gender, race, class, education, and language, place serious limits on one's ability to contribute and persuade (Sossin 1999).

In addition, the abstract, generalized rules that Weber (1997) advocates are far from "impersonal," and the consequences of this formulation on public sector workers are not neutral. Even Weber acknowledged that the rules of the game were designed to ensure predictability for capitalism. He recalls that "in England, where the development of the law was practically in the hands of the lawyers who, in the service of their capitalist clients, invented suitable forms for the transaction of business, and from whose midst the judges were recruited who were strictly bound to precedent, that means, to calculable schemas" (Weber 1999, 111). Powerful interests are built right into the rules, and these rules produce unequal social relations. In Weber's theory, "the members of the administrative staff should be completely separated from ownership of the means of production or administration" (Weber 1997, 331). Capitalism and government are collapsed, and in both cases, the alienation of workers is normalized.

The emphasis that this model of representation places on "neutrality," "impartiality," and "independence" raises particular problems for feminism. Feminists have shown that social scientists have tended to see the world, and public policies, in gender-neutral terms, which ignores the ways in which women and men are situated differently. Stivers (1993) argues that what counts as administrative "expertise" "requires a social order that subordinates women" (7). In the bureaucracy (among other places), women's knowledge and experience has been undervalued.

In a talk about democratic alternatives to neoliberalism, Hillary Wainwright (2002) spoke of the need to value practical knowledge as one of the primary ways to democratize the state. Wainwright's observations highlight one of the fundamental problems of state feminists, who often experience a sense of divided loyalty. Findlay (1988) says that femocrats "inevitably must account to two 'masters,' the government and the women's movement" (8). Levi and Edwards (1990) also note the tension between one's responsibility to feminism and to the bureaucracy, saying that "femocrats serve two 'bosses': the feminist movement as they perceive it and the government bureaucracy itself" (153). In Australia, this dilemma is referred to as one of the missionary versus the mandarin (Levi and Edwards 1990; Kaplan 1996). Geller-Schwartz (1995) explains that public servants are expected to be neutral, but in Canada, "the integration policy implied that civil servants could be internal lobbyists for women's issues" (49). She goes on to say that "holding a job in a women's agency identified them [femocrats] as feminists, a role seen as incompatible with the duty of an unbiased civil servant. As such, their loyalty and discretion could be questioned, and they immediately became suspect" (57).

This is typical of Weberian organization. For Weber, "obedience" is an essential attribute for bureaucrats, who are "subject to strict and systematic discipline and control in conduct of the office" (Weber 1997, 334). Weber believed that bureaucratic organization is "formally the most rational means of carrying out imperative control over human beings" (ibid., 337). Maintaining power and control is the utmost concern (Weber 1997).

State feminism clashes with the dominant bureaucratic culture in Canada, which is "dedicated to neutrality and remains hostile to internal advocacy" (Rankin and Vickers 2001, 12). Chappell (2002) has also identified the intense commitment to neutrality in the Canadian public service as the principal femocratic challenge. The model of neutrality "upholds status quo gender assumptions and makes it difficult for feminist advocates to gain a foothold within the public service" (Rankin and Vickers 2001, 26). Those who could (or would) not conform to the expectation of neutrality were met with animosity because "bureau-crats tend to prefer those who do not rock the boat and whose first loyalty is to the office or agency" (Levi and Edwards 1990, 154). Levi and Edwards (1990) refer to a "distrustful, and often, hostile environment" for femocrats (149). When working on pay equity in the Ontario bureaucracy in the early 1990s, Findlay (1997) remembers her colleagues "warning me that I sounded like an 'advocate' rather than an objective analyst" (314). She describes

> a "chilly climate" that made it difficult for individual women to take up the government's commitments to equal opportunities, and particularly difficult for the women who had been appointed as departmental advisors on the status of women to do their work without harassment ... Feminists were particularly unwelcome. (Findlay 1995, 146)[4]

Findlay (1987) notes that femocrats "faced resistance from the male-dominated bureaucracy ... Advisors were frequently subjected to 'friendly' ridicule or dismissed more aggressively as 'women's libbers' or 'lesbians'" (39), reinforcing both sexism and homophobia. The Australian situation echoes these experiences. Eisenstein (1996) quotes Frances Davies as saying, "Most of the time I was in the Women's Bureau which was eighteen months and seemed like eighteen years, was spent simply justifying existing ... We were actively persecuted" (172). More often, though, resistance is more subtle. A colleague who worked at Status of Women Canada (SWC) once mentioned that at meetings, men would often remark that they were from the "Status of Men Office." Similar experiences in the Ontario Women's Directorate will be seen in the next chapter.

Again, such bureaucratic processes are not just about cultural values. Cultural values act to reinforce power relations. In his analysis of Weber's thought, Maley (2011) stresses the "quite politicized uses of the ideal typical model of bureaucracy" (29), explaining that Weber's promotion of bureaucracy as objective and irreversible had ideological motivations – namely, to argue against socialism and conservatism and to ensure the protection and survival of the capitalist system. Even though his recommendations appear to be rooted in social science principles, there are class politics imbedded in Weber's liberalism (Maley 2011). Maley (2011) shows that bureaucratic neutrality is designed to separate workers and citizens from the "means of administration" (quoting Weber 1997, 37–8), and that public bureaucracies both include and contain citizens.

Sue Findlay (1995) points out that bureaucratic rules and regulations are concrete obstacles to democratic participation and key to the "process of ruling" (420). These rules and values serve to keep some on the inside of decision-making and others marginalized. The outcome is one that excludes the community from the policy process and allows the powerful to maintain a monopoly on policy influence. The concept of social reproduction can provide insight here. Feminist political economy shows how states take on some of the responsibilities for social reproduction. If we go back to Bezanson and Luxton's (2006) broad definition of social reproduction, it includes the caring work necessary to reproduce society, *as well as* the work of reproducing ideas, knowledge, and social and cultural values (3). Within state administration, a dominant set of principles and values gets replicated.

Mahon (1977) maintains that the appearance of neutrality is fundamental to the liberal democratic state (193). The *idea* of neutrality serves to mask the power relations that underlie knowledge production in the state. Most public administration literature now recognizes that, in practice, public servants have their own biases that shape their activities. As Albo (1993) argues, "Separating politics from administration is, of course, a principle most often honoured in the breach: politicians regularly interfere in administration to favour constituents and public officials consistently lobby for their own favoured policy courses" (21).

But the practice of neutrality is flexible not only in the cases of individual public servants, but also on a broader scale through the representation of collective interests and identities. Certain interests in the bureaucracy (i.e., those associated with capitalist economic development), as Mahon shows, are particularly well represented. These interests come to be associated with the general interest, or the common good, and advocating for these interests is taken as the "neutral" position, while the interests of the marginalized are considered "special interests" and advocating for them is seen as biased. Stivers (1993) also wonders how public servants can be said to be protecting the common good when they systematically ignore gender differences in pay, opportunities, and working conditions (32–3).

Mahon (1977) cites Poulantzas, who stresses the importance of "the specific internal ideology circulating within the state apparatuses (the 'neutral' state as the arbitrator above classes, 'service to the nation,' 'general interest,' etc.)" (172). Similarly, a non-feminist (or even anti-feminist) position is the bureaucratic standard, and a feminist position is a deviation from the norm. A feminist political economy approach to representation can provide some clues about how this happens.

First, as a result of popular struggles, a range of interests and identities are represented inside the state, but they are not all represented in the same way, as noted earlier in reference to Mahon. State institutions, and therefore representative structures, reflect the balance of social forces in society. Those located in a dominant position in the power hierarchy (i.e., Finance) are most associated with neutrality and with advancing the general interest. Mahon (1977) uses the example of advancing "the economy" as a prime instance where advocacy and ideological bias are portrayed as neutrality and objectivity. She traces the emergence of these ideas around objectivity and expertise, at least partly, to the professionalization of the public service in Canada in the 1930s. During this time, the Department of Finance took up the role of training civil servants. Finance has played a key role in socializing public servants, or in the social reproduction of the governing ideas, principles, and values. Interestingly, Kernaghan (1978) cites "resocialization to the values of the service" as a main concern expressed in the literature about the viability of representative bureaucracy (493). A more diverse public service would be more difficult to socialize.

Another factor that contributes to the framing of neutrality has to do with the way representation functions within the state. Those structures that are most strongly perceived to be neutral and objective have broad, coordinative functions, and representatives spread throughout the public service. Thus, they are seen as benignly working towards the "general interest." In contrast, those who are more often accused of bias and subjectivity are located in representative structures that are ghettoized and isolated, which creates an institutionalized reinforcement of their "special" interest orientation. The general versus special distinction becomes naturalized through these different forms of representation, serving to both overestimate the objectivity of the powerful and to underestimate the objectivity of the marginalized.

State structures are created with different representative functions. Returning to Mahon, she distinguishes between powerful organs that serve in a coordinative and organizational capacity, and the representatives of subordinate social forces inside the bureaucracy. In the latter case, there is some acceptance that one of the roles of the Department of Labour, or of Indian Affairs and Northern Development, is to represent marginalized interests. Nonetheless, through the Department of Labour, she submits, the second (though far from secondary) representative function is to act as brokers of compromise, managers of conflict, and regulators of social relations, which involves some element of coercion (Mahon 1977). Her analysis warns against exaggerating the extent to which marginalized, and allegedly biased, interests get represented, and understating the representation of powerful, and seemingly objective, interests.

To a certain extent, women's policy machinery fits this pattern of representing marginalized interests. Still, there are some distinctive aspects of women's policy machinery that make its relationship to the values of neutrality and objectivity noteworthy. The representation of women in the public service generally, and the creation of women's policy machinery specifically, has followed a different historical trajectory than that of other organized social forces. This can be explained through a number of factors, including the politics of the first wave of the women's movement, the timing of the emergence of the second wave of the women's movement, and the lack of other avenues of representation, such as political parties, that existed for the working class and farmers. Women came to be represented in the bureaucracy rather late, and through different models of representation.

By the time that ideas seriously emerged about representing women in the public service in the 1970s, debates within public administration about representative bureaucracy were well developed. The representation of francophones, and later of women and Aboriginal peoples, was debated in the literature, with scholars exploring the merits of "passive" (the representation of identity) versus "active" representation (the representation of interests) (Kernaghan 1978, 491; Wilson and Mullins 1978; Selden 1997; Wise 2003). Paralleling more current discussions of procedural and substantive democracy, these earlier conversations questioned whether representation is about simply mirroring the demographic profile of the citizenry, or about being responsive to a social constituency. Kernaghan (1978) reviews these debates in Canada, and even though they take different positions on the issue, most public administration scholars come down on the side of a very liberal democratic notion of symbolic representation, if they accept the idea of representative bureaucracy at all.[5] Kernaghan himself is sceptical of a more substantive form of representation, which seems to put him in line with the prevailing orientation of the time. He submits that "available evidence suggests that the prevailing sense in the Canadian public service is passive" (1978, 510). Wilson and Mullins (1978) come to similar conclusions about interest-based representation in the context of linguistic and ethnic groups (533).

Given the established convention in public administration circles, it is fair to say that the representation of women was seen as acceptable from an identity standpoint, but much less so in terms of interest. This custom clashed with the growing demands from the women's movement, which advanced a notion of representation that was of a different character. Specific structures were sought to represent women's identities *and* interests, and women's policy machinery emerged directly out of women's organizing, including through the Royal Commission on the Status of Women (RCSW). The view from a significant element of the women's movement was that the women staffing these bodies (femocrats) would not simply be brokers, or managers, but rather spokespeople for the movement. Feminists sought a different kind of representation. Ironically, the success of the women's movement (and this is seen in Australia as well), of bringing movement activists into the state, made it particularly vulnerable to criticisms about neutrality and objectivity. That women's structures of representation were introduced at the height of women's movement mobilization and influence, made femocrats visible threats to the bureaucratic status quo.

Weberian bureaucracy is based on a particular gender regime and model of representation and democracy that places high value on rigid rules and "objectivity," and prioritizes representative democracy over more popular forms of representation and citizenship. In this way, the "masculinity of public administration is systemic" (Stivers 1993, 4). This regime poses considerable obstacles for feminist engagement with public administration. Even so, within ideal types, social actors find ways to pressure, challenge, and change institutions from the inside and outside, and to modify the power relations within these regimes. Institutional compromises result from social conflict (Graefe 2007). A central element of a feminist political economy approach is to take seriously the agency of women as political actors, and feminists were able to bring about some positive alterations to the Weberian regime.

Challenging the Weberian Gender Regime

Pressure from the women's movement and other equality-seekers did lead to significant changes to the Weberian model and altered the face of the gender regime. Representation, including inside state administration, was a central demand of second-wave feminism in Canada, as reflected, for instance, by the RCSW. Calling for an adaptation of the "neutrality" principle through the creation of women's policy machinery inside government, and of the "merit" principle through employment equity, feminists were able to expand the notion of representative bureaucracy in public administration. While, as will be elaborated later, feminists differ over whether "representative" refers to numbers – that the public service should mirror, or be a microcosm of, society (procedural representation) – or if it extends to influence on policy (substantive representation), strategies in Canada have tended to pursue both ends. Women's policy machinery, and employment equity, did stretch the boundaries of Weberian organization.

Women's policy machinery, introduced at the federal and provincial scales in the 1970s and 1980s, did not radically alter the nature of state administration. Nevertheless, there was an array of significant structures of representation erected. Federally, the landscape of women's policy machinery included:

- The Women's Bureau, in the Department of Labour[6] – 1954
- Office of the Coordinator for the Status of Women in the Privy Council Office (PCO) – 1971; became Status of Women Canada (SWC) in 1976
- Women's Program, Secretary of State – 1972
- Canadian Advisory Council on the Status of Women (CACSW) – 1973
- Minister Responsible for the Status of Women – 1976
- Women's Health Bureau, Health Canada[7] – 1993
- Office of the Senior Advisor on Gender Equality, Justice Canada – 1996; merged with Diversity, Equality and Access to Justice Division to form the Diversity and Gender Equality Office – 2000
- Gender Equality Initiative, Justice Canada – 1996
- Office of the Senior Advisor on Aboriginal Women's Issues and Gender Equality, Indian and Northern Affairs Canada – 1998; includes the Advisory Committee on Gender Equality and the Women's Issues and Gender Equality Directorate (WIGE)
- Gender-Based Analysis Unit, Citizenship and Immigration Canada – 2000
- Farm Women's Bureau – 1981
- Agriculture and Agri-Food Canada Gender Analysis and Policy (GAP) Directorate, Human Resources Development Canada – 1981
- Gender Equality Division, Canadian International Development Agency – 1998

- Human Rights, Humanitarian Affairs and International Women's Equality section, Foreign Affairs and International Trade – 1998 (Geller-Schwartz 1995; O'Neil and Sutherland 1997; Canada 2000 [Status of Women]; Brodie and Bakker 2007)

Provincially, the configuration of women's policy machinery looked like this:

- Newfoundland – Women's Policy Unit, Newfoundland and Labrador Provincial Advisory Council, Minister Responsible for the Status of Women
- Nova Scotia – Advisory Council on the Status of Women Status of Women
- PEI – Women's Secretariat, PEI Advisory Council on the Status of Women
- New Brunswick – New Brunswick Women's Directorate, New Brunswick Advisory Council, Minister Responsible for the Status of Women, Women's Issues Branch
- Quebec – Ministère responsable de la Condition de la femme – 1979, Secretariat à la condition feminine, Conseil du statut de la femme (CSF)
- Ontario – Ontario Council on the Status of Women/Ontario Advisory Council on Women's Issues, Ontario Women's Directorate (OWD), Minister Responsible for Women's Issues
- Manitoba – Manitoba Women's Directorate, Manitoba Women's Ministry, Minister Responsible for the Status of Women, Manitoba Women's Advisory Council
- Saskatchewan – Women's Secretariat of Saskatchewan, Advisory Council on the Status of Women
- Alberta – Women's Bureau, Alberta Women's Secretariat, Advisory Council on Women's Issues
- BC – Minister of Women's Equality, Ministry of Women's Equality
- Yukon – Yukon Women's Directorate
- NWT – NWT Women's Directorate, Status of Women Council, Special Advisor to the Minister Responsible for the Status of Women, Minister Responsible for the Status of Women
- Nunavut – Minister Responsible for Status of Women Council, Qulliit Nunavut Status of Women Council

(Mitchell 2001, Brodie and Bakker 2007)

These structures of representation did modify the Weberian regime, carving out a (limited) place for advocacy and community participation in the policy process. For instance, through the Women's Program, state funding facilitated the democratic input of organizations.

The introduction of employment equity to the public service also challenged the Weberian model to some extent. It served to problematize the gendered notion of "merit" by recasting it alongside the principle of equity. In fact, one of the core debates about representative bureaucracy within public administration at the time revolved around the question of merit. A number of scholars, public servants, and public sector unions believed that representative bureaucracy was an affront to meritocracy, with some even making the now-ubiquitous charges of "reverse discrimination" (Kernaghan 1978, 500, 508–9). Others saw representative bureaucracy as a reinforcement, and extension, of the merit principle, with it framed as a means for removing barriers that had previously impeded the recruitment of qualified candidates[8] (Kernaghan 1978; Wilson and Mullins 1978). This was thought to require changes to ensure equal access to employment, training, and promotion opportunities, but falling short of "quotas" (Kernaghan 1978; Wilson and Mullins 1978). The government's response, through its equal opportunity strategy, fell into the second category, seeking to "achieve a more proportionate representation," rather than microcosm representation (Kernaghan 1978, 497). Indeed, Kernaghan explains that "the Public Service Commission has described the quota approach as 'undesirable and impractical; ... it would conflict with the merit principle and pose unanswerable questions'" (498).

After the release of the report of the Royal Commission on Bilingualism and Biculturalism, the federal government directed its efforts over the 1960s at increasing the representation of francophones in the public service through active recruitment, the designation of bilingual or French-language positions and units, and language training. By the late 1960s, there was some focus placed on the representation of women, when sex, in addition to race, national origin, colour, and religion, was made a prohibited ground for discrimination under the 1967 Public Services Employment Act. But it was really not until the 1970s, following the RCSW, that a concerted government policy emerged. Starting in the 1970s and early 1980s, governments began to create affirmative action policies internal to the public service. As with francophones, the measures aimed at increasing the representation of women included the creation of new policy machinery (described earlier), active recruitment, training, promotion, and fostering attitudinal change, administered through the Office of Equal Opportunities for

Women, created in 1971 (Kernaghan 1978). Still, these efforts brought only slight improvement (ibid.), resulting in pressure to move from symbolic to more substantial approaches.

Nationally, by the mid-1980s, the reporting of Rosalie Abella's Royal Commission on Equality in Employment provided a legislative framework, not only for the federal government, but also for the provinces. Abella's report coined a change in the lexicon from affirmative action to employment equity, and brought "systemic discrimination" into the policy discourse (Bakan and Kobayashi 2000). The concept of systemic discrimination, based on the idea that discrimination is not always overt and experienced by individuals, but instead is often built into processes and institutions, acting to disadvantage and marginalize identifiable groups, became the basis of the 1986 federal Employment Equity Act, and subsequent provincial legislation and policy.

The strongest employment equity legislation in the country, the Employment Equity Act, was passed in Ontario in 1993. The act included the provincial government and its agencies, as well as the broader public sector (municipal governments, school boards, universities, hospitals, other healthcare facilities) with more than ten employees, the police, and the private sector with more than fifty employees. It also required employment equity plans to remove systemic barriers and an Employment Equity Tribunal to act as an enforcement body (Bakan and Kobayashi 2000). Even this relatively advanced legislation had its critics.[9] What is significant, though, is that employment equity policy constituted state acknowledgment that seemingly neutral principles central to Weberianism, like hiring based on "merit," are tainted by systemic discrimination, and that state action is required to address it. In addition, as will be seen in the next chapter, these challenges to the Weberian model are evident in Ontario's gender regime of public administration from the early 1980s to the mid-1990s.

Clearly, these changes (women's policy machinery and employment equity) did not go far enough in transforming the Weberian gender regime, and feminists continue seeking to push these forward. At the same time, other ideas about public administration came to challenge this paradigm. One, promising flexibility and public empowerment, and emerging within globalization and neoliberalism, gained prominence in liberal democracies, but brought its own gendered implications: the New Public Management (NPM).

Gender and the New Public Management (NPM)[10]

The ideas associated with the New Public Management are generally attributed to Margaret Thatcher's Conservative government during the 1980s. Thatcher emphasized three central elements of bureaucratic reform, or restructuring. Aucoin (2000) identifies these as: increasing individual citizen, while decreasing state, control of public services; reducing the power of the public service; and advancing its "economy and efficiency" (1). Others are less charitable, describing these as privatization, downsizing, and managerialism, respectively. As Albo (1993) shows, "the new watchdogs of public sector management are now easily recited: deficit crisis, downsizing and voluntary terminations (for layoffs), delayering and empowered public consumers (for privatization), entrepreneurial welfare recipients and partnerships in fiscal responsibility (for cutbacks), and so forth" (114). The NPM's basic assumption is that states can, and should, be run like businesses. While Thatcher embraced the neoliberal ideology of the NPM in Britain, she was not alone. States around the world, including Canada, have sought to restructure public bureaucracies based on neoliberal administrative principles (Aucoin 2000), or through increased "marketization"[11] of the state, specifically via privatization, downsizing, and managerialism.

Feminist analysis has demonstrated that neoliberal state restructuring entails a variety of measures that have serious implications for equality (race, class, gender, sexual orientation, ability, age). I will briefly review the extensive feminist discussion of two major projects of the NPM, privatization and downsizing. The third element, managerialism, has received far less feminist treatment, and therefore will be explored here at greater length. All three are chief components of the neoliberal gender regime.

Privatization

One of the central claims of neoliberalism throughout the 1980s and 1990s was that out-of-control public spending had caused massive public deficit and debt. Therefore, states needed to cut such spending (Aucoin 2000). One of the main ways to do so was through privatization: to transfer as many programs and services as possible from the public to the private sector. As Pierre (1995) explains, reforms such as privatization or "contracting out" of public services, the introduction of private sector-type management strategies and objectives into the public sector, the allowance for private involvement in the delivery of public services, and the perception of the recipients of such services as "customers" have contributed to [a] change in the relationship between the public and private sectors. (56)

Aucoin (2000) adds that a wide variety of privatization strategies were employed:

These include interdepartmental cooperation at the point of service delivery; partnership arrangements with other levels of government and non-profit organizations; joint ventures with the private sector; commercializing services; using regulatory instruments in place of direct services; using tax measures in place of spending programs; contracting out the delivery of services; and increased emphasis on voluntary compliance mechanisms in the areas of regulation and tax administration. (201)

While this privatization has generally been justified as a cost-saving measure, other ideological pretexts have operated alongside it as well.

The NPM is based on public choice theory, in which "the root of any failings in the public sector, as seen from this perspective, is the self-interest of bureaucrats" (Peters 1995, 293). Aucoin (2000) explains that "the public service in question was viewed as an institution that sought to perpetuate its own policy preferences, even at times in opposition to those of its political masters" (30). The prevailing "assumption [was] that career public servants are not primarily motivated by the public interest in good government but by the promotion of their own individual or collective self-interests" (Aucoin 2000, 31). Privatization, claims the public choice theorist, rescues the public, or the "taxpayers" from bureaucratic extravagance.

In response to such claims, feminist political economists have emphasized that privatization includes much more than the selling of public assets, and that its many faces are often ignored (Armstrong and Connelly 1997). Privatization is a heavily gendered process that pushes services from the "public" to the "private" sphere, where the "private" includes not only the market but also the family and the voluntary sector. With services placed in the market, citizens are now referred to as "consumers" (Brodie 1995a; Peters 1995; Pierre 1995; Sossin 1999; Shields and Evans 1998), "customers" (Osborne and Gaebler 1993), or "taxpayers"

(Shields and Evans 1998). Despite Aucoin's defence of this language as signalling "a greater willingness on the part of governments, and elected representatives generally, to be responsive to their constituents" (2000, 6), others see it as evidence of the marketization of the state, and the intensification of class, gender, and racial inequalities. The difference between a "citizen" and a "consumer" is quite important, in that the former carries a sense of entitlement, and collective obligation, while the latter emphasizes economic over political power and is based on individualism (Pierre 1995). Many are marginalized by this change in language that raises clear questions of accessibility. One's rights as a "consumer" are significantly circumscribed by the reality of an "unequal distribution of the means to purchase" (Shields and Evans 1998, 82). The ramifications for women, for example, in a society where the feminization of poverty is now part of common language, are not difficult to see.

Beyond the provision of social welfare services, many traditional public policy functions of the state are being turned over to the private sector. The NPM has encouraged the growing use of private think tanks for policy advice (Shields and Evans 1998), and has fostered "a much greater reliance on advisers separate from the career public service" (Aucoin 2000, 81). Notwithstanding his problematic commitment to the idea of "objective" knowledge, Aucoin is right to be suspicious of "[a] politicized state apparatus highly dependent on private-sector contracts for the provision of policy advice and public services" (72). He does not, however, analyse the gender implications of marketized policy advice. For instance, even basic employment equity standards do not apply to the private sector. This became blatantly obvious, for example, when in a 1998 visit to the C.D. Howe Institute, it was discovered that all researchers were male,[12] and "guests" were served by a staff of women of colour.[13]

The NPM also embraces the notion of the "voluntary sector," or the "third sector." Osborne and Gaebler (1993) claim not to advocate privatization, yet spend considerable time focusing on the use of volunteers and the "third sector" (28, 44). Sossin (1999) explains that

> unlike the New Left, which justifies its support for certain voluntary associations on the grounds they provide a voice for vulnerable citizens and can help access public goods and services, the New Right supports voluntary associations because they reduce the size and budget of public agencies, and return public administration, especially in the fields of social welfare, to communities. (15)

It should be stressed that the neoliberal support for the voluntary sector is merely rhetorical in nature, as such organizations have experienced severe cuts to their government funding (Shields and Evans 1998, 94). Regardless, many have identified the problems associated with the voluntary sector, and a return to the "private charity model" that existed in Canada in the nineteenth century. Public sector unions have resisted voluntary sector delivery due to its lower wages (McCuaig 1993). Yet few have acknowledged the gendered implications of further reliance on women's unpaid labour that is already onerous and undervalued in society.[14]

As noted earlier, feminist political economists insist on a definition of privatization that highlights the downloading of the costs of social reproduction onto women's unpaid labour. In this context, women's unpaid labour includes "child care, care for other dependent family members such as the elderly and those with disabilities, and volunteer work of a caregiving nature in the community" (Bakker 1998, 3). With the state continually retreating from the welfare state, social services are being "re-privatized" (Brodie 1995a, 53). Families, or more precisely, women, are left to pick up the slack. Brodie shows that "privatization and the erosion of the welfare state have the effect of forcing health, child, and elderly care back onto the family and the unpaid work of women" (1995a, 54). Feminist economists refer to this as the "buffer effect" or the "hidden costs of adjustment" (Bakker 1998, 7), with the burden of social care increasingly falling onto female relatives (Connelly and MacDonald 1996; Handler 1996; Brodie 1995a, 1996) and female volunteers in the community.

Contradictorily, this re-privatization of social reproduction is happening at the same time that neoliberalism expects women to participate in the labour market equally with men, under a new model of "gender-neutral worker-citizen" (K. Scott 1999, 206). This has led some feminists to speak of a new gender order, marked by the simultaneous erosion and intensification of gender (Fudge and Cossman 2002; Harder 2003). Often this privatization (or re-privatization) is directly linked to the downsizing of public sector jobs. Blaming bureaucrats for the supposed explosion in public spending fuelled the push not only towards privatization, but towards downsizing as well, another element of this gender regime.

Downsizing

Like privatization, downsizing was intended to deal with the dual evils of public expenditure and bureaucratic largesse. Influenced by firms in the private sector that "downsized," or laid off their workers to save money, advocates of the NPM suggested that states "seek to reduce the size of the public service as well as the public service payroll" (Aucoin 2000, 3). Savoie (1994) says that "contracting out held an added bonus for governments who were committed to reducing the size of their bureaucracies, since it transferred jobs from the public to the private sector" (150).

A number of schemes based on the private sector were brought into the federal government in Canada. In 1989, Public Service 2000 introduced the idea that senior managers should adopt practices to "create culture change" in the bureaucracy (Aucoin 2000, 130). But PS 2000 went beyond "culture change," to devolving more control to managers over personnel. In addition, in 1992, the Public Service Reform Act sought to create "a greater capacity for deputy ministers to redeploy, demote and release staff and to appoint certain categories of managers to levels rather than to specific positions" (Aucoin 2000, 131). These measures brought "what managers perceived to be necessary changes in public personnel management. They saw these changes as a way of eliminating the restrictions of the personnel system[; however,] union leaders saw these proposed changes as the way of eliminating the rights of public servants (ibid., 130).

Downsizing is sold by the NPM as part of a package of cost-saving, efficiency, and flexibility. However, understanding downsizing in this way overlooks the ideological motivations behind it. Savoie (1994) stresses "Mulroney's disdain for the public service," with the oft-cited quip that "he promised to give 'pink slips and running shoes to bureaucrats,' once he was elected to office" (91). Downsizing is less about efficiency and more about privatization and limiting the reach of the state, and takes many forms including layoffs, and contracting-out. According to the Canadian Council on Social Development (CCSD, 1997), "between 1992 and 1996, 121,000 jobs across Canada were lost in the public sector," and "public sector jobs dropped from offering one-fifth of all employment in Canada in 1976, to less than one-sixth by 1996." In the recent round of public sector downsizing, as laid out in the 29 March 2012 federal budget, 19,200 federal public sector jobs will be cut (Canada 2012 , 221). The continued failure to acknowledge the gendered implications of these processes is clear in the new, dismissive discourse about cuts affecting mainly the "back office."

Despite the gendered job segregation, the public sector has provided some of the best jobs for women in Canada in terms of wages, benefits, security, and unionization (Bakker 1996a, 45). Therefore, Connelly and

MacDonald (1996) assert that "women are losing some of their best jobs through the erosion and restructuring of the public sector" (84). Private sector employment is more often un-unionized, lacking employment equity standards, and lower paid. For instance, Shields and Evans show that employees of the Victorian Order of Nurses are paid 20–25 per cent less than nurses who are employed in public hospitals (Shields and Evans 1998, 95). Furthermore, in 1996, the CCSD found that "average earnings for women in the public sector are $29,293, compared to $16,038 in the private sector, and $16,603 for those who are self-employed" (CCSD 1997). In addition, "fewer than one-third of women in the public sector earn $20,000 or less per year, compared to nearly two-thirds of those working in the private sector, and 70 per cent of those who are self-employed" (CCSD 1997). The gap remains. A study based on the 2006 census found that women in the public sector earned an average annual income of $45,821, while women in the private sector earned only $43,841 – a 4.5 per cent difference (Sanger 2011).

Not only does downsizing eliminate many "good jobs" for women, but for those left in the public sector, their jobs are coming increasingly to resemble the precarious employment that is characteristic of the private sector. Public sector employment is moving to part-time, temporary (Peters 1995), insecure work, like homework or homecare, and "the public sector is increasingly adopting management philosophies developed in the private sector" (Connelly and MacDonald 1996, 84).

Both privatization and downsizing endeavour to take the public and place it in the private sector. However, the NPM does not stop there, since bringing the private into the public is also one of its central goals. As Aucoin (2000) demonstrates, "These responses [privatization and downsizing] have been accompanied by equally significant efforts to change the structures, systems and practices of public management, broadly defined" (3). The introduction of managerialism, the final element of the gender regime, is raising notable issues for women who remain in the public sector.

Managerialism

Once public services are sufficiently privatized, and the public sector downsized, the NPM posits that what remains within public management must also more closely resemble the private sector. As Aucoin (2000) explains:

The new managerialism in public management has been driven by the same forces experienced in private-sector management, namely a greater need to pay attention to the bottom line in terms of the relationship between revenues and expenditures, on the one hand, and increased demand for quality products and services, on the other ... Governments have sought to enhance their own productivity, in part by resorting to new management practices. (9)

He adds that "governments sought to impose new standards on a broadening range of administrative matters. These included efforts to introduce new management systems applied to traditional corporate concerns as well as new initiatives to extend the corporate dimensions of public management across government" (Aucoin 2000, 99). Aucoin concludes that "enhancing performance in governance to move public management beyond bureaucracy and promote greater economy, efficiency and effectiveness is the bottom line of public management reform" (183).

At the federal scale, during the Mulroney years, several attempts at transplanting these market approaches were made, including Increased Ministerial Authority and Accountability (IMAA), the Centre for Management Development, the Expenditure Review Committee (ERC), the Expenditure Management System (EMS), Public Service 2000 (PS 2000) and Total Quality Management (TQM). Increased Managerial Authority and Accountability (IMAA) began in 1986 to devolve authority and increase productivity. The Ministerial Task Force on Program Review was struck to assess 1000 government programs. EMS set out to create "departmental business plans," and to establish clear goals, targets, costs, and performance measures (Savoie 1994; Aucoin 2000). Beyond the elements mentioned earlier, PS 2000 involved delayering, decentralization, and contracting-out (Savoie 1994), and was influenced by Osborne and Gaebler's best-selling public administration "manual," *Reinventing Government* (Shields and Evans 1998).[15] TQM, transferred from the manufacturing sector to the public service, emphasized the importance of "customer service" and the measuring of results (Savoie 1994; Shields and Evans 1998). The idea of merit pay was also applied to the public service (Peters 1995).

These NPM "reforms" were intended to unleash "an entrepreneurial spirit, allowing organizations to innovate and excel and thus compete in the marketplace of the new global economy" (Aucoin 2000, 90). But, as Aucoin argues, "accepting just about every tenet of management reform advanced by the several, and often competing, schools of management thought in vogue at the time," these reforms generally met with limited success (129, 131). Setting aside for a moment whether its goals are even desirable, Aucoin asserts that given the NPM's claims of good governance, and the decentralization of authority, the results are, at best, contradictory, leading to "greater politicization of governance, and a "simultaneous consolidation and devolution of power" (115).

However, the question is not simply whether the NPM has been successful in fully achieving its objectives. Many find the objectives themselves to be objectionable, and have identified the ways in which even an incomplete project to marketize the state raises critical democratic questions. Notably, managerialism has significantly changed the internal working environment for public sector employees. As seen, it is part and parcel of neoliberalism, and seeks to apply private sector management techniques to the public sector. Savoie (1994) quotes Pollit as saying "managerialism needs to be understood as an ideology" (173). Shields and Evans (1998) agree that it is important to keep "the deeply political nature of managerialism" in mind, since it gives a "technocratic veneer to a political agenda" (71, 73). Managerialism "has been accompanied by a new vocabulary and a new way of conceptualizing the work and purpose of the public sector: concepts like empowerment, total quality management, pay for performance, improved services to clients and value for money" (Shields and Evans 1998, 79).

But what does all of this mean for women and the gender regime specifically? Since the late 1970s, a new configuration of power relations, including a new political and gender order has been consolidated into a neoliberal paradigm. Globalization and neoliberalism have had at least two major impacts on women's relationship to the Canadian state. First, globalization in Canada has entailed a re-scaling of government, largely through decentralization, devolution, and downloading. By re-scaling, I am referring to the spatial reordering or reconfiguration of governance and political action. Mahon (2003) demonstrates that re-scaling is a significant element of welfare state redesign, as it includes downloading, offloading, and decentralizing program responsibilities to sub-national governments. Because of the historical role that the federal government has played in maintaining social programs, and corresponding social rights, re-scaling to the provinces has dovetailed with the neoliberal agenda of limiting the public provision of goods and services and making room for further privatization.[16] Inwood (2000) shows that "globalization has reconfigured the terrain of federal–provincial relations in ways that affect the capability of the national government to impose national standards" in a range of social programs (124). The negative effects of these changes on women have been widely discussed elsewhere, and clearly have ramifications for women's spaces of struggle, and access to social programs. The second area, the restructuring of governance structures in the provinces, has received less attention, but is also very important, and cannot be thought of separately from the first. Both of these changes (re-scaling and restructuring) together constitute an attack on democracy (both procedural and substantive).

Feminists have shown overwhelming evidence of the harmful impact of re-scaling the welfare state, in the form of the decentralization and devolution of social programs on women (Armstrong and Connelly 1997; Brodie 1996; Evans and Wekerle 1997; Bakker 1996a, 1996b). The re-scaling of governance has meant that social programs and services have been downloaded from the federal government to the provinces and municipalities. It also means that "power is moving not just from the national to regional governments, but outward to the market," from public to private (Inwood 2000, 125, 134). This has seriously restricted women's access to those programs that are integral to democratic social citizenship across the country (Brodie 1996). In addition, Linda White (1997) makes the essential point that "what is being pushed for is not simply a reconceptualization of who should deliver programs, but whether any government should deliver these programs" (83). Consequently, feminists have shown that downloading also means that when funding is cut from essential social programs, responsibility for them falls onto the "voluntary sector," and onto families, which, generally, means onto women: as partners, mothers, daughters, sisters, granddaughters (Armstrong and Connelly 1997; Bakker 1998).

In other words, women's unpaid labour picks up the slack. Armstrong and Connelly (1999) add that the public sector "is critical to social reproduction as well as resistance," but neoliberalism is "about the redistribution of power among various scales of the state, a redistribution that has an impact on the form and nature of resistance" (3, 12). Not only has governance moved to different scales, but it increasingly combines state and non-state actors in different ways that have an impact on women's policy activity (Kantola and Outshoorn 2007). Therefore, efforts at democratization (including femocratic administration) must be directed at national and sub-national scales of governance and the voluntary sector. As Rankin (1996) has argued, women's movements face a diversity of sub-national contexts which shape feminist organizing across space and location.

Re-scaling has been accompanied by the restructuring of state forms at all scales of government. In the late 1960s and early 1970s, there was growing demand by Canadian feminists for policy structures for women inside the state, and as seen above, this was one of the central recommendations of the RCSW. The arguments were both procedural – the need for women to be represented in their governing structures – and substantive – the need to have feminist input translated into public policy. Democracy, then, was paramount. Feminists also drew attention to the specific intergovernmental processes in Canada, which have been largely based on the closed, exclusive, elite-dominated practice of executive federalism.[17] Particularly after the Meech Lake Accord, the democratic failings of decision-making by "11 white men in suits" was increasingly criticized.

In response, both federal and provincial governments promised new space for "citizen engagement" in the processes of federalism, through the Social Union (Inwood 2000). However, Inwood (2000) stresses that the federal government's interest in the Social Union is directly related to the influence of the neoliberal New Public Management (elaborated in chapter 4), especially the focus on "partnerships," "empowering citizens," and efficiency. This can be seen in the government's increasing reliance on public reporting as an accountability mechanism in policy areas like early childhood development, learning, and childcare (Anderson and Findlay 2007, 2010; Kershaw 2006; CCAAC 2005). Inwood (2000) predicts that the democratization of the processes of federalism is "unlikely to be realized since globalization has even less respect for citizenship than the traditional elite forms of policy-making that characterize the history of Canadian federalism" (125).

Inwood is right. Citizen engagement has not increased with the Social Union Framework Agreement (SUFA). In fact, the SUFA itself, as well as the three-year review process, has been roundly denounced by social policy advocates including the Canadian Council on Social Development (CCSD), the Poverty and Human Rights Project (PHRP), the National Anti-Poverty Organization (NAPO), the Native Women's Association of Canada (NWAC), the Assembly of First Nations, the Inuit Tapiriit Kanatami (ITK), the Congress of Aboriginal Peoples (CAP), the Métis National Council (MNC), the Voluntary Sector Forum, and the Canadian Union of Public Employees (CUPE). They object to the continuing exclusionary nature of intergovernmental relations, the limited, uneven, unrepresentative, and inaccessible spaces for input from the community across Canada, and the lack of government funding to make participation possible and fair. In the case of Aboriginal organizations, they were only invited to participate in the review and not the agreement itself. They were not treated as parties to intergovernmental negotiations, despite a legal and constitutional obligation to consult, and government rhetoric about respecting the Aboriginal right to self-government. Concerning participation in the review, there was only one submission from a national women's organization (NWAC),[18] and none from any anti-racist or immigrant organizations, LGBT (Lesbian, Gay, Bisexual, Transgender) organizations, or organizations representing people with disabilities (Findlay 2005).

Cameron (2004) argues that the Social Union is really "about relations among the executive branch (Cabinet and/or senior bureaucratic) at the federal, provincial, and territorial levels of government" and as a result of this continued executive federalism, democratic accountability, to both elected legislature, and popular groups, has been weakened (49, 53–5). This is consistent with neoliberal governance approaches.

In general, neoliberal restructuring, including downsizing, privatization, and "rationalization," has brought a marked decline in spaces for democratic participation at all scales of government, and this is certainly true of women's structures of representation. The women's policy machinery that was created at the federal scale, and largely paralleled, albeit very reluctantly in some cases (Malloy 2003), at the provincial scale, has been "restructured," or more accurately in several cases, dismantled. Because these structures across governments have fared so equally poorly in this hostile political climate, arguments outlined earlier that consider provincial and local governments to be more "democratic" must be assessed with this in mind.

Rankin and Vickers (2001) make the link between restructuring and women's representation. They note that "a recent report of the United Nations Experts Advisory Group on National Machineries stated that one of the most significant obstacles that women's equality machinery faces today, throughout the world, is the frequent restructuring of governments" (15). The authors then apply this to the case of women's structures of representation in Ontario, and explain that

the 1995 election of the Harris Progressive Conservative Government in Ontario and its dismantling of important programs for women changed the political opportunity structure for women in Ontario quite radically.

> Increasingly, women in Ontario feel shut out of the process in their home province, yet they also face weak structures federally. (17)

This goes to the point made in chapter 1 that treating federalism as a political shopping mall may not be very helpful if all you have to choose from is the Gap and Old Navy. In other words, with restructuring, the institutions of representation are not particularly democratic at either the federal or the provincial scale. If we are to take seriously some of the claims outlined earlier, namely, those around federalism and local democracy, and federalism and multiple avenues of engagement, then significant transformation of provincial structures of representation is necessary.

Managerialism has affected the configuration of women's policy machinery in Canada. Recall the range of structures that were introduced during the Weberian period outlined above. In the name of "rationalization," several shuffles occurred at the federal and provincial scales in the 1990s–2000s. Since 1993, the CACSW and the Women's Programs were dismantled, with their responsibilities purportedly transferred to Status of Women Canada. The Minister Responsible for the Status of Women went from being a full-fledged cabinet minister to being a junior minister.

These "shuffles" were accompanied by drastic funding cuts and a weakening of support for equality-seeking groups when the policy shifted from core to project-based funding. MacIvor argues that the power of the Women's Program, which provided funding for women's groups and projects, was reduced when Prime Minister Campbell moved it from the Secretary of State to Human Resources Development in 1993. In 1995, in another shuffle under Liberal prime minister Chrétien, it went to Status of Women Canada, a much smaller and weaker department (MacIvor 1996). It should be noted that it was argued at the time that the shuffle would consolidate and strengthen the women's bureaucracy. Currently, SWC encompasses the functions of the now defunct CACSW, and administers the Women's Program, and hence, is a larger department in terms of responsibility than it was previously. These responsibilities, though, were not accompanied by an increase in necessary resources. Drastic de-funding of the Women's Program had occurred by the 1990s[19] (O'Neil and Sutherland 1997, 213). Another round of recent restructuring, already described, followed in 2006.

The provinces saw comparable restructuring. As at the federal scale, women in many provinces have seen their policy machinery "restructured," or destroyed.

The following structures have been dismantled:

- New Brunswick Women's Directorate, plus significant cuts to, then eventual elimination of the New Brunswick Advisory Council (The Women's Issues Branch is now the Women's Equality Branch)
- Ontario – Ontario Advisory Council on Women's Issues (OACWI) (formerly the Ontario Advisory Council on the Status of Women), plus significant cuts to the OWD
- Saskatchewan – Women's Secretariat of Saskatchewan (rolled into the Department of Labour; Status of Women created)
- Alberta – Women's Secretariat and Alberta Advisory Council on Women's Issues (Women's Issues now subsumed under Human Services)
- BC – Women's Ministry (rolled into Ministry of Community, Aboriginal and Women's Services, then the Ministry of Community Services, now the Ministry of Health), Women's Minister demoted to a Junior Minister
- Yukon – Yukon Women's Directorate[20] (as a stand-alone department; Yukon Advisory Council on Women's Issues created in 1992)
- NWT Women's Directorate[21]

Neoliberalism, implemented into the state's administrative processes in the form of the New Public Management, and other attempts to marketize the state, are based on the fundamentally flawed premise that states can, and should, be run like a business. In these terms, "rationalization" posits that overlap in state functions and services should be eliminated. This is the justification for the restructuring of federal women's policy machinery (Rankin and Vickers 2001). Rankin and Vickers note that these changes were "set within an economic rationalist discourse and the argued need to enhance efficiency and effectiveness" (9). Rationalization is a questionable claim in this case because it assumes that all women's policy machinery performs the same function, simply because it deals with women, and therefore can be amalgamated.[22] In reality, each had its own specific function. SWC did research and policy development, the Women's Program funded women's organizations and projects, and CACSW did consultation with the women's movement. Now the latter two functions have almost disappeared from the policy process entirely, not only in practice, but also in theoretical considerations of what are "legitimate" policy activities.

Along with these structural changes, then, the impact of managerialism has been felt at the level of discourse as well. Shields and Evans (1998) indicate that the

> purpose of public management reform is to increase the degree to which public servants manage their operations in ways that enhance economy, efficiency, and effectiveness ... [This] obscures the fundamentally political nature of these changes through the discourse of efficiency, effectiveness and a refoundation of representative democracy. (77–8)

While there is little research thus far on the Canadian context, Australian feminists have shown that this language is in conflict with the priorities of feminism. They have identified their current struggle as one of "femocrats" versus "econocrats," in which the "propaganda of economic rationalism" has become all consuming (Kaplan 1996, 158; Eisenstein 1996, 189). Kaplan (1996) asserts that "an overriding concern with economics diminishes awareness of inequalities and injustice" (155). Hester Eisenstein (1996) agrees that

> by definition the new value system was opposed to the principles and goals of feminism ... The general climate of managerialism included a notion of opposing "social engineering," relying instead on a free market notion that things will take care of themselves. This concept directly countered the feminist argument that one needed intervention on behalf of women, that business as usual would not meet women's needs. (189)

Sawer (1990) shares her experience that "the vast majority of senior officers in the central coordinating departments, Prime Minister and Cabinet, Finance and Treasury, were committed to an economic rationalist agenda of deregulation and less public involvement in the economy" (105). The result is that "the public sector has placed increased faith on economics, one of the social sciences least influenced by feminist critique" (ibid., 250). In the context of intergovernmental relations in Canada, as Cameron (2004) has noted, the predominance of the Department of Finance is also problematic because it is insulated from popular participation (55).

Related, managerialism legitimizes only certain types of knowledge:

> In Australia, specialist knowledge was no longer a requirement for managing equal employment opportunity, just broad knowledge of management skills ... Econocrats were the new arbiters of policy, and other

experts – including femocrats – were being devalued ... The specialist knowledge of femocrats was downgraded in favor of generic managers, who represented the interests of the "economy" as a whole. (Eisenstein 1996, 193, 197)

This appears to echo the reality in Canada as well. Geller-Schwartz (1995) reveals that during the free trade debate, "femocrats within the [federal] government who tried to raise questions about the Government's plans were quickly silenced" (52). Feminist economist Marjorie Griffin Cohen also relates that

[when] we began to talk about economic issues like the budget, trade policy, privatization, deregulation, and the general structure of the Canadian economy, we were going to [sic] far. These were not women's issues: women were not "experts" and therefore our criticism had little credibility. (in Brodie 1995a, 47)

Managerialism has placed substantial limits on the spaces for feminist intervention and analysis. Sawer (1991) sums up the distressing situation well when she says that

the influence of new right agendas and economic rationalism have brought to prominence those trained in insensitivity to gender-specific distributional outcomes and hostile to the forms of social investment needed by women. "Femocrats" often engaged in achieving "least worst" outcomes rather than optimal ones ... The attempt to carry feminist organisational values into government, including an emphasis on process and empowerment ... has been put at risk by managerialism. (275)

The language of the marketplace is ill suited to address public policy from an equity standpoint. Teghtsoonian (2004) gives an excellent example of New Zealand's Ministry of Women's Affairs, where, "in addition to a more hierarchical and managerialist structure, these changes were also reflected in a sometimes awkward business language ... [where] violence against women by abusive partners ("domestic violence") and women's high levels of unemployment are characterized as "important indicators of inefficiency" (11). In a comparative work on Canada and Australia, Sawer (1994) concluded that "in both countries feminist agendas have been adversely affected by the increasing influence of market liberalism and managerialism" (49).

Managerialism and the New Public Management more generally have proved to be difficult to confront. This finds a partial explanation at the level of language, as there appears to be some overlap between neoliberal restructuring of the bureaucracy and feminist prescriptions for change in the public service. This is, in large part, due to the success of the Right in appropriating the discourse of feminism and other social movements. Terms like "empowerment" and "community care," coined by the women's movement, have become the buzzwords of neoliberalism. Shields and Evans (1998) refer to the frequent use of the phrase "consumer empowerment" (2). Osborne and Gaebler (1993), for example, in their popularization of neoliberal public sector restructuring, want to *empower* citizens by pushing control out of the bureaucracy, into the *community*" (19, italics mine). Brodie (1996) adds that the "shift of the health-care burden onto women is being rationalized with specific reference to the progressive discourse of the women's health movement" (17). While this overlapping discourse serves to blur the lines between neoliberal and feminist bureaucratic restructuring, there are radical differences between them. Most notably, feminists are interested in democratizing the state, while neoliberalism, and the NPM in particular, as will be seen further in chapter 4, has served to undermine this democratic project.

Public Administration, Representation, and Democracy

Within political science and political economy, there has been much interest in the democratization of political institutions, ranging from the role and functioning of Parliament to reform of the electoral system, to constitutionalism. Interestingly, much less attention has been placed on state administration, which is curious given its considerable power and influence, combined with its relative immunity from popular participation. And after outlining here the gender regimes associated with both the Weberian and the NPM systems, the need to democratize the structures of public administration is even more evident. In this last section, I will briefly summarize the central differences between the Weberian and NPM gender regimes. I will then move on to identify what Weberian bureaucracy and the NPM share in common, to demonstrate the inherent limitations of both gender regimes. Therefore, I propose that an alternative regime of governance must reconsider the relationship between state feminism, representation, and democracy.

The Weberian and NPM Regimes in Contrast

There are some considerable differences between the Weberian and the NPM regimes. As seen above, the Weberian regime showed some malleability in terms of the representation of marginalized groups. One of the significant adaptations to Weberianism was the introduction of women's policy machinery. While these structures existed within an overarching culture of "neutrality," there was some acceptance that public servants would represent groups that are disadvantaged in the policy process, and that there was a place for the input of "outsiders," supported with state funding. The Weberian gender regime allowed some space for citizenship claims making.

Neoliberalism and the NPM discourage citizens from thinking of themselves as members of groups, and especially groups who make democratic claims. It goes without saying that making such group claims, especially as advocates from inside the state, is an affront to neoliberal sensibilities, which view the world through the lens of competitive individualism and the pursuit of self-interest. To be sure, the label "special interest," has been a pervasive strategy of de-legitimization, rejecting (and simultaneously exaggerating) the influence of collectivities and their representation in the policy process. Overall, managerialism has redefined the role of state administration, shifting it from public to private service.

Another good example of the differences between the Weberian and NPM regime is employment equity. As seen earlier, employment equity provided some real movement towards representative bureaucracy during the Weberian regime. It incorporated equity into the merit principle, and affirmed the existence of, and the state's responsibility for addressing, systemic discrimination. These ideas are at odds with the NPM. As a matter of fact, one of the first actions of the Harris government in Ontario was to repeal employment equity in the province. This marked a "shift ... from one end of the spectrum to the other, moving from a position that ranked at the top of the scale in terms of government support for employment equity, only to be reversed to the most unfavourable orientation in a very short period" (Bakan and Kobayashi 2000, 24).

This shift is evident simply in the title of the bill – An Act to Repeal Job Quotas and to Restore Merit-based Employment Practices in Ontario (Bakan and Kobayashi 2000) – which starkly distinguishes the

Weberian from the NPM regime. Bakan and Kobayashi (2000) lay out well the two different policy approaches:

> Whereas previously the public sector had been identified as an example of the effectiveness of government equity policy, now the priority was shifted to the private sector. Whereas previously the issue of equity was presented as a principle of democratic practice, now workplace equal opportunity was advocated for its contribution to profit maximization. And whereas a general climate in workplace relations previously called for employers to ensure representation among women, Aboriginal peoples, visible minorities and persons with disabilities, now even previously accumulated research records of workplace surveys were to be destroyed. (31)

Indeed, the act *required* that "every person in possession of information collected and compiled exclusively for the purpose of complying with ... the *Employment Equity Act*, shall destroy the information as soon as reasonably possible after this Act comes into force" (Bakan and Kobayashi 2000, 29).

Bakan and Kobayashi (2000) refer to a resulting "process of systemic paper shredding" (29). The erasure of employment equity from official records also represented an erosion of the notion of systemic discrimination as experienced by groups, replaced by discrimination as an anomaly, suffered by isolated individuals (Bakan and Kobayashi 2000, 30–1).

Agócs (2012) has recently pointed to a similar process of erasure federally:

> The Harper government has yet to attempt a repeal of the Employment Equity Act as the Harris government of Ontario did in 1996 ... However the Harper government has made decisions that have had the effect of cutting the legs from under the Act. These decisions have included cuts to the Canadian Human Rights Commission and Citizenship and Immigration Canada, which have monitoring and enforcement responsibilities under the Act, and the scrapping of the mandatory long form of the census, upon which employers and enforcement agencies depend for availability data. Other measures have impaired the ability of the public, researchers and advocacy organizations to monitor employment equity implementation results and voice critical perspectives ... Such actions can amount to a death by a thousand cuts, without the need to incur the political fallout of an attempt at outright repeal of the Employment Equity Act. (9)

Weberian organization and the NPM signify two different notions of representation and democracy. The former, associated with the Keynesian welfare state, entails a positive view of state action and an expansive vision of the public, and seeks to create structures that are ultimately accountable to elected members. The latter, stemming from neoliberal state restructuring, sees the state as the problem, aiming to restrict the public realm and to extend private influence over state structures or public institutions.[23] But they also share more in common than appears at first glance. Both rely heavily on hierarchical forms of organization. Both legitimate very specific kinds of knowledge production. Both adhere to rigid rules and processes. And both advance gendered regimes of representation and democracy.

Continuity across Regimes

Even though the Weberian and the NPM are distinct gender regimes, there are some notable similarities between them. My research questions are in many ways procedural. They have to do with bureaucratic procedures and principles, including hierarchy, neutrality, "expertise," and categorization, and how we might move beyond them. As we have seen, feminists have shown that such forms of bureaucratic organization are particularly problematic for gender democracy in a number of ways. First, bureaucracies are structured hierarchically. Generally, feminist organizational principles emphasize alternatives to hierarchical structures, such as the network, or hub-and-spoke model. Feminists have also highlighted the challenges of representing intersectional identities and experiences within discrete bureaucratic departments and structures. Finally, traditional Weberian bureaucracy is based on the premise of neutrality. This is especially difficult for femocrats, since in their original inception, and in accord with principles of democratization, they were to be advocates of the women's movement from inside the state. In a related manner, revealing the ways in which "knowledge" is socially constructed, and how what constitutes "expertise" is political, has also been a key feminist contribution. In problematizing these structures, feminists seek to transform and democratize them.

But globalization and neoliberalism move us in the opposite direction, towards the NPM, reinforcing, and in many ways intensifying representational problems at all scales of government. Rhetorical claims notwithstanding, "levelling hierarchies" and decentralizing decision-making has not materialized. Instead, neoliberalism has maintained "control from above" (Albo 1993, 25), with greater centralized power in the cabinet and an increasingly politicized[24] upper bureaucracy, combined with extensive downsizing of lower levels of the public service. Aucoin (2000) has referred to this as the "paradox of a simultaneous centralization and decentralization in government structures" (648). Contrary to neoliberal claims, "levelling" has been used as an excuse for downsizing the public sector, but has certainly not "empowered," public-sector workers. Neoliberal public management provides no serious challenge to hierarchical organization because it has no philosophical opposition to the social relations of subordination that hierarchy entails, and in fact promotes such inequalities in myriad ways.

Furthermore, neoliberal public management, not surprisingly, has not responded to feminist concerns about compartmentalization and intersectionality, associated with the Weberian regime. There has been no effort to coordinate policy structures for marginalized women under the NPM. In Ontario, the Race Relations Directorate no longer exists, nor does the Anti-racism Secretariat. While the problems associated with the Weberian regime were related to compartmentalized organizational and representational forms, under the NPM, the very idea of state representation of "special interests" is rejected. As seen earlier, it has been claimed that the restructuring, or more accurately, the dismantling of women's policy machinery, was carried out to "rationalize" and bring together women's policy-related functions under one umbrella. Such a claim is disingenuous. One need only look at the drastic cuts in staff and funding to women's policy structures to measure the interest in, and commitment to, the machinery of gender democracy at all scales of government.

At the same time, the discourse of scientific management, originating with the Weberian model, continues to be portrayed as an unbiased, rational approach to public administration, even as the public service has become more partisan and politicized under the NPM through the marketization of policy advice. Thus, feminist critiques of the principle of "neutrality" have also become more, not less, relevant. This, along with a belief in technocratic knowledge, and the powerful interests it serves, marks continuity across the Weberian and NPM gender regimes.

As addressed earlier, in a marketized state, certain kinds of knowledge are valued. Similar encounters with "economic rationalism" that were cited earlier in reference to Australia have been experienced by Canadian femocrats, but in Canada, neoliberal public management has also taken up the idea of the "feminist expert," with gender-based policy analysis (Rankin and Vickers 2001).[25] Some are beginning to see the potential subversion of democracy that exists: "Sawer ... argues that the move to economic rationalism and public choice approaches to policy analysis constructs women's needs and demands as special interests. Gender-based analysis emerges as 'expert analysis' and is positioned against movement lobbying" (Rankin and Vickers 2001, 20). Even such beacons of neoliberalism as the World Bank have gotten on board with gender-based analysis (GBA) and gender mainstreaming.

Rankin and Wilcox (2004) submit that GBA is quite compatible with neoliberalism because it replaces women's movement participation with technical expertise. It is also a natural extension of Weberian scientific management. Rankin and Vickers (2001) voice the concern that "gender-based analysis may evolve into a status quo approach that represents the perceptions of well-educated, majority women" (35). The democratic, participatory nature of gender budgeting and analysis, as they were originally intended, and have been practised elsewhere, is being lost. One person interviewed went so far as to call gender-based policy analysis "nonsense" because it was being used not as a way to democratize policy, but instead as a way to control the representation of interests. She characterized the new policy research fund within SWC as feminist experts, with no relationship with women's groups, deciding how to give out money. She simply concluded, "This is no good!"[26]

Given these procedural weaknesses, which exist at both the federal and provincial scales of state administration, democratization of these structures is a positive end in itself, but it is also intended to bring about change on the substantive side in terms of policy outcomes. Both are needed for a transformative gender regime.

State Feminism, Representation, and Democracy

As noted in previous chapters, the term femocrat is contested within feminist theory, with some equating it with selling out and de-radicalization and others viewing it as subversive and revolutionary. Under the two dominant gender regimes described above, and examined in more detail over the next two chapters, neither view is entirely correct. State feminists have not simply been co-opted. Femocrats are certainly conscious of power relations. They have developed strategies to challenge the dominant norms and procedures of both gender regimes. They have struggled to be accountable to feminist principles and to the women's movement. But state feminists have also not directly confronted either gender regime of public administration. Femocrats have not always challenged the gendered power relations and procedures of neutrality, expertise, and compartmentalization. In fact, as will be seen in the case studies, some actually actively support these processes. And under the NPM, most femocrats have turned their energies from subversion to mere survival. Nevertheless, state feminism does have the potential to transform public administration. It is important for representation and democracy.

Feminists have worked to re-conceptualize "representation," and in doing so, have made at least two significant contributions which influence my project. First, feminism seeks a broadened scope of action for representational politics beyond the confines of electoral processes. Second, it demands that we deepen the meaning and content of representation to include both procedural and substantive notions. State feminism can play a central role in expanding both of these: the content and the scope of representation.

Feminist political science has insisted that our definitions of the political extend outside of state institutions to include both the public and private spheres, as both provide vital opportunities for representation. Feminist theorists have attempted to go beyond electorally based representation, looking to more complex visions. As Dobrowolsky (2000) maintains:

> Women's representational interventions crisscross institutional/non-institutional or formal/informal divides. They transcend public/private spaces and theorizations (the public refers to the state as well as public discourses, whereas the private encompasses both the market and the family). Standard distinctions fail to take into consideration that feminists have engaged in activities and advanced concerns previously excluded from the conventional, formal political sphere, the world of public institutions and officials, governments and political parties, with their state-sanctioned powers, practices, and discourses. In seeking representation, women have bridged private and public, civil society and state, cultural and political. (3)

Correspondingly, Vickers (1997b) identifies four main sectors of women's representation: Institutions of Official Politics (i.e., legislatures, bureaucracy, judiciary); Institutions of Civil Society (i.e., churches, unions, universities, media); Institutions and Organizations of Autonomous

Women's Movements (i.e., the National Action Committee on the Status of Women [NAC], the Fédération des Femmes du Québec [FFQ], grassroots groups); and Pressure Groups and Social Movements (i.e., environment, peace, anti-racism movements, lobby groups), all being components of a feminist understanding of representation.

These perspectives emphasize that representation, through electoral politics, continues to be relevant. However, a restricted notion of representation that encompasses only electoral politics is inadequate. Electoral politics are not the only (or even primary) avenue of representation and target for democratization. There are other important structures of governance in non-elected structures of the state, such as the legal system and the bureaucracy, and in non-state realms, like participatory democracy and popular movements and groups.

I am taking this wider, and more nuanced, representational focus in arguing for an alternative gender regime of public administration. While I still see electoral politics as a significant structure of representation, there are multiple avenues of representation, and representation beyond the party system is necessary, particularly for marginalized groups. One should also not exaggerate the democratic character of electoral politics, and downplay the serious representational limitations by seeing electoral politics as the only avenue for change, closing off other significant political terrain. Truly democratic representation must move well beyond the electoral system, to look seriously at the current limitations, and the possibilities for transformation, that exist within our structures of bureaucratic administration, including women's policy machinery.

Feminism has also sought to bridge the gap between representative and participatory democracy, and to recognize overlapping forms of representation. For example, direct participation by citizens is often seen as a replacement for, or an alternative to, representative democracy.[27] But participatory democracy does not necessarily bypass representative democracy. Anne Phillips (1991) points out that feminist approaches have challenged the way in which liberal thinking about democracy has relied on the creation of dichotomies – public versus private, or representative versus participatory democracy – which, in reality, are false. Representative and participatory democracy do not have to be at odds with each other. There is an important role for both elected and non-elected representatives to play in facilitating civic engagement. Hilary Wainwright links participatory and representative democracy in a way in which the state (both elected and non-elected) acts as "provider of public support and protection for a variety of forms of popular self-government. In terms of traditional debates about democracy, such an approach would imply a combination of participatory and representative forms" (quoted in Rebick 2000, 32–3). A view of representation that conceptualizes elected and non-elected representatives as facilitators of citizen participation advances a different kind of gender regime of public administration, and an altered role for state feminists, or femocrats, in linking the state and society through women's policy structures.

The femocrat strategy in Australia grew out of the Women's Electoral Lobby (WEL), who came to see that they needed to diversify their political strategy beyond temporary electoral politics, to establish permanent women's policy machinery in the bureaucracy at both the state and national level (Sawer 1990; Eisenstein 1991). Some of this machinery included the Office of Women's Affairs, the Office for the Status of Women, the Women's Bureau in the department of labour, the women's coordinator in the Office of the Prime Minister, women's adviser, departmental units to monitor the impact of programs on women, and advisory bodies (Sawer 1991).[28] As seen above, former Australian femocrat Hester Eisenstein (1996), while identifying some of the contradictions and challenges for feminists working within bureaucratic forms of organization, emphasizes concrete policy gains for women in areas ranging from child care to violence to employment. The origins of the gender budgeting in the early 1980s can also be linked to Australian femocrats (United Nations, UNIFEM 2000). In addition, Australian women's policy machinery influenced other jurisdictions, including Canada.

These structures, despite their flaws, have provided arenas of representation for women, beyond electoral politics, and have served as democratic points of convergence for feminists inside and outside the state. These ties have been weakened by both internal government restructuring and by related cuts to funding for popular organizations (discussed in later chapters), which seriously challenge democratic representation. Recall the observations of Eisenstein, Maillé, and Dobrowolsky in the previous chapter that highlight the significance of forging links between state feminists and the community – something that is necessary for feminist representation and feminist democratic administration. Democratizing the administrative side of the state, and representation within it, therefore, requires not simply resurrecting what was lost to restructuring, but rather creating new, accountable, and participatory structures of representation and linking these strongly to popular movements outside the state. This broadened scope for representation, along with a deepening of the meaning and content of representation, can foster a transformative gender regime.

Feminist political scientists have also contested the meaning and content of representation. They have distinguished between the need to increase the numbers of women elected into politics and improving the way in which women's demands, needs, and identities are represented. These have been referred to as procedural (or descriptive) and substantive representation respectively. Descriptive representation, Tremblay and Trimble (2003) explain, posits that elected representatives should mirror the demographics of those s/he is representing. Substantive representation, by contrast, seeks representatives that not only resemble their constituents demographically, but who also pursue the concerns and interests of those constituents once elected. Similarly, Arscott (1995) makes a distinction between a feminist conception of representation based on numbers and one based on policy outcomes, and Phillips (1991) makes a similar intervention. These definitions underline the need for a deeper understanding of representation, and the importance of considering not only *who* makes decisions, but also *what* the results are. However, they say little about *how* decisions are made, providing a rather limited view of procedural democracy,[29] and tend to portray procedural and substantive democracy in isolation from each other.

Procedural and substantive democracy are directly related. The point of democratization is that it is intended to lead to different policy outcomes than we have currently. But this requires a *substantive process* of representation and democracy. We need to deepen our conceptualization of representation to include not only substantive policy outcomes, but also a more expansive vision of the process itself. Drawing on Dorothy Stetson's framework for gender policy analysis, Newman and White (2006) identify three criteria for evaluating public policy. They ask not only (1) whether women are involved in the process and (2) whether they are able to achieve substantive policy results, but also, (3), *whether women's presence transforms the policy process itself*. Transformation involves reframing policy debates and making the process more inclusive (Newman and White 2006). In the 2005 extension of Mazur and Stetson's pioneering 1995 *Comparative State Feminism*, Lovenduski et al. (2005b) measure the success of women's movements in achieving their goals, and the role of women's policy agencies in that process. In this regard, "success" includes not only direct policy outcomes, but also the inclusiveness of the policy process, and the ways in which policies are framed. Thus, a feminist process of representation and democracy will depend on active participation from outside the state, and systematic interaction between the inside and outside through strengthened ties to the women's movement.

Conclusion

In this chapter, I outlined two models of public administration: Weberian and NPM. I argued that even though both are based on different forms and notions of representation and democracy, and constitute distinct gender regimes, they still share in common a set of values, ideas, and assumptions that have gendered consequences. Weberian administration, revolving around the organizational principles of hierarchy, compartmentalization, and neutrality, has been shown to conflict with feminist principles of equality, interconnectedness, and advocacy. The NPM, embedded in neoliberal state restructuring, with its focus on downsizing, privatization, and managerialism, has also been the subject of widespread feminist criticism due to its impact on women's representation and their labour.

Democratic administration has provided some of the most useful insights into alternative governance approaches to Weberianism and the NPM. However, feminist critiques of bureaucracy complicate the claims made about the democratic potential of the public sector, and have not been well integrated into the analyses within democratic administration. Feminist approaches to representation and democracy can enrich democratic administration by envisioning a transformative gender regime of public administration. Therefore, I suggest that an alternative public administration would make state feminism, representation, and democracy central to its governance models.

The next two chapters will provide a more comprehensive look at the Weberian and NPM governance paradigms and gender regimes in practice, through the case study of the Ontario Women's Directorate (OWD). Chapter 3 examines the opportunities and limitations for state feminism presented by a gender regime of public administration that both challenged and reinforced Weberianism. Chapter 4 explores the neoliberal gender regime, and the place of state feminism within the NPM. The concluding chapter will lay out in more detail a transformative gender regime based on femocratic administration.

3 Experiments with State Feminism in the Weberian Gender Regime

So far, I have maintained that the state is at the intersection of discussions about neoliberalism and globalization, on the one hand, and debates within feminist theory, on the other. I have further asserted that the nation state, as well as sub-national states, and their administrative structures in particular, are central considerations for a feminist model of public administration, based on an alternative vision of representation and democracy, or a transformative gender regime. The need for this alternative vision is reinforced in the feminist literature on gender and institutions that details the role that states and bureaucracies play in (re)producing power relations.

But not all states regulate gender relations in the same way. In the preceding chapter, for instance, I showed that important adjustments were made to the Weberian model, which held more promise for women. Yet I ultimately argued that notwithstanding some central differences between the Weberian and NPM forms, both resulted in gender regimes of governance that circumscribe representational politics. In the next two chapters, I will explore these claims in reference to the specific case study of the Ontario bureaucracy.

Here, I consider state feminism in Ontario, situated at the end stage of the Keynesian welfare state (KWS), with the Weberian gender regime of public administration revolving around the central components of hierarchy, categorization, and neutrality. While some important insights for fashioning an alternative gender regime can be gained from this era, in the end, many in the Ontario Women's Directorate (OWD) were willing only to stretch, but not to break from, the principles of traditional Weberian bureaucracy.

I begin the chapter with a brief overview of the OWD from the 1980s to the early 1990s. I then outline the ways in which this was a Weberian regime with significant modifications, providing greater procedural and substantive opportunities for gender democracy. Overall, I conclude that women's experiences in Ontario within this regime indicate that the Weberian form of organization is indeed problematic and poses a range of limitations and challenges for state feminism. Only by moving beyond it can fundamental change, and femocratic administration, be achieved.

The Ontario Women's Directorate

I will begin by considering roughly the first decade of the OWD. This period spans three governments: the tail end of the Bill Davis Conservatives (until 1985), the David Peterson Liberal minority (1985–7) and majority (1987–90), and the NDP under Bob Rae (1990–5). Despite there being different parties in power, this periodization reflects the responses in interviews, which largely stressed the similarities for the OWD across these governments.[1] Burt and Lorenzin (1997) also submit that the NDP signalled "more of the same" in terms of a commitment to liberal democratic representation and equal opportunity, by building on the policy framework of its predecessor. Therefore, as noted in the introductory chapter, this period represents a particular governance paradigm associated with the Keynesian welfare state, and the modified Weberian gender regime, as outlined in the previous chapter.

As Malloy (2003) indicates, Ontario was slow to introduce similar women's policy structures to those implemented by the federal government after the RCSW in the early 1970s. The first response was to institute the Ontario Council on the Status of Women (OCSW) in 1974, which would later become the Ontario Advisory Council on Women's Issues (OACWI) in 1985. As with other advisory councils, members of the OACWI were appointed by the government of the day, and therefore the council was criticized by the women's movement for its partisanship and lack of autonomy. However, it did provide advice to government, engage in public education, organize formal community consultations, and conduct independent research (Malloy 2003) on a broad range of issues related to women and the environment, women and the economy, single mothers, women and mental health, women and aging, visible minority women, women with disabilities, childcare, new reproductive technologies, constitutional reform, pornography and prostitution, employment standards, and pay equity. It also lobbied for the creation of the OWD (OWD 1993e, "The OWD Is 10"; Malloy 2003).

Bill Davis's Progressive Conservative government created the OWD in 1983 (Malloy 2003), in response to lobbying by the OCSW (OWD 1993e, "The OWD Is 10"). The OWD was to take on the functions of the Women's Bureau in the Ministry of Labour and the Women Crown Employees Office, as well as responsibility for policy and research[2] (ibid.). At that time, a minister responsible for the status of women was also established (Malloy 2003). Status of Women was not an independent portfolio. It was held as additional to the minister's other portfolio, and the OWD was housed within that "home" ministry.[3] The directorate's primary role was to advise government on policy issues related to the status of women.

The directorate had forty-one staff members and a budget of about $4.5 million in 1984 (Malloy 2003). It went through subsequent expansions in 1985–7 under the Liberal minority government and in 1990 under the New Democratic Party (NDP) government (Malloy 2003). Under the Liberals, the OWD had a communications branch, a program branch, and a policy and research branch. Staff numbers reached seventy-six and the budget was just over $22 million in 1991 (Ontario Ministry of Finance 1991). Public servants interviewed estimated that by the mid-1990s, under the NDP, staff levels were close to one hundred.[4]

Lessons for Democratic/Femocratic Governance

Many feminist treatments of bureaucracy do not say much about the democratic potential of the public service. This orientation fails to imagine that within oppressive structures, democratic openings might exist, be created, or be transformed through political struggle and human agency. Due to the contradictory nature of women's relationship to the state, there are still considerable lessons about procedural and substantive democracy that can be learned from the experiences of Ontario state feminists. This is especially true because, during the first decade of the OWD, there were conscious attempts at democratizing the public service, which challenged the Weberian model of public administration.

Procedural Democracy

There are many ways that the state feminism of this period from the mid-1980s to the mid-1990s enhanced the process of governance. The majority of interviews indicated that, in its first decade, there was a very active role for the OWD, with one concluding that the "Director-ate at that time had a very high profile."[5] Generally, both the Liberal and NDP leadership, in their own ways, took the OWD seriously.[6] Several of those interviewed remembered Liberal minister Ian Scott as being a personally committed, influential cabinet minister whose leadership was important for the status of the directorate, especially around pay equity. One public servant said that even though "he would be the last to say he was a strong feminist," Scott had credibility and knowledge of government, and was able to get things through cabinet.[7] Rankin's (1996) research confirms the significance of a com-mitted ministry for women's policy machinery in Ontario. The OWD was seen by the Liberals as a "central advocacy agency,"[8] and this role was seen as legitimate.

For its part, the Rae government was a "stated feminist government," which one participant said was a "powerful message."[9] It had more female legislators and ministers than ever before in Ontario, many of whom were influential. NDP women's ministers Anne Swarbrick and Marion Boyd were very strong and had feminist backgrounds before entering government.[10] There were also several other feminist women in cabinet, which meant the OWD had access to a series of "sympa-thetic" ministers.[11] A former OWD staff member suggested that to be most effective, they needed a "triangle network" consisting of a com-petent, keen minister, another key ministry, and the directorate. During the NDP's term, this was accomplished through the relationship between the OWD, its minister, Marion Boyd (also Community and Social Services [COMSOC] minister and Attorney General at times) and Frances Lankin (Health).[12]

Some of the directorate's assistant deputy ministers (ADMs) were identified as being quite powerful. For instance, Naomi Alboim was an ADM during the 1980s, but was described as operating more like a senior deputy minister. Reporting directly to the secretary to cabi-net, she had high status, went to every cabinet committee meeting, and made sure all policies were reviewed for their impact on women.[13] She was visible and seen as a legitimate "internal advocate for a central agency."[14] In addition, Joan Andrew, ADM in the late 1980s to the early 1990s, was said to be "very pro-active" and to have good visibility and relationships with other ministries dealing with programs for women such as Community and Social Services and Justice. Those after her were thought to have taken a more reactive role.[15]

The directorate provided an opening into the Ontario Public Service (OPS) for many women who otherwise would not have been hired. Furthermore, without downplaying their limited ties to the women's movement, one interviewee stressed that many were often career bureaucrats who had probably never fit into the bureaucracy, and were thrilled to go into the OWD.[16] Because it had a broad mandate and range of policy issues, with no program responsibilities, the directorate had to establish relationships with other ministries. In working with these ministries, the OWD gained advocates in other departments who felt isolated, some of whom were said to have found a "safe haven" when involved with the directorate.[17] One interview was particularly telling, where a public servant recalled a colleague telling her that in her ministry she had actually "left meetings after being spat at."[18] Another commented that one is turned into an advocate when working with other ministries and faced with "brutal and threatening behaviour."[19]

Possibly most fundamental is that during its first decade (about 1983–95), the OWD was a place where feminist debate about the nature of women's relationship to the state was commonplace. In fact, because the majority of those in the directorate had "strong personal feminist values," one participant considered it to be a "thriving place," marked by controversy and committed, passionate people.[20] Another commented that "it was a very different time." There was a lot of debate about feminism and the bureaucracy, which included staff retreats, speakers, and break-out groups about "how to define and establish a feminist bureaucracy ... That kind of debate was very much encouraged at the time."[21] Her colleague remembered active discussions about "how to work and maintain some integrity in one's analysis and one's commitments ... while working within a government bureaucracy." She believed that the feminist debates that were occurring inside the directorate were represented within its own structures. She remarked that "the organizational structure reflected the main differences in feminist analysis," with the social and economic policy department associated with liberal feminism and another department focused on "designated groups," including justice issues and Aboriginal, refugee, and immigrant women. There were "different perspectives in how people approached analyzing the issues." She understood this period as a time when they could deal with fundamental issues, including what the mandate of the directorate was. She is not in contact with the OWD anymore, but senses it is not "intensely debating these things now," as the debate has shifted with the changing nature and role of government.[22]

One of the central discussions within feminism at the time revolved around concerns about how to avoid the marginalization or ghettoization of women's structures of representation. This occurred in a variety of organizations and institutions, including not only the state, but also labour unions, political parties, and community organizations. The OWD was no exception, and there were conscious attempts to prevent the segregation of women's policy and the directorate. One public servant summed up the representational strategy by saying: "If you're serious about equality for women," the idea is to influence the whole structure, otherwise it is "apartheid."[23]

The first ADM, Glenna Carr, sought to bring into the OWD for a period of time people who were experts in particular line ministries, expose them to gender analysis, and then return them to their home ministries to champion women's issues there. It was expected that those who left the OWD would spread feminist analysis throughout the OPS.[24] Several of those, covering different periods over the decade, likened the OWD to an "incubator for a lot of ideas" that were subsequently transferred to other line ministries for implementation.[25] Indeed, many started at the OWD, and then became integrated into line ministries. An interviewee described the directorate as "an ideal training ground," because "the alumni of the OWD are in many places," including Education, Health, Labour, Economic Development, Trade, Treasury Board, and Environment.[26] This strategy saw the OWD as a temporary structure whose functions would eventually become redundant. In an article she wrote about the directorate, former ADM Naomi Alboim (1997) asks, "Should women's issues be integrated into each ministry or department? Isn't the whole point of a change agency to do itself out of a job?" (224).

From its inception, up until the mid-1990s, those in the directorate actively debated their role as advocates and their proper relationship to the women's movement. But these things were not simply the subjects of debate. These discussions resulted in a much different understanding of advocacy and ties to the community than exists now. Procedural democracy was strengthened not only in terms of internal processes, but with improved community access to the state. Those from ACTEW (A Commitment to Training and Employment for Women), for example, described regular consultation and collaboration with the directorate, and funding support, discussed in more detail later.[27] There was also ongoing communication with women's centres and organizations about policy issues, especially in the area of violence against women.[28]

In addition, during the Liberal government, the directorate had almost 100 staff members, and the priority was on public-education (including free publications for teachers) building projects, like employment equity in partnership with the community and private sector and support for, and a collaborative relationship with, stakeholders.[29] Public education was also privileged by the NDP, which had an active communication operation, particularly around public service ads about violence against women.[30]

As a contradictory institution, there were obviously divergent approaches to advocacy and community relations within the directorate, but the dominant orientation to come out of the interviews was to frame the OWD as explicitly feminist, and charged with facilitating social change. This was common across the three governments. The directorate was spoken of as a "legitimate vehicle for equity issues" and a "strategy dedicated to improving women's status."[31] One public servant asserted, "We were employees of the state, but ... that was a tool of improving women's lives."[32] Several agreed that until the mid-1990s, the OWD conceived of itself as an advocacy group. For instance: "There was a period of time, up to the middle 90s where there was a comfort level and an emphasis on interacting with whatever community you happen to be working with, whether it was private sector, broader public sector, or NGOs, so depending on your responsibility, you were encouraged to have that interaction."[33] During the same period of time, a number of former staff also recalled having much more international participation, around events like the Beijing conference, which decreased later on.[34]

As seen with ACTEW, these relationships were supported by the introduction of some funding for community groups. The directorate was not intended to take a program role, but it did provide grants to women's organizations (which will also be elaborated in the next section). Shelters were given start-up money and women's centres received core funding. This was a reflection of the NDP's concern about strengthening the directorate's relationship with the community (Malloy 2003). The NDP also put much more focus on the government's hiring practices as an employer, pursuing staff from the feminist community and working to diversify the representation provided by the OWD.[35]

This was another area of intense discussion within the directorate. Most of those interviewed addressed the efforts to make government more diverse and representative. In light of difficulties with coordination, an Interministerial Consultation on Immigrant Women was struck in 1985 between the OWD and the Ministry of Citizenship and Culture (OWD 1985b, "An Agenda"). In 1989, a cabinet sub-committee was established with representation from the OWD and the Ministry of Citizenship, after consultations with immigrant and visible minority women's groups. Meetings were convened and chaired by the Women's Directorate, and dealt with issues such as access to services, language training, public education, staffing, and, notably, the integration of women's issues within the Multiculturalism Strategy and Race Relations Policy (OWD 1989a, "Cabinet Committee"). Regarding the latter, discussion acknowledged that

> one of the major concerns of immigrant and visible minority women's groups is the lack of explicit focus on their issues in government policy and program development (both process and content). Their issues, they feel, are marginalized within central advocacy organizations, such as the Ontario Women's Directorate and the Ministry of Citizenship (including Race Relations Directorate). Integration of immigrant and visible minority women's issues into the overall policy and program development of line ministries is crucial to ensure equal participation and access. ("Cabinet Committee")

One person noted that the NDP, in particular, stressed inclusivity, and sought to customize programs to target all groups of women, through "culturally sensitive" programs. According to her records, $7.5 million was spent on anti-racism. The NDP insisted that government services must account for racial diversity and respect for Aboriginal distinctiveness. There were five components to its 1991 anti-racism strategy: (1) an Ontario anti-racism policy; (2) an Ontario public sector anti-racism strategy; (3) Public consultations; (4) an Ontario anti-racism secretariat; and (5) an Ontario anti-racism advisory group. She also used the example of the grants program, believing that if one traced its history, it would indicate this change in priorities.[36] In addition, feminist geographer and disability rights activist Vera Chouinard (1999) identified the early 1990s as a time of increased representation of, and consultations with, women with disabilities through the directorate.

Greater attention to diversity is reflected in OWD files and publications, particularly by 1989.[37] These priorities were also expressed through diversifying hiring (Malloy 2003). A participant specifically recalled the hiring of a visually impaired woman. This is a good step on its own, but she saw this more broadly as an instructive lesson in accessibility for the OWD. They learned that active encouragement and outreach were needed, including extending the hiring process to allow more time to apply, and advertising in community newsletters and alternative publications. Accessibility is "not automatic. [It] requires huge effort and special equipment."[38] Another former directorate staff member described similar learning around racism:

> There was a tremendous lot of energy on issues of anti-racism, and there was pressure on the OWD by various women's groups to be less racist ourselves ... to look at all our polices from not only a gender, but also a race perspective, and to make sure that money was equitably distributed. It was very challenging because people had to look at their own racism. We all started out saying, we're not racist ... but you look at the policies you're going after most aggressively.[39]

Some saw a significant change after 1990, when "there was the expectation that the directorate would advocate for the diversity among women, and actively not advocating for the generality of women, or women who were seen to be privileged."[40]

Others reflected on how internal struggles around diversity affected the working environment. A former OWD staff member noted that diversification happened in a very short time, which led to tension: "It took a lot of energy to diversify the organization and while you're doing that, you're diverted from providing the services to women in Ontario." She believed that the tension existed for the entire four-year period of the NDP government. Regardless, she emphasized that it is really important that OWD be representative of the groups it is serving – immigrant, racial minority, Aboriginal, and francophone women. It must represent the feminist groups who have been working for years in Ontario.[41]

The point here is not that the directorate found the right "answers" to these questions, or that it dealt adequately with internal challenges. It is apparent, especially in addressing diversity, that there is still a long way to go. What is significant is that the directorate, rather than being out of touch with the community, was facing the same struggles around representation that were (and are) occurring "outside" in the women's movement. As Mackay et al. (2009) note, drawing attention to such power struggles between actors *within* institutions is one of the strengths of feminist institutionalism.

Kantola and Outshoorn (2007) canvas how women's policy agencies have responded to contemporary debates about diversity and intersectionality. They note that progress across national case studies has been slow in addressing diversity in the policy process, and that state feminists themselves have often resisted an intersectional approach out of "fear that attention to gender will be displaced by other concerns" (279). There have been debates in several countries about possible institutional reforms, yet "many agencies still tend to take women as an undifferentiated category as their point of reference" (Outshoorn and Kantola 2007a, 281). Therefore, comparatively, the directorate seems ahead of its time. And that such fundamental feminist debates were actually happening within the OWD is a striking contrast to the later neoliberal situation that will be explored in the next chapter. With the introduction of the NPM, under Mike Harris's Progressive Conservative (PC) government, state feminism faced a very different set of challenges. This is true at both the procedural and substantive levels.

Substantive Democracy

The OWD provides some interesting insights into procedural democracy, but it also had a substantive impact in the form of concrete policy in its first decade. In fact, one source remembered the whole period being fun because there was "a lot of policy development going on"; it was a "very active period."[42] Here, I will mainly focus on labour market policy or, in the directorate's words, women's economic independence.

In 1984, the directorate's plan of action outlined six main focus areas: affirmative action, childcare, family violence, employment, income support, and justice (OWD 1984d, *Plan of Action*). Initiatives reported for 1983–4 included increased money for childcare, employment supports for single mothers, and affirmative action in the Ontario public service. Gender analysis for cabinet submissions and legislation was also introduced, as well as two programs, Open Doors and Jobs for the Future, that focused on encouraging women to enter non-traditional careers, and provided training for women in new technologies (OWD 1984h, "Third Annual").

These programs were expanded in 1985, after the election of the minority government. A Training Access Fund was started to provide childcare allowances for women in training programs and the Ontario Skills Development Strategy included gender-based considerations such as equal access and part-time workers (OWD 1985j, "Questions and Answers"; OWD 1985g, "New Initiatives"). Attention also turned to wages, overtime protection, worker's compensation for live-in nannies (OWD 1985j, "Questions and Answers"), family law, and pension reform (division of property in divorce) (OWD 1986b, "Minister Responsible"; OWD 1985b, "An Agenda"). Progress continued on affirmative action, particularly in municipalities, school boards, universities, hospitals, and administration, and pay equity was highlighted as a priority (OWD 1985c, "Chatelaine Grades"; OWD 1986a, "Highlights"; OWD 1985b, "An Agenda").

In 1986, 7500 subsidized childcare spaces were created and pension reforms were introduced that extended coverage to part-time workers, continued survivor benefits after re-marriage, and introduced division of pensions upon marital breakdown. The Change Agent program (discussed below) was also established (OWD 1986b, "Minister Responsible"). By the late 1980s, these had expanded significantly. The major policies specifically around women's labour market equality included: employment and pay equity, training, studying the impact of free trade on women's work, the feminization of poverty, women and taxation (partly through the Fair Tax Commission), women and unionization, pensions, family law reform, parental leave, sexual harassment, women in non-traditional occupations, science and technology for girls, working hours, social assistance, settlement, childcare, and an increase in the minimum wage (OWD 1985, *Ontario Labour*, Byrne 1997).[43] There was also an early recognition of the problem of balancing work and family (or in feminist political economy terms, women's paid and unpaid work, or production and social reproduction), through a series of papers, publications, public education materials, and conferences,[44] and the extension of parental leave (through Bill 14) as well as the introduction of consecutive parental leave,[45] flex time, job sharing, and consideration of community design to make women's lives easier. The directorate held or sponsored an array of workshops and conferences on employment equity, recruitment, training, and work/family balance.

Throughout this period, there was an understanding that women's position in the labour market was determined by structural factors (K. Scott 1999). This stemmed from a substantive view of equality, as outlined in the directorate's 1989–90 year-end report, which states: "Although our laws now apply equally to both sexes, the significant differences in the lives of men and women must be taken into account in their application – otherwise laws can actually reinforce women's disadvantaged position" (12). As I will demonstrate in the next chapter, there has since been a monumental shift away from this policy approach and understanding of gender inequality.

During the Davis government, there was some cursory interest in pay and employment equity. A dramatic change occurred in 1985, when the Liberals, under David Peterson, won a minority government that relied on support from the NDP to stay in power. One person interviewed commented that a lot happened during this minority government, and that "bureaucracies love minority governments because they're so active."[46] Due to its relationship with the NDP, pay equity became a central focus of the Peterson government, and this carried through to the New Democrat government. The Equal Pay Coalition, which had been organizing around pay equity in Ontario since the 1970s, had close ties to the NDP (Findlay 1997). It is fair to say that the NDP did not expect to win the 1990 election. Nevertheless, the party had a comprehensive women's policy program that included addressing violence against women, health care and reproductive rights, childcare, family law reform, equal pay for work of equal value (pay equity), affirmative action (employment equity), and unionization since 1982 (Burt and Lorenzin 1997). Marion Boyd cited these policies as one of the main reasons she decided to run in 1985, and thus had a good idea of how her party's platform would play out in policy terms.

Pay equity came under the mandate of the OWD, in addition to employment equity and the prevention of violence against women (Malloy 2003). The high priority placed on pay equity, in particular, raised the profile and influence of the OWD (ibid.). The directorate began working first for pay equity in the public service (OWD 1990, *OWD Year-end Report*), and it was later extended to the private sector (Burt and Lorenzin 1997). Extensive consultations occurred around pay equity, on how to put the principle of equal pay for work of equal value into practice to deal with the gendered wage gap.[47] In Ontario, pay equity started with job-to-job comparisons and was then expanded in 1993 to include a proportional value and proxy method to compare wages in jobs in female-dominated workplaces with men's wages in similar fields. Attempts were also made to speed up pay equity for the lowest-paid workers. In 1994, through the OWD and the Ministry of Labour, $50 million was directed to workers providing home support for seniors and people with disabilities, immigrant services, and library workers (OWD 1994d, "$50 million"). Pay equity started in the OWD, but was eventually moved to the Pay Equity Commission within the Ministry of Labour for implementation.

There were certainly criticisms of pay equity. The proxy method, the most effective in reducing pay inequality, applied only to a small group

of public sector workers and did not address the growing precariousness of women's work (Burt and Lorenzin 1997). However, significantly,
pay equity challenged the idea that assigning value is best left to the
market (Fudge and McDermott 1991). In fact, the early attempts at
introducing equal pay for work of equal value were framed as such. In
a 1985 document, the directorate's arguments for pay equity challenged
several assumptions about the market. In its "Rebuttal against Market
Forces," the OWD (1985i) asserted that: (1) the market is not "free"; (2)
the market cannot eliminate discrimination; and (3) equal value needs
to be determined outside of the market. Also, the proxy method specifically recognized gendered job segregation and the need for substantial
state intervention in order to combat it.

Employment equity was also introduced, starting within the OPS,
then extending to a voluntary approach in the private sector, and finally
a legislated obligation for employers.[48] In its early form, employment
equity took a largely educational approach. For instance, the OWD,
through the Change Agent project, and the Urban Alliance on Race
Relations worked together to develop a handbook for employers on
implementing employment equity for visible minority women. Change
Agent also cooperated with the Cross Cultural Communication Centre
on employment equity in non-profit organizations. There was also a
focus on internal employment equity training of directorate staff (OWD
1989b, "Government Initiatives"). In 1991, the Office of the Employment Equity Commission was created, which eventually became the
Employment Equity Commission that legislated employment equity in
the public and private sectors (OWD 1991, *Year-end Report*). Described in
chapter 2, the Employment Equity legislation took effect in 1994 (OWD
1994c, "Employment Equity"), and was stronger and more inclusive
than its federal equivalent (Burt and Lorenzin 1997). Both the proxy
method for pay equity and employment equity were later repealed by
the Tories in 1995.

The OWD also took a larger role in the administration of grants in
the late 1980s (Malloy 2003). Since the mid-1980s, there had been some
project funding for community groups (OWD 1985h, "OWD Grants
Program"), but a former OWD staff member specifically noted that
when the NDP was elected, "things became possible." There was money
for training and shelters and twenty-six women's centres received core
funding of $50, 000 in addition to other money. Grants were given to
a range of women's groups related to labour market issues, including Women Power Inc., the Employment Equity Network, the Centre

for Employable Workers, Advocates for Training, Women Working with Immigrant Women, the Rexdale Community Micro Skills Development Centre,[49] the Ontario Network of Women in Trades and Technology, the Disabled Women's Network, and the African Training and Employment Centre (OWD 1993c, "The OWD Is 10"). There was a clear shift in funding orientation (as noted by one interview participant cited earlier), with much less emphasis on groups such as those representing female business executives. Community grants were directed to women of colour and women with disabilities to address employment barriers, apprenticeships, non-traditional careers, language and citizenship training, literacy, employment standards, and sexual harassment. Many of these grants also reflected the focus on training in the OWD (OWD 1994a, "Community Grants"; OWD 1994g, "Women Access"; OWD 1989b, "Government Initiatives"; OWD 1985h, "OWD Grants"; OWD 1991a, "Language Training").

Much of these community links were developed through funding in the Community Grants Program and the Change Agent program. The Community Grants Program gave $5000–$10,000 grants for projects in four target areas (OWD 1991, *OWD Year-end Report*). The Change Agent the program fostered cooperation between the OWD, unions, business, and the community. Sometimes in collaboration with the Ministry of Citizenship, funding was often given to projects especially for marginalized women. In 1989–90, $1M in grants was distributed, and $1.4M in 1990–91 (OWD 1990, 1991, *OWD Year-end Report*).

Specific training for immigrant women was introduced and there was emphasis on moving women into non-traditional occupations, skilled trades, and apprenticeship programs. The directorate did a series of promotional posters, targeting high-school guidance counsellors and unions, with the ultimate plan being to get line ministries to take on training and apprenticeships for women. The OWD was aware of the limits to this policy, though.[50] Some directorate staff identified the efforts to get women into male-dominated jobs as one of the hardest things to do, citing different work cultures and harassment as complicating factors.[51] Therefore, the OWD also analysed infrastructure investment with gendered job segregation in mind. One participant explained that the Treasury was working on job creation via capital investment, so the directorate "did an analysis of the employment impact that we called (privately) 'jobs for the boys' ... The analysis was good and showed how skewed the job creation would be." They had to demonstrate that the construction industry is not really going to address women's unemployment unless job segregation was tackled too.[52]

The OWD also worked closely with community groups involved in women's training. ACTEW, known then as Advocates for Community-Based Training and Education for Women,[53] was involved with the OWD in a number of projects. ACTEW was funded by both federal grants by SWC, and provincially by the OWD. One result of their collaborations with the OWD was a booklet entitled *Shortcuts to Career Development Resources for Girls and Women*, which is a compilation of employment resources.

The Ontario Training and Adjustment Board (OTAB), created by the NDP, was another locus of interaction with women's groups. OTAB departed from the bipartite corporatist model to include equity representation alongside business and labour (Haddow and Klassen 2004; Klassen 2000; Bradford 2003), at the insistence of feminist NDP cabinet ministers (Klassen 2000). The board of directors had twenty-two voting members representing seven reference groups: eight business, eight labour, two education/trainers, one francophone, one woman, one visible minority, and one person with a disability, as well as three ex-officio members from the federal, provincial, and municipal governments. This was in addition to the requirement that "business and labour's nominees reflect the ethnic diversity of Ontario, and that a gender balance of the entire governing body be attained" (Klassen 2000, 104). OTAB also played a role in creating local training boards with equity representation (Klassen 2000; OWD 1994h, "Women's Role"). According to one participant, "When I became the deputy of OTAB women's issues were absolutely front and centre," and representatives of women's groups were linked with OTAB.[54]

Labour market policies demonstrated increased attention to marginalized groups (Haddow and Klassen 2004). The directorate participated in creating a booklet called *Your Rights as a Worker*, which put the province's labour law into plain language and translated it into fourteen different languages. This was done in communication with community-based agencies.[55] There was a noticeable shift in directorate publications, with much more emphasis placed on diversity and contingent work.[56] The OWD was also involved in an Inter-Ministerial Council on Women's Economic Status, which investigated home workers and their coverage under the Employment Standards Act,[57] and supported groups such as the Coalition for Fair Working Conditions for Homeworkers, INTERCEDE, and the International Ladies Garment

Worker Union (ILGWU) through grants and conference assistance. The resulting legislation was introduced in July 1994. It included home workers in the Employment Standards Act, regulating hours of work and overtime and holiday pay, imposing a 10 per cent premium on the minimum wage to cover overhead costs, and requiring that employers provide workers with written particulars such as pay and work hours (OWD 1994e, "Improved").

There was significant policy diversity over the decade, made possible by the directorate's larger staff, which allowed for greater specialization, and the "expectation that staff were content experts."[58] Nonetheless, there were obvious policy gaps and contradictions in this agenda. In addition to the limits of pay equity and the lack of employment equity in the private sector, there was little focus on childcare (Malloy 2003), housing, and social assistance as necessary not only for women's labour market equality, but also for women's economic independence more broadly defined. In the case of childcare, advocates were particularly disappointed in the lack of progress considering that several members of the NDP caucus had belonged to the Ontario Coalition for Better Child Care (Burt and Lorenzin 1997). One participant concluded that the OWD has always lacked a clear mandate, that they "never really had an over-arching, or clear notion of what it is they should be doing, what would make a difference."[59] Therefore, feminist theorizing of the limitations of state feminism is of continued consequence.

Limitations of the Ontario Bureaucracy, 1983–1995

In spite of the OWD's growing staff and budget over the mid-1980s to the early 1990s, bureaucratic culture and structure, including hierarchy, compartmentalization, and neutrality, were constant sources of struggle for femocrats. The experiences with, and within, the OWD confirm, in many ways, the feminist critiques of these forms of bureaucratic organization and the contradictory reality of state feminism.

Hierarchy and Power[60]

Rianne Mahon's conceptualization of the unequal structure of representation finds resonance in the OWD. The OWD was created as a central agency, and thus has no direct program responsibilities. Its function is to work laterally with all government departments and ministries. In certain ways, this mitigated some of the coordination problems associated with compartmentalization (discussed below). However, several of those interviewed referred to the directorate's marginal position within the power structures of government throughout the decade. One person interviewed contrasted the directorate with the Conseil du statut de la femme in Quebec, which is housed in the cabinet office, with much more official authority.[61] In Australia too, women's policy machinery was located within the Prime Minister and Cabinet Department (PM&C) (Chappell 2002).[62]

The particular place of the OWD led an interviewee to conclude that to work within the power structures of the bureaucracy, you have to learn to cooperate, and to "get on board," in order to make any progress.[63] Another similarly commented that if you want to move up in the hierarchy, you must accept the goals of the bureaucracy.[64] Some of those interviewed looked back on their initial belief that the right people in the bureaucracy could make the difference, as an unfortunate case of naivety. Even Marion Boyd, minister responsible for women's issues for the NDP government, said that she soon learned that in a bureaucratic setting, she had far less influence than she thought she would have, adding that she used "moral suasion more than anything else. There was some funding power in the violence against women area, but not a lot." Such observations were consistent across the three governments.

The OWD at certain points, especially from the late 1980s to the early 1990s, has had a significant budget, but those interviewed indicated that even during these times, the directorate still lacked leverage, having little control over the money. One public servant stressed that in the OWD, they had to use relationships to influence, and to effect, change. Lacking any real authority, they had to insert themselves into discussions, trying to use research to make arguments.[65] Even this was not easy, however, because those working in the directorate found that accessing the necessary information in order to do research was not straightforward. It was explained in one interview that in 1993, directorate staff met with the feminist policy community to discuss NAFTA and its potential impact on women. The OWD and the minister's staff wanted to determine what they could do, and which resources they could provide to the groups to pursue this project. What the women's community wanted most was research and information, but those in the directorate found that they could not get access to the information that they needed.[66]

One of Malloy's findings is telling for the OWD's location within the structures of power. He quotes a senior Rae official as saying: "You always saw them hanging around. They wore their power suits; they came to all the receptions. But they didn't have any power; no one really listened to them" (Malloy 2003, 104). This seems to confirm the suspicions of a former OWD staff member during the same NDP period, who told me,

> You did get the impression sometimes that you were really seen as a nuisance by the larger Ministries ... You come in at the eleventh hour and say this has a disproportionate impact on women and here it is. They're willing to accept that disproportionate impact because they have this broader policy agenda.[67]

Archival records from the files of former ADM Glenna Carr also indicate some early difficulties getting colleagues to take seriously the requirement for impact-on-women statements. In 1983, guidelines for impact-on-women statements were distributed to Ministries (OWD 1983, "Memorandum"), but in a 1985 memo by Carr, it is clear that the guidelines have had little impact. She says: "Over the past weeks, I have noted with concern an increasing number of Cabinet submissions which either do not contain a section on the potential impact on women or contain an impact statement that appears quite inadequate for our purposes" (ibid.). Submissions from Tourism and Recreation, Education, Skills Development, Transportation, Environment, Health, and the Ontario Youth Investment Program are specifically identified in this regard (ibid.). For example, a submission from Transportation reads: "The specific beneficial impact on women ... remains unknown." Similarly, one from Environment states: "The recommendations contained in this submission will have no disproportionate impact on women" (ibid.). In some notable cases, the conclusions drawn are quite doubtful. A Ministry of Housing impact-on-women statement claims that "the general contracting and building trade elements of the industry have been historically a male preserve. However, there are few barriers to female participation in other elements of the building process, e.g. real estate, the design professions of architecture, engineering and planning" (OWD 1985f, "Memorandum"). At a basic level, a gender-based policy analysis should consider the reality of sex segregation, which does not appear to be the case here. In general, the approach to gender-based analysis was quite superficial. The OWD's assessment of the 1985 budget pointed out that women were not mentioned as a specific target group, not even in reference to training, housing, or violence (OWD 1985a, "1985 Ontario Budget"). It looks like the strategy was simply to consider only what is there, rather than what is not. In other words, as long as there was nothing explicitly discriminatory, the gender analysis was seen to have been accomplished, regardless of whether gender equality resulted from women's omission from policy.

Even by 1990, there still seemed to be resistance to a gender-based analysis. A cabinet document referring to a report on training indicates that "the Ministry of Industry, Trade and Technology suggested that the word 'equity' in the document might send negative signals to the business community" (OWD 1990b, "Deputy Ministers' Committee"). A year later, communication about language training signals similar discomfort with equity analysis, expressing concern that a policy critique would have a "negative impact on the credibility of the OWD ... and put the line ministries on defense" (OWD 1991b, "Memorandum"). In 1993, a series of correspondence points to further issues. It criticizes the exclusion of consideration of immigrant women from a document on language training programs and services, and the lack of input from "clients" on ESL/FSL programs (OWD 1993a, "Memo"; OWD 1993b, "Memorandum"). One memo goes on to question a proposal by the OWD to develop its own paper on language training and immigrant women, arguing that this would "reinforce an inappropriate pattern of marginalization of women's issues, which should be reasonably integrated in a study with such planning resources" (OWD 1993b, "Memorandum"). It is of little surprise, then, that "many grew increasingly impatient with what they saw as the hierarchical, ponderous, and seemingly hidebound environment of the bureaucracy" (Malloy 2003, 103).

Marion Boyd was very explicit about her perception of the directorate's stature:

> We all know that the women's directorate was formed as a gesture. It was never intended to be a pro-active, radical piece. It was a Directorate, not Ministry, so it was without portfolio. It didn't have a Deputy Minister, it just had a Director. The people who were there on the bureaucratic side when I first went into the Ministry, I think were relatively comfortable with that because it meant they didn't have to be terribly accountable ... they were supposed to be coordinating all the activity particularly around the violence against women among the Ministries, but because they didn't

have as much power as the Ministries they were trying to coordinate, they didn't have much clout.

However, Boyd did not simply direct her criticism at bureaucratic forms of organization. While clearly cognizant of its precarious position, she saw the directorate itself as contributing to problematic power relations. Boyd's assessment is that the directorate perceived of itself, and operated as, a victimized unit. She suggested that those in the OWD

> would have seen themselves as being very much the poor sisters, and they would have seen themselves as terribly radical within the bureaucracy, and probably would be insulted to think that some of their Ministers didn't think they were radical enough. [Even in the context of bureaucracy, they were not radical.] Because they felt so oppressed, they acted like oppressed people. They would be defensive, and come across as angry, rather than trying to reach consensus, trying to force people to their view.

She continued to maintain that the Women's Directorate had trouble sharing power. For her, this was curious, since "sharing power is just a basic philosophical tenet of feminism in my view. And yet when the Minister of Citizenship was given the responsibility for employment equity, you'd think the world had fallen apart." She also said that the directorate found collaboration difficult due to "jealousy and territorialism."

While I find Boyd's a rather harsh characterization that seems to downplay the power inequalities she identified earlier, she is pointing to the importance of not discounting agency. This is what is lacking in some of the feminist theories described in earlier chapters, and is picked up again later on in this book. Bureaucratic structures clearly restrict possibilities, but this does not mean that state feminists are immobilized by such constraints, or lack any political autonomy and responsibility. This can be seen in the next section as well, where problems with compartmentalization and coordination are the result of a combination of both structural *and* political factors.

Compartmentalization and Coordination

The OWD, as a central agency, was charged with coordinating any ministry activities related to so-called women's issues. Interview participants spoke of several cases where coordination and collaboration worked quite well. Many recalled that there was always a close relationship between the directorate and the Ministry of Justice, especially with the Attorney General and the Solicitor General, and with the NDP most of all.[68] The creation of the domestic violence court during the NDP government was seen as a particular collaborative success.[69] In the area of wife assault, at one time, thirteen different ministries were involved, including Health, Community and Social Services (COMSOC), Corrections, the Attorney General, Citizenship, Education and Training. On specific issues, like violence against women, coordination was achieved.[70] This was in part, because the NDP women's minister, Marion Boyd, insisted on coordination after she discovered that money set aside by COMSOC for violence against women was being spent elsewhere and that nobody was keeping track of it.[71] This cooperation diminished later on, however, in the mid-1990s, when, as we will see, the policy focus of the directorate shifted away from violence towards women's economic independence. Moreover, attempts at coordination of other programs were less effective, in part because the OWD's advocacy function often resulted in tense relationships with other ministries.

With Christina Gabriel's work on intersectionality and the bureaucracy in mind, I wanted to get a sense of the OWD's relationship with other equity-seeking bodies within the OPS. Some spoke about cross-connections or coalitions, again during the NDP period in particular, with the Anti-Racism Secretariat (ARS), the Office for People with Disabilities (OPD), and the Ontario Native Affairs Secretariat (ONAS).[72] A project on Aboriginal Health and Healing was identified as one instance of collaboration,[73] and there was some involvement with the ARS around violence against women, but this was described as a "fleeting" engagement.[74] One participant noted that although there was an attempt to "consider women from other groups" in the directorate's economic analysis, there was "not huge cooperation" across structures.[75] In general, these relationships did not seem to be well developed, and in some cases were conflictual. Judy Wolfe,[76] a long-time policy analyst and manager at the directorate believed that the OWD suffered when race became more prominent because it occurred within a competitive, rather than a collaborative environment, and many in the directorate became frustrated with other offices, which were perceived to value race over gender. Especially after the early 1990s, under the NDP, she saw visible minority rights as "trumping gender." Another former OWD staff member said that even though they had links with the Ministry of Labour[77] while working on pay equity, she could not recall any conversations or connections with other ministries or secretariats.[78] One remembered having overt "fights" with their counterparts.[79]

One example speaks to the difficulty with coordination, not only between ministries, but also within federalism. A former directorate ADM related that during the NDP government, the OWD was asked to work with the Ministry of Health and the Attorney General on abortion policy. As she recounted:

> It was hard to explain that abortion is covered under the Criminal Code of Canada, and so that's federal ... and that actually Ontario had no right to go there ... If you wanted to improve abortion services provided through the medical system ... but abortion clinics were one of the cutting edges of private providers in the health care system. And no one ever wants to say that, but Morgentaler's clinics were not even non-profit half the time. So the issue of ... how do you want to deal with that in terms of a publicly funded health care system. In small communities where everybody knew each other, stand-alone clinics were probably not an option in terms of service provision. One of the issues too was the training of doctors. It turned out that in Quebec, I believe, its training was, at that time, provided to everybody in their general med school, and training on how to do abortion was only provided as a part of specializing in obstetrics and gynecology in Ontario. So we had a real shortage of providers at the time, trained and qualified providers. [There was a wide range of issues, including issues about prohibiting demonstrations at clinics.] The big, political statement of choice is actually a federal responsibility. They were quite angry about that. So trying to figure out how you could shape something to allow them to have a defining moment was hard work.[80]

In contrast with some feminist analysis emphasizing that federalism is too complicated for activists to understand,[81] it seemed that a lack of substantial coordination, or difficulty coordinating, between femocrats at the provincial and federal levels was the more significant issue in Ontario. Rankin and Vickers (2001) assert that "Rankin's (1996) comparative study of feminist organizing at the provincial and territorial levels has demonstrated that our most serious impediment to effective feminist mobilization on a pan-Canadian basis is limited communication among feminists and femocrats across internal borders" (58). This was reflected in most interviews, when the yearly Federal-Provincial-Territorial (FPT) meetings of ministers responsible for women's issues were raised. Deputy ministers, assistant deputy ministers (ADMs), and working groups have also been involved in these forums. One source said that the day-long FPT meetings were a chance to showcase what they had accomplished over the year. Different provinces would lead the meetings at different times, although Ontario would lead most often.[82] Those from the OWD explained that they would propose agenda items, and would negotiate with their provincial counterparts over meeting agendas and joint policy papers. This was often a challenge.

It was also recounted that some in the OWD came up with the idea of doing something around work and family, which at that time was not a concept that was used much. They took it from the International Labour Organization (ILO), wanting to capture economic and family issues together in one package. However, it was not easy:

> The problem with working with different jurisdictions is that each government has its own agenda and they're not necessarily compatible. I remember at the time, for example, with Alberta, they didn't even want to use women's issues in any document ... or there was some word like women's issues, or affirmative action, I can't remember what the term [was], but they didn't want to see that ... We had to come up with something that each Premier could go back to their government and say, hooray, we did this. So this paper started out at about twenty pages long and I think it ended up about two pages long with an appendix, and it had to be negotiated with my counterparts in all the other provinces. And in fairness to them, they were trying to be helpful by producing something that they felt their Minister Responsible for Women's Issues would take.[83]

In the end, the document was very vague, and "very motherhood-focused." She added that ministers wanted to be seen as doing something about women, but that it was very difficult to get anything through in that (FPT) process.[84] Harder (2003) tells a related story where those in the Alberta Women's Secretariat were not allowed to use the term "pay equity" due to its association with feminism.

OWD archival records pointed to similar complications, noting in particular, reluctance in New Brunswick and Alberta, in the early 1980s, to specifically address women's issues. In addition, finding common ground was a challenge. One document provides a good sense of the array of policy priorities for women across the provinces and territories:

– Ontario – tax policy, training, technological change and women
– Manitoba – equal pay, pensions, child care, affirmative action

- Alberta – affirmative action, wage gap
- Northwest Territories – all of the above and international trade
- Newfoundland – education and training, affirmative action, childcare, pensions
- Saskatchewan – all of the above, and entrepreneurial and business skills
- British Columbia – female poverty
- Quebec – wage gap, training, taxation, poverty, social security[85]

Eventually, in 1984, the ministers responsible for the status of women identified childcare as a key issue to focus on. But the archival records reveal ongoing trouble in trying to address childcare through the FPT process. It was difficult to even strike the FPT Working Group on Child Care, recommended by Ontario minister Robert Welch, because Alberta, Quebec, and British Columbia had to consult their cabinets before joining the working group. Once the working group was formed, Alberta was very concerned about interfering with "provincial flexibility and mandate on child care," and this became persistent source of contention.[86] By 1985, Manitoba was insisting that any new cost-sharing arrangement between the federal government and the provinces not include commercial childcare services, while other provinces wanted to determine the conditions themselves, and Quebec stressed the need to reaffirm its exclusive jurisdiction over child care (OWD 1985b, "FPT"). One OWD alum's comment that there was "always an outlier province," often Alberta, and sometimes Quebec,[87] certainly seems appropriate.[88]

Former Ontario minister responsible for women's issues Marion Boyd had a different take on the FPT process, referring to the annual meetings as "wonderful." She described them as a place for women's ministers to meet from across country and speak frankly about what they could and could not do, or what their governments would accept. It was very policy-focused and she remembered having "great respect for their wisdom about what might be desirable versus what might be possible." What others saw as "foot-dragging" she characterized as "good political sense" and "laying the groundwork for evolutionary change." Because she also worked in several other ministries (Education, Community and Social Services, and Attorney General), with programs that intersected with the Women's Directorate, she could bring a range of issues to the FPT tables. She did note that they could be much more radical in that era than now, but that it was also more difficult then because there were few models to follow for women's policy.

And there are some instances of successful collaboration. Sometimes there was pooling of money for research, or campaigns, such as violence against women, with joint development of materials, so provinces could share educational materials. Several public servants noted that this was often useful for provinces to access federal research resources from SWC, and other sources,[89] with one specifically mentioning the importance of federal information in the early development of what was then called affirmative action in Ontario.[90] Some added that it was useful for other provinces to share the resources of a bigger Ontario bureaucracy that could administer the joint projects.[91] Others also recalled that provincial women's ministries and offices worked together often, for both the formal annual ministers' meetings and other things.[92] Possibly the most useful was not the FPT itself, but the "strong informal networks" for information between jurisdictions at the staff level.[93]

Specific projects were discussed including the "Workplaces That Work" document, produced by Ontario for the FPT ministers, which gives advice to employers on how workplaces can be more friendly to women,[94] and "Fast Forward," about entrepreneurship for women.[95] It was said that the main purpose of the FPT meetings was to provide leverage for ministers, "to allow them to say, Ontario has to do something on X, because everybody else is going to do something on X, so it gave you some clout in your own jurisdiction."[96] This echoes Harder's (2003) findings in Alberta.

Overall, we can see more contradictions. Most thought that the FPT meetings were a weak mechanism for substantial cooperation. Several people said that while they met and reported to each other, they had no real powers to implement anything. This is largely because most of this machinery in Canada has a policy-coordination, rather than a program, function, so the FPT process results in few statements about concrete actions.[97] One specifically noted that at her last FPT meeting, the ministers agreed to look at the gendered aspects of caregiving (child and adult care), but since the agreement was only to "look at it," it was not clear if anything would actually happen, with no commitment made by Ontario's women's minister.[98] Others added that the outcomes were largely symbolic, involving the setting of standards, with minimal commitment, and that it was difficult to manage the need for internal agreement.[99] Similarly, a source mentioned that SWC had some federal-provincial meetings, which she thought could have started during International Women's Year (IWY), but that, again, this involved more reporting than analysis and action.[100]

Some could not remember having any intergovernmental interaction at all. One conclusion summed up the contradictory character of the FPT meetings by saying that "it was a mixed bag,"[101] while another referred to them as the "annual who ha."[102] Unquestionably the most scathing assessment of these processes was provided by a former OWD staff member who remembered her colleague's version of FPT: "F–ing Pointless Tasks!"[103] These difficulties point to two conclusions that will be elaborated in the final chapter: the need for systematic coordination and cooperation between federal and provincial femocrats, as proposed by Rankin and Vickers (2001), and for active community participation in the policy process, including the FPT process.

The combination of working across ministries and jurisdictions and a very complicated set of policy issues created a demanding situation for the directorate. Possibly the most difficult aspect of bureaucratic structure and culture for those in the OWD is the expectation of political "neutrality."

Neutrality, Relations with the "Outside," and the Construction of "Expertise"

As outlined in the previous chapter, the public service is expected to be politically neutral, non-partisan, and impartial in carrying out the policy decisions of the government. In this light, feminist analyses of the bureaucracy have shown that state feminists often feel caught between their loyalty to the government and their responsibility to the women's movement. This is a running theme in both Canadian and Australian femocrat literature, and Malloy's book title, *Between Colliding Worlds*, highlights precisely this tension. It was also a recurring issue for the Ontario state feminists I interviewed, across the Davis, Peterson, and Rae governments, with one interviewee referring to splits between "those who saw themselves as feminists first, or civil servants first."[104] While almost all in the directorate would identify themselves as feminists, some were more advocacy-focused, and others more public-service-oriented, and the OWD lived a contradictory existence.

It was very difficult for many in the Women's Directorate to fit into bureaucratic norms. A 1984 document referred to a Hansard debate in which the OWD was described as "a shade too political" (OWD 1984a, "Estimates Office"). Similarly, a former ADM explained that the Peterson Liberals saw the OWD as "out there" "rabble rousers" who were primarily pushing an NDP agenda. Ironically, when the NDP formed the government, there was a high level of distrust of the bureaucracy, including those in the Women's Directorate, who were considered "Liberal sell-outs, bureaucratic sell-outs."[105] Furthermore, many within the larger public service had a problem with the idea of representative bureaucracy. According to one interviewee, "It was highly resented by the upper management, mainly male managers, people who think the bureaucracy should be managed by experts. That whole idea of representation … didn't make sense to them."[106]

Struggles around "neutrality" were not simply about the imposition of bureaucratic norms and values onto state feminists without agency. Those in the OWD themselves, throughout the decade, had very different understandings of their advocacy roles. Some clearly saw their primary responsibility as being with the government. One spoke of non-partisanship as a core value of bureaucracy, and related to the public good, drawing a distinction between the personal opinions of public servants and the values of a professional public service and between partisan positions and evidence-based policy and advice.[107] Judy Wolfe made this point most strongly:

I am definitely a public servant. I grew up in a public servant household and I have a degree in political science, I study political theory, and I worked as a Parliamentary intern as well, so working for MPPs, I spent a lot of my career working closely with politicians. So that's who make the decisions. They are accountable. I'm not, at the end of the day … It's not up to me to decide what policy is … If there was a spectrum, I would be extreme at one end of the spectrum in terms of the Women's Directorate on that point. Most parts of government, this would never be a question, but in advocacy organizations like the Women's Directorate it was a daily question … In that first period in particular, there were lots of people who had much more connection with the women's movement than I did and with the academic world than I did, and they would sometimes be advocating positions that they believed were right, and didn't care if that would be completely opposed to what the government had been elected on, or what the Minister had said she wanted.

Others also discussed the issue of advocacy:

When you go out to the community, you're the face of government. You can't really be that advocate. I think the problem was with some individuals managing that. Because you can't go out to the community and, although personally you agree there was a bad policy decision somewhere, and you're hearing that from the community, you can't really forget that you're always the face of government ... I think that was the tension.[108]

You're not there to advocate for women, you're there to support the Minister's ability to advocate for women. There's a big difference between those two. The government are the ones who are elected. Nobody elected me. The taxpayer isn't paying me to go out and encourage pressure to be put on the government to do something. That's not what I'm paid to do. But in the Women's Directorate, certainly there was the responsibility to bring issues to the Minister.[109]

I believe pretty passionately in civil service values, and I am concerned about their erosion on any ground. I don't think a civil servant's job is advocacy; ours is to make a fair case for all the points of view and ensure decision-makers have the information they need to make good decisions. And I believe that a "good" decision made by a responsible politician is quite often not what is "best" from either a technical or advocacy position – it's a complex balancing of those concerns plus broader questions of public interest, the overall government direction, constituent interests, etc. ... I recall when we had a new Minister in Peterson's government, Mavis Wilson – she was pretty comfortable with women's groups like Zonta and Business and Professional Women, she was NOT initially comfortable with trade unionists, community activists, welfare advocates, etc. But our job was to make sure she met all of them and understood their points of view too, so that she had a full understanding of the implications of any decision she might make or urge her Cabinet colleagues to make. Not that she had to agree with them, just so that she would have a good sense of what their reaction would be ... So I was disappointed with the next [NDP] minister, who initially seemed OK with union and activist types but actually resisted meeting the business types ... Just because as a feminist I might have "agreed more" with Anne Swarbrick's assumptions and preferences, my job as a civil servant was to get her to understand the views of those she didn't necessarily agree with or was sympathetic to.[110]

These comments are profoundly Weberian. Weber insisted that in the case of conflicting policy ideas, "if his superior insists on its execution, it is his duty and even his honor to carry it out as if it corresponded to his innermost conviction, and to demonstrate in this fashion that his sense of duty stands above this personal preference" (Weber 1997, 115).

Some saw advocacy as more central to their mandate. Despite defending the idea of a non-partisan public service, one public servant went on to maintain,

You are advocates for women. It's like the Ministry of the Environment – our job is to be advocates for the environment in the ministry. I was joking the other day about the Ministry of Agriculture and Food who really are like spokespeople for the farmers of Ontario. I said, when I was at the Women's Directorate we weren't nearly as good. People called us an advocacy ministry but we had nothing on the Agricultural guys.[111]

She added that it was not always the case, but now at senior levels, everybody understands the agricultural ministry, or Northern Development and Mines, as advocates. For the latter, their job is to advocate for the North. Everybody comes to the cabinet table representing an interest (e.g., municipal affairs) yet still "it's way harder advocating for minority positions ... Advocating for racial minorities or people with disabilities or women, those are harder things to do."[112] Also, it is clear that only particular "interests" are associated with advocacy. While the purview of advocacy has been expanded to include things like agriculture and the environment, ministries that represent very powerful interests, such as Finance, continue to be seen not as advocating for a particular constituency, which I will return to later on.

While identifying themselves with an advocacy role, many described the need for a strategic approach to negotiating neutrality:

The advocacy is a different kind of advocacy. I was a public servant before I went into the Women's Directorate. I think it is harder for people who come straight from the women's movement into the civil service, I don't think they understand the culture. But understanding ... your job is to advocate, but it's to advocate within the civil service. Your job is to get your Minister on side and build the coalitions you can build to get the policies you want developed ... Some people are better and some people are not so good at doing it. I think that the issue that always plagues the Women's Directorate is the extent to which you can be public about your advocacy and the extent to which, in a Cabinet government, you can pre-judge the decision Cabinet will make. You can't say we're going to propose X and then risk that your Minister can't get it through Cabinet and they look like a dork because then they're lame-duck forever, not only with their colleagues, but with the women's community. I think it's the issue in the women's movement sometimes of the extent of transparency people want in the community versus what you really can and can't be transparent about within a Cabinet decision-making in government.[113]

I understood my role as a conduit. So that the politicians needed to understand why it was good and useful for their mandate to support community group X, and community group X needed to understand what it was that they needed to deliver in order to get support. And I was the interpreter. And on one level, you could say that that's not an appropriate role for a bureaucrat to play, because maybe a bureaucrat should be more closely aligned with the government, but in fact, the government isn't going to get what it wants if it doesn't have some kind of [permeable] membrane.[114]

One participant saw the OWD as a bureaucracy that has an advocacy function – "Its role is to work with programs that affect women and to advocate in the policy making realm."[115] An "outsider" perspective on this tension was that

you can be a civil servant and not sell your soul to the devil ... But if you want the devil to pay for the dance, you have to dance ... [You have to] play nice ... In bureaucracy you have to dance to two masters. You have to keep your passion under your desk. Some are very skilful. They're not on the frontlines demonstrating, but they do consistent, feminist work.[116]

But some were less comfortable playing this role. One former OWD staff member described feeling guilt and anxiety about being a "turncoat" when joining the OWD, where her salary was 98 per cent more than for her previous work in the anti–violence against women community.[117] This particular situation, and the general differences in understandings of the role of state feminists, are largely reflections of the varying backgrounds of those in the OWD.

In interviews, it was clear throughout all three governments that even though OWD staff consisted of a mixture of career public servants, members of the women's movement (anti-violence, women's employment advocacy), the labour movement, and social services, the majority came from within the OPS.[118] Malloy (2003) found that

it was firmly assumed by both politicians and bureaucrats that the OWD would be staffed by public servants with prior experience and career aspirations in the Ontario public service ... Public servants were hired as lawyers or economists, rather than "women's issues" specialists … They were not expected to remain at the OWD for more than two or three years, after which they would return to their previous ministries and serve as future OWD contacts and "ambassadors." Little effort was made to recruit staff directly from women's groups and external organizations. (95)

Like its federal counterpart, Status of Women Canada (SWC),[119] the OWD was mostly staffed from other places in the bureaucracy. One person interviewed remembered that some OWD staff members in the late 1980s and early 1990s had been involved in the Ministry of Labour, but was not sure she would consider them to be feminists. They were not from the feminist community. They were bureaucrats who were concerned with women's employment issues.[120]

Some of those interviewed were quite forthcoming about their lack of ties to the women's movement, or familiarity with women's policy. It was common to hear in interviews that the directorate was seen as a place for women to get into the public service, or to gain managerial experience. For instance, a former staff member said the OWD was an opportunity for women to get a foot in the public service. Many would not be able to get jobs in other places first, like Treasury, but once in the civil service, they could move through the bureaucracy.[121] Another described the directorate as a "training ground for women in management," "trampoline for their careers," and an opportunity for younger women to get into the public service, but added that there was a stigma attached to working in the OWD. She saw her stint in the directorate during the NDP period as part of a "path to public service," and a way to broaden her experience, rather than to concentrate on women's issues. She had no connections to organized women's groups.[122] In fact, Sue Findlay (1995) recalls that during the NDP government, community activists hired as policy advisers had to resign from their community organizations (431).

Some staff was drawn from the community. A former public servant said she was hired in the OWD during the Peterson government because she had an interesting trade union and feminist background, which "counted for them, but not anybody else" in the OPS.[123] One former ADM also spoke of trying to strike a balance between stable, public service experience ("insiders") and creating a directorate that was reflective of women outside of the public service. She sought those who were active in a diversity of communities – racial minority communities, women with disabilities, and Aboriginal women, "so the directorate could be the interpreter of government to the community and the interpreter of community to the government."[124] Still, "before 1990 the OWD staff had been overwhelmingly of white European descent, a pattern reinforced by the strategy of recruiting from within the permanent bureaucracy" (Malloy 2003, 103). One interviewee characterized the OWD as primarily a "white crowd, a straight crowd,"[125] and another referred to it as "basically a white middle class women's bastion."[126] In this way, the OWD fit comfortably within Weber's vision of bureaucrats as educated, middle-class professionals (Maley 2011).

Others spoke of the difficulty in bringing in "outsiders" to the directorate, and the struggles to make the transition to working within the government.[127] This was also common across the three governments, although there was a more active attempt at addressing it under the NDP. One interviewee framed it as a problem with such staff not understanding how government works, and that advocacy from the outside is different than that from the inside.[128] One of the resulting problems was that many women's organizations could not relate to the directorate, and felt that its agenda did not speak to their communities. Some former OWD staff said there were definitely elements of the women's community who felt the OWD did not represent them.[129]

There was always dissension in the OWD about how to respond to criticisms from the community. Some agreed that OWD had to be more responsive to diversity, while others thought differently (Malloy 2003). It was evident that there were very different analyses among those interviewed regarding diversity and the directorate. One public servant recalled that one of her strongest memories at the OWD was that "there were identity politics played out daily."[130] While she added that she did not want to marginalize the issues, which were real issues in the community that people were worried about, I sensed that she was referring to "identity politics" pejoratively. This seems to reflect one of the sentiments uncovered in Malloy's research that the "Ontario Women's Directorate became, in the words of one mid-level staff member, 'a dysfunctional organization,' where staff were divided by 'a hierarchy of oppression'" (Malloy 2003, 103). Attention to diversity was especially pronounced after the election of the NDP.

Some were well aware that the directorate consisted of largely white women, middle-class women, and spoke of efforts to address this. Wolfe said that addressing racism within the OWD during the late 1980s and early 1990s was "very painful." She learned a lot, and many were pushed by colleagues to understand that their "behaviour is not benign." According to another former staff member, people tended to focus on the ideas they were aware of, which meant that the directorate's activities reflected the experiences of a small, fairly privileged, group of women.[131] She went on to explain that once this was acknowledged, they did make efforts to be more sensitive to immigrant women through papers on labour market issues, and free trade (largely focusing on the impact on certain industries, such as textiles, where immigrant women are heavily concentrated).

This interviewee added that problems existed in that there were some women from the "ethnic community" in the OWD, and the "ethnic community" felt they were there to promote their interests. She thought it was understandable for them to have that expectation, but noted that bringing in someone from a particular ethnic group sometimes includes some perspectives and not others, and so they "all need[ed] to make a conscious effort to reach beyond their own circumstances."[132] Even though, at a surface level, her conclusion seems innocuous, there appears to be an underlying concern about the dangers of "identity politics" seen earlier. This also seems to be reflected in another participant's statement that she learned about racism, but this "doesn't mean I changed."[133]

Marion Boyd identified real difficulties in the directorate concerning both racism and classism awareness. She believes that "there were hardworking, well-meaning, very dedicated, very committed feminists, just having a hard time seeing how feminism intersects with other forms of inequality." She elaborated, saying,

They weren't radical in that I would have expected that ... they would have constantly been trying to lobby me around issues like Spouse in the House, and the levels of Welfare, and frankly, they weren't interested in that kind of social justice. They talked a real good line, but I never felt any pressure, not very much, from Women's Directorate around those kinds of equity issues. Equal pay for work of equal value, absolutely – all the pay equity stuff for women who were earning, but from my perspective, a real class orientation, and very grave difficulty hearing any class analysis of what was going on. And they were at that point having a very difficult time making the transition in terms of racism and sexism. Again, talking a good line, but having some difficulty making it real ... I think the class stuff was probably the most serious. I think there was an awful lot more openness about the race issues ... but because of the strong class bias ... aware that there wasn't equity, but not [a] sense that you had to reach out to make sure that people were welcome. And very much a "them and us" kind of thing, so that the feminists in other ministries, and there were lots of them, who never felt as though their feminisms were recognized, never felt as though there was real understanding that feminism could express itself in different policy ways.

Although Boyd's interpretation does not address the connections between race and class, it does correspond with the observations of women of colour in key ministries, and in the anti-violence community who saw the OWD as derailing their projects, and with feminist analysis of the limitations of pay equity.[134] An OWD alum also pointed out that "there were so many areas of interest in terms of women's economic status, and I think we always knew that pay equity was most accessible to middle class women. It's just harder for other women in other jobs ... We just felt it was something that was not really available to poorer women."[135] She believed the directorate needed to think about the feminization of poverty and what to do about women who cannot access pay equity, by focusing on things like the minimum wage. Another, with years of directorate experience, stressed the need to talk about education equity, rather than pay equity, to help women join unions, to work on income tax and pension reform, childcare, and the lowering of poverty levels.[136]

In addition, Malloy (2003) found that

> feminist activists and groups criticized this "corporate" focus and derided the OWD staff and their outside professional counterparts as the "Lipman's crowd" (according to one former OWD head) after an upscale fashion retailer. These activists accused the OWD of downplaying and even deliberately ignoring other issues such as child-care, same-sex rights, anti-racism efforts, private sector employment equity, and particularly economic issues such as the effect on women of trade agreements, tax policies, and social spending cuts. (101)

A directorate alum also remembered internal jokes about the "silk set executives" (including former ADM Glenna Carr, who had her own personal shopper), who were more career- than advocacy-focused, and saw the OWD as a stepping stone.[137] Not surprisingly, then, especially in its early years, the directorate had a reputation for having few links to feminists outside the state. Many in the OWD thought that consultation was the job of the OACWI (Malloy 2003).[138] As Malloy (2003) explains, "Little direct attention was paid to the relations with movement activists and organizations, other than developing contacts with upper-middle class networks of businesswomen and professionals such as lawyers ... Most activists and organizations were sceptical of the OWD's comprehension of the broad range of opinions and priorities in the women's movement" (98). The lack of connections to the community resulted in policy lapses. Marion Boyd gave an example of sexual assault centres and shelters in rural and remote areas, most of which have not been successful because they lacked the community base to build them in places like North Bay and Kenora. She believed the directorate had good intentions, but because the importance of a grassroots basis was ignored, it was not good public policy.

There were debates within the directorate throughout the decade about what its relationship should be to groups in the community, and these reflected the backgrounds of those in the OWD. One participant said there were "a wide range of perspectives" on their relationship to outside groups, depending on the personal experiences of staff. Those with government experience often saw stakeholders as outsiders who do not understand government. Those with other experience, such as in social services, were accustomed to forging links with service delivery and other groups.[139] A similar observation was made that there was "ongoing friction" over competing visions of the organization depending on whether one had a civil service background or a community group background.[140] Some in the OWD saw relating with the community as a nuisance, while "others had a very well-developed approach ... recognizing that in a democratic decision-making process there are a variety of push and pulls and having well-informed or articulate or effective advocates on the outside is going to be helpful."[141] These debates spanned all three governments.

Such differences reverberate in the ways that OWD staff members described their relationship to groups, and where they placed the onus of responsibility for effective consultations throughout the decade. Some were very concerned about balancing the need to develop a relationship with stakeholder groups, with the fact that "the ultimate decision-making authority rests with Cabinet."[142] Judy Wolfe had a similar perspective, maintaining that it was important to know the organizations, such as the Older Women's Network (OWN), and the Disabled Women's Network (DAWN) and their issues in order to do good research and get relevant policy information. Ultimately, however, "they did not drive our agenda. If the government wasn't interested in talking about that issue, too bad." Another was cautious in relating to the community because "there was a kind of obligation to maintain a certain distance, otherwise you got yourself in conflict of interest." Others faulted community groups themselves for shortcomings in consultations: "Some groups were more effective in recognizing the different roles and responsibilities. I felt certainly when I first went to the OWD and at various points along the way, a lot of ambivalence and guilt about how I was perceived in the feminist community. There was this 'us' and 'them' attitude."[143] Wolfe also said that because the community thought the directorate had much more influence than it did, they sometimes expected more than what was possible. She described the situation at the OWD as one of "constant negotiation and compromise" and developing "the art of the doable" within the government's priorities.

In contrast, others in the directorate placed themselves as central to ensuring links are made with the community. Malloy (2003) submits that state feminists "provide the necessary conduits between public administration and external activists" (x), and the concept of "conduit" was used frequently by those I interviewed. For example:

> I remember having real disagreement with colleagues who said we should be (or were) "vanguards" in the women's movement. I felt that for $50,000 a year I wasn't in the vanguard of anything. The most I could do would be to gain some space for the vanguard to act inside. We had to do things like (e.g.) "sell" how higher auto insurance for women was "better" (more equal ...), and at the end of the day our first loyalty was supposed to be to government. Or at least that's how I felt. I suppose I felt in contact with the "real" women's movement (trade union and outside) through friendships and connections, but I didn't feel my role was "part of" what I conceived of as the "real" (vanguard, outside, radical, challenging) women's movement so much as ensuring they could be heard within "the system." A couple of examples – we were doing a report on the (first) Free Trade Agreement and Women, my boss asked me to find out what women's groups thought, I went through my phone book and called all the organizations I could think of and ones recommended to me over the course of a couple of days and got "their views" (sometimes they hadn't yet thought to have a view, so they had to call back) and summarized it all for the report. Or another time the feds I think had released some report on training, and I asked a collection of women's community based trainers to write an analysis of it for the OWD, which we could then use to brief/inform within government. So I guess I saw us/me as a conduit rather than a leader.[144]

One interviewee thought her most important task in the OWD was

> being able to be a successful interpreter, and to see a benefit to the community of working with government. The only reason I'm interested in government being happy about working with the community is so that government will continue to work with the community. So that's my rationale for making government happy. But being able to see the community benefit from that relationship is great. And also being able to see how such a small amount of money from government can legitimize an activity that will benefit a community, and also can release a huge amount of in-kind energy. It's quite amazing how on a wing and a prayer, and 2000 bucks from government ... things happen.[145]

Another added that "governments need political pressure from outside of the government ... and they need the bureaucrats inside to channel it in a way where governments can use it."[146] Working together with women on the inside and outside "understanding their different roles, but their complementary roles" was seen to be the primary responsibility of the directorate.[147] Some thought that much more needed to be done to facilitate these relationships, with one person pointing out that while SWC used to fund advocacy, but now only funds research, the OWD has never been committed to "funding for advocacy."[148] Another said their inability to adequately fund groups was disappointing to the directorate and its constituents.[149]

Therefore, there are certainly limitations to state feminism in Ontario, even with rather extensive modifications. Hierarchy, compartmentalization, and neutrality are forms of bureaucratic organization and cultural norms that put significant constraints on those working in the OWD, and at the same time are often reinforced and reproduced by state feminists themselves.[150] In this way, gender regimes are not merely structured and regulated by the state, they are replicated through social relations. The OWD did not represent a femocratic administration.

Reconsidering Gender and Bureaucracy

It is evident from the Ontario case study that feminist theories of the state and bureaucracy can provide important insights into gendered administrative relations and structures. Nevertheless, some of these theories are overwhelmingly pessimistic and provide little room for political agency and strategy. Porter (2003) emphasizes the importance of "the role of women as subjects and political actors" (17), and the experiences of state feminists in Ontario demonstrate not simply co-optation and the preservation of the status quo, but rather a complicated combination of limitations and opportunities for change. In making sense of these opportunities for change, democratic administration can make a considerable contribution to constructing an alternative gender regime.

Feminist critiques of bureaucracy and democratic administration are complementary in that they both provide a challenge to traditional ideas about administration. Where they depart is that the extension of some feminist analyses, as seen in chapters 2 and 3, is that bureaucracies are *inherently* and *irreversibly* patriarchal, and therefore not worth practical feminist attention. In contrast, democratic administration wants to transform, rather than abandon, the administrative state, as its principal political project. For its part, however, the bulk of democratic administration approaches lack a feminist analysis of the state and the bureaucracy. We can draw lessons from the experiences of state feminists in Ontario in order to draw a more realistic picture of the relationship between theory and practice and to have this inform the insights of democratic administration more directly. In order to do so, I will return to the point made earlier about the ongoing debates within the OWD related to diversity and advocacy.

For most of its life, the directorate's staff has not reflected the diversity of those it is supposed to represent, and for only a short time, in the early 1990s, was there much attempt to remedy this situation. Malloy (2003) portrays the NDP period especially as fraught with internal strife and animosity around diversity, leaving the OWD with no internal or external credibility (103, 105). He argues that because they became "caught up in the tumultuous world of the women's movements, the directorate became even further detached from the world of public administration" and "the OWD appeared to lose effectiveness as a policy unit once it became caught up in the turmoils of the women's movement in the late 1980s to 1990s" (104, 186). It is striking that when the directorate most reflected the women's movement, and provided the strongest challenge to the status quo, it was seen as least "effective." In a related way, it is significant that for Malloy, and some of those interviewed, internal struggles are seen as nuisances or distractions from the "real business" of public administration. What they do not consider is that such struggles are examples of democracy in practice, and that we might learn from them.

Malloy's assessment fits with his general (Weberian) public administration orientation. He will accept that the OWD depart from traditional
public administration only to the extent of maintaining an "ambiguous"
existence. Malloy argues that the tension or ambiguity allows agencies
to accommodate the conflicts and tensions inherent in the relationship
between governments and social movements. Unlike other larger and
less ambiguous state structures, the very flexibility and adaptability of
special policy agencies may present the best opportunities for building
relationships between governments and social movements. But in the
end, he believes that the directorate failed on this account because it
"never really established itself in a state of true ambiguity – rather, it
radically tilted towards one or the other world depending on the party
in power" (Malloy 2003, 187). In other words, it can bend the rules of
neutrality, but it can never break them. The task for women in the public
service continues to be to "manage the tension" (Stivers 1993, 8). Malloy stops far short of suggesting that state feminists might, or should,
substantially challenge the process and substance of public administration. As a result, his prescriptions hint of the "equal opportunity focus"
that Stivers (1993) rejects as "seeking a piece of the existing pie rather
than questioning its ingredients" (18).

From a democratic administration perspective, informed by feminist
theory, the problem with Malloy's evaluation is that the goal should
not simply be "accommodation" of the community. It should be a more
substantial challenge to governance. The work of Sue Findlay, which
brings together democratic administration and feminist theory, stresses
that state feminism must not simply be about representation (or the
transmitting and translation of community input to the government);
it needs to be about transformation. For one interviewee, her job in
the OWD was to "transform government" by affecting how ministries
work, by using different tools of analysis and alternative sources of
information and data, and by connecting to new groups in the community.[151] But Findlay would disagree with the above commentator,
who went on to assert that the idea of the public servant as advocate
is wrong because they are "challenging the entire civil service, but not
challenging the idea of the civil service."[152] Findlay and many of those
I interviewed are challenging the *idea* of the civil service as neutral and
detached from the communities they serve.

Democratic administration recognizes this and seeks to shift accountability to the people. This model of accountability was proposed by
Stephen Lewis in his capacity as Advisor on Race Relations to Premier

Bob Rae. Lewis "urged the government to create a Cabinet Committee on Racial Relations, calling for a 'terribly ambitious' experiment in democratic participation and accountability, in which racial minority communities would set or negotiate the agenda" (OWD 1994, "Letter to Stephen Lewis"). Some of those cited earlier, who explicitly identified themselves as advocates for the women's movement, share such an understanding of accountability. One person interviewed described not the government, but community groups as "the accountability mechanism for the OWD."[153] This former directorate staff member's analysis supports the conclusions of Australian femocrats that pressure from the "outside" is essential to their work. Where democratic administration departs is in the direction where I think state feminism must move, towards fostering the participation of the community beyond organized groups. I will return to this in the concluding chapter.

In considering the debates within the directorate about diversity and advocacy, some feminist theory would downplay these aspects in favour of stressing co-optation and the nature of bureaucracy as an oppressive form of organization. Such an analysis is not misplaced. But as feminist political economy insists, the state and bureaucracy are contradictory – representing both the institutionalization of power relations *and* a site of struggle and contestation.

Conclusion

The point is not to romanticize this period in Ontario, or to engage in the kind of nostalgia that Janine Brodie has warned against. There were clear limitations related to the bureaucratic structure and culture, including the ways that some in the directorate themselves reinforced these problems. In the end, the OWD did not go far enough in challenging the Weberian gender regime, as it remained largely committed to the basic principles of Weberian bureaucracy. However, it is important to consider the place of state feminism within the process of democratization, and thus the relationship between feminist state theory and democratic administration. How can this inform the evolution of feminist theories of bureaucracy and the state more generally, for an alternative gender regime?

A heightened profile, vigorous feminist debates over fundamental issues of representation and transformation, and a rich policy agenda for the OWD signal advances in both procedural and substantive democracy. The period stands in marked contrast to the subsequent neoliberal form of governance. Increasingly, the Weberian style of bureaucracy was challenged, less from social democratic influences than from the Right. The late 1980s and 1990s became the "watershed decade in the transformation of Western public bureaucracies" and "in contrast to the rigid and hierarchical structures associated with the welfare state, the New Public Management's vision of a more client-centred and streamlined public service gained ascendancy" (Shields and Evans 1998, 56, 79). According to Pierre (1995), the "public sectors in most countries in Western Europe and North America appear to be gradually transforming from Weberian organizational structures into private sector-modeled organizations" (57).[154] Unfortunately, the limitations of state feminism, particularly related to top-down and expert-focused administration, were amplified under the Tory government. In addition, a new set of gendered consequences were introduced in Ontario through the New Public Management, the focus of the next chapter.

4 Gendered Governance and the New Public Management Regime

Accounts of state restructuring continue, in large part, to ignore the gendered nature of these processes. Of course, there is a body of feminist literature that highlights the negative impact of state restructuring on women, but this literature tends to focus on either women as users of state programs and services, or as public sector workers. While this chapter draws upon both, I will mainly examine how neoliberal strategies aimed at the administrative structures of the state, specifically through the New Public Management (NPM), have affected the process and substance of policy for feminists working in the state bureaucracy in Ontario by introducing a gender regime revolving around downsizing, privatization, and managerialism.

As seen in the previous chapter, there were some efforts to democratize the bureaucracy throughout the 1980s, often based on progressive critiques of bureaucratic organization. However, the critique from the Right, that bureaucracy is cumbersome and inefficient, became dominant. In this chapter I will examine the period of the Harris Progressive Conservative government during which neoliberal bureaucratic restructuring failed to remedy, and in fact exacerbated, a gendered public administration, and further undermined women's structures of representation. I explore these gendered consequences of state restructuring through the case study of the Ontario government's approach to public management in the mid-1990s–2000s.

Focusing on the activities of the Ontario Women's Directorate, and other women's policy machinery, specifically in relation to labour market policy, I demonstrate that a democratic shift occurred within the Ontario bureaucracy. This change is evident at the procedural level, where the representative function of women's policy structures has been seriously eroded, and at the substantive level of women's labour market policy, which has moved away from advocating for women as workers, and addressing structural inequalities, towards promoting the development of women's entrepreneurial initiative and individualism. These neoliberal administrative strategies have clear consequences for gender democracy, and continue to be a powerful force in the Ontario state today.

The NPM in Ontario

In chapter 2, I focused mainly on the NPM at the federal scale in Canada, but similar restructuring has occurred provincially as well.[1] Here, I turn to the specific case study of Ontario. I argue that changes under the auspices of the NPM in Ontario, largely under the Harris Progressive Conservatives (PCs), have been detrimental to both procedural and substantive democracy. Procedurally, women's access to democracy has been limited by the weakening of women's structures of representation within the Ontario bureaucracy. These effects have also been felt substantively, in the form of policy outcomes for women, specifically labour market policy in Ontario.

Borrowing from Thatcher and the American Right, the PCs in Ontario argued during their 1995 election campaign, and subsequent government, that the restructuring and shrinking of government, and the reduction of deficit and debt (in addition to lowering taxes) were paramount (Ralph 1997; Bradford 2003). Indeed, "the main theme behind the Common Sense Revolution [was] the call to re-invent the role and responsibility of government in Ontario" (Clarke 1997, 31). A large part of this "reinvention" involved reducing the size of the state, by cutting a large range of programs and services, including health care, education, welfare, childcare subsidies, health and safety enforcement, environmental protections, job training, pay equity, public housing, and transfers to municipalities (Dare 1997), while eliminating others such as labour protection laws, and employment equity. Following the NPM recipe also meant downsizing (laying off public sector workers), privatization, commercialization, and appeals to volunteerism (Browne 1997; Régimbald 1997).

Many have also pointed out that in Ontario, as Aucoin found at the federal level in Canada, and in other jurisdictions, like Britain, Australia, and New Zealand, the NPM is really about a centralization of power in the cabinet (Clarke 1997; Browne 1997). The Tories wanted to curtail the influence of both the public service and the community (Bradford 2003). The Harris government was able to radically restructure government, along the lines of the NPM, through one, very controversial, Omnibus Bill, the Savings and Restructuring Bill. The Omnibus Bill, which was introduced in December of 1995, sought to introduce or amend over forty pieces of legislation, and gave the cabinet wide-ranging powers (Weinroth 1997). Weinroth explains that the bill was

> a "surgical cut" through the "red tape" of a bureaucratic protocol which, while admittedly tedious, has often been a way of securing due process and preventing arbitrary decision making by high-ranking ministers. The Omnibus Bill purposely legitimizes and grants exclusive prerogative to such high-standing politicians ... The passing of authoritarian legislation such as the Omnibus Bill could be justified on the grounds that bureaucracy was duplicative, its red tape exasperating and convoluted. The arbitrary will of ministers could, in his [Harris's] eyes, effectively cut through the administrative tangles. (63–5)

This obsession with "red tape," culminated with the invention of the "Red Tape Secretariat." According to the secretariat's website:

> The government created the Red Tape Secretariat to help eliminate existing red tape and prevent unnecessary rules and regulations from being created in the future. The Secretariat reviews proposed Cabinet policies and regulatory measures that affect business and institutions, and intervenes on behalf of business, institutions and members of the public seeking assistance with provincial red tape problems. The Secretariat reviews and reports on ministries' annual red tape reduction plans. It also coordinates legislation that reduces barriers to business, investment and job creation. (Ontario Red Tape Secretariat 2002a, "About Us")

The website reads like a how-to manual on implementing the NPM. In explaining "Who We Are," the secretariat lists seven functions, including: improving competitiveness (creating a positive business environment); fostering a cultural shift (against red tape); eliminating red tape now (through legislation and ministry plans); preventing red tape in the future (justifying and limiting regulation); intervening in red tape matters (investigation and resolution of red tape problems); taking action on special problems (to eliminate and prevent red tape); and improving customer service (customers first) (Ontario Red Tape

Secretariat 2002b, "What We Do"). These functions do well in meeting the ends of the NPM, and advance a very particular set of interests and power relations. They prioritize deregulation and limited government, they highlight economy and efficiency, they recast citizens as customers within the market model, they assert greater political control over the public service, and, most important, they demonize the bureaucracy.

The bureaucracy was a central target of the Harris Tories. The text of the Common Sense Revolution specifically mentions the reorganization of government as a priority (Régimbald 1997). The bureaucracy was portrayed by the PCs as an irresponsible and inefficient monstrosity that wasted and mismanaged taxpayer money. For Weinroth (1997), "in exploiting the two perceived weaknesses of big government – heavy taxation and sprawling bureaucracy – Harris has contributed to the construction of an administrative beast deemed unruly and in need of massive constraint" (61). Harris promised to "create partnerships with private business and open our administrative operations to outside competitions, where this can save taxpayers money" (quoted in Weinroth 1997, 60).

While not the primary focus of this study, it should be noted that even though under the Liberals since 2003 the hard edge has dissipated with less outward disdain for the public service, NPM techniques such as performance measurement and public-private partnerships continue to support neoliberal governance. Coulter (2009) maintains that

> although the current Liberal government in Ontario engages in rhetoric about the value of public services, its Third Way approach ensures that neoliberal policy approaches prevail, although in camouflaged and modified forms. In this way, neoliberalism is deepened and normalized, and discussion of gender and socioeconomic inequality is largely avoided by government politicians. (24)

The Liberal government operates based on fiscal conservatism and political constraint (Coulter 2009). This is typical of reformulated versions of neoliberalism that seek to put a gentler public face on largely the same market-oriented policies. With its new emphasis on children and the social, McKeen (2007) has referred to a "neoliberal wolf in lamb's clothing" and Coulter to "the evolution and repackaging of neoliberalism in its mature, camouflaged Third Way costumes" (Coulter 2009, 41). Some have identified this as a new type of "social investment" liberalism, beyond neoliberalism (Jenson 2008), yet others are pointing to contextualized "varieties of neoliberalism" (Albo and Fast 2003; Cerny 2004; Larner 2003) or "variegated neoliberalization" (Brenner et al. 2010) to explain the emergence of neoliberalism in new forms over time and place.

This view of bureaucracy, put into practice through the NPM, has gendered effects. Sauer et al. (2007) note that in the majority of countries they studied, the restructuring of women's policy machinery undermined women's substantive representation, and negatively affected links between state feminists and the autonomous women's movement. In their comparative collection, Outshoorn and Kantola (2007b) also find that NPM techniques led to budget cuts for women's policy agencies, a loss of autonomy for state feminists, and a weakened relationship with the women's movement.[2] I find such results in Ontario as well, as I explore the impact of the NPM gender regime on procedural and substantive democracy for women.

Procedural Democracy: The NPM and Women's Structures of Representation

As outlined in previous chapters, there is a variety of women's policy machinery, at both the federal and provincial levels. Although inadequate, structures were created which recognized that women have particular policy needs, and that they have a democratic right to be represented within the structures of the state. As described in chapter 4, in Ontario this largely occurred through the OWD. Under the Ontario PCs, and their pursuit of the NPM, this understanding of representation clearly changed, which negatively impacted equality-oriented structures, such as the directorate. One participant summed up this change well, noting that "when the Tory government came in, they had no use for the OWD at all."[3] This is made clear through the determined process of marginalization, the imposition of managerialism, and the undermining of community representation that the directorate experienced under the NPM gender regime.

Marginalizing the OWD

A series of indicators point to a concerted effort at marginalizing the OWD. Recall Rankin's (1996) findings about the centrality of ministerial support. One of the ways the government's commitment to the directorate can be gauged is by examining the Tory ministers responsible for women's issues. According to interviews, the women's ministers under the PC regime were weak in terms of decision-making, with little power or credibility in the government. Former minister for women's issues under the NDP government Marion Boyd described both the Tory women's ministers, Dianne Cunningham and Helen Johns, as very "inactive." For Boyd, "neither of them were proactive, neither of them would describe themselves as feminists ... I don't think they understood what was going on in the Directorate. They felt like outsiders, they both told me." Malloy's study supports this. His examination of the OWD indicates that both the women's ministers under the PCs were marginal, even more so than others in the highly centralized Harris government (2003).

Dianne Cunningham was the women's minister for most of the Tory government. For a brief period, she was replaced by Helen Johns, who according to an interviewee "was a disaster."[4] Another said that she became particularly frustrated with the second mandate of the Tories, which was "very difficult" largely because of Minister Johns. Johns was described as a "huge problem" who "hated women, hated women's issues."[5] It was explained in one interview that Cunningham quickly came back, but she was also minister of training, colleges, and universities, and did not have time to devote to the directorate. This public servant believed that even though Cunningham said she loved the women's portfolio, she really only liked the economic side, and was not interested in the violence side of the directorate's mandate. Her assessment is that the minister "always claimed it was something close to her heart ... But actions speak louder than words and there wasn't a whole lot of action." Any of the policy progress that was made happened "regardless of the fact that she was Minister."[6] She went on to say: "We did not see her [Cunningham] physically for over a year ... Her office was a floor below us, and she wouldn't even show up for staff meetings. We didn't see her until she was leaving. We had a good-bye party for her ... [The Minister would disagree,] but from a staff level, we really felt ignored, completely ignored."[7]

There are many other indications of the PCs' lack of interest in, and support for, the OWD. In 1996, the women's ministry, previously stand-alone, was rolled into the new Ministry of Citizenship, Culture and Recreation (Malloy 2003). Judy Wolfe maintained that "the way it was handled was abysmal" and that the OWD became "submerged" in the Ministry of Citizenship. This ministry, responsible for women, immigrants, people with disabilities, seniors, volunteerism, and honours and awards, was dubbed by one source "the Ministry of People We Don't Care About."[8]

The Tories also reduced both the budget and the numbers of staff in the OWD[9] (beyond the cuts made by the NDP). The budget reached a peak in 1992 at $23 million, and in 1994–5 had fallen to $21.1 million. It began a major decline in 1995, with a budget of $17.6 million, and then $17 million in 1996–7 (Malloy 2003).[10] It did start to rise again briefly from 2004 to 2006, and then fall once again. The 2011 budget at $17.8 million was barely higher than it had been in 1987 (Ontario Ministry of Finance 1987, 2011), and is actually 40 per cent lower than in 1987 if adjusted for inflation.

A former OWD policy analyst correctly estimated that "the staff was reduced to about 40 per cent of what it had been. She also observed that there were "massive changes to the structure." In the past, "the organizational structure reflected the main differences in feminist analysis," representing liberal feminist concerns as well as "designated groups" – Aboriginal women, refugee and immigrant women – which allowed for "different perspectives in how people approached analyzing the issues. [However,] that all got swept away because the place went from four branches down to two."[11] A number of OWD alum said that the directorate was stripped of both its resources, or size, and its mandate, or capacity,[12] with one commenting that the OWD website even lacked basic statistics on women and was marked by a general lack of presence.[13] Another was more pointed in her assessment, maintaining that the OWD "floundered" after a "conscious undoing" by the Tories, which she saw as "a clearly articulated agenda."[14] Similarly, when asked about the OWD, a community worker, previously with ACTEW, and then with the Canadian Labour Congress, replied that the "Tories decimated them."[15]

This community advocate also pointed out that neoliberal restructuring at the federal level affected them as well. She noted that when her organization found that Ontario's labour market policies lacked focus, it made sense to turn to the Ontario branch of the National Action Committee on the Status of Women (NAC),[16] but, as another put it, "NAC's funding was slashed to smithereens"[17] by the federal government. One former Ontario minister responsible for women's issues also focused on the way in which changes at one level of government can negatively affect another, indicating that the "destruction of Status of Women ... affected everybody else." The result was felt concretely, in that the provincial women's policy machinery relied on seed grants from the federal Secretary of State (and then SWC), and at the rhetorical level, where policy thinking about women and equality, specifically substantive equality, corroded.[18] Evidently, forum shopping is of little value in these circumstances.

I interviewed a public servant who started at the directorate as a manager. She said when she arrived, she had three staff members – a temporary administrative assistant, a permanent policy analyst, and one other policy analyst there on a secondment. Since there had not been a manager there for a while, the policy analyst was also acting as the manager. Because the administrative assistant was a temp, she did not have a purchasing card and so she could not even buy supplies. This former manager stressed that she does not have very high standards, but that the directorate had furniture from the 1950s, and the computer was sitting on a tripod. She thought it looked like an "orphaned" unit, and "you could tell already the Women's Directorate just wasn't considered as important because if a unit really was considered critical, then you don't let it run down like that."[19] One other OWD alum explained that in the early 1990s, the OWD was a rather large organization with an expanded mandate. With nearly one hundred staff members, she said it was like a small ministry. When the PCs were elected, they completely restructured the directorate. When she returned to the new government after being on leave, "the organization was completely different," one-third to one-half of the staff were gone, and whereas before they had three to four senior managers, these had been reduced to two and then eventually one.[20] The ADM, Mayann Francis, was also replaced.[21] Another commented that "now the Directorate has a staff of 20 people on a good day. When I first started working there about 15 years ago … we were like *one hundred* 20."[22]

Budget and staffing cuts were matched with diminishing policy influence. Implicit in a lot of the descriptions that were given of the previous governance regime is recognition of what has changed, and what has been lost, for state feminism over the decade. Most of those interviewed said that at one time, the OWD was much stronger, and differentiated that from the current context where the directorate's presence has definitely been weakened.[23] Groups like ACTEW agreed that this decline in presence has affected their relationship with the directorate. For instance, in the past, the directorate had a role in both devising new policies and analysing all policies with a gender lens. A former manager at the OWD recalled that during the time of the Harris government, the profile and the role of the Women's Directorate was certainly being downplayed ... I came on board to lead a policy unit, and frankly, there was no policy work going on ... Basically the position of the government at that time was that they were not interested in policy specifically directed at women ... In the past, the OWD had played a much more dynamic role.[24]

She added that it wasn't just women, "they downplayed interests groups in general," and that all equity groups were "getting short shrift."[25] Although she had never heard the terminology of the NPM, she explained perfectly the NPM changes that Aucoin writes about, saying:

I did find it frustrating not to be able to work on policies. In a sense, there was a trend in government, under the Conservative government ... Traditionally, civil servants played a very active role in recommending policy directions. It's always the role of the politicians to make the decisions, but we traditionally played a very active role in researching different policy directions, coming forward with options and recommendations, and then the politicians would decide which way they wanted to go. Under the Mike Harris government, that changed all across government, not just in the women's area. What happened is you had a small cadre of political advisors around the Premier who would basically decide on the political direction, and the civil servant's role became strictly implementation. And it really took a lot away from the interest and the usefulness of the whole policy role ... It was as though the expertise of the civil service wasn't valued any more.[26]

Judy Wolfe confirmed that it was hard to find anything to work on because they knew in the directorate that the government was not going to consider any legislation. Aggravating the situation was the fact that the Tories took away the ability to get data based on gender and race, making their policy work very difficult. The OWD previously had a much more dynamic role in shaping policy direction. Another staff member revealed that the directorate used to be involved in the development of equity materials for educators for things like women's history month, until it was considered cheaper to just "farm it out."[27]

When the profile of the directorate was shrinking, a former OWD manager believed, the FPT meetings were important avenues,[28] and this was seen in one interview as especially important during the Harris period.[29] She believed that the FPT process was a vehicle for the minister to gain credibility: "If you can get it tabled and in discussion at the FPT level, then it gives you a way to come back to Ontario and start talking about it."[30] Contradictorily, she added that the FPT meetings also provided a venue for looking at women's economic status in new ways that fit the Ontario government's agenda, which, as will be shown later in the chapter, was very problematic for women.[31] Furthermore, someone else recalled that there used to be regular FPT meetings of ministers responsible for women's issues and the civil servants working in women's policy structures in the mid-1980s. She called this period the "heyday," because women's issues were addressed in first ministers' conferences, but noted that this is not the case now, and that women's issues are no longer on first ministers' agendas. There are still meetings, which act mostly as information exchanges.[32] There was, then, a general shrinking of the policy environment at both levels of government.

Another indication of the OWD's diminished policy presence is in the area of gender-based analysis (GBA). Many recalled the practice where the directorate's assistant deputy minister (ADM) would get all cabinet submissions and an opportunity to comment on their impact on women, but noted this was no longer the case since the Tories held office.[33] Several also identified a general lack of consciousness within the PC government about the impact of policies on women. One participant asserted that the OWD was

> supposed to be a place where the gender analysis of policy happens. But we don't always see things. And we don't always see things in time that gives us an opportunity to have a major or minor impact on it ... [They say] we need this back by noon, and you get it at nine ... just as it is going to Cabinet or committee ... Policy staff claim that all of their policies are gender neutral. Well they can't be.[34]

She said that because the directorate lacks the capacity for full gender analysis, its efforts end up being "hit and miss."[35] Another public sector worker told me that she was working on the development of gender-based analysis in an international context, and so this got her thinking about GBA in Ontario. She noticed an irony that while GBA is now mandatory in Canada, and that other countries are looking for "Western" models to follow, this analysis is not actively happening in Canada, and especially not in Ontario since 1995. The Harris government put much less priority on GBA. She recalled that in the Rae government, ministers were interested in the impact of policies on women, and that the OWD had to be consulted. The impact of policies on Aboriginal peoples, racial minorities, and people with disabilities was also analysed. To her recollection, "there was an equity overlay that people knew when preparing materials they better address equity," and equity questions were encouraged. In contrast, in the Harris period, "it was no secret that those were not the questions that the Harris government would ask."[36] There ceased to be any gender review of policies,[37] or the incubation of new policies. This was no longer seen as the mandate of the OWD.

State Feminism Meets Managerialism

The shift in approach to the OWD is indicative of managerialism. One of the main functions of the directorate historically was to act as an advocacy agency for women's policy. However, under managerialism, advocacy, even more so than under the Weberian gender regime, is seen as illegitimate. As one interviewee explained, "The role of central agency was not accepted ... The word advocacy was not accepted under the Tory government."[38] In fact, Marion Boyd recalled that

> there was an absolute injunction against bureaucrats taking an advocacy role, which was very unusual. Even back in the early, early, days of the Women's Directorate ... it was expected the Women's Directorate would be on the edge, that they would be demanding much more than the government they served would allow, but that was their role. If you're going to have window dressing, that's what you do.

A public servant added that during her time at the OWD, it conceived of itself as an advocacy group, but she was sure this was no longer the case. She said: "I bet you if you found a phone book from that period of time, that you would see advocacy, advocates on behalf of women, you would see the language that now would be entirely forbidden. It's just unthinkable that something akin to a central agency in government would be using terminology like that."[39] In fact, in a pamphlet from the early 1990s, the directorate does describe itself as "a central advocacy agency within the Ontario government, reporting to the Minister Responsible for Women's Issues" (Ontario n.d., OWD, "The OWD: Who We Are"). Similarly, in its *Year-end Report, 1989–1990*, the directorate is described as "an advocacy agency that works both within the provincial government and in Ontario's communities to further the economic, legal and social status of women" (Ontario 1990, 3).

In the subsequent report, the directorate is said to act as "an advocate and critic on behalf of women by consulting with ... line ministries" (Ontario 1991, *OWD Year-end Report, 1990–1991*, 15). Until the late 1990s, the directorate is consistently identified as having an advocacy role. However, by its *1998–1999 Business Plan*, the OWD identifies itself as "a coordinator and key policy advisor on issues of concern to women, consistent with the need to promote women's economic independence and ensure safe communities" (Ontario, OWD 1998, 2). The notion of advocacy, and its link to democracy, is replaced with the market and a law-and-order agenda.

This change in discourse was played out in practice as the advocacy function of the OWD was strictly curtailed under the NPM regime. A public servant noted: "In the early 90s, you had much more freedom to really be the advocate in government, to have those concerns taken to a higher level, taken much more seriously. Just a different agenda, a much more equity-seeking agenda. Later, the shift is completely differ-ent across government in terms of what the priorities are."[40] The expec-tation of "neutrality" tightened up considerably under neoliberalism in Ontario. As a former OWD manager put it:

> The thing that we always had to be a bit careful about, and I was told this right when I was interviewed [for the job] ... about the neutrality ... we had to be very careful there because the women's directorate had in the past had some members of it who were very openly pro-active in the women's movement. And particularly during that period of government, that was frowned upon. So when I came on board, I was told very clearly that I was expected to be a corporate player and balance any personal feelings I might have with the rules we were expected to play. There was almost a bit of a conflict of interest at the time if you were an open advo-cate of the women's movement working for the Women's Directorate. That isn't to say that some people weren't, but you kind of had to temper it, and keep it to yourself a certain amount.[41]

The Harris government was very interested in the OWD acquiring a much more "traditional" administrative character. Malloy (2003) found that "according to several interviews, the new deputy minister was explicitly charged with 'cleaning things up' and returning the OWD to the bureaucratic fold" (105).[42] In this way, the NPM is not a com-plete departure from the Weberian regime of administration. Instead, it extends further Weberianism's emphasis on political neutrality.

Nevertheless, there is an important difference between the NPM's commitment to the principle of "neutrality," and that identified with Weberian bureaucracy. Despite its claims, the NPM, as noted earlier by Aucoin, has certainly not "de-politicized" the bureaucracy.[43] In reality, neoliberal public administration aims to limit the discretion of public servants and to impose greater political control over them. These objectives appear to be reflected by one OWD staff member's interpretation of bureaucratic neutrality. She commented:

> If you do believe that a non-partisan public service is key to democracy, at a certain point you have to sit there and say … the people of Ontario have voted for this government. I've never run for public office. These people got elected on this platform. They were very clear about killing employment equity and cutting welfare rates and all of that other stuff, and that's it … To be fair … I've been asked to do things that I thought were bad public policy by governments of all three persuasions.[44]

In seeing herself as primarily responsible to the governing party of the day, and for implementing its agenda, she has slipped from the Weberian belief in non-partisan, technical expertise,[45] to the idea that bureaucrats are simply the instruments for implementing party politics.

There is evidence that the NPM's focus on "de-politicizing" the bureaucracy[46] has not only affected feminists working inside the state, but is filtering into women's community organizations as well. In her work on fiscal policy and the re-privatization of social reproduction, Lisa Philipps (2002) has shown that tax laws governing the assignment of charitable status are forcing women's groups to reorient themselves away from advocacy and towards service delivery, de-radicalizing themselves in the process.[47] Fudge and Cossman (2002) also illustrate that

> charitable organizations and a range of other voluntary associations are being called upon to provide everything from food to health research funding; at the same time, they are being transformed by the requirement that they emulate the market sector and market actors. Organizations that operate in terms of business plans, provide client services, and emphasize professionalization appear to be thriving in the era of neoliberalism, while other advocacy-based groups seem to be under attack. Equality-seeking groups are increasingly being recast as special interest groups and are no longer regarded as entitled to government funding. (24)

Both affirm the conclusions of Jenson and Phillips (1996) that organizations are being steered away from advocacy towards service provision, and are becoming increasingly professionalized. This is reinforced by Harder's (2003) research on Alberta, where many feminist organizations "have curtailed their advocacy work in the interests of service provision and continued access to the few public dollars that remain available to them" (158). The 2006 changes made to the funding guidelines of the federal women's program further entrench managerialism's silencing of community advocacy.

These findings were also reflected in Ontario by community representatives I spoke to, who explained that to make up for funding shortfalls, they applied for charitable status, but were rejected because they used to have the word "advocates" in their name. In order to reapply successfully, they made internal changes, including changing their name and agreeing to no public discussion of advocacy. They expressed frustration that they had a position paper and tool kit prepared,[48] but could not say anything about it and risk their application. They commented that advocacy must be done in a certain way, with one noting, "We call it education." She added that they had to "become de-programmed and find new ways of speaking."

Self-censorship seemed to be a key strategy for many in the OWD too. Boyd said that "a whole lot of people just simply hunkered down to try and wait it out." Due to the extent of the cuts, people in the directorate felt extremely defensive, and had "tremendous frustration with the lack of commitment to women's issues." Boyd suggested: "I think they were fearful of the political staff in a way that I don't think they really were with us [the NDP]."[49] They were afraid the Tories would scrap the directorate, and so "they became very quiet, and not very inventive." Public servants made comparable assessments, with one noting that "to many people's amazement, the OWD survived. It took on a much more limited mandate, a more focused mandate."[50] A former OWD policy analyst sensed that when she was rehired at the directorate , her manager needed reassurance that she "wouldn't be too much of a shit disturber" and could work within such a mandate. She said that cautious management was valued at that time because the directorate was "a pretty big target."[51] Sawer and Grey (2008) confirm that the international trend has been for femocrats to take a defensive stance towards neoliberal and neoconservative forces.

As seen earlier, the Harris government was preoccupied with the bureaucracy. When asked specifically about the introduction of new ideas and management models, people were quick to recall examples. Someone remembered active searches for options to restructure departments and ministries and for new governance models, including interest in the British model of a small inner cabinet of senior ministers combined with junior ministers.[52] Another discussed a number of cost-cutting measures and constraint exercises, which even went as far as "cutting muffins in half" at meetings.[53] All of this draws inspiration from the NPM.

It was not simply the government's structural changes, but also its underlying ideological motivation that placed it within the NPM. A source explained that she has been in civil service for nineteen years. She believed that the majority of public sector workers joined the government not for monetary reasons, but to serve the public, and for the opportunity to shape policy. However, the label of "special interest groups," applied consistently by the PC government, made it difficult for those working in equity-seeking areas (women, Aboriginal peoples, seniors) to feel the same pride in their work. She entered the civil service during the Peterson government, and had been through the Liberal, NDP, and PC periods. While there were changes with each, after the Harris government came in, "there was a huge shift."[54] She continued to say:

> Under the Conservative government, we were very much made to feel as scapegoats and whipping boys because the government at the time very publicly took the stance that if anything is going right, well, the politicians get credit because it was our decision, if anything's going wrong ... well they've [bureaucrats] lost the cheque or this or that ... It just played havoc with morale ... You've basically taken a group of people, you've taken away the most meaningful parts of their job, and then you['re] basically openly and to the public saying if there's anything wrong it's their fault and oh, by the way, anybody could come off the street and do their job and we've got to save money so the best way to do that is get rid of those lazy civil servants![55]

With disappointment, she alluded to the success of the anti-bureaucrat discourse, saying, "They've done surveys, and we're down there with car salesmen and lawyers and politicians."[56]

Also central to the NPM, Aucoin (2000) found that "in the 1980s, a new priority was given to the management of government ... [The public service] paid less and less attention to the development of policy alternatives" (68). There

was a decline "in the proportion of senior managers who are knowledge-
able about the substantive aspects of the policy areas in which they are
expected to provide policy advice." This situation was exacerbated by
the increase in deputy and associate deputy ministers with no experience
in the line departments to which they were appointed as the top public
service executives ... The failure to recognize the importance of technical expertise and experience in the provision of policy advice, and thus
in problem solving, meant that those with such attributes and experience
were overtaken by those perceived to have better skills at managing the
policy process. (Aucoin 2000, 67)

The Ontario case study confirms this. Regardless of whether they came
from within, or outside of, the public service, one interviewee insisted
that from the early 1980s to the mid-1990s, all OWD staff "absolutely
considered themselves feminists. [However,] [s]ome of the people that
were hired in the mid-90s and beyond weren't even so sure they wanted
to be those terms."[57] One community advocate observed that the OWD
had a project officer who "didn't know anything, wasn't a feminist,
and wasn't all that interested."[58] A former OWD manager said: "I was
honest and said I came in for managerial experience, but we had a lot
of women on the staff who were very committed to the women's movement ... I care about that too ... This is going to sound terrible, but I did
have some reservations about working in an all-female environment."[59]
   A public servant who is no longer in contact with the OWD also
identified a change in focus and personnel at the directorate. Debates
over feminist theory were common in the early OWD, but she guessed
it is not intensely debating these things now, and that the debate has
changed with the nature and role of government shifting.[60] Another
saw this move manifested in management styles at the OWD, where
her manager, a career bureaucrat, was process- and detail-oriented,
with "not much discussion at the ideological level. She wasn't interested in debate related to feminist theory." This manager was focused
on ensuring that changes in the mandate were pushed through.[61] The
former OWD policy analyst concluded that

   the organization, from my perspective, when I started to work there,
   was pretty much, I'll say, in quotes, "mission-driven." People were there
   because they had strong beliefs in terms of women's equality or women's
   issues. It wasn't just straight government work. They came with an interest in women's issues. The second time around, with some of the changes

in mandate [around 1997], there had been a number of personnel changes and the expectation that people had a grounding in feminist theory was gone ... I was struck, I was actually surprised, to be working alongside people who, from my perspective, they didn't know anything, and didn't really have any interest in feminism. So it shifted from being a place that informed policy development with feminist theory, to a place where women were kind of like a demographic factor.[62]

Therefore, with the loss of self-identification with feminism and feminist theory, the active debates within the OWD, described in chapter 3, were no more.

This reflects what a community worker called a "bureaucratization of the bureau," whereby people were not trained in their portfolios.[63] A directorate staff member confirmed that restructuring occurred such that "the policy people are multi-tasking. We're supposed to know about everything." She said this might be a good idea in theory, but now there is nobody in the policy branch.[64] As Albo (1993) demonstrates, so-called multi-skilling also entails an intensification of work, and a decline in service to the public.

Community advocates also spoke of internal restructuring leading to unevenness of staff and high turnover.[65] When asked about changes under the NPM, one OWD alumnus laughed, adding, "When I started there, I used to have a new manager every week. I'm exaggerating, but I was hired by a woman named ... she resigned and left ... Then there was a period of a lot of people doing 'acting management.'"[66] Another OWD staff member told a comparable story about turnover:

In the last two and a half years, when I started there, there was a manager in my unit. She left. The position was not filled for six months ... Another woman came in. She was there for six months. Hated it. She left. And now we're without a manager again. She came because she wanted management experience, but it was so horrible ... She went back to her home position, which was a step down.[67]

This participant said there was a lot of "internal trouble" there because they had gone through many managers and suffered from a lack of leadership. While the directorate has always had high turnover, in the past this was because it was seen as a place for women in OPS to go and get management experience, and then "disseminate through the OPS ideas around looking at policy through a gender lens." But the "turnover now is because they are unhappy." The turnover has become a "huge problem" and is making the situation "so horrible."[68] A former manager ascribed a "revolving door" scenario at the directorate.[69]

This lack of continuity in staff also contributed to a dearth of long-term vision, or planning for future action. A public sector worker noted that there have always been minor shifts in governance approaches,[70] but remembered one shift in particular, taken by a manager from another ministry, who came into the OWD. She recounted:

> Essentially it was how to do outcomes based planning and outcomes based measuring. [It was three or four years ago since the first time it filtered down to her work.] Now, it seems that over that period of three or four years ... everything's a buzz word, everything's a format, this has got to be done in this way, with very little thought or vision ... or planning about what the content is. It's the structure that's driving it. And now, there's a whole new focus on results-based planning. So for the last few days, people have been scrambling trying to figure out how to put stuff into that template, as opposed to the previous template ... It seems like it's all rule-driven, so there can be no individual decision-making judgment ... These templates that now run our life ... is there a way that they could be used and not feel so oppressive? I am so close to focussing on not being here anymore. The worst part of working for the government is having bureaucratic leadership that is non-visionary and disorganized.[71]

This was contrasted with a time when "there was an acknowledgment and expectation that staff were content experts, and so we were expected to have a vision for the agency and put it all together and we had dreams. And now we get told what to do ... Why would anybody of vision ... put themselves in a position of having to deal with those issues?"[72] Another agreed that "there's no place to bring new ideas. There's no place for the staff to say, I've got this great idea, I'd like to develop it further ... It just doesn't happen."[73] The desire for vision by those in the OWD conflicted with the NPM orientation of the government. Malloy (2003) discovered that "a senior person involved in the Harris-era restructuring said the plan was to make the directorate a very tightly focused policy analysis unit working within the bureaucracy and expressed frustration at broad visions which did not fit this internal policy strategy: 'For example, I don't know why the hell they're still involved in grants'" (105). From the perspective of the NPM, the Women's Directorate should operate like any other administrative structure.

Aucoin (2000) identified the constraints it places on visionary thinking as one of the main weaknesses of the NPM. He asserts that bureaucrats "must have ideas about what is to be done ... It is the force that drives change in the management of the state" (68). But instead of the NPM regime fostering innovative ideas from public sector workers, many identified a drastic reduction in trust and a lack of tolerance for discretion. For example, one participant recalled that "there were periods of time when if I was invited to go on a panel show on TVO [TV Ontario], I went on a panel show on TVO. I wouldn't be allowed now, or if I were allowed, I wouldn't be allowed unless they vetted my script."[74]

Such stories reinforce Aucoin's point that the NPM seeks to assert control over the public bureaucracy and to centralize its functions. He refers to

> the widespread perception by political leaders ... that the career public service, or state bureaucracy, had assumed too great an influence over the management of the state. In each case, public management reform has tried to check, counter and constrain this influence ... Governments ... have sought to reassert political control over the state apparatus. (Aucoin 2000, 3)

This accurately describes the experiences of Ontario public sector workers, who noted that quality management and service standards and accountability mechanisms were introduced, that all divisions and ministries had business plans, that spending had to be in harmony with those business plans, and that it was very difficult to get money that did not fit into the plan.[75] The first directorate business plan was created in 1996 (Malloy 2003).

Dianne Cunningham highlighted her government's call for business plans for all ministries, hailing it as "the best thing to ever happen to the OWD."[76] She believed it forced the directorate, which had been involved in some program delivery in spite of its coordinating function, to get focused, monitor its goals, identify "best practices," and show results. When the minister came in, the OWD "had a huge budget," with no business plan. She stated that she was "fed up with reports," and wanted the OWD to be more results-focused and stop trying to do too much. She denounced criticism against her for pulling back, contending that the nine ministries involved in violence against women was indicative of the directorate's lack of focus. Instead, she sought to "build on programs that work," insisting that technical programs for women grew under her government, and are still growing, because they work.[77]

Judy Wolfe also supported the introduction of business plans, which she says were "a god-send to the public sector," which was isolated from the reality of the world, and needed to demonstrate how they had succeeded. Such an idea, as will be seen, was very controversial at the directorate. Wolfe discussed the unpopular changes made to women's centres, which involved "pushing the economic agenda hard." This moved the focus to getting women jobs and meant "a shift in relationship from the Women's Centres driving the policy to being driven by the policy." The centres were not happy when they were required to produce outcomes measures, which Wolfe acknowledged is very difficult when some results, like increased self-esteem for women, are hard to quantify.

Cunningham's adherence to neoliberal governance practices was also clear when the minister explained that her government cut back on public service advertisements related to violence against women. They were able to get the private sector to do it because "big companies – they don't want their women coming to work every day violated." Her rationale reads like it was drawn directly from an NPM manual on privatization: "That's the way it should be. We in Ontario and Canada depend on the government to do things that we should be doing for ourselves."[78]

The *1998–1999 Business Plan* was also rife with NPM discourse. In describing the OWD's role, the plan explains that the "Directorate acted as a catalyst by initiating cross-sectoral partnerships in communities across the province to maximize client service and develop new solutions to issues faced by women" (Ontario 1998, 3). Further, the OWD was a "catalyst to encourage cooperation and partnerships to facilitate the use and sharing of innovative best practices and to develop collaborative plans for models of excellence with other ministries" (5). The plan goes on to say that the directorate was putting much more emphasis on program accountability, and on introducing performance measures.

Cunningham still maintained her support for the directorate, saying, "I had huge respect for the people there because I knew how hard it was," and that she appreciated their "excellent advice" and expertise, and the opening they provided to women outside in the community.[79] This comment notwithstanding, her evaluation of the situation appears to be at odds with that of OWD staff. For instance, the minister claimed,

"I think after we [the Tories] were there, when we made it [the OWD] smaller and more effective and efficient, I think they liked their jobs a lot because they actually were truly respected … I think it's true of many programs. They get too big. They're not effective and efficient. You pull them back, you get good leadership." What Cunningham has provided is an endorsement of the central principles of the NPM, not an accurate understanding of the perspectives of the directorate's staff.

When asked specifically about business plans, one public servant replied that the Tories "thought the business plans were great. Personally, I think trying to do policy in a business plan model is the most ridiculous thing I've ever heard of."[80] In terms of results-based measuring, while she saw nothing wrong in theory with showing that what you are doing has an effect, the problem is how to measure the results in practice. She gave an example to illustrate the difficulties in quantifying some outcomes. Because it is not program-focused, one of the directorate's tasks might involve consulting other ministries on their policies on the wage gap, and on women in different occupations. How does the OWD measure the results of such an activity? She also emphasized the incomplete information that is often gained from these processes, pointing out that the directorate could survey the people they are directly affecting, such as those in the Women in Skilled Trades (WIST) program to find out if women actually end up working in their desired industry. This would satisfy the results-based test, and might show that the program was successful in putting women into skilled occupations. However, she questioned if it is actually a success, if a year later, "they all drop out," due to the culture of the industry and this goes unmeasured.[81] Chappell (2002) has noted similar problems for femocrats operating within a managerialist policy environment in Australia.

The subsequent Liberal government has continued to focus on accountability, results-based planning, evaluation, logic models, outcomes, outputs, and performance measurement (Coulter 2009). In *Breaking the Cycle: Ontario's Poverty Reduction Strategy*, targets, outcomes measurement, and evaluation are underscored. Public reporting on income, school readiness, education, health care, and housing is celebrated to improve accountability (Ontario, Cabinet Committee on Poverty Reduction 2013). "Measuring results" is also the key message in the housing strategy (Ontario, Ministry of Municipal Affairs and Housing 2010). This shift towards "new" accountability mechanisms in Canada has not led to real improvements in public policy for women (Anderson and Findlay 2010).

Several of those interviewed also spoke of the introduction of "pay for performance," and the discourse of "empowerment" and "competency." One worker commented that these ideas had become a "very powerful model" that is "essentially [about] control mechanisms."[82] Another reported that

> in terms of labour policy, the women's directorate had been doing their own kind of analysis of data to look at trends in labour force participation. The Harris government centralized a lot of functions and we had a much closer relationship with the Ministry of Finance, and so in terms of the kinds of data that we were going forward with, the government wished to have some control in terms of what was going out. So from a government perspective I understand that, you don't want one department saying one thing and somebody else saying another. On the other hand, the way they generated the numbers, they produced documents that it just looked like nothing but good news. They wanted only good news.[83]

The control of communication was also mentioned by a former OWD manager, who maintained that "a big one [challenge] under the Harris government was spin, communication spin. Sometimes you were just ready to scream the amount of times that house notes and briefing notes and correspondence would get re-written."[84] Judy Wolfe added that they had disputes with the Premier's Office because no public education was allowed. Pre-1995, the directorate could do things like ad campaigns to deliver messages to the public, "but post-95, [it was] impossible. There was so much control over messaging from the centre, and so little interest in what the Women's Directorate was doing, that you couldn't get a message through."

The desire for control is seen not only with public sector workers, but with communities outside the state as well. While the NPM professes to value, and support, citizen engagement, this does not appear to be the case. Albo (1993) asserts that "the new right has hacked away at even modest forms of participatory administration – citizen advisory boards, funding for citizens' groups, rights of procedural justice" (25). Several examples confirm this. In Alberta, Harder (2003) found that,

> for those arguing that the Alberta state had lost control of its fiscal management capacity and that spending reductions were meant to reassert that control, political contestation was viewed as a divisive process, one that was not conducive to efficient public management, and a distraction

from the facilitation of the effective functioning of the market. A neoliberal project of state restructuring was, thus, highly attractive since it involved the evacuation of politics from the realm of the state. (16)

This corresponds with similar changes in Ontario, where one element of the Tories' Omnibus Bill was to eliminate a range of bodies for public consultation and local participation (Browne 1997).[85]

Representation and the Policy Community

If one considers the relationship between feminists inside the state and activists outside in the community during this period in Ontario, it is clear that democratic participation was wanting. As Bradford (2003) explains:

> Legislative amendments were made in labour relations, employment equity and social assistance to limit the resources and policy voice of unions, social equity movements and anti-poverty activists. In turn, the Premier's Council, the SPF [Sector Partnership Fund], and OTAB, structures that had institutionalized a policy role for civil society representatives, all disappeared in the government's first year. When unions and social movements protested the pace and direction of change in a series of "Days of Action," Premier Harris repeated that "no special interest group or lobby will stop us." (1018)

A spokesperson from a community organization said that when the Tories were elected, "real consultation plummeted," and "phony consultations"[86] increased. When consultation did occur, it was much less public, and input from consultation was rarely integrated. For her, this constituted a "lockdown on policy" by the Tories, when, for long periods of time, there were no calls for proposals or projects from the women's policy community and was no clear funding cycle.[87] According to one source:

> There was an explicit expectation when I was first there that you are talking to women's community groups. The OWD funded women's centres, so we had a link with communities through the women's centres, but we also liaised with women's groups, we had contacts, we would call to talk about issues. When the Harris government came in, it was basically, you don't talk to anybody. It really felt like you were working in a vacuum.[88]

Another added that "of course the previous government didn't care what the stakeholders thought ... There was the long, dark era under the Conservative government when we weren't allowed to talk to people."[89] In addition, an interviewee recalled that

> there was a period of time, up to the middle 90s where there was a comfort level and an emphasis on interacting with whatever community you happen to be working with, whether it was private sector, broader public sector, or NGOs, so depending on your responsibility, you were encouraged to have that interaction. When the previous [Tory] administration was elected, I was actually shocked to go out to a community group, people I had known for over a decade, they thought *I'd* changed. They treated *me* differently.[90]

She adds, however, that changes to their relationship with outside groups were "mostly due to workload and staff cuts, not necessarily because the groups were less receptive."[91] Marion Boyd observed that bureaucrats "were no longer seen as advocates by the women's community based services, but as obstructionists."[92] But she noted that this is an unfair judgment by the community, and is based on their lack of understanding of the little power that feminist bureaucrats actually had.

It is not the case that there were no consultations with the community, but the Tory government had a very particular view of who was included in their "community." A participant indicated that there was "Partners for Change," which involved community partnerships around initiatives for economic security for women. However, she stressed that the stakeholders were primarily

> friends of the Ministry.[93] They were high powered, executive women. They were not the immigrant women counseling groups. It was consultation, but at a different level ... It was more consulting with stakeholders that would be supportive of the government as opposed to ones that would be critical of the government. Anything that was likely to be critical, not so interested in getting their opinion. We know they don't like us, so why would we listen to what they have to say? Because we're going to go ahead and do it anyway, right?[94]

The Business and Professional Women's Association was one of the key organizations for the Tory government. This person continued to say that beyond relating to such groups, over the last few years, the directorate has been unsure what its relationship to the outside should be. There is a lack of leadership from its director, or ADM. She noted that her unit was supposed to do "stakeholder relations," and that her job was to make a list of groups and talk to them, but wondered how to maintain a relationship with the community when there is nothing happening in the directorate to talk to them about. She was disappointed that in the past there "was more action going on," but now there is no generation of new ideas or opportunities to develop new stakeholder relationships.[95]

It was common to hear those interviewed describing feeling of despair within the OWD, with one concluding that "in terms of day to day, what it's like to work there, it's pretty awful right now. People are pretty unhappy ... It used to be great and now it's lousy. We used to do cool stuff, now we don't."[96] Several confirmed that it was much more difficult for them to keep connections to the community due to a lack of field staff to keep in touch with groups, due to the breakdown in information from the community to the state, and due to the lack of value placed on the input of "special interest groups."[97] Many struggled with the situation. As an interview participant explained:

> It's when you're externally working with those stakeholders, you can't really be seen as the advocate and playing that role that you know you play internally. It's a different role. It's a role of managing the relationships, but also being able to communicate effectively out what the government agenda is. And frankly, that was very difficult for many people working there, particularly at that time, given what the [PC] government agenda was. And people were lost to the organization because of that, because they just couldn't play that role ... They didn't really want to be the face of that government when they were out in the community groups.[98]

To one staff member, it seemed that the focus on efficiency and accountability was about "accountability more to the inside, than the outside,"[99] underscoring Sue Findlay's (1997) conclusions. She maintains that shielding the public service from democratic participation is key to maintaining power relations, and that it is not surprising that restructuring has meant that the bureaucracy is even less open to "outsiders" now (1997).

Regardless of the changing rhetoric about partnerships and collaboration, community representation in the policy process is currently shallow. In the Liberals' Poverty Reduction plan, the government commits only to provide "support to co-ordinate community revitalization projects" (Ontario, Cabinet Committee on Poverty Reduction 2013, 3). Clearly steering, rather than rowing, is still the order of the day. Coulter argues that the Ontario Liberals, operating through a persona of "niceness," engage in consultation that "constructs the appearance of dialogue, while postponing the need for action" (Coulter 2009, 32–3), echoing the aforementioned "phony consultations" from the PC era.

Paralleling the situation federally, the provincial deficit provided the pretence to explore what needed to be cut. In addition to social welfare programs, the provincial government turned its attention to structures within the public service. Besides the OWD, the other main structure of representation for women was the Ontario Advisory Council on Women's Issues (OACWI) (formerly the Ontario Advisory Council on the Status of Women). Unlike the cuts to the OWD, the OACWI was scrapped completely. It is important to note that the loss of the OACWI was not strongly resisted by the women's movement. The advisory council was criticized for its political appointment process and its lack of connections to the feminist community. One participant was especially blunt, commenting that the council was "absolutely useless ... they did nothing." However, she added that they had little budget, or staff,[100] while others had more positive assessments of the OACWI. A source with extensive knowledge of women's policy machinery at all three levels of government suggests that advisory councils in liberal democracies do provide at least a limited form of representation that links society to the policy process.[101] Another thought that while the representation of class interests was weak, that the councils did provide racial representation.[102]

And even though the OACWI's legitimacy within the women's movement was suspect, this was not the main basis for its dismantling. The loss of the OACWI was part of the larger restructuring and attack on gender democracy through women's structures of representation. One person interviewed indicated that "in the early 1990s, all governments had a retrenchment ... Part of it is bureaucratic retrenchment, there are just fewer staff, and what people saw as being 'perks,' like women's bureaus ... tended, like a variety of other add-ons" to be targeted.[103] Another commented that the OACWI "was not seen as a core business, or a real need," so it was one of the first things to be cut. She went on to say that the Tories believed they didn't need policy advice, and they cut those things that were not mainstream – "women's policy issues were not at the top of agenda, they were not on the radar screen."[104] Furthermore, Marion Boyd asserted that there was "a real repression under the last [Tory] government of ideas they did not concur with."

This reality led a number of people to wonder whether the restructuring was simply a symptom of the more significant problem of the government's anti-equity agenda. For example:

> I'm not sure that restructuring government ... If the government decides that you're not a priority, you're not a priority. So I'm not sure it would be structure ... I actually don't believe necessarily that you need a stand-alone Women's Directorate to have clout in government. I think that if you had a robust policy and research unit, community liaison and outreach, it could be within a bigger Ministry ... But if you starve it of resources ... If a government, by every public statement it makes, says that these issues are not of concern to them. First of all, it means over time, civil servants are careerist in the sense that you don't go looking for a job where nothing is going to be done in the next three or four years. And second of all, if nothing is being done, the people who are there start to leave. If you're not on the radar screen.[105]

While an important point, it is difficult to separate the restructuring of government from the set of ideas that devalue equality seeking, since the NPM is both an ideology and a political practice that work in concert. But under the Tory government, it is clear that women's issues were given very low priority. Furthermore, when women's policy issues were taken up, it was done so in a way that departed significantly from past practice. This is evident in women's labour market policy.

Substantive Democracy: The NPM and Women's Labour Market Policy

Even though women's policy was certainly not a main focus of the PCs in Ontario, it did receive some attention. One interviewee was careful to refer to these government responses as addressing *women's issues*, rather than as *feminist policy*, instructing me to "note no use of the word feminist in there."[106] Under the Tories, as with previous governments, the focus of women's policy was on two main areas: violence against women and women's economic independence. Here, I will address only the latter.[107]

Restricting the Policy Field

Labour market policy for women during this period consisted mainly of encouraging women's entrepreneurialism and their entrance into male-dominated "non-traditional" occupations.[108] For the former, other ministries provided small business loan programs for women, in combination with the OWD's own grant distribution. Nevertheless, as Malloy (2003) argues, the economic independence stream was "overwhelmingly service-oriented; it produced publications, such as, 'Advancing Women's Economic Independence: Ontario's Success Story' and 'Fast Forward: A Resource for Women and Entrepreneurship in Canada,' that emphasized women succeeding in business and as business owners" (108).

On the website for the Tory Government of Ontario, primary emphasis was placed on "Supporting Women's Entrepreneurship." The 2003 website explained that "the OWD works with business leaders and community organizations to encourage and support female entrepreneurship ... Women entrepreneurs are making a vital contribution to the provincial economy" (Ontario, OWD 2003i, "Supporting"). The government made grand claims on the website: "Entrepreneurship poses an attractive career alternative, and Ontario's women entrepreneurs boast tremendous successes. Ontario women are turning good ideas and a little start-up money into thriving, growing businesses" (ibid.).

Of course, the website failed to mention that self-employment is one of the lowest-paying, and gendered forms of employment. There is the impression that the self-employed are high-paid consultants and contractors, when, in reality, almost half of the self-employed were earning less than $20,000 a year at the time (De Wolff 2000), despite working longer hours, on average (Burke, Mooers, and Shields 2000). In addition, the gender gap in self-employment is the highest of any form of employment, with women making only 59 per cent of what men make (Hadley 2001). Cranford and Vosko's (2004) research also points to the gendered and racialized nature of self-employment, showing that immigrant women with small businesses have much less access to, and support from, unpaid family labour than men.

Such considerations do not mesh with neoliberalism, which sees gender inequality not as systemic, or structural, but rather as a problem of individual women. This is evident in the website's showcasing of women's success stories (including photographs). The following are two examples:

1. Catherine Ferguson, Dyno-Pink Enterprises, Thunder Bay

"Selling is hard," says Catherine Ferguson, owner of Dyno-Pink Enterprises, which sells portable greenhouses and garages in Thunder Bay. It's a lot harder than transporting dynamite on contract, another side of her business. Catherine found she wasn't taken seriously when she first went into business for herself in 1995. "They pat you on the head and say you've got a cute little dream, but …" So Catherine joined a lending circle through PARO: A Northwestern Ontario Women's Community Loan Fund. A lending circle is a good way to find financing when traditional methods fail, says Catherine. "The six women in my circle all own businesses. We go over each others' business plans. If we agree the plans are viable, we authorize a loan. The first loan can be up to $1,000. We don't have to jump through hoops to get the money either," says Catherine. "The circle does a lot more than just give me a loan when I need one. We exchange information and give each other moral support and advice. It's a support group that can help you over some rough patches. Being a business owner can be really stressful, and the circle provides a non-threatening place to relax." In return, Catherine says, the women in the lending circles help raise money for the organization by running special events. "We've been so successful, we've got a contract to run a government program that teaches unemployed women how to start a business," she reports with pride. As for the dynamite, Catherine began transporting it on a dare from her husband. It turned out to be something she enjoys and does well. She sees it as a growth opportunity and wants to take on more contracts and eventually buy her own truck. (Ontario, OWD 2003c, "Catherine")

2. Sibongile Matheson, Sibongile, Toronto

Sibongile Matheson was at a low ebb of her acting career when she decided to open a business. She had a family to support, $100 and an interest in her heritage. "It was easy to choose African art and textiles." That was in 1993. Today, Sibongile, whose name means "We thank you" in her native tongue, has moved from her home office to a leased space in downtown Toronto. "I feel I have visibility as a business person now," says Sibongile, who imports from Africa and exports to the United States. Although it wasn't easy starting with so little capital, she had both moral support from her husband and practical support from mentors she met at trade shows. "Several exhibitors taught me how to set up more effective displays. They set me on the right road to learning about import and export. They even referred customers to me." Life hasn't been easy for Sibongile. A Zulu, she fled South Africa during the Apartheid troubles, settling in Toronto after stays in England and Zimbabwe. "It was a desperate time in my life. I asked for help, and it came." What is most important when starting a business? "Seek information. There's lots if you look for it. Ask questions. Keep asking until you get to the right department or person. Keep focused. Do your homework until you find what you need." Sibongile's dream is to develop her business into a centre where people can learn about Africa. "It will be a centre that encompasses African art, books, music, travel and film. Many people could benefit, not just Africans or black people." Sibongile's dream began with some tough lessons. "I'm from a different culture, and I have to deal with that. Sometimes, it isn't easy." But she has faced many challenges and maintains a positive outlook. "Don't let other people spoil your dream," she says. "I have family, good friends and business mentors. The rest is up to me." (Ontario, OWD 2003h, "Sibongile")

It is significant that none of the examples refers to any form of government assistance, from the OWD or otherwise. They privilege private sources of support (market, family, and community), combined with individual initiative. Recall that for Sibongile, "I have family, good friends and business mentors. The rest is up to me." The state is conspicuously absent from this equation. In fact, many of the cases displayed are not even in Ontario. The message is that these enterprising women did not need the Ontario government to help them to achieve their goals. It is difficult to disagree with one public sector worker who described this policy approach as "pathetic from my perspective."

In addition to concentrating on women's entrepreneurialism, the OWD website paid some attention to job segregation. But much has changed since the times when the main approach (pre-Tories) to deal with the problem of job segregation, and one of the central projects of the OWD, was pay equity. The Tory solution to women's job ghettoization can be found in simply exhorting women to expand their occupational horizons, and by providing inspirational stories to aid in this task. Under the heading "Job Segregation?"(with the question mark presumably casting doubt on the scope and strength of segregation), the website exhibits the story of Louise Arbour, former Supreme Court Justice:

"There's no limit to what law offers in terms of challenges and opportunities," says Louise Arbour, a Supreme Court Justice. You must have a very strong idea of who you are, but still be open-minded and progressive. All aspects of life are affected by laws" … Louise says: "You have to be curious about the world that surrounds you and must be willing to have an impact on it, however small." (Ontario, OWD 2003d, "Job Segregation?")

While certainly one would not want to discourage women from becoming Supreme Court justices, it might not be the best strategy to address the structural problem of job segregation and women's concentration in low-paid, insecure, non-unionized jobs.

Other role models are displayed as well, including:

1. Pat Oakes-Scattergood, Ironworker … "I was a young, divorced, North American Indian with two small children.` I worked in an office. I didn't make enough money and it wasn't very satisfying. I got a chance to take a structural steel welding course. Welding isn't as hard as I expected and neither was the apprenticeship. It gives you a sense of freedom, like you've conquered something." (Ontario, OWD 2003e, "Pat's Moving Up")
2. Carol Bee, Trucker … "Nine years ago, when I started trucking, women truckers were already on the road. Today you see a lot more, and I can understand why. I've been to all 10 provinces and 50 states. There's a real sense of freedom in trucking. And the pay is good" (Ontario, OWD 2003a, "Carol's Got Wheels")
3. Carole Harrison, Machinist … "I worked on the assembly line for seven years before deciding to become a machinist. My father, brother and sister are all in the skilled trades and work for the same company as I do. It helped a lot that my sister was there ahead of me and had gone in as a pipefitter. It's challenging work and I have no complaints about the pay." (Ontario, OWD 2003b, "Carole Can Fix It")

Each story ends with exactly the same message:

[insert name] is a great example of the increasing number of women who have chosen new and different occupations. They are proof that women can do the work. Training in math and science is often needed to get into non-traditional jobs, or apprenticeship programs for women offered by employers. The prospects are good – and the rewards are well worth the effort.[109]

Again, gender inequality is individualized. Sex segregation is depicted by the OWD as a problem of individual choice. Women can solve the problem of sex segregation, and low pay, simply by making different career choices, just like Pat Oakes-Scattergood did.[110]

This is another consistent element over time. In the current guidelines for OWD grants to community organizations, the priorities include projects related to micro-lending for low-income women to start small businesses, supporting entrepreneurialism, and Women in Skilled Trades and Information Technology Training. As in the Tory era, the OWD continues to put "recognizing women" at the forefront through "The Leading Girls, Building Communities and Leading Women, Building Communities Awards [to] recognize and celebrate girls and women who demonstrate exceptional leadership in working to improve the lives of others in their communities" (Ontario, OWD 2011b, "Recognizing Women").

There is little evidence that the Liberal agenda involves much more activity on women's labour market policy than did their predecessors'. In many instances, women's economic independence is overshadowed by violence against women (or "domestic violence"). Public education campaigns and resources and links are all focused on violence, with little mention of women's economic equality (Ontario, OWD 2011c, "Resources"; Ontario, OWD 2012a, "Key Programs"). Connections between poverty and violence against women are not made clear (Coulter 2009). Rhetoric on poverty reduction has not been met with action, and poverty continues to be individualized (ibid.). There have not been significant changes made to welfare policy (ibid.), and the clawback of the National Child Benefit Supplement was only phased out in the face of a court challenge. In her study of the McGuinty Liberals, Coulter (2009) found that

> the neoliberal ideological project ... reinforces the political culture that emphasizes and promotes individualism, individual responsibility, and choice, without any accompanying discussion about existing inequities in power and economic status or between genders, and how these influence the ability of people to make choices in their lives. (28)

As noted before, the NPM gender regime extends beyond any given political party in power.

Gender and Neoliberal Labour Market Policy

Many OWD staff members were not satisfied with such an approach to women's labour market policy. When asked about women's labour market policy and the directorate, one person quickly replied that "nothing" is happening. She then clarified: "It's not entirely that nothing's happening, there are some targeted employment projects, specifically around women and non-traditional skills."[111] But it was clear that she saw this as inadequate. One public servant described such programs as treating women as "labour capital," to make up labour and skill shortages.[112] Another acknowledged that the shortage in skilled trades people made this a very convenient focus for women's labour market policy.[113] Sears (2000) has called this approach the "new vocationalism," based on disciplining workers, and fitting them into, rather than challenging, the existing labour market.

The Information Technology Training for Women (ITTW) program is a good example. It is described on the 2002 OWD website as follows: "A partnership between the Ontario government, the private and the voluntary sectors, ITTW provides low-income women in Ontario with government-funded specialized training that will help them qualify for entry level jobs in IT" (Ontario, OWD 2003g, "Program Trains"). The program is intended to train women to be webmasters, database administrators, and software developers. While it is mentioned that the program "will let them [disadvantaged women] leave poverty behind for sustainable careers as technical office professionals," it is emphasized several times that "ITTW is part of Ontario's strategy to address skill shortages in high-tech industries" (ibid.; Ontario, OWD 2003f, "Pilot Project"; Ontario, OWD 2001, "Ontario Government Invests"). Women's labour market equality barely competes for attention against the Ontario government's preoccupation with bolstering the IT sector.

This was not the first time the directorate focused on getting women into non-traditional careers, including training in technology. As seen earlier, programs like Open Doors and Jobs for the Future, began under the Davis Tories, and continued under subsequent governments. The difference is that previously such programs were but one aspect of a much broader women's policy agenda. During the Harris government, these initiatives became the primary emphasis for women's labour market policy and this emphasis has been maintained under the Liberals. In the Liberal poverty reduction strategy ITTW is one of the few policies described that is directed specifically to women (Ontario, Cabinet Committee on Poverty Reduction 2013.). The OWD lists programs on skilled trades and information technologies as its highlights (Ontario, OWD 2012b, "News").

Several of those interviewed pointed to the weaknesses in this strategy,[114] including the reality that for women who do enter male-dominated workplaces, there are often extensive harassment issues and what one source called an "old boys atmosphere."[115] Given the individualized, market-based approach to women's policy, one woman interviewed expressed her frustration:

You have two things that have always been described as the core business –
the prevention of violence against women and achieving women's economic independence. One can see clearly why white boys in suits would
get behind the prevention of violence against women ... "You can't do
that to girls, that's bad"... but there is no understanding of what it would
take to achieve women's economic independence ... and along with that,
at a higher level, no understanding of how power operates in society. That
isn't part of the political process, not part of political consideration ... If
there were visionaries, and there was some kind of plan, and if someone
really understood power relations, and what it was appropriate for government to do about women's economic independence. Or maybe they do
have the discussion but they don't think we have anything to contribute
to it. And I don't know because nobody would tell me.[116]

Others also noted the absence of key programs necessary for wom-
en's economic independence, and further stressed that, in a related
manner, the PC government operated with a very different conception of equality. For instance, one civil servant explained that while
working for a framework for the FPT meeting, the management of
the OWD was

trying to get a focus for the women's directorate. For the Harris government, of course, it was all about the economy. So it was a natural fit, on
the positive front to say, women have a contribution to make that is being
under-utilized ... The things that weren't factored into an understanding
about women and work, it was mostly children, or ... care of dependents ...
[and] informal caregiving. Issues around female-dominated occupations,
primarily public sector work that was being hard hit by some of the policies of the government was a non-starter. There wasn't interest in looking
at labour force participation that way.[117]

She explained that there was "no mention of childcare anywhere. It was
mostly stuff that was getting stripped out. What was getting stripped
out was any acknowledgment that women start from a not-equal place.
The ideology of the Harris government was the equal, not the equitable kind of understanding of how stuff works."[118] One public servant
expressed disappointment at the now predominant idea that "we've
done that." She says they have to keep "reminding people that women
are still making less, that women are still having to bear the economic
burden of being the caregiver both of their children and of their parents,

and of the impact on their ability to earn a living, have a decent pension, etc., etc."[119]

Those from ACTEW also detected a lack of understanding of what it means for women to have real economic independence, stressing that programs like childcare and housing, which "dropped out" under the Tories, are essential for women's economic independence. Such contradictions abound in the Tory agenda, the most obvious being their resurrection of the regressive "spouse-in-the-house" rule,[120] which is, as Kitchen (1997) describes, "a manifestation of the deeply entrenched gender stereotyping of women as dependants of men" (109). Thus, for the Harris government, and neoliberals alike, economic independence is not about gender equality, it is about reducing women's dependence on the state. One person interviewed made this point very clearly in the context of discussing a pilot project to increase women's participation in the auto-parts industry. She believed these efforts were largely "symbolic," concluding that the Tory government "would like women to be independent because they don't want women on social assistance, and they certainly don't want women with children on social assistance for long periods of time."[121]

Community groups clearly have a different vision of women's economic independence and labour market policy in mind. They expressed concern that the province had not clearly articulated a labour market development policy that considers older workers, women, workers with disabilities, and immigrants. Especially with the Tories, there was a lack of an integrated approach to women's labour market policy, which the ACTEW representatives described as "hit and miss."[122] A former OWD staff member also noticed a drastic change in the way diversity among women was treated, saying that "with the Harris government, everything was just kind of washed away. It was like women were one big lump."[123] Bakan and Kobayashi (2000) add that "in the aftermath of the repeal of employment equity legislation, the term 'diversity' was used to imply a very different meaning: literally everyone, with no consideration of the systemic processes of exclusion, or positive measures to promote inclusion" (7). Policy reflected this limited version of equality.

Under the Liberal government, gender equality continues to be absent from policy discourse. In the poverty reduction plan, even though the report figures prominently on the OWD's website, the policy agenda for women is very meagre. There is about one page of text, much of which focuses on gender-neutral "domestic violence." This is embedded in the overarching goal in the plan to reduce "child poverty" by 25 per cent in five years (Ontario, Cabinet Committee on Poverty Reduction 2013, *Breaking the Cycle*). This is actually an improvement on *Ontario's Long-Term Affordable Housing Strategy* (Ontario, Ministry of Municipal Affairs and Housing 2010) and *Open Minds, Healthy Minds: Ontario's Comprehensive Mental Health and Addictions Strategy* (Ontario, Ministry of Health 2011), which also appear on the directorate's website, but fail to mention women at all, not even in reference to "domestic violence" in the housing plan (2010). As Coulter (2009) shows, the current Liberal government "promotes de-gendered, class-less neoliberal subjects, while actively avoiding consideration of the systemic causes of poverty and collective solutions that challenge the neoliberal policy paradigm" (25).

Subverting Substantive Democracy

In many cases, the problem was not simply a lack of a clear approach to women's labour market equality; it was that Tory polices, backed up by NPM arguments, directly undermined that goal. Armstrong and Connelly (1997) note that the PCs "used the deficit and new discourse of eliminating red tape and global competition to justify direct attacks on pay equity legislation and wage gains in the state sector" (3). Their assault on unions, especially provisions making it more difficult to unionize, further undermined the already limited ability of women concentrated in precarious employment to collectively organize. Furthermore, the assumption underlying Tory policies, that equality equals labour market participation, has been challenged by many immigrant women and women of colour who, despite having very high labour-market participation rates, overwhelmingly lack equality (with men or other women).

For many interviewed, what came to mind first in terms of women's labour market policy under the Tories was the cuts made to things like the Pay Equity Commission, Ontario Jobs Training, childcare, and health and safety enforcement, and the elimination of employment equity and OTAB, including the equity representation on local boards.[124] For instance, a once-OWD policy analyst noted that

> things sort of floundered on women's issues ... From '95 on, the government ... dismantled the employment equity commission, they abolished the legislation, they dismantled the programs in the broader public sector. That was a conscious decision of the previous [Tory] government to do all

that. So employment equity ... for all intents and purposes disappeared. Pay equity ... there was just no policy agenda to move.[125]

Judy Wolfe recalled that "once the Conservatives were elected ... there was a moment when I was sitting in my office ... in October of 1995 ... when I was listening to the news and every single thing I had ever worked on was cancelled. That was a disheartening moment ... I still can feel that feeling." Another saw the loss of employment equity as the loss of the more substantive understanding of equity beyond sameness. She said they were "naive" in the OWD, believing that once rights were gained, they could not be lost, but the Tories did take rights away and "in such a mean-spirited way, that equity became a bad word."[126] Wolfe also highlighted the loss of gender-inclusive language that was nurtured when the Liberals were in office, saying that "employment equity was expunged from the language after 1995. You could not use anything that sounded like that."[127] Bakan and Kobayashi (2000) confirm that "in practice, even verbal use of the term 'employment equity' was considered a feature of past practice, neither relevant to, nor acceptable in, the current context" (29). Katherine Scott (1999) has called these policy actions "a systematic dismantling of many of the important gains that the women's movement has made over the last 20 years" (230).

In view of such a reality, it must be acknowledged that in several interviews, the difficulty of developing a women's policy agenda during the Tory period was stressed. One person interviewed explained the struggle like this:

In the context of the previous government, trying to sort out an agenda on women's issues that people could move forward with ... it took a fair amount of time and energy. And because Dianne Cunningham was both our Minister [Education and Training] and the Minister of Women's Issues, in some ways, I don't think people understood how much energy she put into figuring out what a women's agenda that she could move forward would be. And she really did care about the issues. So in a way she settled on something that was completely within her domain because she owned both sides of the issue and wasn't dependent on a colleague to sort it through. To be honest, I think that's why stuff like women's access to apprenticeship and ... She had a very strong gut feel about women on their own trying to make a living. [She thinks she was a single parent for some time.] So I think the labour market stuff became what was safe to do. Women's access to apprenticeships, those kinds of things.[128]

Another agreed that considering the context, Cunningham led the OWD with the "odds stacked against it."[129] Someone else commented that the minister "found her own ways of maintaining the profile of the Women's Directorate without getting in trouble with the party's general direction ... Counter-balancing the government apathy about women's policy was a Minister who personally cared a lot about it and found other routes of promoting it."[130] She said that Cunningham was good at interpersonal relations, organized provincial forums and focus groups, and solicited letters from her constituents to raise the profile of women's issues, and she admired her as a "dynamic" minister.[131] Judy Wolfe agreed that Cunningham had a lot of knowledge and connections, and was an effective politician, who focused on women's successes in the provincial forums, and sought to "find out what's good and focus on that."[132] She added that because promoting business was important to the Tories, Cunningham created Partners for Change with women from the private sector, and pursued a money management program for girls. Nonetheless, given her position within the power structure of a government arduously pursuing the NPM agenda, there was little in the form of substantive results for women in Ontario.

These policies have not rebounded much under the Liberals. The Poverty Reduction plan refers briefly to full-day learning, but makes no mention of employment and pay equity. It notes improvements to employment standards to address precarious work, but also venerates paid work (regardless of quality) through measures such as the Ontario Child Benefit (Ontario, Cabinet Committee on Poverty Reduction 2013), and is fully committed to a market-based approach to housing (Ontario, Ministry of Municipal Affairs and Housing 2010). Markets and children (future market engines) are the proper subjects of public policy. As a case in point, in the Mental Health and Addictions strategy, the Ontario state "will focus on early intervention and support to protect our children from the many associated costs of mental illness and addictions and help steer them on the road to safe, healthy, and happy futures" (Ontario, Ministry of Health 2011, *Open Minds*, 4).

These findings emphasize the importance of feminist policy ideas inside the state. Through the concept of "gender framing," Lovenduski et al. (2005a) explore the ways in which political ideas are structured in public discourse. Using the example of the under-representation of women in politics, Lovenduski (2005) notes that the policy problem can be framed in terms of gender discrimination or, alternatively, as an issue of women's choices, and that each leads to different policy solutions. Strong women's policy agencies are able to get issues defined in a way that advances women's movement claims and takes place on feminist policy terrain. This reinforces my own conclusions about women's structures of representation in Ontario and the role of femocrats in the social reproduction of knowledge inside the state. The framing of women's labour market inequality as an issue of women's career choices, rather than one of systemic discrimination, marks a significant shift in the power and influence of the OWD. However, it would be misguided to attribute too much control over this framing process to state feminists themselves without regard for the overarching neoliberal context. Through neoliberal forms of governance, women's policy agencies are remobilized towards implementing a neoliberal policy agenda (Lovenduski 2005).

Conclusion

As we saw in the introduction to this book, one public sector worker aptly asked, "Is that the state's business [considering power relations]? Maybe it isn't. How does the state deal with power relations? Does it adjust for them? ... It gets itself involved [in power relations] in a variety of ways."[133]

The NPM has definitely produced a particular and enduring system of power relations, which privileges private, market relations, understands inequalities in power not as a collective phenomenon, but as the result of individual circumstance, and radically restricts the role of communities in the policy process.

I began by suggesting that the NPM has dominated ideas about the role and form of government in Canada, including Ontario, since the 1980s and 1990s. I then went on to examine the ways in which the NPM gender regime, based on privatization, downsizing, and managerialism, resulted in different, and intensified, problems for women. In outlining some of the gender consequences of managerialism specifically in chapter 3, I noted that the majority of literature in this area focuses on Australia. The case study, then, sought to explore the gendered effects of the NPM, with a particular focus on Ontario. Using the Ontario Women's Directorate, and other women's policy machinery in Ontario, as an example, I argued that the NPM has undermined democracy – both procedural and substantive democracy.

Procedurally, the NPM rejects the central principles of women's structures of representation, namely, that women's policies and feminist ideas about policies are important, that feminists within these bureaucracies should advocate for women, and that they should consult with women in the community. Substantively, traditional approaches by the OWD to women's labour market policy, which used to see gender inequality as related to a complicated set of structural factors, have been rejected in favour of market-based, individualized solutions.

But this is not just a historic moment, easily changed through shifting electoral tides. Neoliberalism and NPM strategies are not about any one political party. These ideas continue to resonate in Ontario politics today. Under subsequent Liberal governments, the directorate's presence has not significantly improved and major advancements in women's representation and public policy have not occurred. Gender democracy has not fared well under neoliberal New Public Management, which points to the need to focus greater attention on the gendered governance regimes at sub-national levels and how they might be transformed. The following chapter will provide some concluding comments on this transformation, through femocratic administration.

Conclusion: Building a Femocratic Administration

I sought to do several things in this book. I placed my study within an era of neoliberalism and globalization, in which strategies of resistance based on the democratization of the state are needed. I stressed, however, that such strategies must be informed by feminist insights into the gendered nature of the state. They also must recognize the federal character of the Canadian state, by addressing democratic deficits at both the national and the sub-national level, and in their relations with each other. Through the case of the Ontario Women's Directorate (OWD), I examined the place of femocrats, or state feminists, within the broader project of democratization. During two distinct periods of public sector experimentation, and under two different gender regimes, I identified the possibilities and limitations of state feminism within a largely social democratic and Weberian context, and then analysed the consequences for gender democracy associated with the neoliberal governance approach, the New Public Management (NPM). It is clear from both cases that procedural and substantive democratic weaknesses exist in the Ontario public service. Furthermore, in the latter case, neoliberal state restructuring has had a particularly negative impact on feminists working within, as well as outside of, the Ontario state. So what does this mean for women's movement strategies focused on the state and for those in opposition to neoliberalism?

As I noted earlier, democratic administration is an important piece in the struggle against neoliberalism. However, democratic administration either ignores, or says very little about, gender. In this project, I have tried to bring together democratic administration with certain forms of feminist state theory and state feminist practice, in order to begin imagining what a feminist democratic administration, or a "femocratic administration" would look like, and will develop this idea further here.

A Transformative Gender Regime

Central to an alternative gender regime is feminist democratization, including femocratic administration. Femocratic administration is only one part of feminist democratization, a broad project aimed at a range of institutions of governance including the electoral system, the party system, the legal system, and the bureaucracy. It also includes non-state institutions such as labour unions, workplaces, non-governmental organizations, and religious institutions. However, my project is limited to the administrative state.

It was evident in chapters 2 and 3 that the state and public policy are important for feminism, but some would prefer to target electoral politics rather than state administration. They stress the importance of progressive forces gaining political office. Feminist democratization certainly includes a focus on electoral politics. However, electoral politics have received rich feminist attention, whereas for state administration, this has been much less so outside of Australia. Moreover, it is fundamental to my argument that simply gaining political office is not enough. As the case of the Ontario NDP shows, such change is not permanent, and therefore not transformative. Progressive changes brought in by one government can be wiped out by the next. As Bakan and Kobayashi (2000) point out with the case of employment equity, policy positions do not always fall neatly along partisan lines. My study puts much less emphasis on party politics than on regimes of governance, particularly gender regimes, and on the importance of mobilizing social forces as central to a democratic political project. But maybe most important is that focusing only on electoral politics ignores the power of, and lack of accountability in, state administration, and the possibilities that exist there for change.

Feminists have made progress in influencing law and public policy, yet without fundamental restructuring of the institutions and processes of governance, such progress will always be limited. This is because of the institutionalization of power relations. Inequalities have been built into state structures and processes, including public administration. Institutionalization implies some durability in the structuring of power relations, while at the same time involving a constant process of negotiation and renegotiation. In the Ontario case, this is evident in a number of ways. For instance, unequal power relations are institutionalized in both the Liberal/NDP and the Tory periods. This is seen in the ways in which bureaucratic structure and culture reinforce power and privilege. The case study in chapter 3 demonstrates how hierarchy, categorization, and neutrality are key to isolating, marginalizing, delegitimizing, and dismissing alternative knowledges and perspectives, and chapter 4 shows the enduring nature of such bureaucratic norms, as well as the institutionalization of new ones.

At the same time, however, the two periods entail different projects for restructuring power relations. This is reflected both in the different ways that the directorate itself was treated over these two periods, and in the policy outcomes for women. The divergent ways that each understood equality, and the way this became translated into policy, is an important shift in the way in which inequality was entrenched. These distinctions indicate the importance of seeing variations in states across time and place, and the possibilities for change.

The institutionalization of power relations is also an indication of the balance of social forces in a given place and time. The marginal place of the OWD within the Ontario state, and its weakened state during the Tory period in particular, is not simply about state pursuits. It is also a reflection of the weakened women's movement (due to a number of internal and external factors, including at the federal level). This is why an emphasis on mobilizing on the outside, and changing the movement's relationship with the state is as important as restructuring the institutions themselves, and why femocratic administration is imperative for feminist practice.

It was evident when speaking to some former or current state feminists in the Ontario public service that they saw their roles as disruptive of the status quo, and therefore democratizing. One participant came to believe that subverting the government could be achieved simply by giving helpful answers to the people who called.[1] Another, who worked in the Pay Equity Commission, admitted that sometimes she did not do the things she did not agree with and was able to do so because she "knew the tricks of heel-dragging."[2] Speaking about changes brought in under the NPM, one public servant commented that "just because the ideologies around management change doesn't mean that everybody changes their behaviour. Some people feel good when they feel subversive."[3]

Such responses echo those encountered by Malloy (2003): "One common reaction, also found in interviews for this study, was to adopt public accountability to the bureaucracy, but private accountability to the women's movement – possibly by leaking information and documents" (35). Based on interviews with social assistance recipients, Margaret Little (1998) also recounts stories of social workers who, seeing themselves first and foremost as advocates for the poor, actively advised their "clients" on how to hide income gained from former partners, or gifts from parents (171). While interesting, these actions do not, on their own, challenge the overall bureaucratic climate, and are not, in any real sense, democratic or accountable. Femocratic administration, as a strategy to move beyond neoliberalism, must be a broad-based project that moves beyond individual acts of resistance, towards a radical transformation of the state and the development of an alternative gender regime.

Sossin (1999) has observed that "the feminist analysis of the state embraces contradictory tendencies. While one stream of feminist analysis conceives of ways to transform the nature of the state; another conceives of new strategies for feminist representation in state institutions" (13). A femocratic administration must do both: transform the state and provide representation within it. It must also incorporate a third element that reconfigures the relationship between state and society. These will be referred to as feminist bureaucratic restructuring, representative bureaucracy, and democratic administration respectively. Each will be discussed in turn.

Feminist Bureaucratic Restructuring

As Panitch (1993) asserts, hierarchical bureaucracy, "an institution that thrives on secrecy and prefers a passive citizen to administer is an institution that is ill-suited to the development of democracy" (7). It is also ill suited to feminism. There is a semblance of congruence between feminist and neoliberal discourse on bureaucratic restructuring. But when feminists speak of flatter hierarchies, and decentralization, the terms take on much different meanings than those espoused by neoliberals. Chapter 4 showed that despite claims of levelling hierarchy, neoliberal restructuring has maintained "control from above" (Albo 1993, 25). Even if one ignores the disjuncture between neoliberal rhetoric and reality, there is still a significant gap at the level of motivation between the neoliberal and feminist concerns about hierarchy. At its root, neoliberalism seeks to limit government (and democracy), and removing levels of bureaucracy accomplishes this goal. Unlike feminism, neoliberalism has no philosophical opposition to the social relations of subordination that hierarchy entails, and in fact promotes such inequalities in the market.

It also appears that feminism and neoliberalism have in common their support for the decentralization of power. Once again, though, this agreement is at little more than the superficial level of discourse. When neoliberals demand decentralization, what they really mean is greater centralized power in the cabinet and an increasingly politicized upper bureaucracy combined with extensive downsizing of lower levels of the public service, as noted in chapter 4. Aucoin (2000) has referred to this as the "simultaneous consolidation and devolution of authority" (115).

The decentralization being pursued by neoliberals illustrates its divergence from feminism. Sue Findlay (1987) refers to "a new decentralizing of federal programs, which in the case of the Women's Program meant the control of resources by regional staff dominated by men who were largely insensitive – if not overtly hostile – to the activities of both the women's movement and the Women's Program" (42). The neoliberal decentralization is actually an obstacle to the kind of change advocated by feminists. As Rebick attests, "Women's groups have always been against big bureaucracies delivering services in health care and social assistance, but it is hard to come up with more democratic forms of service delivery when the Right is pushing for privatization" (Rebick and Roach 1996, 29). Feminist advocacy for community-based delivery of social services is not the same as the NPM's preference for (re)privatization. One OWD staff member stressed that there are many things that the private sector cannot do, because they are unprofitable, like providing social housing and environmental protection. She also drew attention to the pressures on the voluntary sector, commenting that "you can't always be expecting non-profit philanthropists to be doing everything."[4]

In addition, decentralization in Canada, a federal system, has a variety of applications. It refers to both the decentralization of authority within the bureaucracy and to the decentralization of powers from the federal to the provincial (and municipal) government. Neoliberals in Canada have been more interested in the latter than the former, and specific problems for women are raised by the decentralization of federalism – funding and standards for social programs. Decentralization of federalism can have negative consequences for women, particularly outside of Quebec and the First Nations. Feminist restructuring must secure women's access to substantive democracy, in the form of uniform social programs across Canada. It must also address the gaps in procedural democracy associated with elite-driven, and secretive, executive federalism, and the need for coordination among state feminists across jurisdictions, which I will return to later.

Decentralization in the feminist sense means something very different than that sought by neoliberals. Peters (1995) distinguishes between two diverging perspectives by saying that "in the participatory model, decentralization is intended primarily to channel control to a different set of bureaucrats, or to the clients, rather than being used as a means of creating competition among service providers so that a market can work" (305).

Nevertheless, the distinction between neoliberalism and some forms of feminist action is increasingly blurred (Fraser 2009; Findlay 2013). For instance, this can be seen in the discussion of "forum shopping" in chapter 2. It is true, as Sawer and Grey (2008) celebrate, that "activists look for new spaces where women's movement activism can take flight" (10). But movements should not be romanced by the promise of shifting scales and new spaces. Andrew (2008) warns that local sites are "teetering between being new spaces for the women's movement and being new spaces for government co-option" (127). And such flexibility towards the "new" reality of neoliberalism must not simply relinquish the "old" spaces, created through struggle. I disagree with Maddison and Jung (2008), who posit that, "as the femocracy crumbles perhaps it is time to turn away from the state, and to develop a renewed focus on networks and organizations" (45). As developed below, both state feminism *and* strong women's organizations are necessary. For femocratic administration, each needs the other.

Phillips (1991) reminds readers that "the women's movement took participation almost as its definition of bureaucracy" (142), and thus developed corresponding organizational strategies. Many feminist organizational techniques can be applied to the bureaucracy. Feminists prefer a network model to a hierarchical one (Sawer 1990), in which relations between departments are for purposes of coordination rather than control. This has also been called a wheel, or a hub-and-spoke model (ibid.). Furthermore, in consciousness-raising groups, feminists experimented with rotating responsibilities and speakers,[5] task division via a lot, and skills sharing to illicit a more "democratic division of labour" (Phillips 1991, 128), and to prevent the monopolization of knowledge. The budget council in Porto Alegre, Brazil, has adopted these organizational principles, using a system of rotating seats and term limitations (Wainwright 2003, 58). In its early years, women also worked part-time in the OWD, and part-time in other ministries to allow cross-fertilization and to prevent ghettoization (Alboim 1997). Some of these methods might also be employed to more adequately address women's intersectional identities.

As discussed earlier, bureaucratic compartmentalizing is quite problematic. Gabriel explores some of the measures to better reflect women's intersectionality. The Coalition of Visible Minority Women and the Ontario Advisory Council for Women's Issues (OACWI) met and developed proposals for: an interministerial committee to coordinate the functions of the OWD and Race Relations Directorate (RRD); increased representations of women of colour in both bureaucracies; and an impact on visible minority women reviews (Gabriel 1996). There was also a greater focus on immigrant, visible minority, Aboriginal, and disabled women within the OWD (Alboim 1997). Finally, stronger ties to a diverse range of women's groups outside the state, as will be discussed later, are necessary. While these alone will not overcome the problem of compartmentalizing, they are a step in the direction of greater recognition of intersectionality.

Coordination is also necessary across levels of government for improving structures for gender democracy. Both "democracy" and the "nation state" in Canada are made more complex by different scales of governance, or federalism. Because federal and provincial structures of representation are similar, lessons about how to democratize them might be translated from one level to the other. And transformation of structures of representation at the sub-national level is important to avoid what Mahon (2003) calls a "singular focus on the national" (2).[6] This is particularly relevant given the gendered nature of Canadian federalism and the constitutional division of powers (Cameron 2006; Vickers 1994). Further, especially in the current context of globalization and neoliberalism, with the restructuring and rescaling of governance, democratization, or more specifically gender democracy, must be introduced to conceptualizations of federalism and intergovernmental relations. Gender, federalism, and democracy must be considered together. The democratization of provincial states is essential, but it must occur in concert with the transformation of the relationship *between* provincial states and the federal government, namely, through intergovernmental processes and institutions of executive federalism.

Gender-based policy analysis, for instance, has been required practice by the federal government since 1995, when it signed on to the UN

Platform for Action and introduced the Federal Plan for Gender Equality, a five-year strategy, and then again in 1997, with the Convention on the Elimination of All Forms of Discrimination against Women (CEDAW). It has introduced gender-based policy analysis into areas such as the Department of Justice, Health Canada, the Canadian International Development Agency, and Human Resources and Development Canada (Rankin and Vickers 2001). Yet the process must be universalized to all government policies and programs, and has been used very unevenly and superficially across the provinces, with some showing particular resistance, namely, Alberta and Harris's Ontario (ibid.). And we continue to have clear examples of systemic gender discrimination in federal policies, Employment Insurance (EI) being just one (Vosko 1996; Canadian Labour Congress 2000; Porter 2003), indicating that such initiatives must not simply go through the motions, they must be binding.

Access to such structures of gender democracy is important for women's equality in all provinces. However, it is crucial that not only the presence, but also the process, of GBA be coordinated across Canada. Gender-based policy analysis, as mentioned earlier, has the danger of undermining democracy if it becomes simply a tool of the privileged, or of "experts." But gender-sensitive budgets and policymaking need not be exclusionary. In South Africa, the women's budget is conducted by several non-governmental organizations (NGOs) and the Parliamentary Joint Committee on the Improvement of the Quality of Life and Status of Women, and popular education initiatives have been developed, with material written in plain language, to demystify the budget for people. In other countries too, the gender budget is collaborative, in Switzerland, for instance, between labour unions and NGOs, and in Uganda between the Parliamentary Women's Caucus and an NGO called the Forum for Women in Democracy. The United Nations Development Fund for Women (UNIFEM) also provides assistance through workshops and technical support in gender budgeting (United Nations 2000). These are good steps that can be expanded beyond organized groups to communities. The ultimate goal should be participatory gender-based policy analysis and gender budgets: a democratic budget and policy process that represents the priorities of people. Gender-based policy analysis must be taken back to its original conception as a participatory process between citizens, organized social forces, and the state (Bakker and Elson 1998). And it must be employed universally across the country.

So when we speak of democratization, federalism cannot be forgotten. A core question for femocratic administration is how can democratization of both intergovernmental relations and women's policy structures facilitate coordination between femocrats across levels of government? According to Rankin and Vickers (2001), alliances between feminists in the bureaucracy at both levels of government have been key in Australia to women's policy development:

> We identify the effective coordination and strategic co-operation among femocrats working at the Commonwealth and state levels as especially important to successes in policies and programs in the violence field. Our Canadian research suggests that successes at the sub-national level in Canada, most notably in the case of anti-violence strategies in Quebec, can be traced to the same factors. (25–6)

In Australia, it is also significant that femocrats at both levels of government cooperate around the use of the Commonwealth spending power in developing policies for women (Rankin and Vickers 2001). The relevance to Canada, where there is "limited coordination among governments and minimal coordination among femocrats working at the various levels" (ibid., 57), is quite evident, and the voices of state feminists on the spending power are absent.

Following the Australian practice wherein a "systematic structure of co-operation" was developed, Rankin and Vickers (2001) recommend an annual conference that brings together activists, femocrats, and politicians at the federal and provincial levels. Although there are existing inter-governmental links, Rankin and Vickers have something much more comprehensive and participatory in mind. This seems to mesh with many of those I interviewed from the Ontario public service, who had some positive things to say about cross-jurisdictional cooperation, but would like to see it developed much further. In her more recent work, Vickers (2011) stresses the importance of "multi-level femocrat networks" for advancing women's equality in federations (141).

Another central concern for feminist bureaucratic restructuring is the place of women's structures of representation within the overall power structures of the state. Some believe that it is very important for women's structures of representation, like the OWD, to be stand-alone, with a central, concentrated role. Others, worried about marginalization and ghettoization, prefer an integration model. These differences were evident in interviews. One interviewee who favoured the first, saw the OWD as functionally stand-alone, but without a full minister, and argued that if women's issues were the minister's only portfolio, the issues would get more priority in cabinet and more time and attention from the minister.[7] While a former staff member cautioned that it could become a problem if women's policy machinery becomes too isolated or independent, she thought the best scenario would be a Ministry of Equity Issues, like the new Children's Ministry under the Liberals, with its own stand-alone ministry and minister. The second-best option for her would be to subsume the directorate into the most powerful, most influential place, the Cabinet Office.[8]

Some saw this as the ideal – to house the directorate within a central ministry, but noted the real possibility that underfunding and limited status and authority could undermine its effectiveness. One source used a federal example as an illustration, suggesting that if SWC were to be placed in the Privy Council Office (PCO), there is the possibility it would simply become integrated, which she believes is what has happened to multiculturalism.[9] Another asserted, "I actually don't necessarily think it has to be stand-alone ... I think there are pros and cons to a stand-alone agency ... There could be real advantages to being part of a bigger department if it meant you had more clout at civil service or Cabinet tables."[10] This reaffirms Sue Findlay's (1989) point, building on Mahon's unequal structure of representation, that women's policy machinery is located on the margins of bureaucratic power (9). But Findlay also stresses that the powerlessness of state feminists is related not only to structure, but also to their relationship to the women's movement.

This is why I was also convinced by many of those I interviewed who put less emphasis on structure than on personnel, agency, and political context. Despite her comments above, one participant insisted that there is "not a structural answer." What is most important for her is the people, how they perceive their roles, their leadership, and their vision. She saw Joan Andrew as a very effective ADM due to her proactive approach that went beyond focusing on the gender impact of policies, and was based on building visibility and relationships with other ministries dealing with programs for women, like COMSOC and Justice. She believed that no longer having their own ADM was a great loss, but she maintained that it is the minister's commitment that might matter most in the end.[11] These are reinforced by the observations made in chapter 4 that government hostility trumped any structural issues. Yet this is not to say that structure is irrelevant.[12] Both political mobilization and structural change are important. Key to femocratic administration is creating democratic, feminist structures whose ultimate power is drawn from the community.

The need to simultaneously address bureaucratic structures and processes while building a culture of participation is clearly illuminated by the case study of the OWD. The directorate's experience demonstrates that the governing principle of neutrality, as one example, functions as a serious obstacle to feminist representation. Therefore, the notion of neutrality is also important to femocratic administration. Lipsky's (1980) model of the "street-level bureaucrat" who has a close relationship to citizens better conforms to feminist ideals of service delivery. Evans and Wekerle (1997) point out that "women's mobilization and activism has been most apparent in the public sector, a sector in which women have made inroads both as workers and in obtaining programs and legislation directed at promoting greater gender equality" (22). Selden (1997) also makes a link between procedural democracy, through strengthened representation, and substantive democracy. In her study of the Farmers Home Administration's Rural Housing Loans program in the United States, her findings indicated that "administrators who perceive their role as that of an advocate or representative of minority interests are more likely to make decisions that benefit the minority community" (140).

In assessing the effectiveness of women's policy agencies in eleven jurisdictions, Lovenduski et al.'s RNGS study sets advocating for the women's movement as a central criterion. Their project reinforces through comparative empirical evidence, the importance of state feminist structures that identify with, and are responsive to, women's movement demands (Lovenduski 2005; Lovenduski et al. 2005b).[13] The RNGS model describes state feminists operating in this vein as "insiders" (Lovenduski 2005; Haussman and Sauer 2007b). It is appropriate, therefore, that Findlay (1995) has referred to her role as a femocrat as an "outsider on the inside" (40). This is the raison d'être of state feminism. It is (or should be) a branch of the women's movement that exists within the state. Its ultimate goal is to advance a feminist agenda, or to become, as Wainwright (2002) calls it, the "enabling state." In an enabling state, state feminists would not simply advocate *on behalf* of communities, they would support communities in advocating *on their own behalf*. This requires shifting energies towards coordination, the empowerment of the excluded, and the creation of networks (Stivers 1993). For Stivers, this is the truly legitimate role of state administrators: "Public servants deserve our approbation not because they understand the public interest better than the rest of us but because they are willing to bear more of the burden for facilitating its accomplishment" (ibid., 135).

In chapter 3, it was apparent that not all state feminists in Ontario share this vision of an insider culture of advocacy and power sharing. Some identified themselves within the traditional public administration model based on ministerial accountability and neutral, professional expertise. They fall within the "restoration of professional management" model of Albo's (1993) typology.[14] Stivers (1993) also critiques this defensive stance within public administration, viewing it as an attempt at "mobilizing support for administrative business as usual" (3). However, others explicitly framed themselves primarily as advocates for, and accountable to, the women's movement, and thus, fit comfortably within the mould of femocratic administration.

This advocacy orientation is imperative for rethinking accountability mechanisms, and reconceptualizing knowledge, expertise, and advocacy. Traditional public administration holds that the accountability mechanism involves public servants being ultimately responsible to the government of the day, not necessarily to the community. In this way, ministerial accountability serves to undermine democracy. Burt and Lorenzin (1997) provide a useful illustration, where once elected, feminists in the Ontario NDP came to see "themselves as the spokespeople for responsible government" who had to distance themselves from the very movements and "special interest" groups in which they were once active (226). It does not bode well for the representative claims of government when advocating for citizens by the public service is seen as contrary to its interest, which should be, after all, democracy. A transformative gender regime of public administration would position state femocrats as advocates for the communities they represent, and as facilitators of popular participation.

It should be noted that such an understanding of advocacy is not a complete break from current governance practices. There has been a historical understanding in Canada that certain departments are to be advocacy-oriented. Some participants emphasized this in reference to Agriculture or Environment. As was seen in the preceding chapters, the problem is that the function of "advocacy" is used to marginalize some departments, namely, those representing the less powerful, while others, often the strongest advocates for their constituents, are framed in coordinative terms, and as acting for the "general interest."

Mahon (1977) uses the Department of Finance as an example where the appearance of independence masks its pursuit of a particular form of political economy, and its relationship to dominant social forces. She reminds us that "all 'representatives' are not equal" and that the "quality" of representation provided depends on one's position within the power structures of the state. Some representatives are able to gain valuable concessions for those they represent, while others are more likely to gain only limited concessions, or to end up making them to the more powerful (ibid.). Therefore, "all social forces achieve a form of representation – although the relations among the representatives express the inequalities established in civil society" (Mahon 1977, 193). This is precisely what Mahon means by an unequal structure of representation.

Following Mahon, what I am suggesting is that, currently, all departments should be properly understood as engaging in advocacy. Some are simply better able to fulfil this function due to their place in the structures of power. Within this context, marginalized advocates, like state feminists, can only draw their power from the communities they represent, and by strengthening their accountability to them. And this is also not unprecedented. Pross (1995) has used the concept of "policy communities" to draw attention to the standing relationships between government agencies, the media, academia, and interest groups around specific policy issues. Even though my approach departs from Pross's pluralist framework by challenging bureaucratic notions of neutrality and expertise, and by emphasizing the role of state feminists in *actively* mobilizing those on the "outside,"[15] he speaks to existing policy practice that can be broadened and deepened to advance a gender regime based on more popular forms of democracy and substantive representation.

My research indicates that such a gender regime has resonance with many state feminists. The struggle to develop and strengthen ties between the directorate and the community was an ongoing theme in the interviews. A recurring metaphor used by the participants was that of the conduit, with some envisioning their role in more benign terms, as a pathway, or intermediary, between state and society, and others going much further, identifying themselves as facilitators of participation and dialogue. In fact, concern about movement away from advocacy under the NPM was one of the central preoccupations for those in the OWD, signalling a thirst for democratic change inside the public service.

Femocratic administration involves a shift in accountability from the government to the community, and therefore does entail some departure from the current model of ministerial accountability, where civil servants provide "neutral" advice, on which elected officials then act. But as Albo (1993) argues, the original democratic principles on which accountability rested have been blunted. Democratic accountability has actually come to mean that civil servants are responsible for implementing the governing party's agenda, rather than ensuring accountability to the people. Beyond the fact that this current form of ministerial accountability assumes a democratic electoral system that is illusory,[16] it is also the source of a central contradiction faced by the directorate that I identified in chapter 4, namely: what happens when a government is elected that is hostile to the principles of equality on which state feminism rests? Is the OWD's role then to implement an anti-equity agenda because it is ultimately responsible to the government of the day? Or, are state feminists responsible for identifying, and then translating, the feminist community's issues and interests to those elected to represent all citizens?

Femocratic administration is not about bypassing "democratically" elected representatives. It is not about increasing the personal power of femocrats. It is about empowering communities. It is about supporting and strengthening the autonomous women's movement. It is about helping to mobilize those who are marginalized in the political system to make their political claims heard, ultimately strengthening the accountability of elected members to their citizens. Femocratic administration challenges the growing centralization of power in cabinets and the insulation of politicians from popular control. In the end, democratic accountability still remains with elected officials, but it exists alongside new forms of accountability that prioritize inclusion and community engagement (Feldman and Khademian 2001).

At a basic level, such a change requires placing the onus of responsibility for community participation on state feminists, rather than the reverse, which continues to be prevalent. Rankin and Vickers (2001), for instance, give advice to women's organizations that they "don't wait to be asked" for their input. Although their point is for groups to upset government control of policy consultations, Rankin and Vickers perpetuate the idea that it is the responsibility of groups themselves, and not the state, and in this case, state feminists, to ensure their participation. They propose that groups must begin to take more initiative in building relationships with public servants willing to play the femocrat role on specific issues. That is, women's orga- nizations must accept more responsibility for building policy networks – networks of potential femocrats in various departments whose jobs give them an interest in the specific policy or program. In particular, women's groups can help potential femocrats educate themselves, especially about diversity and minority women's views and needs by providing them with information, including them in e-mail and list-servers, and inviting them to group meetings and conferences. (Rankin and Vickers 2001, 55)

Here, it is the responsibility of already overburdened and underfunded women's groups not only to seek out the attention of femocrats, but also to "educate" them about diversity. Such thinking is echoed in Carty and Brand's (1993) recounting of an Ontario conference on "vis- ible minority" women that "was not a conference to question state practices which produce inequality. Instead, it became a conference to question the various constituencies' 'shortcomings' in making their demands heard by the state" (176). Panitch (1993) has also emphasized that communities, for a variety of reasons, ranging from passivity to marginalization, are not always organized, or prepared to participate, and need state assistance in doing so. While communities are certainly pivotal in keeping the state accountable, femocrats need to take the facilitation of participation and organization as one of their principal responsibilities.

A substantial degree of discretion is required to allow femocrats to pursue the role of an advocate for the disempowered, rather than as a "neutral" analyst, so it must not be forgotten that discretion can be problematic. Lipsky (1980) reminds us that while discretion is meant to promote *advocacy*, it can also allow for discrimination, or further the privileges of the advantaged.[17] There is no easy answer to this dilemma, but as we have seen, it would be naive to think that the line between politics and administration is currently a clear one, or that bureau- crats do not already have significant discretion and social biases (Albo 1993). To avoid replicating these problems, Albo (1993) advocates the strengthening of "procedural justice: appeals processes, ombudsper- sons, and advocacy bodies with real resources and powers of admin- istrative sanction to ensure equality of treatment" (30). Sossin (1993) also stresses that increased discretion must necessarily be accompanied by greater accountability, and an empowered citizen ability to critique (392). He sees public participation as necessary to "undermine the privilege of expertise in the formation and implementation of public policy" (383).

It can be added that rethinking the idea of what is "expertise," or "valid knowledge" (Wainwright 2003, 21), rather than rejecting it, would place greater value on lived experience. Stivers (1993) maintains that administration's "preference for hard data over soft data is a reflection of cultural preferences for the masculine over the feminine," and that its bias towards detached knowledge must be challenged in order to create space for "genuine dialogue with *citizens*, whose opinions can more easily be discounted or dismissed because they are not considered expert" (39, 49). She advances a "feminist *phronesis* [practical wisdom] [that] seeks connection with marginalized people in order to ground practice in the real conditions of their lives" (143).

Femocratic administration exposes the artificial division between politics and administration, and challenges the construction of expertise based on elitism and the exclusion of popular knowledges. It is not only male bureaucrats who have constructed notions of expertise. Within the directorate there were disagreements about whose feminist knowledge "counted" – that of elected members or bureaucrats – and there was little emphasis on popular knowledge. Wainwright (2002) stresses the need to move beyond the notion of the state as "knowing agent." She argues that practical knowledge has not been valued, even by social democratic parties, who also rely on the knowledges of elites (1993). Femocratic administration takes seriously "other forms of knowledge – as expressed, for example, in the daily lives of ordinary people and in the media of popular culture" (Wainwright 1993, 114).

Valuing this knowledge advances both procedural and substantive democracy by fostering participation and providing new ways of thinking about public policy problems and solutions. Albo (1993) suggests that taking popular knowledge seriously would avoid public policy gaffes where, for example, "daycare centres are located far away from transportation nodes ... [or] community centres are open only during working hours" (23). According to Susan Phillips (1993), "citizen groups ... serve as vehicles for direct participation, alternative sources of policy expertise, effective mechanisms for communication of information and vocal watchdogs over governments" (12). This was seen in practice at the municipal level with Britain's Greater London Council (GLC) in the 1980s. The GLC reached out to, and funded, community groups, and the groups elected representatives to council committees to work together on ideas and strategies. This approach to political decision-making recognizes the specialized knowledge and experience that community groups can contribute to the policy process (Rebick 2000). Fostering popular knowledge is part of state feminism's accountability to the community. The bureaucracy, though, must also be representative of those to whom it is accountable.

Representative Bureaucracy

Women's representation in state institutions is the subject of much feminist debate. For example, "radical/cultural feminism rejects strategies of engagement based on the view of the state as a potential ally for women, believing that change is a matter of consciousness, not of political strategy, organization, or action" (Vickers 1997b, 30). Postmodern feminists, such as Chantal Mouffe, see representation as impossible, leading to some women artificially "speaking for" other women (ibid.). Nonetheless, chapter 1 demonstrates that some quite sophisticated feminist theories of the state have been developed that are able to capture the paradox of strategic interaction with the state, and the continued significance of representation for women.

Despite her strong critique of bureaucracy, Ferguson (1984) understands that "people have to resist from where they are, not from where they would like to be" (208). She accepts that "entry into the public world, now almost exclusively a bureaucratic world, is necessary to some extent, if for no other reason than to be able to speak against it" (208). Ferguson concludes that "to challenge bureaucracy in the name of the values and goals of feminist discourse is to undermine the chain of command, equalize the participants, subvert the monopoly of information and secrecy of decision-making, and essentially seek to democratize the organization" (209). Surely, "democratization" cannot occur if the representation of men and "fortyish, publicly heterosexual, able-bodied, white, well-educated and urban" women (Vickers 1997b, 26) remains dominant. A representative bureaucracy involves the active recruitment of women from the diverse communities that state feminists are there to represent.

Not only feminists share a concern for a more representative bureaucracy. Feminists are part of a larger movement trying to emphasize that at the very least "the composition of the bureaucracy should reflect in fair proportion certain demographic characteristics of society" (Brooks 1994, 310). Femocratic administration, therefore, must reflect the diversity of Canadian women. Unfortunately, there is a long way to go.

Vickers (1997b) reminds us that "nowhere in the world are women present in state-level institutions in numbers that reflect their proportion of the population" (21). While in 1997, women made up roughly half of the federal public service, they were still heavily concentrated in clerical jobs, with 84.0 per cent of "administrative support" performed by women, but only 23 per cent of those in the executive (Kernaghan and Siegel 1999).

In terms of recent hiring into the federal public service,[18] this trend remains consistent, as in 1998, 81.7 per cent of "administrative support" jobs were filled by women, but only 28.6% of those in the executive (Canada, Treasury Board Secretariat 1998). In 2002–3, 52.8% of all federal public service employees were women, but only 33.8% had executive positions (Canada, Treasury Board Secretariat 2004). The representation of persons with disabilities and persons in a visible minority is even more deficient. In 1997, persons with disabilities made up 4.8% of the available workforce, yet were only 3.3% of the public service. By 2002–3, the representation of persons with disabilities in the federal public service was 5.6% (ibid.). Those in a visible minority staffed only 4.7% of the public service in 1997, despite representing 9% of the overall workforce (Kernaghan and Siegel 1999). The figure for 2002–3 was 7.4%, with 83.8% of visible minorities holding "indeterminate" positions and with heavy concentration in administration (Canada, Treasury Board Secretariat 2004). Similar patterns of unstable and administrative positions exist for Aboriginal peoples (ibid.). For women, people with disabilities, visible minorities, and Aboriginal peoples, the hiring of "indeterminate" employees is on the rise (ibid.), indicating the growing precariousness of government employment for all designated groups.[19] Agócs uses 2011 data to demonstrate that in spite of federal employment equity policy, women, Aboriginal peoples, and people with disabilities continue to be over-represented in temporary and lower salary positions in public administration, and visible minorities are particularly under-represented (2012). With the recent round of federal cuts to the public service, the picture is unlikely to improve (Agócs 2012).

These figures raise serious questions about the commitment to employment equity policies that have existed now for two decades at the federal level and even more so at the provincial level in Ontario, where employment equity policy is completely lacking. They also elucidate the challenges that a femocratic administration faces. Magnusson (1993) asserts that "only if movements are present in the operations of the state can representation from without be really effective ... Social movements are both inside and outside the oppressive relations that have to be changed. Thus the movement for democracy radiates from centres inside and outside the state" (127). Findlay (1987) has also stressed the importance of representation arguing, that "both the under-representation of women in the bureaucratic decision-making process and lack of expertise on women's issues made it difficult to argue that the state could act in the interest of women's equality" (37).

Agócs (2012) outlines several justifications, both procedural and sub-stantive, for representative bureaucracy. The first is symbolic, under-scoring the responsibility of the public sector to act as "model employer" (1). In addition, Agócs (2012) maintains that "citizens and taxpayers have a right to expect that they, and their children, can find careers in the public service they support if they so choose and have appropriate qualifications" (2). Finally, she makes an argument about substantive representation, showing that in the United States, the "literature shows that public organizations with larger proportions of women and/or minorities in decision-making roles are more likely to produce out-comes compatible with the interests of women and/or minorities than similar organizations with fewer women and/or minorities" (2).

As important as numerical representation is, Findlay (1993a) rightly points out that traditionally "solutions focused on obtaining represen-tation in the state, rather than transforming the state itself" (156). Like Findlay, others stress a more substantive definition of representation. Vickers notes that representation in the state is not enough, and must be combined with the democratization of civil society (Vickers 1997b). Findlay emphasizes participation more than representation, arguing that "a struggle for a 'different kind of *relationship* between state and society' rather than a 'different kind of state'" (Findlay 1993a, 166) is required. This prospect will now be explored.

Democratic Administration

Sawer and Grey (2008) point out that "there is no guarantee that struc-tures created within, and alongside, the state will continue to serve as spaces for women's empowerment" (10). This is why ongoing and active participation is so vital.

Democratic administration is about a transformation of the state, not based on periodic shifts brought on by electoral and party politics, but on a permanent, although constantly developing, process of democra-tization and shifting power relations. In order to displace the power relations embodied in the state, the empowering of social movement organizations and citizens is needed. This "involves the reallocation of power to subordinate or relatively powerless people ... empowerment involves altering power relationships. Because underlying inequalities are not disturbed, and because underlying inequalities shift over time, empowerment is never permanent" (Handler 1996, 217–18). It is clear from the Ontario case that empowering communities constitutes a major threat to neoliberalism. Undermining the advocacy role of femocrats and disrupting ties between the women's movement and the OWD was central to the NPM strategy of the Harris government.

Empowerment entails a reconfiguration of the relationship between state and society or, for femocratic administration, between feminists inside and outside of the state. One aspect of this accountability, as both Albo and Panitch suggest, is to rely less on the appointment of administrators, and more on their direct election by those they represent (Albo 1993; Panitch 1993). Panitch gives an example of workers affected by health and safety legislation electing the inspectors. Similarly, its constituents, such as those in the violence against women community, or those working on women's labour market issues, could elect certain positions in the OWD. In archival documents, there is also reference to suggestions that the former OACWI base its appointments on recommendations from community groups (Ontario, OWD 1984a, "Estimates Office").

Adamson et al. (1988) make a distinction between two types of feminism in Canada, institutionalized and grassroots feminism: "Institutionalized feminism operates within traditional institutions – inside political parties and government ministries, for example – while grassroots feminism is more community-based, emphasizing collective organizing, consciousness-raising, and reaching out to women 'on the street'" (12).

The goal of femocratic administration is to dull these distinctions. Strong ties between femocrats and the outside women's movement must be strengthened and maintained (Findlay 1987; Mackintosh 1993; O'Neil and Sutherland 1997; Grant 1988; Franzway et al. 1989; Sawer 1990). In their comparative work, Outshoorn and Kantola (2007a) link the power of women's policy agencies to the strength of autonomous women's movements. Likewise, Findlay (1995) states:

What I learned from my own experience in the 1970s was that there were moments when feminists could use the structures of representation to good advantage, but that their success depended on a strategy that would

> link insiders and outsiders in struggles to make women's perspectives the
> basis for policy and program development. (111)

The early years of the federal Women's Program in the Department of
the Secretary of State have been held up as a model. Geller-Schwartz
(1995) states that "according to one of its former directors, the staff of
the Women's Program considered themselves accountable to the agenda
of the women's movement rather than to government priorities" (45).
The program, though, which sought to empower grassroots feminists
groups, became weakened by an increasingly bureaucratized funding
procedure (Geller-Schwartz 1995), a point that I will return to later on.

A close relationship to women's groups was also important to the
Women's Bureau in the Ministry of Labour (Geller-Schwartz 1995).
Geller-Schwartz maintains that

> femocrats have worked directly, indirectly, or even surreptitiously, using
> external organizations to further their own institution's policy goals. On
> the one hand, they marshalled their resources within the state through
> research, public education, and, when possible, direct subsidy, to foster
> pressure from domestic lobbies, and on the other, they exerted pressure
> for compliance with Canada's international commitments. (50)

Dobrowolsky (2000), discussing women's struggles around the development of the Charter of Rights and Freedoms, points out how important
it was that "work from 'within' was bolstered from 'without'" (722).
Porter (2003) makes similar observations in regard to pregnancy
and maternity-related policy. Inside information provided by femocrats was also invaluable to NAC's lobbying for pay equity (Geller-
Schwartz 1995).

The Australian case demonstrates most dramatically the effect of
the *lack* of a strong relationship between feminists inside and outside
of the state. The femocracy was originally spawned from the women's
movement, and was "widely seen as the arm of the women's movement in government" (Eisenstein 1991, 32). It was recognized that "a
femocrat's power within the bureaucracy was crucially dependent
upon the extent of the pressure being exerted on government and politicians by activist feminist groups outside the bureaucracy" (ibid., 34).
By the 1980s, though, these connections increasingly disintegrated, as
the strength of the Australian women's movement began to decline
(Eisenstein 1991, 1996; Sawer 1990).

There are also numerous examples from the Canadian bureaucracy, where a lack of accountability to the women's movement is evident. Cohen (1993) says that "the bodies established by government appointees often provided important support for feminist initiatives, but since they were not accountable to the women's movement itself, they often acted in ways that received a great deal of criticism from the movement" (21). The absence of ties to the women's movement (and unrepresentativeness of femocrats) was evident when the Canadian Advisory Council on the Status of Women (CACSW) published a report in 1988 entitled *Immigrant Women in Canada: A Policy Perspective*. The report, which seemed to insinuate that immigrant women had greater job opportunities than Canadian-born women, was widely criticized by women's groups. As Eisenstein (1991) points out, "it is entirely possible to empower women to oppress their sisters once they achieve high office" (32), and so accountability to the women's movement is an essential ingredient in femocratic administration.

Ties to the women's movement not only maintains accountability, it also supports the role of a femocrat as an "inside activist." The problem faced by femocrats, as seen by Adamson et al. (1988), "is that they lose the power they could wield through being part of a larger constituency, and at the same time are separated from a body of support that could help to offset pressures within the system to conform" (183). Lamoureux (1987) has identified the fact that in Quebec, the "CSF [Conseil du statut de la femme] is well aware that it only has power to the extent that its demands are backed up by an organized women's movement" (61). Close ties between the CSF and women's groups have been very important in securing policy advancements in Quebec (Lavigne 1997; Lamoureux 1987). Likewise, Alboim (1997) argues that the

> best way for the Ontario Women's Directorate to achieve its goals is to form a partnership between the inside and outside structures ... When a partnership is formed, the best features of both sides come to bear on a given issue. The strength of the internal group is its knowledge of government process, priorities, and personalities. External groups are independent and are closer to the front-line problems. (224)

Mackintosh (1993) explains that "one of the strongest lessons of the Greater London Council economic policy was that it was working relations with outside groups, and pressure from outsiders, that turned general ideas into effective policies" (44).

There seems to be agreement among many I interviewed in the Ontario bureaucracy that strong pressure from the outside and mobilizing communities is very important. One person interviewed saw more democracy and participation as the only way forward. Because of the "difficulties of a unit like the OWD in terms of relating to the outside and having some kind of impact on the inside," she emphasized an ongoing connection with the outside. She insisted that they "can't govern without it … [Participation] must permeate all political processes in their specificity." For this former public servant, democratizing the state's relationship with the community requires an understanding of "how they try to respond to the demands that a community of women might make, different communities of women, and yet do it in a way that does, in the end, limit the kinds of policies that are produced, and the number of policies."[20] Others were also concerned about how to enhance connections to the outside, and how to move away from the "consultation model" where governments usually know in advance what they are willing to do.[21]

These public sector workers confirm Panitch's (1993) point "that pressure for democratizing the state does not come entirely from outside the government: it also comes from those who work in the public and para-public sectors themselves" (7). Accordingly, in chapter 3, I stress that feminists inside the state have political agency, and thus can be powerful forces for democracy. But equally important is linking these inside forces to those on the outside. Therefore, this book is about a strategic reorientation of the women's movement, towards mobilizing around the democratization of the Canadian state, including all levels of the state, and the relationships between them.

Drawing attention to the relationship between federalism, feminism, and democracy is important in this regard. Gender democracy depends on developing institutions of popular participation and planning in the realm of intergovernmental relations to displace the top-down process of executive federalism.[22] This will entail a shift in focus away from the Social Union Framework Agreement (SUFA) model – where citizen groups are simply monitoring the products of executive federalism – towards the creation of structures where social actors can take an active role in determining both the "who" (process) and the "what" (substance) of social policy. Although it is clear from femocrat accounts that women's ministers participate only on the margins of executive federalism, the model of elite decision-making is, nevertheless, reproduced in these FPT processes. None of those interviewed discussed any input from the women's policy community at the FPT level, reinforcing conclusions by Inwood and Cameron, and social policy participants in the SUFA review, that stress the closed, exclusive, and undemocratic nature of intergovernmental relations.

Opening the intergovernmental process to the community is essential to moving beyond executive federalism. In executive federalism, the only "legitimate" policy voices, as Cameron (2004) has argued, are first ministers and senior bureaucrats (49). These voices are then considered to be representative of regional concerns, even though, in reality, they are speaking for very specific interests. In the case of childcare, the difficulty negotiating the FPT process and the exclusionary nature of executive federalism stands out as the real obstacle to progress on social policy. It is only by excluding advocates from the discussion that such a divided policy perspective could emerge. Had the policy process around childcare that occurred in the 1980s (and this is still true today) actively involved citizens and groups, a much clearer consensus on the need for a national childcare system would become readily evident.[23] Thus, I concur with White's (1997) call for the creation of structures for including social actors as "key decision makers and standard setters in social security" in order to protect the rights of social citizenship and to ensure that programs and services are "accountable to the women who use them."

There were places in the OWD archival records where direct links were made between the limitations of certain policies and the exclusion of groups from the policy process. Some correspondence about the federal Language Instruction for Newcomers to Canada (LINC) program voiced concern about the lack of consultation with communities, particularly immigrant women. In this case, it was also pointed out that the federal government was narrowly addressing the issue of language training within its own jurisdictional frame, instead of considering the community's broader perspective. A representative of the Ontario Women's Action on Training Coalition pointed out that "ESL is a training issue, not merely a citizenship issue" (OWD 1992b, "Memo re: Integration"). For this group, their understanding of the policy issues crossed jurisdictions. Therefore, ideas like those seen from Rankin and Vickers (2001) for regular conferences that include federal and provincial femocrats and feminist activists are one interesting way to begin to address this problem.

While all of this is theoretically powerful, the practical implications are such that, in the present environment, the resources required for extensive interaction between state and societal feminists do not exist.

Many have discussed the participation that was nurtured through the Greater London Council in Britain during the 1980s, partly through the provision of government funding.[24] State funding of women's groups is, therefore, absolutely essential (Rebick 1998; Albo 1993; Handler 1996; Langille 1993).

The issue of state funding for organizations is a highly contested issue within the Canadian women's movement and other popular movements. Many believe that state funding has deleterious effects including de-radicalization, co-optation, and loss of autonomy (Loney 1977; Ferguson 1984). Carty and Brand (1993) are particularly suspicious of state funding, asserting that it makes the National Action Committee on the Status of Women (NAC)[25] "a conduit of legitimation" and "an arm of the state" (178, 179). This debate was also ongoing among members of NAC itself, some of whom preferred to maintain independence and others who felt a sense of entitlement to government funding (Vickers et al. 1993). In her book conversation with former NAC president Judy Rebick, Kiké Roach asserts that "for most of its life, NAC has been about 80 per cent funded by government. But today, only about 20 per cent of NAC's budget comes from the feds. I think that is a good thing, because the less feminists rely on government, the more self-determining – and critical of government – we can be" (Rebick and Roach 1996, 99). The concerns raised about state funding are warranted. The seemingly partisan nature of funding by the Tories during the 1980s (where NAC, increasingly radical, and anti–free trade and anti–Meech Lake Accord, saw drastic cuts to its funding, while the anti-feminist group REAL Women [Realistic, Equal, Active, for Life] received state funding for the first time) reinforces the threat to independence associated with state funding.[26] But in such cases, the larger problem is that there is no autonomous mechanism in place to secure funding, making groups vulnerable to partisan interference.

Public funding does also raise the complication that not all of civil society is progressive (Maley 2011), and state funds may be used to support anti-feminist or other reactionary organizations. This cannot be entirely avoided, but it can be mitigated. Absolutely, groups receiving public funding must be engaged in activities that are compatible with Canada's equality commitments in the Charter of Rights and Freedoms, and the UN Convention on the Elimination of All Forms of Discrimination against Women (CEDAW). Furthermore, organizations must be accountable and transparent, with membership information publicly available to support their representational claims. Ultimately, the democratic importance outweighs the risks.

There are substantial issues of representation involved in the public funding of community groups. Phillips (1993) maintains that "a necessary function of the state is to compensate for the inherent inequalities by including representatives of the less privileged groups in political institutions and consultations, and by providing assistance to these groups (perhaps in the form of public funding) so that they, too, can have a voice" (12). Moreover, political parties receive state funding, yet are highly inadequate in representing the interests and identities of women and other marginalized groups. Teghtsoonian (2004) cites Laurel Weldon's conclusions that "women's policy agencies and women's community-based activism 'in combination ... give women a stronger voice in the policy-making process than does the presence of women in the legislature'" (3). Popular organizations have legitimate claims to funding given their importance in making up for the failings of other institutions of representation in Canada. For instance, it is particularly difficult for visible minority immigrants to participate in the Canadian electoral system, as they often feel a sense of disappointment in the racism and lack of representativeness in the system (Simard 1991). As Simard argues, visible minorities often see participation in community groups as better alternatives to political parties.

This is also true for women, as women's organizations in Canada have been functioning as alternative avenues of representation. NAC, for instance, called itself a "parliament of women," making clear representational claims. In the face of such representational promises, it struggled to maintain a nationally based focus and membership, and a main reason for accepting state funding was that, "given the country's vast territory and sparse population, few pan-Canadian or even provincial/territorial groups could survive without government support" (Vickers et al. 1993, 28). For organizations, like NAC, that commit to accessibility, requiring translation services and sign interpretation, bilingual publications, regional offices, and (well) paid staff, the funding requirements are considerable (ibid.). Chouinard (1999) has documented comparable challenges in maintaining a national strategy for women with disabilities after the federal cuts to funding for the Disabled Women's Network (DAWN). State funding for popular organizations is a basic right of citizenship (Albo 1993), as it is fundamental to the functioning of democracy.

This right of citizenship is the reason the funding of women's and other organizations has a history in Canada. The early mandate of the Women's Program was based on the principle that, in a democratic society, groups must be funded to adequately provide alternatives. NAC explains that the Women's Program "fund was a creation of what is referred to by many women as an equality fund. It recognized the fact that women had a right to democratic participation in Canadian society and that given our political, social and economic inequality, the necessary financial and other resources must be provided as a proactive measure" (NAC 1998). Support has also been provided in kind. In the past, the Toronto Board of Education and City Hall have been committed to working with community organizations, providing space, food, transportation, and childcare for participants. They have fostered an advocacy model "permitting the movements to become co-architects of policy development and implementation" (McCuaig 1993, 227).

Regretfully, we are moving further and further away from this model. The retaliatory cuts[27] made at the federal level by Brian Mulroney in the late 1980s were not reversed by the Chrétien and Martin Liberals, and have been met with a new round of cuts by the current minority and majority Conservative governments.[28] The changes made to funding under the Liberals were strongly opposed by NAC and other women's organizations. The federal government ended core funding, and as NAC (1998) states, "under new criteria, NAC's work will be measured on a project by project basis and this is contrary to our mandate. Women's lives are not short term projects" (3). Further changes in 2006 to the funding criteria have eliminated support for advocacy and research through the Women's Program altogether, and raise grave concerns for democracy. NAC has stressed that "it is through the access to financial resources of the Women's Program Fund that women's groups have been able to participate to a large degree in the democratic political processes of this country. A cut to this funding is a cut to women's democratic rights" (2).

By 2004, NAC was on the verge of financial collapse, and attempts to rebuild through a short-term government grant have met with little success. This is precisely why one of the Canadian Women's March Committee's thirteen demands was $30 million in core funding for equality-seeking women's organizations, as part of the "Our Fair Share" campaign, which asks for $2.00 for every woman and girl child in Canada (Canadian Women's March Committee 2000). The work that is being done around the need for reinstating federal funding of women's groups is fundamental to strengthening "inside/outside" ties and remobilizing the women's movement. Public funding needs to exist at the provincial and local levels too.

The financial challenges of women's groups are directly related to women's subordinate place in the economy. Thus, the democratization of the public sector is only one side of the coin, and requires a corresponding democratization of the market (Albo 1993; Panitch 1993) and the family. As Panitch has pointed out, democratic administration "still leaves a private sector in which the corporations that control our economy and culture are not democratically structured at all" (5) and so democratization of the state must be combined with, and will contribute to, democratization of the market,[29] including global trade and finance and domestic labour conditions and working time.[30] It must be noted, though, that efforts at developing democratic administration and a democratic workplace consistently fail to consider specific issues of gender, race, class, nationality, sexuality, ability, age, etc.[31] A feminist[32] democratization, or a "femocratization" of the state and the market must be the focus of political struggles.

Democracy is about the participation of individuals, and groups, so greater direct citizen participation, beyond organized groups, is necessary for democratic administration, but there are practical barriers to full citizen participation. The reality of women's complicated relationship to the public and private must be recognized. Panitch, while providing useful suggestions for a more participatory state, does not acknowledge many of the gendered barriers to this participation. The persistent gendered division of labour in the family, in which women's unpaid work interferes with full political participation, is often not scrutinized. Participation takes time, and time is gendered. Phillips (1991) stresses that "in societies where the division of labour is ordered by sex (that is, every society we know), time becomes a crucial constraint on women and meetings an additional burden" (21). She reminds us that the "position women occupy in contemporary societies is one that (a) discourages women from participating equally in meetings that are open to both women and men; and (b) discourages the majority of women from the intense involvement that a women's movement can mean" (142). Phillips has identified the "tyranny of domestic commitments" (38) as one of the largest obstacles to participatory democracy. She argues that "democratic government is subverted and denied by the blatantly undemocratic ways in which our social (usually working) lives are organized, and that a more substantial democracy will depend on restructuring the workplace to permit genuine and equal participation" (38). Women's citizenship is circumscribed by their responsibility for social reproduction (Stivers 1993).

Women's paid work is central to this project of democratization. Globalization has brought increasingly precarious employment, and much of this work is done by women. It includes part-time, temporary, contract, and home work. Almost all of this work is un-unionized, and it is only recently that unions in Canada have shown any interest in organizing such workers. Organizing marginalized and precarious workers is essential to any strategy aimed at reversing and resisting globalization and promoting democracy (Ross and Martin 1999; Carchedi and Carchedi 1999; White 1993; Warskett 2000; Huws 1999; Vosko 2000; Yalnizyan 1993).

For women, a shorter work week (or workday), as advocated by Albo (1994), has been shown not only to reduce the "double-burden" of paid and unpaid work,[33] and allows more time for democratic participation (White 1993; Panitch 1994). Feminist work on valuing women's unpaid labour is also essential in this regard. Many are beginning to identify new ways in which this unpaid work could be valued that range from placing a market value on these services to (re)socializing more of the costs of social reproduction.[34] This type of research is fundamental to any effort at democratizing the market and the family for women and men.

Waring (2000a) concludes that devolution of responsibilities to the "community" raises important policy questions since "time-use studies demonstrate that there aren't a large bank of human resources sitting about in the community with time on their hands just desperate to take over the devolution of services." This fits nicely with the work that Bakker has done. In a report for Status of Women Canada, Bakker (1998) argues that "policy makers are rarely explicit about how such assumptions [of unpaid work] guide their decision-making. Yet, policy development in Canada is informed by implicit models of the macroeconomy as well as the family" (viii). The downloading of social services to the family or voluntary sector does not consider the costs in terms of women's unpaid work, and thus Bakker suggests that "policy makers must make explicit their assumptions which underpin macroeconomic policies ... When governments choose to forego lost revenues in exchange for savings on health expenditures partly realized through unpaid activities in households and communities, such a policy decision should be stated clearly" (4). That it seems radical for both Waring and Bakker to emphasize that policies should be aimed at reducing the burden of women's unpaid work, not increasing it, is a testament to the extent to which gender inequality is entrenched in society.[35]

Participation in democracy is more difficult for women who dispro-portionately carry the burden of social reproduction, for immigrant women who lack the language skills to participate, for disabled women who face physical access barriers, for women whose working hours do not allow participation, and for gays, lesbians, and transgendered people, who still face hostility from men and other women. This is why polices that socialize social reproduction and reduce working time are essential. Due to the gendered nature of time, the state must provide childcare and other support services, to ensure that all are free to par-ticipate, as exemplified in Porto Alegre, Brazil. There, women make up half of those involved in the participatory budget process, and working-class people are the majority of participants. The Brazilian case also demonstrates the symbiotic relationship between participa-tory and representative forms of democracy (Earles and Findlay 2003), so I stress the continued importance of representation, in addition to participation.

It is also expected that democratization of the "public" sphere will support democratization of the "private" sphere (Albo 1993). Panitch (1993) says that democratic administration "still leaves a private sec-tor in which the corporations that control our economy and culture are not democratically structured at all. Yet it is now clear that only far more democratized public institutions will ever have the creativity and popular strength necessary to democratize the private sector" (5). Shields and Evans (1998) see democracy as necessary to challenge neoliberalism, since it "threatens a policy of monetary stabilization because governments must contend with voter demands to supply them with public goods of various kinds" (68). And Magnusson (1993) concludes that "individual and collective empowerment can occur only at the expense of the main institutions of social control – most notably the state, the market, and the patriarchal family. In this sense, demands for democratization are inherently revolutionary" (128).

Fundamentally, democratization, of which femocratic administration is a part, will only result from what Panitch (1993) calls a "democracy movement" (16), which must seek the transformation of the both the state and everyday life (Wainwright 2003, xix). Fortunately, there is a multitude of contextualized democratic experiments ranging from the local to the global, to provide inspiration for such a vision. Rather than a global civil society, based on universalism, let us forge a global move-ment of mutual learning about, and support for, democracy in a diver-sity of contexts.

Conclusion

In 2013, the OWD celebrated its thirtieth anniversary. This is a fitting time to pause and reflect on the place for state feminism in democratic struggles. We need to question the growing willingness of progressive movements, including feminism, to eschew the state, and democracy along with it, in favour of more distant and abstract spaces of struggle. This orientation is bolstered by certain tendencies in feminist theory, as Adamson et al. (1988) warn, that "presenting the state as a monolith of patriarchal power rather than as a structure vulnerable to pressure, and ... making only criticisms of the state rather than viable suggestions for change ... robs women of any belief that social change can take place and that what they do could make a difference" (186). Feminists must actively contribute to debates about state restructuring by offering critiques, and by moving beyond what Susan Ferguson (2000) calls the "politics of preservation" (276) towards imagining alternatives.

Picturing democratic possibilities is no easy task. As Stivers (1993) reminds us: "Because most of us have so little experience with any such arrangements and because business as usual seems so firmly entrenched, most such ideas are dismissed as terribly impractical" (74). Add to this the reality that "feminist theorizing is somewhat like trying to think in a language that does not yet exist" (ibid., 128). This concluding chapter, then, is one modest attempt at moving the conversation on gender and democratic governance forward. It described how a combination of feminist bureaucratic restructuring, representative bureaucracy, and democratic administration are essential to building a "femocratic administration."

Femocratic administration is about keeping the state at the forefront of contestations over equality, participation, and democracy. It is imperative that feminists continue not only to investigate how the state maintains unequal relations of power, but also to envision how it can be transformed.

Notes

Introduction: Gender, Governance, and Democracy in Ontario

1 Stivers (1993) questions the priorities of public administration as a field of study, pointing out that "facts such as that women are paid less than men, generally do most of the lower-level work, do not fit accepted managerial roles, experience sexual harassment in organizations, and work a double-shift of home and job responsibilities are as tangible as many other factors in the real world of public administration to which observers have given considerably more attention" (7).

2 It must be kept in mind then that many of the measures I am describing here are based on the Canadian context, and are not easily transferable to other locations. This is particularly true for "femocratic administration," where the landscape for women's policy differs significantly from that of other places. Hester Eisenstein makes this point in reference to Australia, where the "femocrat" (feminist bureaucrat) strategy was based on a particular, historic, set of social relations (1996, 205).

3 Although such disagreements about signifiers also exist. For instance, Hirst and Thompson (1992) argue that such markers of globalization are widely exaggerated. David McNally (2000) also calls for caution in overestimating the extent of global integration.

4 Evans, McBride, and Shields (2000) similarly refer to globalization as "the contemporary expression of eighteenth century economic liberalism" (95).

5 As many have pointed out, however, neoliberalism does not always mean less state intervention, and in fact, has resulted in increased coercion, and often, when linked with neoconservatism or social conservatism, increased moral regulation. See Burke, Mooers, and Shields (2000) and Fudge and Cossman (2002).

6 Representative administration, though, while noted in democratic administration, becomes much more important in femocratic administration.
7 Rebick, like many others, stresses the need for a system of proportional
representation (PR).
8 It should be noted that while Australia once acted as a model for state feminism, over the 1990s, it underwent a major process of restructuring. In 1997,
the Women's Bureau was dismantled, a cut of 40% was made to the Office of
the Status of Women's budget, and in 2004 its position was further undermined when it was moved from the Prime Minister's Department to the
Office of Women in the Department of Family and Community Services.
In the mid-1990s, the following were eliminated: the Office of Indigenous
Women, the Migrant Women's Advisor, the Gender and Curriculum Unit,
the Equal Pay Unit, the Work and Family Unit, the Women's Health Unit,
the Women's Sport Unit, the Women's Policy Unit in Social Security, and
the Women's Subcommittee of the Australian Health Ministers Advisory
Committee. Gender budgeting and analysis was weakened and operating
funding for women's groups was replaced with project-based funding. (See,
for instance, Sawer 2007.) It will be shown that similar changes have occurred
in Canada.
9 Although in some contexts, particularly Nordic countries, state feminism
is also used more broadly to refer to feminists in electoral politics.
10 These Canadian sources are in addition to the extensive Australian body
of work, including Eisenstein 1996, 1991, 1990; Franzway et al. 1989; Sawer
2007, 1994, 1991, 1990; Watson 1992; and Yeatman 1990.
11 For an elaboration see Porter (2003) and Dobrowolsky (2000). Similar examples, also reviewed by Dobrowolsky, are the cases of sex discrimination
under the Indian Act of *Lavell* and *Bedard*.
12 For a comparative approach on provincial policy on violence against
women, see Collier 2009.
13 Sauer et al. (2007) also found that centre and left-wing governments did
not guarantee a positive environment for state feminism.
14 These include factors such as waged and unwaged labour, caring labour, reproduction, and emotional and sexual life. For an elaboration, see Walby 2004.
15 This can be seen with Malloy (2003), for instance, who emphasizes
the competing norms and ideals of social movements and public
administration.
16 But they also draw from a variety of other approaches including public
choice, political culture, and legal-institutional.
17 Although Graefe departs from them with an explicit political-economy
orientation.

1. A Feminist Political Economy of Representation

1 Given the popularity of historical institutionalism within FI, it will be the main focus here.
2 Kenny and Mackay (2009) conclude, for instance, that "Amanda Driscoll and Mona Lena Krook's bold ambition to create a feminist rational choice institutionalism seems likely to flounder because of epistemological incompatibilities" (273).
3 Although discourse analysis is synonymous with post-structuralism, discursive institutionalism takes a divergent view of discourse and institutions. For a good explanation of the difference between discursive institutionalist and post-structuralist approaches, see Rönnblom and Bacchi, 2011.
4 Feminist institutionalists themselves are aware of these weaknesses. Mackay (2011) and Lovenduski (2011) recognize the need for a better understanding of change and agency.
5 As a case in point, Ferguson (1984) insisted that the state must be viewed as both structure and process, and that bureaucratic relations exist in social context.
6 Indeed, MacKinnon (1989) even specifies that she is analysing how "the *liberal state* coercively and authoritatively constitutes the social order in the interest of men as a gender – through its legitimizing norms, forms, relation to society, and substantive policies" (162, emphasis mine), acknowledging variations in state types.
7 This is ironic since one of FI's main critiques of neo-institutionalism is its lack of analysis of power and for Kenny (2007), "a gendered approach to the study of institutions would make power a central analytical focus" (96).
8 For Young (2000), the women's movements are synonymous with organized groups, such as the National Organization of Women (NOW) and the National Action Committee on the Status of Women (NAC), indicative of a pluralist approach to group politics.
9 Young (2000) refers to institutions as "exogenous factors," explicitly setting them outside of society (12).
10 Mahon and Collier (2010) make this point in reference to childcare advocacy in the provinces (outside of Quebec) and through international instruments. Brennan (2010) also points out that in Australian childcare, "tactical agility does not always result in policy success" (49).
11 Increasingly, this triad is being expanded to include the voluntary sector.
12 See, for instance, Burstyn 1983.

13 One need only look at the continuing sex-segregation in the state's own structures of the public service and its resistance in settling its pay equity claims, at the persistent commitment among many provincial states to the infamous "spouse in the house" rules around social assistance benefits, at the state's failure to act around the promised national child care program, or at the clear gender discrimination in the Employment Insurance (EI) Program, to see this reality.

14 For example, see Simeon and Robinson 1990; Cameron 2006; Graefe 2003.

15 The category of "post-colonial" is quite problematic in capturing a very diverse set of perspectives, in that some of them draw from Marxism, while others are more closely associated with post-structuralism.

16 See, for example, McGrath and Stevenson 1996; Koshan 1997; Crenshaw 1991; Bannerji 1996; Millbank 1997; Monture-Angus 1989, 1995; Driedger 1996.

17 Koshan 1997; Crenshaw 1991; Forell 1991; Monture-Angus 1995; Native Women's Association of Canada 1991.

18 Millbank (1997), though, is cautious of a "rights-based claim to 'privacy'" (280).

19 For an exception, see Gabriel 1996.

20 For instance, many Aboriginal women remind us that historically, matriarchal forms of kinship are more familiar to them than patriarchy, and Afro-American feminists have insisted that their families have often served as support systems in a racist society (see Koshan 1997; hooks 1981; Bhavnani and Coulson 1986; King 1997; Dua 1999; and Porter 2003).

21 Green 1993; Hill-Collins 1990; King 1997; Das Gupta 1995. Although in some cases, this too, may be overstated. Michèle Barrett (1980), writing in the 1970s, notes that very few families actually resembled the male-breadwinner model.

22 See, for example, O'Brien and Weir 1995; Cossman 1996; and Gavigan 1996.

23 For instance, Mahon 2005, 2007; Mahon et al. 2007; Jenson 2008; Jenson et al. 2003.

24 While it is beyond the scope of this chapter, an unsettled question is whether the goal is for each to integrate gender into these existing paradigms, or to create a new and autonomous feminist political science framework.

25 For an elaboration, see Sainsbury 1999 and O'Connor 1993, as well as chapter 3.

26 For more see concluding chapter.

27 However, this is a major point of contention among feminists. As seen with Carty and Brand, and also discussed by Bystydzienski and Sekhon (1999), state funding is seen by many as a threat to autonomy. Nevertheless, in Canada, with the financial collapse of NAC, these arguments are a bit of an abstract luxury. This reality is reflected in the fact that one of the thirteen demands of the World March of Women was $30 million in core funding for equality-seeking women's organizations (part of the "Our Fair Share" campaign, which asks for $2.00 for every woman and girl child in Canada). I develop this point in the concluding chapter.

28 Eisenstein (1996) is aware that the Australian femocrat strategy was the product of a particular historical conjuncture and set of social relations. It cannot simply be translated to other times and spaces. However, there are general democratic lessons that can be drawn from her case study.

29 But I believe that representation is important to supporting this.

2. Gender Regimes of Public Administration

1 Wilson and Mullins (1978) also demonstrate this through the example of francophones in the public service. They note that scientific management, introduced to the Canadian public service in 1918, "packaged together goodness, merit, morality, neutrality, efficiency, science and the Protestant work ethic into one conceptual lump" (521). One of the results was that "these reforms closed one of the principal avenues by which francophones had previously been recruited to the federal public service" (521). This "rationalization" also included a built-in bias for anglophone education and experience (524).

2 See Ann Porter's discussion of UI/EI, for instance: Porter 2003.

3 Agócs (2012) also shows that, actually, there was more diversity in the public sector under the patronage system.

4 Findlay borrows the term "chilly climate" that was coined at the University of Western Ontario to describe the hostile environment for women, and feminists especially, on university campuses.

5 Kernaghan (1978) cites Porter, Rowat, Wilson, and Mullins. While Rowat, Wilson, and Mullins defend the principle of representative bureaucracy, they do so from the perspective that merit and neutrality will not be harmed.

6 In 1995, the Women's Bureau became the Gender Analysis and Policy Directorate, with a changed focus on gender analysis within Human Resources Development Canada (HRDC) (National Governmental Organizations, n.d.).

7 Now the Bureau of Women's Health and Gender Analysis.

8 For example, in the context of francophone representation, Kernaghan (1978) explains that "the government's response to this merit versus representation issue is that bilingual competence is an element of merit and that by increasing the number of positions requiring bilingual competence the government 'will increase the opportunities for qualified francophones and thus at one and the same time preserve the merit principle and achieve the goal of a more representative Public Service'" (500).

9 For an elaboration, see Bakan and Kobayashi (2000). It is notable that one of the main critiques of employment equity is the lack of targets or quotas. In early debates about representative bureaucracy (described above), quotas were seen to be in direct violation of the merit principle, and this argument continues to have currency.

10 Some have described the "the marketization of the state" (Pierre 1995, 56), while others have referred to the "market model" (Peters 1995, 289). Both capture basically the same grouping of decentralization, downsizing, privatization, and managerialism.

11 Here, I am relying on Pierre's (1995) definition of marketization: "to employ market criteria for allocating public resources and also to measure the efficiency of public service producers and suppliers according to market criteria" (56).

12 This has improved only slightly since. In 2004, one of the Institute's economists was a woman, one senior fellow was a woman, and three women (out of 22) were listed as research fellows (C.D. Howe Institute 2004). By 2006, there was no change in the first two categories and in fact, in the third area, there appears to be a decline in representation (three out of 26). In 2014, little progress could be observed.

13 When this situation was pointed out and the hiring process was questioned, it was revealed that rather than an internal employment equity policy, the Institute prefers to function by "word of mouth." It was further pressed that such a process seems like a reliance on the "old boy's network." Needless to say, the Institute did not take this interpretation seriously.

14 See Bakker 1998, for an in-depth discussion of how women's unpaid labour is ignored in macroeconomic policy.

15 Which Aucoin (2000) describes as the "popular, but flawed, manifesto of David Osborne and Ted Gaebler" (250).

16 For example, key to my project, the area of labour market policy (i.e., labour relations and training), falls under provincial jurisdiction, but has, in the past, had a more significant federal presence. The federal

involvement in training, in particular, has largely been lost under decentralization (Haddow and Klassen 2004).

17 These critiques parallel those made by feminists of the top-down, exclusive nature of Weberian bureaucracy. I will return to this point in the concluding chapter.

18 See NWAC 2002.

19 This happened at the same time as the federal Tories decided to fund the anti-feminist group REAL (Realistic, Equal, Active, for Life) Women (O'Neil and Sutherland 1997).

20 In the Yukon, where the Women's Directorate was closed, the former Status of Women minister was actually quoted as accusing "feminazis" of preventing her from expressing her opinions (although she later resigned from her portfolio) (Mitchell 2001).

21 As of November 2007. See, for example, Mitchell (2001).

22 Malloy (2003) also shows that in the case of Ontario, discussed more in chapter 4, the Ontario Advisory Council on Women's Issues (OACWI) was thought to be duplicating the responsibilities of the Ontario Women's Directorate (OWD), even though the OWD played no role in organizing formal consultations with the community, or in producing independent research. One interviewee noted, however, that the OWD actually did try to organize formal consultations. She also stressed that the OACWI could not be said to have produced independent research either (interview 15b, 26 April 2005).

23 Bakan and Kobayashi (2000) show how these two sets of policy principles play out differently in the case of employment equity in Ontario. One principle sees employment equity from the perspective of proactively addressing systemic discrimination, while the other sees employment equity as an unjustified, special measure.

24 Pierre (1995) argues that the "marketization of the state" involves a "depoliticization of the state" (67), but the appointment of private-sector advisers, etc. has not led to a depoliticization, but rather a repoliticization, of the bureaucracy (Savoie 1994). Pierre later identifies "a simultaneous depoliticization and politicization of the public administration" (Pierre 1995, 75). Similarly, Peters (1995) has drawn attention to the attempts by Reagan, Thatcher, and Mulroney to increase their own influence over the bureaucracy, and Shields and Evans (1998) point to the growing use of "outside" advice from right-wing think tanks such as the C.D. Howe and Fraser Institutes.

25 Although with its recent cuts to Status of Women Canada, the current Conservative federal government appears to be moving away from even

this very limited form of representation towards a *neoconservative* approach that is more virulently anti-"special interest" as well as anti-"expertise."

26 Interview 3, 5 March 2004.

27 This idea was discussed in the previous chapter in reference to the work of Sue Findlay.

28 As noted in chapter 1, however, most of this machinery has been eliminated.

29 They also focus strictly on electoral politics, which I will address later on.

3. Experiments with State Feminism in the Weberian Gender Regime

1 These commonalities, especially due to minority government, include a more flexible view of advocacy, stronger ministerial support, a more active policy agenda, continuity in policy, staffing, and numbers, etc.

2 The OWD was to be policy- rather than program-focused, responsible for development and coordination, while line departments were to take care of implementation (Malloy 2003).

3 For instance, the first minister responsible for women's issues in Ontario, Robert Welch, was also deputy premier at the time (Malloy 2003). One interviewee commented that the women's portfolio was always an additional portfolio and, therefore, was "never a full-time job" (interview 15a, 21 Oct. 2004).

4 Interview 2, 24 Feb. 2004; interview 14, 15 Oct. 2004; interview 18, 27 Jan. 2005. As Malloy (2003) explains, exact employment levels are not available because under the NDP's "Social Contract," employment levels were no longer made public.

5 Interview 4, 23 April 2004.

6 One exception was Liberal minister responsible for women's issues Greg Sorbara, who was not committed to women's issues, not very powerful, and very concerned about interfering in ministry boundaries (Malloy 2003).

7 Interview 4, 23 April 2004.

8 Interview 1, 20 Nov. 2003.

9 Interview 4, 23 April 2004.

10 Boyd, for instance, was active in the anti–violence against women community. An interesting difference in perspectives was offered in a few interviews that is worth noting. Some thought it was very important to have an explicitly feminist minister, with one saying it was a "nuisance" if the minister was not interested in women's issues (interview 5, 12 May 2004). Others thought that it was actually easier to work with a minister who

does not really know about the issues. For example: "If you're providing advice to someone who also has experience in that sector, you're essentially screwed. Because they will know a different example, they will know more, they will want to demonstrate their expertise ... [She advised people who knew nothing about the issues and respected her experience. This was a] good position to be in" (interview 2, 24 Feb. 2004). This was seen as a problem with the NDP ministers, who were feminists and thought that they could play the role of advocate better than the OWD. It is also important to point out Burt and Lorenzin's (1997) findings that all four female NDP cabinet ministers they interviewed (Boyd, Carter, Haslam, Mathyssen) described themselves as feminists, but had very different definitions of what that meant to them. Byrne (1997) found similar results.

11 Interview 5, 12 May 2004.
12 Interview 5, 12 May 2004.
13 Interview 4, 23 April 2004.
14 Interview 1, 20 Nov. 2003.
15 Interview 14, 15 Oct. 2004.
16 Interview 8, 18 June 2004.
17 Interview 10, 3 Sept. 2004.
18 Interview 11, 3 Sept. 2004.
19 Interview 19, 27 Jan. 2005.
20 Interview 5, 12 May 2004.
21 Interview 10, 3 Sept. 2004.
22 Interview 11, 3 Sept. 2004.
23 Interview 15a, 21 Oct. 2004.
24 Someone called this a "process of infection" (interview 15a, 21 Oct. 2004). However, one former OWD staff member said that while there is still a network of connections throughout the OPS with the OWD, and many tried to take gender analysis outside to other ministries, this was sometimes not a possibility. It was easier in some places, like Health and COMSOC, than in others (interview 19, 27 Jan. 2005).
25 For example, interview 1, 20 Nov. 2003; interview 17, 8 Nov. 2004; and interview 2, 24 Feb. 2004. However, Rankin (1996) shows that the downside to this strategy was high staff turnover and lack of continuity.
26 Interview 10, 3 Sept. 2004.
27 Interview 6, 20 May 2004, and interview 7, 20 May 2004.
28 Interview 12, Oct. 3 2004; interview 2, 24 Feb. 2004; interview 5, 12 May 2004; interview 14, 15 Oct. 2004; interview 17, 8 Nov. 2004.
29 Interview 17, 8 Nov. 2004.
30 Interview 14, 15 Oct. 2004.

31 Interview 10, 3 Sept. 2004.
32 Interview 10, 3 Sept. 2004.
33 Interview 2, 24 Feb. 2004.
34 Interview 12, 3 Oct. 2004; interview 15a, 21 Oct. 2004. The OWD's international links were also highlighted in their fall 1994 newsletter. See Ontario 1994b, "Directorate Is Prime Resource."
35 Interview 1, 20 Nov. 2003; interview 2, 24 Feb. 2004; interview 3, 5 March 2004; interview 8, 18 June 2004; interview 9, 25 June 2004; interview 10, 3 Sept. 2004; interview 11, 3 Sept. 2004; interview 14, 15 Oct. 2004; interview 18, 27 Jan. 2005.
36 Interview 5, 12 May 2004.
37 See, for instance, Ontario, OWD 1990a; 1989a; 1989b; *Women in the Labour Market: Focus on Racial Minority Women*, 1992; *Women in the Labour Market: Focus on Women with Disabilities*, 1992.
38 Interview 4, 23 April 2004.
39 Interview 5, 12 May 2004.
40 Interview 2, 24 Feb. 2004.
41 Interview 14, 15 Oct. 2004.
42 Interview 4, 23 April 2004.
43 As reflected in directorate publications including: *The Free Trade Agreement and Women*, 1987; *The North American Free Trade Agreement: Implications for Women*, 1993; *Employment Equity for Aboriginal Women: Putting Skills to Work*, 1990; *Employment Equity for Visible Minority Women, A Guide for Employers: A Change Agent Project*, 1990. Also, indicated in archival records: "Update on Family Law Reform Amendment Act," 18 June 1984.
44 See, for example: OWD 1993f, "'Work and Family'"; OWD and CAMCO 1992, *Flexible Working Arrangements*; OWD and Union Gas 1992, *Sharing the Balance*; OWD and United Food and Commercial Workers Union, 1992, *Balancing Work and Family Responsibilities*. In addition, in 1989–90, the directorate produced a video on family friendly policies (OWD 1990, *OWD Year-end Report, 1989–1990*). In 1994, they held a symposium on "Families and the Economy" (see OWD 1994i, "Work & Family Symposium," 2).
45 Judy Wolfe explained that there was considerable resistance among unions and some in the directorate towards consecutive parental leave, favouring concurrent leave instead. In the end, the argument for consecutive leave, largely based on the gender-equality impact, won out.
46 Interview 4, 23 April 2004.
47 Interview 4, 23 April 2004; interview 5, 12 May 2004; interview 7, 20 May 2004; interview 9, 25 June 2004; interview 10, 3 Sept. 2004; interview 11, 3 Sept. 2004; interview 12, 3 Oct. 2004; interview 15a, 21 Oct. 2004; interview 17, 8 Nov. 2004.

48 One person interviewed, who had worked on affirmative action very early in its development, made an important point about policy legacy, emphasizing that by the time employment equity was scrapped by the Tories, many had already implemented and committed to it in places like school boards and hospitals (interview 19, 27 Jan. 2005).

49 Interview 5, 12 May 2004.

50 Interestingly, this is one of the only directorate projects to survive the PC government.

51 Interview 17, 8 Nov. 2004; interview 4, 23 April 2004.

52 Interview 15a, 21 Oct. 2004. Early in the OWD, there was significant attention paid to women in non-traditional careers, technology, and small business ownership. For instance, in 1984 the Business Ownership for Women Program was established (OWD 1984, *Plan of Action*). By the early 1990s, these were much lower priorities. However, they provided a solid foundation for the Tories to build their market-oriented approach to women's policy once elected in 1995. Burt and Lorenzin argue that, in general, the NDP policies "reflected a continuing shift in the party away from socialist policies toward a market-driven agenda" (222).

53 As explained further in chapter 4, ACTEW has changed its name to A Commitment to Training and Employment for Women.

54 Interview 1, 20 Nov. 2003. One ACTEW representative thought that the NDP made a credible effort at consultation, but believed that with OTAB, consultation took too long and degenerated into a local "road show" (interview 6, 20 May 2004). Judy Wolfe also noted that union resistance to inserting gender was a problem with OTAB, as well as with other NDP projects. Others have discussed the shortcomings of OTAB too. For examples see Bradford (2003), Haddow and Klassen (2004), and Klassen (2000).

55 Interview 9, 25 June 2004.

56 See, for example, *Employment Equity for Aboriginal Women* (OWD 1991); *Employment Equity for Visible Minority Women* (OWD and the Urban Alliance on Race Relations, 1990); *Focus on Aboriginal Women* (OWD 1993a); *Focus on Racial Minority Women* (OWD, 1993b); *Focus on Women with Disabilities* (OWD 1993c).

57 An interviewee concluded by saying, "I'm sure that's not something that Mike Harris persevered with" (interview 4, 23 April 2004).

58 Interview 2, 24 Feb. 2004.

59 Interview 3, 5 March 2004.

60 Most of those interviewed had negative impressions of bureaucratic hierarchy and power relations, but one response was distinct, noting that, in some ways, it is at least easier to negotiate a system where the structure

is "overt and explicit," than one where it is unofficial, "but exists nonetheless" (interview 15a, 21 Oct. 2004).

61 Interview 1, 20 Nov. 2003.

62 However, most of those interviewed believed that while structures can make things more difficult or easy, on their own, they do not make *the* difference. This will be discussed in the concluding chapter.

63 Interview 5, 12 May 2004.

64 Interview 2, 24 Feb. 2004.

65 Interview 1, 20 Nov. 2003.

66 Interview 5, 12 May 2004.

67 Interview 14, 15 Oct. 2004.

68 For instance, interview 10, 3 Sept. 2004, and interview 14, 15 Oct. 2004.

69 Interview 14, 15 Oct. 2004.

70 Interview 9, 25 June 2004.

71 Interview 8, 18 June 2004.

72 Interview 9, 25 June 2004; interview 10, 3 Sept. 2004; interview 12, 3 Oct. 2004.

73 Interview 9, 25 June 2004.

74 Interview 10, 3 Sept. 2004.

75 Interview 15a, 21 Oct. 2004. She added that there was much more done in British Columbia, where they had their own disability secretariat, and seconded Aboriginal women from an Aboriginal women's organization into the ministry twice to build capacity in understanding how government works, and to help them become more effective lobbyists.

76 As noted in the introductory chapter, while most of those interviewed wished to remain anonymous, some agreed to use their names.

77 This was especially the case when Anne Swarbrick, who had strong labour movement connections, was minister responsible for women's issues.

78 Interview 11, 3 Sept. 2004.

79 Interview 9, 25 June 2004.

80 Interview 9, 25 June 2004.

81 Interview 7, 20 May 2004. This can be seen by one representative of ACTEW, who seemed to have a very sophisticated knowledge of federalism. For instance, in the strategy taken by ACTEW, on the one hand, they directed criticism to the federal government for their cuts to the Canadian Jobs Strategy, and to community groups as well as the changes to UI for their impact on immigrant and refugee women, people with disabilities, older, linguistic, and racial minorities, and farm workers, while on the other hand, continued to call upon the province for "support and intervention" (OWD 1992a, "ACTEW Letter").

82 Interview 4, 23 April 2004.

83 Interview 4, 23 April 2004.

84 Interview 4, 23 April 2004.

85 "Summary of Proceedings, FPT Meeting of Officials," Ottawa, 10 October 1984.

86 OWD 1984b, "FPT Ministers Conference"; OWD 1984c, "Memorandum to: Members of the Ontario Delegation"; OWD 1984e, "Preliminary Summary Record"; OWD 1984f, "Proposed Terms of Reference." This is still very familiar in the current context as is the other key point of disagreement – non-profit administration.

87 Interview 19, 27 Jan. 2005.

88 This might be taken as evidence for the "federalism as obstacle" to social policy stance noted in chapter 1. However, rather than being a problem of federalism itself, I believe it is more indicative of the exclusion of the community, in this case, the childcare advocacy community, from the policy process. I will return to this point in the concluding chapter.

89 Interview 19, 27 Jan. 2005; interview 17, 8 Nov. 2004; interview 12, 3 Oct. 2004; interview 9, 25 June 2004; interview 3, 5 March 2004.

90 Interview 19, 27 Jan. 2005.

91 Interview 2, 24 Feb. 2004; interview 12, 3 Oct. 2004; interview 19, 27 Jan. 2005.

92 Interview 4, 23 April 2004; interview 8, 18 June 2004; interview 11, 3 Sept. 2004; interview 14, 15 Oct. 2004. One interviewee explained that for a period of time, the directorate was also more involved internationally, but this has since declined in focus (interview 12, 3 Oct. 2004).

93 Interview 17, 8 Nov. 2004.

94 Interview 1, 20 Nov. 2003.

95 Interview 18, 27 Jan. 2005.

96 Interview 9, 25 June 2004.

97 Interview 3, 5 March 2004; interview 14, 15 Oct. 2004; interview 17, 8 Nov. 2004; interview 18, 27 Jan. 2005.

98 Interview 17, 8 Nov. 2004.

99 Interview 14, 15 Oct. 2004; interview 18, 27 Jan. 2005.

100 Interview 2, 5 March 2004.

101 Interview 12, 3 Oct. 2004.

102 Interview 15a, 21 Oct. 2004.

103 Interview 12, 3 Oct. 2004.

104 Interview 19, 27 Jan. 2005.

105 Interview 11, 3 Sept. 2004.

106 Interview 3, 5 March 2004.

107 Interview 13, 7 Oct. 2004.
108 Interview 14, 15 Oct. 2004.
109 Interview 4, 23 April 2004. It is interesting how this public servant has adopted the supposedly (gender) neutral language of "taxpayers" and equates democracy only with elections.
110 Interview 15a, 21 Oct. 2004.
111 Interview 9, 25 June 2004. Another interviewee, however, disagreed that the Ministry of the Environment would identify with an advocacy role (interview 15b, 26 April 2005).
112 Interview 9, 25 June 2004.
113 Interview 9, 25 June 2004.
114 Interview 2, 24 Feb. 2004.
115 Interview 14, 15 Oct. 2004.
116 Interview 7, 20 May 2004.
117 Interview 10, 3 Sept. 2004.
118 Although, as will be seen, there was more focus under the NDP on diversifying the directorate staff.
119 One interviewee noted that at the federal level, only those in the Women's Program in the Secretary of State were brought in from outside the public service (interview 3, 5 March 2004).
120 Interview 3, 5 March 2004.
121 Interview 10, 3 Sept. 2004.
122 Interview 14, 15 Oct. 2004.
123 Interview 15a, 21 Oct. 2004.
124 Interview 1, 20 Nov. 2003.
125 Interview 11, 3 Sept. 2004. Although another agreed that the OWD staff was largely white, she did not have the same recollection of it as a "straight crowd" (interview 15b, 26 April 2005).
126 Interview 8, 18 June 2004.
127 Interview 3, 5 March 2004; interview 4, 23 April 2004; interview 8, 18 June 2004; interview 17, 8 Nov. 2004.
128 Interview 9, 25 June 2004. It was not clear to me, however, whether the problem was a lack of understanding about how government works or a fundamental lack of agreement about how government should work.
129 Interview 11, 3 Sept. 2004; interview 8, 18 June 2004; interview 4, 23 April 2004; interview 5, 12 May 2004; interview 2, 24 Feb. 2004; interview 3, 5 March 2004; interview 18, 27 Jan. 2005.
130 Interview 11, 3 Sept. 2004.

131 It is important to keep in perspective that I am mainly talking about the difficulties of relatively privileged women. One interviewee made this very clear when she explained: "I'd had some pretty rotten jobs before (waitress, library clerk) and my father was a bureaucrat so I thought the general working environment and the job were great, personally. I made twice what I had at my previous job, I was paid to sit and think and learn and talk to people, I was exposed to some very bright people who challenged me continually, and there were always some interesting constraints and parameters to work with" (interview 15a, 21 Oct. 2004).

132 Interview 4, 23 April 2004.

133 Interview 18, 27 Jan. 2005.

134 See, for example, the essays in Fudge and McDermott 1991, *Just Wages*, and Findlay 1997. Judy Wolfe also indicated that while the process and symbolism of job comparison was important to unions and the NDP, the administration of proxy pay equity was very difficult.

135 Interview 5, 12 May 2004.

136 Interview 5, 12 May 2004.

137 Interview 18, 27 Jan. 2005.

138 This is interesting because the OACWI was seen in the community as even less open than the OWD, with some in the community actually wanting to get rid of it.

139 Interview 10, 3 Sept. 2004.

140 Interview 14, 15 Oct. 2004.

141 Interview 10, 3 Sept. 2004.

142 Interview 14, 15 Oct. 2004.

143 Interview 10, 3 Sept. 2004.

144 Interview 15a, 21 Oct. 2004.

145 Interview 2, 24 Feb. 2004.

146 Interview 4, 23 April 2004.

147 Interview 1, 20 Nov. 2003.

148 Interview 2, 24 Feb. 2004.

149 Interview 5, 12 May 2004.

150 Sue Findlay (1995) makes a similar point in reference to exclusionary practices in feminist organizations.

151 Interview 15a, 21 Oct. 2004.

152 Interview 15a, 21 Oct. 2004.

153 Interview 14, 15 Oct. 2004.

154 Pierre (1995) questions the extent to which this change is more rhetoric rather than reality.

4. Gendered Governance and the New Public Management Regime

1 This point, about the interconnectedness of federal and provincial struc-
    tures, was stressed in chapter 1.
2 Overall, though, Outshoorn and Kantola (2007a) offer an optimistic
    assessment of the current state of women's policy agencies, concluding
    that despite the damage of neoliberal restructuring in some places
    (Australia, the Netherlands and the United States), "on the whole, most
    have survived and consolidated or even improved their position within
    the national bureaucracies" (284). The Ontario case study does not seem to
    fit this pattern of resilience.
3 Interview 1, 20 Nov. 2003.
4 Interview 17, 8 Nov. 2004.
5 Interview 19, 27 Jan. 2005.
6 Interview 17, 8 Nov. 2004.
7 Interview 17, 8 Nov. 2004.
8 Interview 17, 8 Nov. 2004.
9 Malloy (2003) specifies that staff departures were "both voluntary and
    involuntary" (105).
10 The budget did begin to increase again in 1997, but has never returned to
    the levels of the early 1990s (Malloy 2003). (In the 1998–9 Business Plan,
    the budget is listed as $18.5M, with 35 staff.) In an interview with Dianne
    Cunningham, she acknowledged this change herself, commenting that the
    OWD "used to be well-funded" (interview 16, 5 Nov. 2004).
11 Interview 12, 3 Oct. 2004.
12 For instance, interview 9, 25 June 2004; interview 10, 3 Sept. 2004; inter-
    view 11, 3 Sept. 2004; interview 12, 3 Oct. 2004; interview 13, 7 Oct. 2004;
    interview 14, 15 Oct. 2004.
13 Interview 10, 3 Sept. 2004. A directorate staff member also noted that they
    wanted to develop an Internet site with basic statistics about the economic
    reality of Ontario women, to demonstrate why gender policy analysis is
    needed, and why policy impacts differently on women than men (inter-
    view 17, 8 Nov. 2004), but as will be shown, gender analysis is no longer
    seen as a priority.
14 Interview 11, 3 Sept. 2004.
15 Interview 7, 20 May 2004.
16 Interview 6, 20 May 2004.
17 Interview 2, 24 Feb. 2004.
18 Interview 6, 20 May 2004. This interviewee reinforces the contradictory
    nature of federalism as both an obstacle and an opportunity. She clearly

saw federalism as an obstacle to coherent labour market policy. With employment programs and services for immigrant women specifically in mind, she thought that certain issues are treated as a "hot potato" between jurisdictions. Yet at the same time, she identified federalism as providing important political opportunities when faced with a hostile Ontario Tory government. Others did not have much optimism about the federal government as second resort.

19 Interview 13, 7 Oct. 2004.
20 Interview 14, 15 Oct. 2004. In NPM style, it was not just the OWD that was targeted. The PCs downsized the entire government, with 20% of the civil service being cut (interview 14, 5 Oct. 2004).
21 Interview 14, 15 Oct. 2004. Francis came up numerous times in interviews, but she was not willing to be interviewed. Malloy (2003) refers to a similar situation, also being unable to sort out the details of her departure.
22 Interview 17, 8 Nov. 2004.
23 Although it was not the focus of my research questions, for those still at the OWD, it seemed that under the subsequent Liberal government the directorate's presence had not significantly improved.
24 Interview 13, 7 Oct. 2004.
25 Interview 13, 7 Oct. 2004.
26 Interview 13, 7 Oct. 2004.
27 Interview 17, 8 Nov. 2004.
28 Interview 13, 7 Oct. 2004.
29 Interview 12, 3 Oct. 2004.
30 Interview 12, 3 Oct. 2004.
31 Interview 12, 3 Oct. 2004. This was also paradoxical, though, because on the one hand, Ontario saw the FPT as a way to push forward its agenda, while on the other hand, the federal government was funding evaluations of Ontario's programs for women. As this participant put it, "Ontario was not happy" (interview 12, 3 Oct. 2004).
32 Interview 1, 20 Nov. 2003.
33 For example, interview 4, 23 April 2004; interview 8, 18 June 2004; interview 12, 3 Oct. 2004; interview 13, 7 Oct. 2004; interview 14, 15 Oct. 2004; interview 17, 8 Nov. 2004.
34 Interview 17, 8 Nov. 2004.
35 Interview 17, 8 Nov. 2004.
36 Interview 10, 3 Sept. 2004.
37 However, one interviewee, who was at the directorate for a short time, seemed to have a different recollection. While very frustrated by the lack of policy development at the OWD, she remembered reviewing cabinet

submissions for their impact on women and saw this as one of the only ways they were still able to influence policy indirectly (interview 13, 7 Oct. 2004). Minister Cunningham also indicated that the "gender lens was big" when she was there, and that she was influenced by Hedy Fry at the federal level on gender policy analysis (interview 16, 5 Nov. 2004).

38 Interview 1, 20 Nov. 2003. This is similar to British Columbia, where the minister of women's equality "determined that advocacy 'was not a core service'" (Teghtsoonian 2004, 26).

39 Interview 11, 3 Sept. 2004.

40 Interview 14, 15 Oct. 2004.

41 Interview 13, 7 Oct. 2004.

42 The OWD did not have its own deputy minister (DM). Here he is referring to the DM from the women's minister's other ministry.

43 For an elaboration, see Pierre (1995), Savoie (1994), and Peters (1995).

44 Interview 8, 25 June 2004. Although in this case, the participant had a more complicated position on advocacy, as seen in her subsequent elaboration of her role, cited in chapter 3.

45 Which itself has been problematized for its gendered assumptions.

46 Keeping in mind what was said above, that "de-politicizing" is misleading.

47 Philipps (2002) also argues that tax laws are facilitating the re-privatization of social reproduction by increasing incentives for voluntary sector involvement. An interviewee expressed similar concerns as Philipps, and the feminist political economists cited earlier, that with government cuts, more work to support women is falling to the non-profit area "to fill the vacuum." Interestingly, archival records of a 1985 cabinet submission from Citizenship and Immigration actually predicted that the "value of volunteer activity is likely to increase with limits on government spending." It goes on to say that "with increasing numbers of women entering the work-force, new sources of volunteers must be found; senior citizens and part-time workers are a resource which could be developed further in this regard" (Ontario, OWD 1985d, "Implementation"). The Peterson Liberals were in power then, so clearly NPM techniques, while more predominant in the Harris government, did not begin there.

48 In time for the June 2004 federal election.

49 Although Boyd did qualify this remark to say that often those in the OWD were impatient with (but not fearful of) her political staff, allowing that her staff probably weren't as sensitive as they could have been.

50 Interview 10, 3 Sept. 2004.

51 Interview 12, 3 Oct. 2004.

52 Interview 9, 25 June 2004.

53 Interview 11, 3 Sept. 2004.

54 Interview 13, 7 Oct. 2004.

55 Interview 13, 7 Oct. 2004. While the Harris government was demoniz-
ing bureaucrats as selfish and lazy, this interviewee had a very different
analysis, often seeing dedication at their own expense, with civil servants
"beavering away doing something that was going to eliminate their job
eventually."

56 Interview 13, 7 Oct. 2004. Albo (1993) outlines two schools of resistance
to NPM – one calling for a return to professional management, and one
seeking to democratize administration. This interviewee, along with some
others, clearly belongs to the former category. I will return to this in the
concluding chapter.

57 Interview 1, 20 Nov. 2003.

58 Interview 7, 20 May 2004.

59 Interview 13, 7 Oct. 2004.

60 Interview 11, 3 Sept. 2004. She added that debates were intense in the community, however, about whether or not to work with the Tories. This was
particularly the case in the violence against women community, because in
order to get money, they would have to accept the de-gendered language
of "domestic violence."

61 Interview 12, 3 Oct. 2004.

62 Interview 12, 3 Oct. 2004.

63 Interview 7, 20 May 2004.

64 Interview 17, 8 Nov. 2004.

65 Interview 6, 20 May 2004, and interview 7, 20 May 2004.

66 Interview 12, 3 Oct. 2004.

67 Interview 17, 8 Nov. 2004.

68 Interview 17, 8 Nov. 2004.

69 Interview 13, 7 Oct. 2004.

70 Likewise, another commented that "every government fiddles," moving
things around to other departments, but generally most saw neoliberal
government restructuring to be of a very different scale and character
(interview 9, 25 June 2004).

71 Interview 2, 24 Feb. 2004.

72 Interview 2, 24 Feb. 2004.

73 Interview 17, 8 Nov. 2004.

74 Interview 2, 24 Feb. 2004.

75 For example, interview 5, 12 May 2004; and interview 17, 8 Nov. 2004. The
subsequent Liberal government has continued to focus on results-based
planning, logic models, outcomes, outputs, and performance measures.

Teghtsoonian (2004) shows that business plans were also introduced by the NDP to the Ministry of Women's Equality in British Columbia.

76 Interview 16, 5 Nov. 2004.

77 Interview 16, 5 Nov. 2004.

78 Interview 16, 5 Nov. 2004.

79 Interview 16, 5 Nov. 2004.

80 Interview 17, 8 Nov. 2004.

81 She also added that not all the managers even understand these strategies in order to implement them (interview 17, 8 Nov. 2004.)

82 Interview 5, 12 May 2004.

83 Interview 12, 3 Oct. 2004. She went on to elaborate that the OWD had funded a project by an organization under an earlier government. The organization produced a booklet that "was explicitly critical of the Harris government. And there it is on the front page: 'We want to acknowledge with thanks funds from the Women's Directorate.' This is like a big no-no."

84 Interview 13, 7 Oct. 2004. When I spoke with Dianne Cunningham, we reviewed some of these communications, and she drew my attention to "how we always tried to put the good spin on it" (interview 16, 5 Nov. 2004).

85 One key exception is the PCs' pursuit of public-private partnerships with the business community. For an elaboration see Bradford (2003). The directorate's *1998–1999 Business Plan* specifically refers to public-private partnerships in the context of community consultation (Ontario 1998, 2).

86 They refer specifically to the "Roadmap to Prosperity," referring to it sarcastically as "that lovely document" (interview 6, 20 May 2004, and interview 7, 20 May 2004).

87 Interview 6, 20 May 2004. This problem is directly related to the issue raised earlier about the professionalization of groups. The OWD used to provide core funding to women's groups and centres. The funding process changed so that in order to get funds, groups now have to give project submissions, and the OWD then selects the "most worthy" (interview 13, 7 Oct. 2004).

88 Interview 12, 3 Oct. 2004.

89 Interview 17, 8 Nov. 2004.

90 Interview 2, 24 Feb. 2004.

91 Interview 2, 24 Feb. 2004. Although Malloy (2003) found that some groups stopped contacting the directorate due to limited resources, and a sense of futility. He points to the double dilemma that the OWD's legitimacy with the outside was undermined at the same time as it had very little credibility on the inside.

92 Interview 8, 18 June 2004.

93 Interestingly, Dianne Cunningham identified Partners for Change as non-partisan (interview 16, 5 Nov. 2004).

94 She specifically referred to cuts in funding, lifetime bans on welfare, and the reintroduction of the Spouse in the House rule (interview 17, 8 Nov. 2004).

95 Interview 17, 8 Nov. 2004.

96 Interview 17, 8 Nov. 2004.

97 Interview 2, 24 Feb. 2004; interview 3, 5 March 2004; interview 13, 7 Oct. 2004; interview 17, 8 Nov. 2004.

98 Interview 14, 15 Oct. 2004.

99 Interview 3, 5 March 2004.

100 Interview 1, 20 Nov. 2003.

101 Interview 3, 5 March 2004.

102 Interview 2, 24 Feb. 2004.

103 Interview 10, 3 Sept. 2004.

104 Interview 1, 20 Nov. 2003.

105 Interview 9, 25 June 2004.

106 Interview 2, 24 Feb. 2004.

107 Unfortunately this reflects the artificial policy separation used by the OWD and is not to deny that women's economic independence and violence against women are certainly interrelated. This is especially important because several pointed out that from 1995 onward, much more emphasis was put on economic independence than violence against women, and the strong relationship between the directorate and the justice ministry, under Minister Marion Boyd, were severed. The focus on women's economic independence, then, which was problematic in itself in a number of ways discussed later, also occurred at the expense of violence against women initiatives. The government increasingly dealt with violence against women through a law-and-order approach. As Judy Wolfe noted, the Tories also believed that having a job would solve women's problems, including violence.

108 As noted in chapter 3, this was also a focus during the previous Liberal and NDP governments, but it became much more central in the PC agenda. Dianne Cunningham specifically mentioned the attention placed on "celebrating small business" and women and computing skills (interview 16, 5 Nov. 2004). Teghtsoonian (2004) also found a heightened emphasis on women in business in her study of British Columbia's (former) Ministry for Women's Equality.

109 Interestingly, one interviewee informed me that these quotations were taken from a poster series, which she described as very successful in the

1980s (interview 15b, 26 April 2005). As I note in chapter 3, this earlier policy focus provided a basis on which to build a neoliberal women's policy agenda.

110 Trickey (1997) makes a similar point about the repeal of the Employment Equity Act. She asserts that the systemic understanding of racism that had been developed over time was replaced by the Tories with an individualized approach to discrimination, largely left to the Ontario Human Rights Commission, which is based on an individual complaint model.

111 Interview 17, 8 Nov. 2004.

112 Interview 2, 24 Feb. 2004.

113 Interview 13, 7 Oct. 2004.

114 One source pointed out that there is a more substantive way to approach the training of women in non-traditional jobs, and gave an example from British Columbia. When the new "Fast Cat Ferries" were introduced, they were made of aluminum, so the trained welders in the province were not able to work without retraining. The B.C. Women's Ministry insisted that training be given to women and First Nations people.

115 Interview 13, 7 Oct. 2004.

116 Interview 2, 24 Feb. 2004.

117 Interview 12, 3 Oct. 2004.

118 Interview 12, 3 Oct. 2004.

119 Interview 17, 8 Nov. 2004.

120 Boyd argues this is a problem within the OWD itself, which, from her perspective, was always much more interested in issues like pay equity than in levels of welfare and the Spouse in the House rule (interview 8, 18 June 2004). But another interviewee stressed that the directorate was not consulted about welfare levels (interview 15b, 26 April 2005).

121 Interview 12, 3 Oct. 2004.

122 They added that in Canada in general, there is no overall industrial strategy that encompasses employment, training, and credential recognition, and that this problem is further complicated by overlapping federal-provincial jurisdiction, which makes it difficult to develop policy (interview 6, 20 May 2004 and interview 7, 20 May 2004).

123 Interview 12, 3 Oct. 2004.

124 Also see Scott (1999).

125 Interview 9, 25 June 2004.

126 Interview 8, 18 June 2004.

127 This was despite the fact that it was national policy language.

128 Interview 9, 25 June 2004.

129 Interview 14, 15 Oct. 2004.

130 Interview 13, 7 Oct. 2004.
131 She saw Cunningham as a "red Tory" (interview 13, 7 Oct. 2004).
     Another maintained that Cunningham does identify as a feminist –
     "What she means by that might be different from what an NDP person
     might mean, but she would" (interview 2, 24 Feb. 2004).
132 Wolfe also credited Cunningham with the survival of the directorate
     (interview 18, 27 Jan. 2005).
133 Interview 2, 24 Feb. 2004.

Conclusion: Building a Femocratic Administration

1 Interview 2, 24 Feb. 2004.
2 Interview 5, 12 May 2004.
3 Interview 2, 24 Feb. 2004.
4 Interview 17, 8 Nov. 2004. Another participant made the important point
   that downloading to the voluntary sector also fails to recognize the need
   for adequate staff to coordinate volunteer labour (interview 18, 27 Jan.
   2005).
5 Often disks or chips were used. When one wanted to speak, they used
   one of their chips. This was done to discourage a few from monopolizing
   discussions (Phillips 1991).
6 But Mahon (2003) also emphasizes the interconnectedness of scales. Given
   the nature of Canadian federalism, and specifically the interdependence
   created by federal funding arrangements, provincial structures
   cannot be examined in isolation from the federal scale and intergovernmental relations. Regard must be given to the wider structures and
   processes of federalism, in which sub-national structures are imbedded, in
   order to understand the potential for procedural and substantive (social
   rights) democracy both at, and between, different levels of governance.
7 Interview 17, 8 Nov. 2004.
8 Interview 14, 15 Oct. 2004.
9 Interview 3, 5 March 2004.
10 Interview 9, 25 June 2004.
11 Interview 14, 15 Oct. 2004.
12 However, these debates do seem to pose the structural options as either/
    or, which discounts the possibility of multiple structures of representation
    for women's equality, based on a variety of models.
13 However, the study found that for a structure to be successful, a merely
    symbolic connection to the women's movement was not enough (Loven-
    duski et al. 2005b).

14 Based on my discussion in chapter 4, I would also place Malloy's work in this grouping.

15 Pross (1995) also conceives of the policy community as important mainly in terms of a "perpetual review process" (266) rather than "popular control over the design and delivery of programs," as Langille (1993) advocates (236).

16 Very briefly, it assumes that the electoral system actually reflects the popular will of the electorate, which is unfounded given the current Single Member Plurality system. It also assumes that the party system provides equal representation to all citizens, when there is abundant evidence to the contrary. See, for example, Earles and Findlay 2003.

17 Sossin (1993) demonstrates how discretion in tax administration has served to aid the elite taxpayer, who is already advantaged.

18 Federal statistics are being used because equivalent information is not available in Ontario owing to the end of employment equity.

19 One interviewee pointed to the irony that in Ontario, in total numbers, there are probably more women in the public service now than men, and there has even been an increase of women in managerial positions. But this is happening at the same time as men are leaving the public service and moving to the private sector. She thought this might be a sign that government is not the best place to work anymore. Restructuring has certainly changed the character of work in the public sector (interview 13, 7 Oct. 2004).

20 Interview 3, 5 March 2004.

21 Interview 17, 8 Nov. 2004. And, as Albo (1993) maintains, this "locks in existing inequalities of representation" (30). Wainwright (2003) adds that the possible options are usually predetermined by policy "experts" (20).

22 In many ways, executive federalism and Weberian bureaucracy share much in common.

23 This is not to say that there is no disagreement within the childcare community. However, there is broad agreement on fundamental issues including the need for federal funding and national standards assuring quality, universality, accessibility, and affordability.

24 Mackintosh (1993) argues that better funding of groups was needed.

25 Although their article refers to a period of time when NAC had a very different funding relationship with the federal government than it has now.

26 As do the current changes made by the Harper Conservatives to the Women's Program within Status of Women Canada.

27 After its vocal opposition to the Canada-U.S. Free Trade Agreement, NAC's funding was cut drastically, and the Tories refused to participate in NAC's annual lobby (Geller-Schwartz 1995).

28 In September 2006, the Harper Conservatives announced a $5 million cut to Status of Women Canada. This is in addition to the elimination of other significant democracy- and social-justice-oriented bodies such as the Court Challenges Program and the Law Commission of Canada. For a complete list of cuts, see "Government cuts to 66 programs announced in September 2006." CBC News 2006. http://www.cbc.ca/news2/background/ parliament39/budgetcuts-list.html.

29 Hopefully this does not replicate the false dichotomy between the economic and the political. The purpose of democratic and femocratic administration is, after all, to bring back together the public and private, economic and political, which have, as Ellen Wood (1995) has shown, been separated in capitalism. In speaking of "democratizing the market," I am making two assumptions. First, I am influenced by feminist work on the public/private divide, which has shown that one's ability to participate in the public sphere depends on significant change in the private (i.e., the household and market) sphere. (For example, see Phillips 1991.) Second, I believe that democratizing the state will make it more possible for people to seek democracy in their everyday lives.

30 See Panitch 1993; Albo 1994; Jackson 1999.

31 It is curious how often feminist contributions are ignored in the democratic administration literature. In *Shrinking the State: Globalization and Public Administration "Reform,"* Shields and Evans, for instance, even while citing Janine Brodie (who has provided one of the leading feminist critiques of neoliberalism in Canada), largely bypass all of the gendered consequences of neoliberal restructuring. They cite both Brodie and Hilary Wainwright without mentioning gender.

32 This requires a feminism that is concerned not only with gender equality, but that of class, race, nationality, sexuality, ability, and age.

33 The shorter work week frees up time for both men and women, allowing for a more equitable division of domestic labour. This is, of course, no guarantee that such an equitable division will occur, and so the patriarchal structure of the family must remain an essential target of struggle for both women and men.

34 See Waring 2000b; Bakker 1998.

35 It must be noted that, as Meg Luxton as shown, time-use studies on their own are unable to measure important factors such as working conditions, efficiency and work quality, multiple tasks, and household variations, and therefore need to be supplemented with other strategies. For more on time-use studies, see Luxton 1997. Measuring time use, however, does have the advantage of avoiding commodification, and advancing democratization.

Bibliography

Archival Sources

Ontario. OWD. (1994). "Letter to Stephen Lewis from Elaina Zienba, Minister of Citizenship and Marion Boyd, Attorney General and Women's Issues." May. Archives of Ontario. RG 69–1.

Ontario. OWD. (1993a). "Memo re: Study of ESL/FSL programs." June. Archives of Ontario. RG 69–1.

Ontario. OWD. (1993b). "Memorandum re: Updating of ESL/FSL programs." Archives of Ontario. RG 69–1.

Ontario. OWD. (1992a). "ACTEW Letter." 23 April. Archives of Ontario. RG 69–1.

Ontario. OWD. (1992b). "Memo Re: Integration of Women's Issues within Joint Survey on ESL/FSL." Archives of Ontario. RG 69–1.

Ontario. OWD. (1991a). "Language Training and Immigrant Women." May. Archives of Ontario. RG 69–1.

Ontario. OWD. (1991b). "Memorandum re: Language Training Paper." 16 October. Archives of Ontario. RG 69–1.

Ontario. OWD. (1990a). "Cabinet Committee on Race Relations: Report." 19 June. Archives of Ontario. RG 69–1.

Ontario. OWD. (1990b). "Deputy Ministers' Committee on Education, Training and Adjustment Report." 19 April. Archives of Ontario. RG 69–1.

Ontario. OWD. (1989a). "Cabinet Committee on Race Relations Information Item: Government Initiatives Relating to Immigrant and Visible Minority Women." May. Archives of Ontario. RG 69–1.

Ontario. OWD. (1989b). "Government Initiatives Related to Immigrant and Visible Minority Women." May. Archives of Ontario. RG 69–1.

Ontario. OWD. (1986a). "Highlights." Archives of Ontario. RG 69–1.

Ontario. OWD. (1986b). "Minister Responsible for Women's Issues Summary of Key Announcements." July 1985–April 1986. Archives of Ontario. RG 69–1.

Ontario. OWD. (1985a). "1985 Ontario Budget: Analysis of Impact on Women." Archives of Ontario. RG 69–1.

Ontario. OWD. (1985b). "An Agenda for Reform: Proposals for Minority Parliament." May. Archives of Ontario. RG 69–1.

Ontario. OWD. (1985c). "Chatelaine Grades the Provinces on Women's Issues." April. Archives of Ontario. RG 69–1.

Ontario. OWD. (1985d). Citizenship and Culture. "Implementation of Lead Role in Volunteerism." Cabinet Submission. 22 November. Archives of Ontario. RG 69–1.

Ontario. OWD. (1985e). "FPT Working Group on Child Care: Report to Meeting of Ministers Responsible for the Status of Women." Winnipeg, Manitoba. June. Archives of Ontario. RG 69–1.

Ontario. OWD. (1985f). "Memorandum to: Robert D. Carman, Secretary of Cabinet, Subject: Impact on Women Statements in Cabinet Submissions." From Glenna Carr. 26 September. Archives of Ontario. RG 69–1.

Ontario. OWD. (1985g). "New Initiatives for Women: Proposed and Announced." 7 May. Archives of Ontario. RG 69–1.

Ontario. OWD. (1985h). "OWD Grants Program." 19 February. Archives of Ontario. RG 69–1.

Ontario. OWD. (1985i). "Policy Issue: Rebuttal against Market Forces." Archives of Ontario. RG 69–1.

Ontario. OWD. (1985j). "Questions and Answers: Women's Issues." 2 April. Archives of Ontario. RG 69–1.

Ontario. OWD. (1984a). "Estimates Office of the Deputy Premier, October–November 1984. Summary and Analysis. Policy Planning and Analysis Unit, Policy and Research Branch." December. Archives of Ontario. RG 69–1.

Ontario. OWD. (1984b). "FPT Ministers Conference." 4 December. Archives of Ontario. RG 69–1.

Ontario. OWD. (1984c). "Memorandum to: Members of the Ontario Delegation to the Third Annual Meeting of F-P-T Ministers Responsible for the Status of Women." Archives of Ontario. RG 69–1.

Ontario. OWD. (1984d). "A Plan of Action for the Women of Ontario." Cabinet Submission to Deputy Premier's Office. 18 April. Archives of Ontario. RG 69–1.

Ontario. OWD. (1984e). "Preliminary Summary Record of Discussion." FPT Meeting of Ministers Responsible for Women. Ottawa, 4 December. Archives of Ontario. RG 69–1.

Ontario. OWD. (1984f). "Proposed Terms of Reference, FPT Working Group in Child Care." 18 June. Archives of Ontario. RG 69–1.

Ontario. OWD. (1984g). "Synthesis of the Proceedings at Niagara-on-the-Lake." Office of the Deputy Premier, May. Archives of Ontario. RG 69–1.

Ontario. OWD. (1984h). "Third Annual FPT Conference of Ministers Responsible for the Status of Women: Summary Report on Initiatives Taken by Provincial Governments, 1983–1984." Archives of Ontario. RG 69–1.

Ontario. OWD. (1984i). "Update on Family Law Reform Amendment Act." 18 June. Archives of Ontario. RG 69–1.

Ontario. OWD. (1983). "Memorandum to: Cabinet Committee Secretaries re: Statements on Women in Cabinet Submissions." From Glenna Carr. 18 October. Archives of Ontario. RG 69–1.

Government Documents

Canada. Minister of Finance. (2012). *Jobs Growth and Long-Term Prosperity: Economic Action Plan 2012*. Ottawa. 29 March. http://www.budget.gc.ca/2012/plan/pdf/Plan2012-eng.pdf.

Canada. Status of Women Canada. (2000). "Canada's National Response to the UN Questionnaire to Governments on Implementation of the Beijing Platform for Action (1995) and the Outcome of the Twenty-Third Special Session of the General Assembly (2000)." http://www.un.org/womenwatch/daw/followup/responses/Canada.pdf.

Canada. Treasury Board Secretariat. (2004). "Employment Equity in the Federal Public Service 2002–2003." http://publications.gc.ca/collections/Collection/BT1-9-2003E.pdf.

Canada. Treasury Board Secretariat. (1998). "Table 9: Hirings into the Federal Public Service by Designated Group and Occupational Category." *Employment Equity in the Federal Public Service 1977–1998*.

Ontario. Cabinet Committee on Poverty Reduction. (2013). *Breaking the Cycle: Ontario's Poverty Reduction Strategy*. http://www.children.gov.on.ca/htdocs/English/documents/breakingthecycle/Poverty_Report_EN.pdf.

Ontario. Ministry of Finance. (2011). *Public Accounts of Ontario*.

Ontario. Ministry of Finance. (1991). *Public Accounts of Ontario*.

Ontario. Ministry of Finance. (1987). *Public Accounts of Ontario*.

Ontario. Ministry of Health. (2011). *Open Minds, Healthy Minds: Ontario's Comprehensive Mental Health and Addictions Strategy*. http://www.health.gov.on.ca/en/common/ministry/publications/reports/mental_health2011/mentalhealth_rep2011.pdf.

Ontario. Ministry of Municipal Affairs and Housing. (2010). *Ontario's Long-Term Affordable Housing Strategy*. http://www.mah.gov.on.ca/Page9187.aspx.

Ontario. OWD. (2012a). "Key Programs: Public Education Campaigns."
   http://www.women.gov.on.ca/english/keyprograms/education.shtml.
Ontario. OWD. (2012b). "News Highlights." http://www.women.gov.on.ca/
   english/news/index.shtml.
Ontario. OWD. (2011a). "For Organizations: Grant Information." http://
   www.women.gov.on.ca/english/grants/index.shtml.
Ontario. OWD. (2011b). "Recognizing Women." http://www.women.gov.
   on.ca/english/recognizing/index.shtml.
Ontario. OWD. (2011c). "Resources and Links." http://www.women.gov.
   on.ca/english/resources/gettinghelp.shtml.
Ontario. OWD. (2003a). "Carol's Got Wheels."
Ontario. OWD. (2003b). "Carole Can Fix It."
Ontario. OWD. (2003c). "Catherine Ferguson."
Ontario. OWD. (2003d). "Job Segregation?"
Ontario. OWD. (2003e). "Pat's Moving Up."
Ontario. OWD. (2003f). "Pilot Project Provides Information Technology Train-
   ing for Women."
Ontario. OWD. (2003g). "Program Trains Disadvantaged Women for the IT Sec-
   tor, $300,000 Presented during International Women's Week." 5 March 2002.
Ontario. OWD. (2003h). "Sibongile Matheson."
Ontario. OWD. (2003i). "Supporting Women's Entrepreneurship."
Ontario. OWD. (2001). "Ontario Government Invests in Information Technol-
   ogy (IT) Training for Women." 27 April.
Ontario. OWD. (1998). *OWD 1998–1999 Business Plan*. Queen's Printer for
   Ontario.
Ontario. OWD. (1994a). "Community Grants Address Diversity." *Currents* 4
   (11, Spring): 4.
Ontario. OWD. (1994b). "Directorate Is Prime Resource for International
   Women's Organizations, Governments." *Currents* 4 (12, Fall): 5.
Ontario. OWD. (1994c). "Employment Equity Takes Effect." *Currents* 4 (12, Fall): 3.
Ontario. OWD. (1994d). "$50 Million Pay Equity Down Payment Helps Low-
   Paid Women." *Currents* 4 (12, Fall): 7.
Ontario. OWD. (1994e). "Improved Working Conditions for Homeworkers."
   Currents 4 (12, Fall): 2.
Ontario. OWD. (1994f). "Students Need to Understand Sexual Harassment."
   Currents 4 (12, Fall): 6.
Ontario. OWD. (1994g). "Women Access New Funding." *Currents* 4 (11,
   Spring): 2.
Ontario. OWD. (1994h). "Women's Role Strengthened in Training and Labour
   Adjustment Decision-Making." *Currents* 4 (11, Spring): 8.

Ontario. OWD. (1994i). "Work & Family Symposium a First." *Currents* 4 (12, Fall): 2.

Ontario. OWD. (1993a). *Women in the Labour Market: Focus on Aboriginal Women*.

Ontario. OWD. (1993b). *Women in the Labour Market: Focus on Racial Minority Women*.

Ontario. OWD. (1993c). *Women in the Labour Market: Focus on Women with Disabilities*.

Ontario. OWD. (1993d). *The North American Free Trade Agreement: Implications for Women*.

Ontario. OWD. (1993e). "The OWD Is 10 Years Old." *Currents* 4 (9, Spring): 1–2.

Ontario. OWD. (1993f). "'Work & Family': Acting on Workplace Realities." *Currents* 4 (10, Fall): 3.

Ontario. OWD. (1991). *OWD Year-end Report, 1990–1991*.

Ontario. OWD. (1990). *OWD Year-end Report, 1989–1990*.

Ontario. OWD. (1987). *The Free Trade Agreement and Women*.

Ontario. OWD. (1985). *Ontario Labour Legislation of Interest of Women*.

Ontario. OWD. (1984). *Plan of Action for the Women of Ontario*.

Ontario. OWD. (N.d.). "The Ontario Women's Directorate." Government of Ontario. Toronto.

Ontario. OWD. (N.d.). "The Ontario Women's Directorate: Who We Are, What We Do, How We Work." Government of Ontario. Toronto.

Ontario. OWD and CAMCO. (1992). *Flexible Working Arrangements: A Change Agent Project by the OWD and CAMCO Inc*.

Ontario. OWD and the Ontario Métis and Aboriginal Association. (1991). *Employment Equity for Aboriginal Women: Putting Skills to Work*.

Ontario. OWD and Union Gas. (1992). *Sharing the Balance. The Union Gas Experience: A Change Agent Project by the OWD and Union Gas*.

Ontario. OWD and United Food and Commercial Workers Union. (1992). *Balancing Work and Family Responsibilities: A Change Agent Project by the OWD and the United Food and Commercial Workers Union*.

Ontario. OWD and the Urban Alliance on Race Relations. (1990). *Employment Equity for Visible Minority Women, A Guide for Employers: A Change Agent Project*.

Ontario. Red Tape Secretariat. (2002a). "About Us." 15 October.

Ontario. Red Tape Secretariat. (2002b). "What We Do." 15 October.

Interview Sources

Interview 1. Phone interview. 20 Nov. 2003.

Interview 2. In-person interview. Toronto, Ontario. 24 Feb. 2004.

Interview 3. In-person interview. Toronto, Ontario. 5 March 2004.
Interview 4. In-person interview. Toronto, Ontario. 23 April 2004.
Interview 5. In-person interview. Toronto, Ontario. 12 May 2004.
Interview 6. In-person interview. Toronto, Ontario. 20 May 2004.
Interview 7. In-person interview. Toronto, Ontario. 20 May 2004.
Interview 8. In-person interview. London, Ontario. 18 June 2004.
Interview 9. In-person interview. Toronto, Ontario. 25 June 2004.
Interview 10. In-person interview. Toronto, Ontario. 3 Sept. 2004.
Interview 11. In-person interview. Toronto, Ontario. 3 Sept. 2004.
Interview 12. Phone interview. 3 Oct. 2004.
Interview 13. In-person interview. Toronto, Ontario. 7 Oct. 2004.
Interview 14. In-person interview. Toronto, Ontario. 15 Oct. 2004.
Interview 15a. Phone interview. 21 Oct. 2004.
Interview 15b. Follow-up, email. 26 April 2005.
Interview 16. In-person interview. London, Ontario. 5 Nov. 2004.
Interview 17. In-person interview. Toronto, Ontario. 8 Nov. 2004.
Interview 18. In-person interview. Toronto, Ontario. 27 Jan. 2005.
Interview 19. In-person interview. Toronto, Ontario. 27 Jan. 2005.

Secondary Sources

Adamson, Nancy, et al. (1988). *Feminist Organizing for Change: The Contempo-rary Women's Movement in Canada*. Toronto: Oxford University Press.
Agócs, Carol. (2012). "Representative Bureaucracy? Employment Equity in the Public Service of Canada." Paper presented at the annual meeting of the Canadian Political Science Association. 13–15 June. http://www.cpsa-acsp. ca/papers-2012/Agocs.pdf.
Agócs, Carol. (1997). "Institutionalized Resistance to Change: Denial, Inaction and Repression." *Journal of Business Ethics* 16 (9): 917–31.
Albo, Gregory. (1994). "Competitive Austerity and the Impasse of Capital-ist Employment Policy." In *Socialist Register 1994: Between Globalism and Nationalism*, ed. Ralph Miliband and Leo Panitch, 144–70. London: Merlin Press.
Albo, Gregory. (1993). "Democratic Citizenship and the Future of Public Man-agement." In *A Different Kind of State? Popular Power and Democratic Admin-istration*, ed. Gregory Albo, David Langille, and Leo Panitch, 17–33. Toronto: Oxford University Press.
Albo, Gregory, and Travis Fast. (2003). "Varieties of Neoliberalism: Trajectories of Workfare in the Advanced Capitalist Countries." Presented at the Annual

Meetings of the Canadian Political Science Association Congress of the Humanities and Social Sciences, Dalhousie University, Halifax, Nova Scotia.

Alboim, Naomi. (1997). "Institutional Structure as Change Agent: An Analysis of the Ontario Women's Directorate." In *Women and the Canadian State/ Femmes et L'État Canadien*, ed. Caroline Andrew and Sanda Rodgers, 220–27. Montreal: McGill-Queen's University Press.

Allen, Judith. (1990). "Does Feminism Need a Theory of the State?" In *Playing the State: Australian Feminist Interventions*, ed. Sophie Watson, 21–38. London: Verso.

Anderson, Lynell, and Tammy Findlay. (2010). "Does Public Reporting Measure Up? Federalism, Accountability and Child Care Policy in Canada." *Canadian Public Administration* 53 (3): 417–38.

Anderson, Lynell, and Tammy Findlay. (2007). *Making the Connections: Using Public Reporting to Track the Progress on Child Care Services in Canada*. Child Care Advocacy Association of Canada. November.

Andrew, Caroline. (2008). "Women in Cities: New Spaces for the Women's Movement?" In *Women's Movements: Flourishing or in Abeyance?* ed. Sandra Grey and Marian Sawer, 116–27. New York: Routledge.

Armstrong, Pat. (1996). "The Feminization of the Labour Force: Harmonizing Down in a Global Economy." In *Rethinking Restructuring: Gender and Change in Canada*, ed. Isabella Bakker, 29–54. Toronto: University of Toronto Press.

Armstrong, Pat, and M. Patricia Connelly. (1999). "Introduction: Feminism, Political Economy and the State: Contested Terrain." In *Feminism, Political Economy and the State: Contested Terrain*, ed. Pat Armstrong and M. Patricia Connelly, 1–21. Toronto: Canadian Scholars' Press.

Armstrong, Pat, and M. Patricia Connelly. (1997). "Introduction: The Many Forms of Privatization." *Studies in Political Economy* 53 (Summer): 3–9.

Arscott, Jane. (1995). "A Job Well Begun ... Representation, Electoral Reform, and Women." In *Gender and Politics in Contemporary Canada*, ed. François-Pierre Gingras, 56–84. Toronto: Oxford University Press.

Aucoin, Peter. (2000). *The New Public Management: Canada in Comparative Perspective*. Montreal: Institute for Research on Public Policy (IRPP).

Bacchi, Carol. (1999). *Women, Policy and Politics: The Construction of Policy Problems*. London: Sage.

Bakan, Abigail, and Audrey Kobayashi. (2000). *Employment Equity in Canada: A Provincial Comparison*. Ottawa: Status of Women Canada.

Bakker, Isabella. (1999). "Neoliberal Governance and the New Gender Order." *Working Papers in Local Governance and Democracy*, 1: 49–59.

Bakker, Isabella. (1998). *Unpaid Work and Macroeconomics: New Discussions, New Tools for Action*. Ottawa: Status of Women Canada.

Bakker, Isabella. (1996a). "Deconstructing Macro-economics through a Feminist Lens." In *Women and Canadian Public Policy*, ed. Janine Brodie, 31–56. Toronto: Harcourt Brace & Company Canada Ltd.

Bakker, Isabella. (1996b). "Introduction: The Gendered Foundations of Restructuring in Canada." In *Rethinking Restructuring: Gender and Change in Canada*, ed. Isabella Bakker, 3–28. Toronto: University of Toronto Press.

Bakker, Isabella, and Diane Elson. (1998). "Towards Engendering Budgets." In *The Alternative Federal Budget Papers 1998*, 297–319. Ottawa: Canadian Centre for Policy Alternatives.

Bannerji, Himani. (1996). "On the Dark Side of the Nation: Politics of Multiculturalism and the State of 'Canada.'" *Journal of Canadian Studies/Revue d'Études Canadiennes* 31 (3): 103–24.

Barrett, Michèle. (1980). "Feminism and the Politics of the State." In *Women's Oppression Today: Problems in Marxist Feminist Analysis*, 227–47. London: Verso.

Bezanson, Kate, and Meg Luxton. (2006). "Introduction: Social Reproduction and Feminist Political Economy." In *Social Reproduction: Feminist Political Economy Challenges Neoliberalism*, ed. Kate Bezanson and Meg Luxton, 3–10. Montreal, Kingston: McGill-Queen's University Press.

Bhavnani, Kum-Kum, and Margaret Coulson. (1986). "Transforming Socialist-Feminism: The Challenge of Racism." *Feminist Review* 23 (1): 81–92.

Block, Sheila, and Grace-Edward Galabuzi. (2011). *Canada's Colour Coded Labour Market: The Gap for Racialized Workers*. Ottawa: Canadian Centre for Policy Alternatives. March. http://www.policyalternatives.ca/sites/default/files/uploads/publications/National%20Office/2011/03/Colour%20Coded%20Labour%20Market.pdf.

Bradford, Neil. (2003). "Public-Private Partnership? Shifting Paradigms of Economic Governance in Ontario." *Canadian Journal of Political Science* 36 (5): 1005–33.

Brennan, Deborah. (2010). "Federalism, Childcare and Multilevel Governance in Australia." In *Federalism, Feminism and Multilevel Governance*, ed. M. Haussman et al., 37–50. Burlington, VT: Ashgate.

Brenner, Neil, Jamie Peck, and Nik Theodore. (2010). "Variegated Neoliberalization: Geographies, Modalities, Pathways." *Global Networks* 10 (2): 182–222.

Brock, Kathy. (2010). "Capturing Complexity: The Ontario Government Relationship with the Social Economy Sector." In *Researching the Social Economy*, ed. L. Mook et al., 131–53. Toronto: University of Toronto Press.

Brodie, Janine. (1996). "Canadian Women, Changing State Forms, and Public Policy." In *Women and Canadian Public Policy*, ed. Janine Brodie, 1–30. Toronto: Harcourt Brace & Company Canada Ltd.

Brodie, Janine. (1995a). *Politics on the Margins: Restructuring and the Canadian Women's Movement*. Halifax: Fernwood Publishing.

Brodie, Janine. (1995b). "The Women's Movement Outside Quebec: Shifting Relations with the Canadian State." In *Beyond Quebec: Taking Stock of Canada*, ed. Kenneth McRoberts, 333–57. Montreal, Kingston: McGill-Queen's University Press.

Brodie, Janine. (1990). *The Political Economy of Canadian Regionalism*. Toronto: Harcourt Brace Jovanovich.

Brodie, Janine, and Isabella Bakker. (2007). "Canada's Social Policy Regime and Women: An Assessment of the Last Decade." Ottawa: Status of Women Canada. March. http://publications.gc.ca/collections/collection_2007/swc-cfc/SW21-156-2007E.pdf.

Brooks, Steven. (1994). "Bureaucracy." In *Canadian Politics*, 2nd ed., ed. James P. Bickerton and Alain-G. Gagnon, 307–27. Peterborough, ON: Broadview Press.

Brown, Wendy. (1995). "Finding the Man in the State." In *States of Injury: Power and Freedom in Late Modernity*, 166–90. Princeton: Princeton University Press.

Browne, Paul Leduc. (1997). "Déjà Vu: Thatcherism in Ontario." In *Open for Business, Closed to People: Mike Harris' Ontario*, ed. Diana S. Ralph, André Régimbald, and Nérée St-Amand, 37–44. Halifax: Fernwood Publishing.

Burke, Mike, Colin Mooers, and John Shields. (2000). "Introduction: Critical Perspectives on Canadian Public Policy." In *Restructuring and Resistance: Canadian Public Policy in an Age of Global Capitalism*, ed. Mike Burke, Colin Mooers, and John Shields, 11–23. Halifax: Fernwood Publishing.

Burstyn, Varda. (1983). "Masculine Dominance and the State." In *Women, Class, Family and the State*, ed. Varda Burstyn and Dorothy E. Smith, 45–89. Toronto: Garamond Press.

Burt, Sandra. (1993). "Legislators, Women and Public Policy." In *Changing Patterns: Women in Canada*, 2nd ed., ed. Sandra Burt et al., 212–42. Toronto: McClelland & Stewart Inc.

Burt, Sandra, and Elizabeth Lorenzin. (1997). "Taking the Women's Movement to Queen's Park: Women's Interests and the New Democratic Government of Ontario." In *In the Presence of Women: Representation in Canadian Governments*, ed. Jane Arscott and Linda Trimble, 202–27. Toronto: Harcourt Brace & Company.

Byrne, Lesley Hyland. (1997). "Feminists in Power: Women Cabinet Ministers in the New Democratic Party (NDP) Government of Ontario, 1990–1995." *Policy Studies Journal: The Journal of the Policy Studies Organization* 25 (4): 601–12.

Bystydzienski, Jill M., and Joti Sekhon. (1999). "Introduction." In *Democratization and Women's Grassroots Movements*, ed. Jill Bystydzienski and Joti Sekhon, 1–21. Bloomington: Indiana University Press.

Cameron, Barbara. (2006). "Social Reproduction and Canadian Federalism." In *Social Reproduction: Feminist Political Economy Challenges Neoliberalism*, ed. Kate Bezanson and Meg Luxton, 45–74. Montreal, Kingston: McGill-Queen's University Press.

Cameron, Barbara. (2004). "The Social Union, Executive Power and Social Rights." *Canadian Women's Studies* 23 (3 & 4): 49–56.

Canadian Council on Social Development (CCSD). (1997). "Public Sector Downsizing: The Impact on Job Quality in Canada." Report commissioned by the Canadian Union of Public Employees. 3 October.

Canadian Labour Congress (CLC). (2000). Analysis of UI Coverage for Women.

Canadian Women's Foundation. (2013). *Fact Sheet: Moving Women out of Poverty*. January. Toronto. http://www.canadianwomen.org/sites/canadian-women.org/files/PDF-FactSheet-EndPoverty-Jan2013.pdf.

Canadian Women's March Committee. (2000). "It's Time for Change? The World March of Women." *Canadian Women's Studies* 20 (3): 21–3.

Carchedi, Bruno, and Guglielmo Carchedi. (1999). "Contradictions of European Integration." *Capital and Class* 23: 119–53.

Carty, Linda, and Dionne Brand. (1993). "'Visible Minority Women': A Creation of the Canadian State." In *Returning the Gaze: Essays on Racism, Feminism and Politics*, ed. Himani Bannerj, 169–81. Toronto: Sister Vision.

CBC News. (2006). "Government cuts to 66 programs announced in September 2006." 27 September. http://www.cbc.ca/news2/background/parliament39/budgetcuts-list.html.

C.D. Howe Institute. (2004). "The Institute's Economists."

Cerny, Philip G. (2004). "Mapping Varieties of Neoliberalism." In *IPEG Papers in Global Political Economy 12, Department of Government*, 1–18. Manchester: University of Manchester. http://www.bisa-ipeg.org/wp-content/uploads/2013/06/12-Philip-Cerny.pdf.

Chappell, Louise. (2002). *Gendering Government: Feminist Engagement with the State in Australia and Canada*. Vancouver: UBC Press.

Child Care Advocacy Association of Canada (CCAAC). (2005). "Fact Sheet # 1 – Public Funding and Child Care Policy: How Do We 'Make the

Connection?'" September. http://www.ccaac.ca/mtc/en/pdf/mtc_fact-sheet1.pdf.

Cho, Sumi, Kimberlé Williams Crenshaw, and Leslie McCall. (2013). "Toward a Field of Intersectionality Studies: Theory, Applications, and Praxis." *Signs* 38 (4, Summer): 785–810.

Chouinard, Vera. (1999). "Body Politics: Disabled Women's Activism in Canada and Beyond." In *Mind and Body Spaces: Geographies of Illness, Impairment and Disability*, ed. Ruth Butler and Hester Parr, 269–94. New York: Routledge.

Clarke, Tony. (1997). "The Transnational Corporate Agenda behind the Harris Regime." In *Open for Business, Closed to People: Mike Harris' Ontario*, ed. Diana S. Ralph, André Régimbald, and Nérée St-Amand, 28–36. Halifax: Fernwood Publishing.

Cohen, Marjorie Griffin. (1997). "From the Welfare State to Vampire Capitalism." In *Women and the Canadian Welfare State: Challenge and Change*, ed. Patricia M. Evans and Gerda R. Wekerle, 28–67. Toronto: University of Toronto Press.

Cohen, Marjorie Griffin. (1993). "The Canadian Women's Movement." In *Canadian Women's Issues. Volume 1: Strong Voices: Twenty-Five Years of Women's Activism in English Canada*, ed. Ruth Roach Pierson et al., 1–31. Toronto: James Lorimer & Company.

Cohen, Marjorie Griffin, and Stephen McBride. (2003). "Introduction." In *Global Turbulence: Social Activists' and State Responses to Globalization*, ed. Marjorie Griffin Cohen and Stephen McBride, 1–10. Burlington, VT: Ashgate Publishing.

Collier, Cheryl N. (2009). "Violence against Women or Violence against 'People'? Assessing the Impact of Neoliberalism and Post-neoliberalism on Anti-Violence Policy in Ontario and British Columbia." In *Women and Public Policy in Canada Today: A Study of Continuity and Change*, ed. Alexandra Dobrowolsky, 166–86. Toronto: Oxford University Press.

Comack, Elizabeth. (1999). "Theoretical Excursions." In *Locating the Law: Race/Class/Gender Connections*, ed. Elizabeth Comack, Sedef Arat-Koc, Karen Busby, et al., 19–68. Halifax: Fernwood Publishing.

Connell, R.W. (2002). *Gender*. Malden, MA: Blackwell Publishers Inc.

Connell, R.W. (1990). "The State, Gender, and Sexual Politics." *Theory and Society* 19 (5): 507–44.

Connelly, Patricia, and Martha MacDonald. (1996). "The Labour Market, the State, and the Reorganization of Work." In *Rethinking Restructuring: Gender and Change in Canada*, ed. Isabella Bakker, 82–91. Toronto: University of Toronto Press.

Cossman, Brenda. (1996). "Same-Sex Couples and the Politics of Family Status." In *Women and Canadian Public Policy*, ed. Janine Brodie, 223–54. Toronto: Harcourt Brace & Company Canada Ltd.

Coulter, Kendra. (2009). "Deep Neoliberal Integration: The Production of Third Way Politics in Ontario." *Studies in Political Economy* 83: 191–208.

Cranford, Cynthia, and Leah Vosko. (2004). "Gender, Nation and Precarious Self-Employment among Immigrant Women and Men: Reflections on the Canadian Case." Paper presented at the Gender and Work Database: Knowledge Production in Practice conference. York University, Toronto, Ontario. 1 October.

Crenshaw, Kimberlé. (1991). "Mapping the Margins: Intersectionality, Identity Politics and Violence against Women of Colour." *Stanford Law Review* 43 (6): 1241–99.

D'Agostino, Maria, and Helisse Levine. (2011). *Women in Public Administration: Theory and Practice*. Sudbury, MA: Jones & Bartlett Learning.

Dare, Bill. (1997). "Harris's First Year: Attacks and Resistance." In *Open for Business, Closed to People: Mike Harris' Ontario*, ed. Diana S. Ralph, André Régimbald, and Nérée St-Amand, 20–6. Halifax: Fernwood Publishing.

Das Gupta, Tania. (1995). "Families of Native Peoples, Immigrants and People of Colour." In *Canadian Families: Diversity, Conflict and Change*, ed. Nancy Mandell and Ann Duffy, 141–74. Toronto: Harcourt-Brace.

De Wolff, Alice. (2000). "The Face of Globalization: Women Working Poor in Canada." *Canadian Woman Studies* 20 (3): 54–9.

Dobrowolsky, Alexandra. (2000). *The Politics of Pragmatism: Women, Representation, and Constitutionalism in Canada*. Don Mills, ON: Oxford University Press.

Driedger, Diane. (1996). "Emerging from the Shadows: Women with Disabilities Organize." In *Across Borders: Women with Disabilities Working Together*, ed. Diane Drieger, Irene Feika, and Eileen Giron Batres, 10–25. Charlottetown: Gynergy Books.

Driscoll, Amanda, and Mona Lena Krook. (2009). "Can There Be a Feminist Rational Choice Institutionalism?" *Politics & Gender* 5 (2): 238–45.

Dua, Enakshi. (1999). "Beyond Diversity: Exploring the Ways in Which the Discourse of Race Has Shaped the Institution of the Nuclear Family." In *Scratching the Surface: Canadian Anti-Racist Feminist Thought*, ed. Enakshi Dua and Angela Robertson, 237–60. Toronto: Women's Press.

Earles, Kimberly, and Tammy Findlay. (2003). *Renewing Democracy: Rethinking Representation in Canada*. Law Commission of Canada.

Eisenstein, Hester. (1996). *Inside Agitators: Australian Femocrats and the State*. Philadelphia: Temple University Press.

Eisenstein, Hester. (1991). "Speaking for Women? Voices from the Australian Femocrat Experiment." *Australian Feminist Studies* 6 (14): 29–42.

Eisenstein, Hester. (1990). "Femocrats, Official Feminism and the Uses of Power." In *Playing the State: Australian Feminist Interventions*, ed. Sophie Watson, 87–104. London: Verso.

Evans, B. Mitchell, Stephen McBride, and John Shields. (2000). "Globalization and the Challenge to Canadian Democracy: National Governance under Threat." In *Restructuring and Resistance: Canadian Public Policy in an Age of Global Capitalism*, ed. Mike Burke, Colin Mooers, and John Shields, 80–97. Halifax: Fernwood Publishing.

Evans, Pat M., and Gerda R. Wekerle. (1997). "The Shifting Terrain of Women's Welfare: Theory, Discourse, and Activism." In *Women and the Canadian Welfare State: Challenge and Change*, ed. Pat Evans and Gerda Wekerle, 3–27. Toronto: University of Toronto Press.

Feldman, Martha S., and Anne M. Khademian. (2001). "Principles for Public Management Practice: From Dichotomies to Interdependence." *Governance: An International Journal of Policy, Administration and Institutions* 14 (3): 339–61.

Felice, Mary. (1998). "A Timeline of the Public Service Commission of Canada." Public Service Commission of Canada. http://web.archive.org/web/20070703131234/http://www.psc-cfp.gc.ca/research/timeline/psc_timeline_e.htm.

Ferguson, Kathy. (1984). *The Feminist Case against Bureaucracy*. Philadelphia: Temple University Press.

Ferguson, Susan. (2000). "Beyond the Welfare State? Left Feminism and Global Capitalist Restructuring." In *Restructuring and Resistance: Canadian Public Policy in an Age of Global Capitalism*, ed. Mike Burke, Colin Mooers, and John Shields, 276–86. Halifax: Fernwood Publishing.

Ferrao, Vincent. (2010). "Paid Work." In *Women in Canada: A Gender-Based Statistical Report*. Statistics Canada. http://www.statcan.gc.ca/pub/89-503-x/2010001/article/11387-eng.pdf.

Findlay, Sue. (1997). "Institutionalizing Feminist Politics: Learning from the Struggles for Equal Pay in Ontario." In *Women and the Canadian Welfare State: Challenges and Change*, ed. Patricia M. Evans and Gerda R. Wekerle, 310–29. Toronto: University of Toronto Press.

Findlay, Sue. (1995). "Democracy and the Politics of Representation: Feminist Struggles with the Canadian State, 1960–1990." PhD dissertation, University of Toronto.

Findlay, Sue. (1993a). "Democratizing the Local State: Issues for Feminist Practice and the Representation of Women." In *A Different Kind of State? Popular*

Power and Democratic Administration, ed. Gregory Albo, David Langille, and Leo Panitch, 155–64. Toronto: Oxford University Press.

Findlay, Sue. (1993b). "Reinventing the 'Community': A First Step in the Process of Democratization." *Studies in Political Economy* 42 (Fall): 157–67.

Findlay, Sue. (1988). "Feminist Struggles with the Canadian State: 1966–1988." *Resources for Feminist Research* 17 (3): 5–9.

Findlay, Sue. (1987). "Facing the State: The Politics of the Women's Movement Reconsidered." In *Feminism and Political Economy: Women's Work, Women's Struggles*, ed. Heather Jon Maroney and Meg Luxton, 31–50. Toronto: Methuen Publications.

Findlay, Tammy. (2013). "Femocratic Childcare Governance." In *The New Politics of Critical Social Work*, ed. Mel Gray and Stephen A. Webb, 174–94. Basingstoke: Palgrave.

Findlay, Tammy. (2011). "Gender, Democracy and Multilevel Governance: Early Childhood Development Roundtables in British Columbia." Paper presented at the 2011 Meeting of the Canadian Political Science Association, Wilfrid Laurier University, 19 May 2011.

Findlay, Tammy. (2008). "Femocratic Administration: Gender, Democracy and the State in Ontario." Doctoral dissertation, Faculty of Graduate Studies, York University.

Findlay, Tammy. (2005). "Social Policy and Social Citizenship: An Analysis of the Social Union Framework Agreement (SUFA) Three-Year Review." Paper presented at the Canadian Social Welfare Policy Conference, University of New Brunswick, 16 June.

Forell, Caroline. (1991). "Stopping the Violence: Mandatory Arrest and Police Tort Liability for Failure to Assist Battered Women." *Berkeley Women's Law Journal* 6: 215–62.

Franzway, Suzanne, et al. (1989). *Staking a Claim: Feminism, Bureaucracy and the State*. Sydney: Allen & Unwin.

Fraser, Nancy. (2009). "Feminism, Capitalism and the Cunning of History." *New Left Review* 56: 97–117.

Fudge, Judy, and Brenda Cossman. (2002). "Introduction: Privatization, Law, and the Challenge to Feminism." In *Privatization, Law, and the Challenge to Feminism*, ed. Brenda Cossman and Judy Fudge, 3–37. Toronto: University of Toronto Press.

Fudge, Judy, and Patricia McDermott, eds. (1991). *Just Wages: A Feminist Assessment of Pay Equity*. Toronto: University of Toronto Press.

Gabriel, Christina. (1996). "One or the Other? 'Race,' Gender, and the Limits of Official Multiculturalism." In *Women and Canadian Public Policy*, ed. Janine Brodie, 173–95. Toronto: Harcourt Brace & Company, Canada.

Gavigan, Shelley. (1996). "Family Ideology and the Limits of Difference." In *Women and Canadian Public Policy*, ed. Janine Brodie, 255–78. Toronto: Harcourt Brace & Company Canada Ltd.

Geller-Schwartz, Linda. (1995). "An Array of Agencies: Feminism and State Institutions." In *Comparative State Feminism*, ed. Dorothy McBride Stetson and Amy Mazur, 40–58. Thousand Oaks, CA: Sage Publications.

Grace, Joan. (2011). "Gender and Institutions of Multi-Level Governance: Child Care and Social Policy Debates in Canada." In *Gender, Politics and Institutions: Towards a Feminist Institutionalism*, ed. Mona Lena Krook and Fiona Mackay, 95–111. Basingstoke: Palgrave Macmillan.

Graefe, Peter. (2007). "Political Economy and Canadian Public Policy." In *Critical Policy Studies: Contemporary Canadian Approaches*, ed. Michael Orsini and Miriam Smith, 19–40. Vancouver: UBC Press.

Graefe, Peter. (2003). "Tipping the Scales: Conceptualizing Social Reform beyond the Centralization-Decentralization Dynamic." Paper presented at Questioning the Boundaries of Governance: A Graduate Workshop on the Theory and Practice of Federalism, Decentralisation and Multilevel Governance, University of Toronto, 14–15 February 2003.

Grant, Judith E. (1988). "Women's Issues and the State: Representation, Reform and Control." *Resources for Feminist Research* 17 (3): 87–9.

Gray, Gwendolyn. (2010). "Feminism, Federalism and Multilevel Governance: The Elusive Search for Theory?" In *Federalism, Feminism and Multilevel Governance*, ed. Melissa Haussman et al., 19–36. Burlington, VT: Ashgate.

Green, Celia. (1993). "Thinking Through Angela Y. Davis' *Women, Race & Class*." In *Returning The Gaze: Essays on Racism, Feminism and Politics*, ed. Himani Bannerji, 153–66. Toronto: Sister Vision.

Haddow, Rodney, and Thomas R. Klassen. (2004). "Partisanship, Institutions and Public Policy: The Case of Labour Market Policy in Ontario, 1990–2000." *Canadian Journal of Political Science* 37 (1): 137–60.

Hadley, Karen. (2001). *And We Still Ain't Satisfied: Gender Inequality in Canada, A Status Report for 2001*. Toronto: CSJ Foundation for Research and Education and National Action Committee on the Status of Women (NAC).

Handler, Joel. (1996). *Down from Bureaucracy: The Ambiguity of Privatization and Empowerment*. Princeton: Princeton University Press.

Harder, Lois. (2003). *State of Struggle: Feminism and Politics in Alberta*. Edmonton: University of Alberta Press.

Harding, Sandra. (1991). *Whose Science? Whose Knowledge?: Thinking from Women's Lives*. Ithica: Cornell University Press.

Haussman, Melissa, and Birgit Sauer, eds. (2007a). *Gendering the State in the Age of Globalization: Women's Movements and State Feminism in Postindustrial Democracies*. New York: Rowman & Littlefield Publishers.

Haussman, Melissa, and Birgit Sauer. (2007b). "Introduction: Women's Movements and State Restructuring in the 1990s." In *Gendering the State in the Age of Globalization: Women's Movements and State Feminism in Postindustrial Democracies*, ed. M. Haussman and B. Sauer, 1–17. New York: Rowman & Littlefield Publishers.

Hill-Collins, Patricia. (1990). *Black Feminist Thought*. Boston: Unwin Hyman.

Hirst, Paul, and Grahame Thompson. (1992). "The Problem of 'Globalization': International Economic Relations, National Economic Management and the Formation of Trading Blocs." *Economy and Society* 21 (4): 357–96.

hooks, bell. 1981. *Ain't I a Woman: Black Women and Feminism*. Boston: South End Press.

Hutchinson, Janet R., and Hollie S. Mann. (2006). "Gender Anarchy and the Future of Feminisms in Public Administration." *Administrative Theory & Praxis* 28 (3): 399–417.

Hutchinson, Janet R., and Hollie S. Mann. (2004). "Feminist Praxis: Administering for a Multicultural, Multigendered Public." *Administrative Theory and Praxis* 26 (1): 75–95.

Huws, Ursula. (1999). "Material World: The Myth of the Weightless Economy." In *Global Capitalism versus Democracy: Socialist Register 1999*, ed. Leo Panitch and Colin Leys, 29–55. New York: Monthly Review Press.

Inwood, Gregory J. (2000). "Federalism, Globalization and the (Anti-)Social Union." In *Restructuring and Resistance: Canadian Public Policy in an Age of Global Capitalism*, ed. Mike Burke, Colin Mooers, and John Shields, 124–44. Halifax: Fernwood Publishing.

Jackson, Andrew. (1999). "The Free Trade Agreement – a Decade Later." *Studies in Political Economy* 58 (Spring): 141–60.

Jenson, Jane. (2008). "Citizenship in the Era of 'New Social Risks': What Happened to Gender Inequalities?" In *Gendering the Nation-State: Canadian and Comparative Perspectives*, ed. Yasmeen Abu-Laban, 185–202. Vancouver: UBC Press.

Jenson, Jane, Rianne Mahon, and Susan D. Phillips. (2003). "No Minor Matter: The Political Economy of Childcare in Canada." In *Changing Canada: Political Economy as Transformation*, ed. Wallace Clement and Leah F. Vosko, 135–60. Montreal, Kingston: McGill-Queen's University Press.

Jenson, Jane, and Susan D. Phillips. (1996). "Regime Shift: New Citizenship Practices in Canada." *International Journal of Canadian Studies* 14 (Fall): 111–36.

Kantola, Johanna, and Joyce Outshoorn. (2007). "Changing State Feminism." In *Changing State Feminism*, ed. Joyce Outshoorn and Johanna Kantola, 1–19. New York: Palgrave.

Kaplan, Gisela. (1996). *The Meagre Harvest: The Australian Women's Movement, 1950s–1990s*. Sydney: Allen & Unwin.

Kenny, Meryl. (2011). "Gender and Institutions of Political Recruitment: Candidate Selection in Post-Devolution Scotland." In *Gender, Politics and Institutions: Towards a Feminist Institutionalism*, ed. Mona Lena Krook and Fiona Mackay, 21–41. Basingstoke: Palgrave Macmillan.

Kenny, Meryl. (2007). "Gender, Institutions and Power: A Critical Review." *Politics* 27 (2): 91–100.

Kenny, M., and Fiona Mackay. (2009). "Already Doin' It for Ourselves? Skeptical Notes on Feminism and Institutionalism." *Politics & Gender* 5 (2): 271–80.

Kernaghan, Kenneth. (1978). "Representative Bureaucracy: The Canadian Perspective." *Canadian Public Administration* 21 (4): 489–512.

Kernaghan, Kenneth, and David Siegel. (1999). "Representative Bureaucracy, Employment Equity, and Managing Diversity." In *Public Administration in Canada*, 4th ed., 575–95. Toronto: International Thomson Publishing.

Kershaw, Paul. (2006). "Weathervane Federalism: Reconsidering Federal Social Policy Leadership." *Canadian Public Administration* 49 (2): 196–219.

King, Deborah K. (1997). "Multiple Jeopardy, Multiple Consciousness: The Context of a Black Feminist Ideology." In *Feminist Social Thought: A Reader*, ed. Diana Meyers, 220–41. New York: Routledge.

Kitchen, Brigitte. (1997). "'Common Sense' Assaults on Families." In *Open for Business, Closed to People: Mike Harris' Ontario*, ed. Diana S. Ralph, André Régimbald, and Nérée St-Amand, 103–12. Halifax: Fernwood Publishing.

Klassen, Thomas R. (2000). *Precarious Values: Organizations, Politics and Labour Market Policy in Ontario*. Montreal, Kingston: McGill-Queen's University Press.

Knuttila, Murray. (1987). "New Criticism and the Challenge of Feminism." In *State Theories: From Liberalism to the Challenge of Feminism*, 129–43. Toronto: Garamond Press.

Koshan, Jennifer. (1997). "Sounds of Silence: The Public/Private Dichotomy, Violence, and Aboriginal Women." In *Challenging the Public/Private Divide: Feminism, Law & Public Policy*, ed. Susan Boyd, 87–109. Toronto: University of Toronto Press.

Krook, M.L., and F. Mackay. (2011). "Introduction: Gender, Politics, and Institutions." In *Gender, Politics and Institutions: Towards a Feminist Institutionalism*, ed. M.L. Krook and F. Mackay, 1–20. Basingstoke: Palgrave Macmillan.

Kulawik, T. (2009). "Staking the Frame of a Feminist Discursive Institutionalism." *Politics & Gender* 5 (2): 262–71.

Lamoureux, Diane. (1987). "Nationalism and Feminism in Quebec: An Impossible Attraction." In *Feminism and Political Economy: Women's Work, Women's Struggles*, ed. Heather Jon Maroney and Meg Luxton, 51–68. Toronto: Methuen Publications.

Langille, David. (1993). "Putting Democratic Administration on the Political Agenda." In *A Different Kind of State? Popular Power and Democratic Administration*, ed. Gregory Albo, David Langille, and Leo Panitch, 229–43. Toronto: Oxford University Press.

Larner, Wendy. (2003). "Neoliberalism?" *Environment and Planning. D, Society & Space* 21 (5): 509–12.

Lavigne, Marie. (1997). "Structures institutionelles en condition féminine – le cas du Conseil du statut de la femme du Québec." In *Women and the Canadian State / Femmes et L'État Canadien*, ed. Caroline Andrew and Sanda Rodgers, 228–40. Montreal: McGill-Queen's University Press.

Levi, Margaret, and Merideth Edwards. (1990). "The Dilemmas of Femocratic Reform." In *Going Public: National Histories of Women's Enfranchisement and Women's Participation within State Institutions*, ed. Mary Katzenstein and Hege Skjeie, 141–72. Oslo: Institute for Social Research.

Lipsky, Michael. (1980). *Street-Level Bureaucracy: Dilemmas of the Individual in Public Services*. New York: Russell Sage Foundation.

Little, Margaret Jane Hillyard. (1998). "'Manhunts' and 'Bingo Blabs': Single Mothers Speak Out." In *No Car, No Radio, No Liquor Permit: The Moral Regulation of Single Mothers in Ontario, 1920–1997*, 164–81. Toronto: Oxford University Press.

Loney, Martin. (1977). "A Political Economy of Citizen Participation." In *The Canadian State: Political Economy and Political Power*, ed. Leo Panitch, 446–73. Toronto: University of Toronto Press.

Lovenduski, Joni. (2011). "Foreword." In *Gender, Politics and Institutions: Towards a Feminist Institutionalism*, ed. Mona Lee Krook and Fiona Mackay, vi–xi. Basingstoke: Palgrave Macmillan.

Lovenduski, Joni. (2005). "Introduction: State Feminism and the Political Representation of Women." In *State Feminism and Political Representation*, ed. Joni Lovenduski et al., 1–19. New York: Cambridge University Press.

Lovenduski, Joni, et al. (2005a). "Conclusions: State Feminism and Political Representation." In *State Feminism and Political Representation*, ed. Joni Lovenduski, et al., 260–93. New York: Cambridge University Press.

Lovenduski, Joni, et al., eds. (2005b). *State Feminism and Political Representation*. New York: Cambridge University Press.

Luxton, Meg. (2006). "Feminist Political Economy in Canada and the Politics of Social Reproduction." In *Social Reproduction: Feminist Political Economy Challenges Neoliberalism*, ed. Kate Bezanson and Meg Luxton, 11–44. Montreal, Kingston: McGill-Queen's University Press.

Luxton, Meg. (1997). "The UN, Women and Household Labour: Meaasuring and Valuing Unpaid Work." *Women's Studies International Forum* 20 (3): 431–9.

Mackay, Fiona. (2011). "Conclusion: Towards a Feminist Institutionalism?" In *Gender, Politics and Institutions: Towards a Feminist Institutionalism*, ed. Mona Lena Krook and Fiona Mackay, 181–96. Basingstoke: Palgrave Macmillan.

Mackay, Fiona. (2008). "The State of Women's Movement/s in Britain: Ambiguity, Complexity, and Challenges from the Periphery." In *Women's Movements: Flourishing or in Abeyance?* ed. Sandra Grey and Marian Sawer, 17–32. New York: Routledge.

Mackay, Fiona, Surya Monro, and Georgina Waylen. (2009). "The Feminist Potential of Sociological Institutionalism." *Politics and Gender* 5 (2): 253–62.

Mackay, Fiona, and Georgina Waylen. (2009). "Feminist Institutionalism." *Politics & Gender* 5 (2): 237.

MacIvor, Heather. (1996). *Women and Politics in Canada*. Peterborough, ON: Broadview Press.

MacKinnon, Catharine. (1989). *Toward a Feminist Theory of the State*. Cambridge, MA: Harvard University Press.

Mackintosh, Maureen. (1993). "Creating a Developmental State: Reflections on a Policy Process." In *A Different Kind of State? Popular Power and Democratic Administration*, ed. Gregory Albo, David Langille, and Leo Panitch, 36–50. Toronto: Oxford University Press.

Macpherson, C.B. (1965). *The Real World of Democracy*. Toronto: Canadian Broadcasting Corporation.

Maddison, Sarah, and Kyungja Jung. (2008). "Autonomy and Engagement: Women's Movements in Australia and South Korea." In *Women's Movements: Flourishing or in Abeyance?* ed. Sandra Grey and Marian Sawer, 33–48. New York: Routledge.

Magnusson, Warren. (1993). "Social Movements and the State: Presentation and Representation." In *A Different Kind of State? Popular Power and Democratic Administration*, ed. Gregory Albo, David Langille, and Leo Panitch, 122–30. Toronto: Oxford University Press.

Mahon, Rianne. (2005). "Rescaling Social Reproduction: Childcare in Toronto/Canada and Stockholm/Sweden." *International Journal of Urban and Regional Research* 29 (2): 341–57.

Mahon, Rianne. (2003). "Yet Another R? The Resign *and* Rescaling of Welfare Regimes." Working Paper no. 55. School of Public Policy and Administration, Carleton University.

Mahon, Rianne. (1977). "Canadian Public Policy: The Unequal Structure of Representation." In *The Canadian State: Political Economy and Political Power*, ed. Leo Panitch, 165–98. Toronto: University of Toronto Press.

Mahon, Rianne, and Cheryl Collier. (2010). "Navigating the Shoals of Canadian Federalism: Childcare Advocacy." In *Federalism, Feminism and Multilevel Governance*, ed. Melissa Haussman et al., 51–66. Burlington, VT: Ashgate.

Mahon, Rianne, et al. (2007). "Policy Analysis in an Era of 'Globalization': Capturing Spatial Dimensions and Scalar Strategies." In *Critical Policy Studies*, ed. M. Orsini and M. Smith, 41–64. Vancouver: UBC Press.

Maillé, Chantal. (1997). "Challenges to Representation: Theory and the Women's Movement in Quebec." In *In the Presence of Women: Representation in Canadian Governments*, ed. Jane Arscott·and Linda Trimble, 47–63. Toronto: Harcourt Brace.

Maley, Terry. (2011). *Democracy and the Political in Max Weber's Thought*. Toronto: University of Toronto Press.

Malloy, Jonathan. (2003). *Between Colliding Worlds: The Ambiguous Existence of Government Agencies for Aboriginal and Women's Policy*. Toronto: University of Toronto Press.

Maroney, Heather Jon, and Meg Luxton. (1997). "Gender at Work: Canadian Feminist Political Economy since 1988." In *Understanding Canada: Building on the New Canadian Political Economy*, ed. Wallace Clement, 85–117. Montreal, Kingston: McGill-Queen's University Press.

Mazur, Amy G., and Dorothy McBride Stetson, eds. (1995). *Comparative State Feminism*. Thousand Oaks, CA: Sage Publications.

McBride, Stephen. (2001). *Paradigm Shift: Globalization and the Canadian State*. Halifax: Fernwood Publishing.

McCuaig, Kerry. (1993). "Social Movements and the NDP Government of Ontario." In *A Different Kind of State? Popular Power and Democratic Administration*, ed. Gregory Albo, David Langille, and Leo Panitch, 219–28. Toronto: Oxford University Press.

McGrath, Ann, and Winona Stevenson. (1996). "Gender, Race, and Policy: Aboriginal Women and the State in Canada and Australia." *Labour/Le Travail* 38: 37–53.

McIntosh, Mary. (1978). "The State and the Oppression of Women." In *Feminism and Materialism: Women and Modes of Production*, ed. Annette Kuhn and Ann Marie Wolpe, 254–89. London: Routledge & Kegan Paul Ltd.

McKeen, Wendy. (2007). "The National Children's Agenda: A Neoliberal Wolf in Lamb's Clothing." *Studies in Political Economy* 80: 151–73.

McNally, David. (2000). "Globalization, Trade Pacts and Migrant Workers: Rethinking the Politics of Working-Class Resistance." In *Restructuring and Resistance: Canadian Public Policy in an Age of Global Capitalism*, ed. Mike Burke, Colin Mooers, and John Shields, 262–75. Halifax: Fernwood Publishing.

Millbank, Jenni. (1997). "Lesbians, Child Custody, and the Long Lingering Gaze of the Law." In *Challenging the Public/Private Divide: Feminism, Law and Public Policy*, ed. Susan Boyd, 280–303. Toronto: University of Toronto Press.

Mitchell, Penni. (2001). "Women's Policy Units Wiped Out." *Herizons*,
Summer.

Mohanty, Chandra Talpade. (2013). "Transnational Feminist Crossings: On
Neoliberalism and Radical Critique." *Signs* (Chicago) 38 (4): 967–91.

Monture-Angus, Patricia. (1995). "Organizing against Oppression: Aboriginal
Women and the Canadian State." In *Thunder in My Soul: A Mohawk Woman
Speaks*, 169–88. Halifax: Fernwood Publishing.

Monture-Angus, Patricia. (1989). "A Vicious Circle: Child Welfare and the First
Nations." *Canadian Journal of Women and the Law* 3 (1): 1–17.

National Action Committee on the Status of Women (NAC). (1998). "Going for
the Gold on Women's Equality: Challenging the Government's New Funding Initiatives for Women's Programs." February. 1–4.

National Governmental Organizations. (n.d.). Policy, Action, Research List
(PAR-L).

Native Women's Association of Canada (NWAC). (2002). NWAC Position
Paper: The Social Union Framework Agreement (SUFA). March.

Native Women's Association of Canada (NWAC). (1991). *Voices of Aboriginal
Women: Speak Out about Violence*. Ottawa.

Newman, Jacquetta, and Linda White. (2006). *Women, Politics, and Public
Policy: The Political Struggles of Canadian Women*. Toronto: Oxford University
Press.

O'Brien, Carol Anne, and Lorna Weir. (1995). "Lesbians and Gay Men Inside
and Outside of Families." In *Canadian Families: Diversity, Conflict and Change*,
ed. Nancy Mandell and Ann Duffy, 111–39. Toronto: Harcourt Brace and
Company.

O'Connor, Julia S. (1993). "Gender, Class and Citizenship in the Comparative
Analysis of Welfare State Regimes: Theoretical and Methodological Issues."
British Journal of Sociology 44 (3): 501–18.

O'Neil, Maureen, and Sharon Sutherland. (1997). "The Machinery of Women's
Policy: Implementing RCSW." In *Women and the Canadian State / Femmes et
L'État Canadien*, ed. Caroline Andrew and Sanda Rodgers, 197–219. Mon-
treal: McGill-Queen's University Press.

Ontario Common Front. (2012). *We Are Ontario*. Toronto. 8 December. http://
weareontario.ca/wp-content/uploads/2013.5.21-December-8-Report.pdf.

Osborne, David, and Ted Gaebler. (1993). *Reinventing Government*. New York:
Penguin Books.

Outshoorn, Joyce, and Johanna Kantola. (2007a). "Assessing Changes in State
Feminism over the Last Decade." In *Changing State Feminism*, ed. Joyce Outshoorn and Johanna Kantola, 266–85. New York: Palgrave.

Outshoorn, Joyce, and Johanna Kantola, eds. (2007b). *Changing State Feminism.* New York: Palgrave.

Panitch, Leo. (1994). "Globalisation and the State." In *Socialist Register 1994: Between Globalism and Nationalism,* ed. Ralph Miliband and Leo Panitch, 60–93. London: Merlin Press.

Panitch, Leo. (1993). "A Different Kind of State?" In *A Different Kind of State? Popular Power and Democratic Administration,* ed. Gregory Albo, David Langille, and Leo Panitch, 2–16. Toronto: Oxford University Press.

Panitch, Leo, and Sam Gindin. (2000). "Transcending Pessimism: Rekindling Socialist Imagination." In *Socialist Register 2000: Necessary and Unnecessary Utopias,* ed. Leo Panitch and Colin Leys, 1–22. Halifax: Fernwood.

Peters, Guy. (1995). "The Public Service, the Changing State, and Governance." In *Governance in a Changing Environment,* ed. B. Guy Peters and Donald J. Savoie, 288–322. Montreal, Kingston: McGill-Queen's University Press.

Philipps, Lisa. (2002). "Tax Law and Social Reproduction: The Gender of Fiscal Policy and an Age of Privatization." In *Privatization, Law and the Challenge to Feminism,* ed. Brenda Cossman and Judy Fudge, 41–85. Toronto: University of Toronto Press.

Phillips, Anne. (1991). *Engendering Democracy.* University Park: Pennsylvania State University Press.

Phillips, Susan D. (1993). "A More Democratic Canada?" In *How Ottawa Spends: A More Democratic Canada?* ed. Susan D. Phillips, 1–41. Ottawa: Carleton University Press.

Phillips, Susan D., Brian R. Little, and Laura A. Goodine. (1997). "Reconsidering Gender and Public Administration: Five Steps beyond Conventional Research." *Canadian Public Administration* 40 (4): 563–81.

Pierre, Jon. (1995). "The Marketization of the State: Citizens, Consumers and the Emergence of the Public Market." In *Governance in a Changing Environment,* ed. B. Guy Peters and Donald J. Savoie, 55–81. Montreal, Kingston: McGill-Queen's University Press.

Porter, Ann. (2003). *Gendered States: Women, Unemployment Insurance, and the Political Economy of the Welfare State in Canada, 1945–1997.* Toronto: University of Toronto Press.

Pringle, Rosemary, and Sophie Watson. (1992). "Women's Interests and the Post-Structuralist State." In *Destabilizing Theory: Contemporary Feminist Debates,* ed. Michèle Barrett and Anne Phillips, 53–73. Stanford: Stanford University Press.

Pross, Paul. (1995). "Pressure Groups: Talking Chameleons." In *Canadian Politics in the 1990s,* 4th ed., ed. Michael S. Whittington and Glen Williams, 252–75. Toronto: Nelson Canada.

Ralph, Diana. (1997). "Introduction." In *Open for Business, Closed to People: Mike Harris' Ontario*, ed. Diana S. Ralph, André Régimbald, and Nérée St-Amand, 13–19. Halifax: Fernwood Publishing.

Randall, Melanie. (1988). "Feminism and the State: Questions for Theory and Practice." *Resources for Feminist Research* 17 (3): 10–15.

Randall, Vicky. (1988). "Gender and Power: Women Engage the State." In *Gender, Politics, and the State*, ed. Vicky Randall and Georgia Waylen, 185–205. New York: Routledge Press.

Rankin, Pauline L. (1996). "Experience, Opportunity and the Politics of Place: A Comparative Analysis of Provincial and Territorial Women's Movements in Canada." PhD dissertation, Carleton University.

Rankin, Pauline L., and Jill Vickers. (2001). *Women's Movements and State Feminism: Integrating Diversity into Public Policy*. Ottawa: Status of Women Canada.

Rankin, Pauline L., and Krista D. Wilcox. (2004). "De-gendering Engagement?: Gender Mainstreaming, Women's Movements and the Canadian Federal State." *Atlantis: Critical Studies in Gender, Culture & Social Justice* 29 (1): 52–60.

Rebick, Judy. (2000). *Imagine Democracy*. Toronto: Stoddart.

Rebick, Judy. (1998). "Controversies: The Women's Movement and the Trudeau Era." *Media and Politics: The Trudeau Era*. Winters College, York University, North York, Ontario.

Rebick, Judy, and Kiké Roach. (1996). *Politically Speaking*. Vancouver: Douglas & McIntyre.

Régimbald, André. (1997). "The Ontario Branch of American Conservatism." In *Open for Business, Closed to People: Mike Harris' Ontario*, ed. Diana S. Ralph, André Régimbald, and Nérée St-Amand, 45–53. Halifax: Fernwood Publishing.

Reinhartz, Shulamit. (1992). *Feminist Methods in Social Research*. New York: Oxford University Press.

Roberts, Helen, ed. (1990). *Doing Feminist Research*. 2nd ed. London: Routledge.

Rönnblom, Malin, and Carol Bacchi. (2011). "Feminist Discursive Institutionalism – What's Discursive about It? Limitations of Conventional Political Studies Paradigms." Paper presented at the 2nd European Conference on Politics and Gender, Budapest.

Ross, George, and Andrew Martin. (1999). "Through a Glass Darkly." In *The Brave New World of European Labour: European Trade Unions at the Millennium*, ed. Andrew Martin and George Ross, 368–97. New York: Berghahn Books.

Sainsbury, Diane. (1999). "Gender, Policy Regimes and Politics." In *Gender and Welfare State Regimes*, ed. Diane Sainsbury, 245–75. Toronto: Oxford University Press.

Sanger, Toby. (2011). *Battle of the Wages: Who Gets Paid More, Public or Private Sector Workers?* Ottawa: Canadian Union of Public Employees (CUPE). December. http://cupe.ca/updir/Battle_of_the_Wage_ENG_Final-0.pdf.

Sauer, Birgit, Melissa Haussman, and Dorothy McBride. (2007). "Conclusions: State Feminism and State Restructuring since the 1990s." In *Gendering the State in the Age of Globalization: Women's Movements and State Feminism in Postindustrial Democracies*, ed. Melissa Haussman and Birgit Sauer, 301–24. Rowman & Littlefield Publishers.

Savoie, Donald. (1994). *Thatcher, Reagan, Mulroney: In Search of a New Bureaucracy*. Toronto: University of Toronto Press.

Sawer, Marian. (2007). "Australia: The Fall of the Femocrat." In *Changing State Feminism*, ed. Joyce Outshoorn and Johanna Kantola, 20–40. New York: Palgrave.

Sawer, Marian. (1994). "Feminism and the State: Theory and Practice in Australia and Canada." *Australian-Canadian Studies* 12 (1): 49–68.

Sawer, Marian. (1991). "Why Has the Women's Movement Had More Influence on Government in Australia than Elsewhere?" In *Australia Compared: People, Policies and Politics*, ed. Francis Castles, 258–77. Sydney: Allen & Unwin.

Sawer, Marian. (1990). *Sisters in Suits: Women and Public Policy in Australia*. Sydney: Allen & Unwin.

Sawer, Marian, and Sandra Grey. (2008). "Introduction." In *Women's Movements: Flourishing or in Abeyance?* ed. Sandra Grey and Marian Sawer, 1–14. New York: Routledge.

Sawer, Marian, and Jill Vickers. (2010). "Introduction: Political Architecture and Its Gender Impact." In *Federalism, Feminism and Multilevel Governance*, ed. M. Haussman et al., 3–18. Burlington, VT: Ashgate.

Scott, Katherine. (1999). "The Dilemma of Liberal Citizenship: Women and Social Assistance Reform in the 1990s." In *Feminism, Political Economy and the State: Contested Terrain*, ed. Pat Armstrong and M. Patricia Connelly, 205–35. Toronto: Canadian Scholars' Press.

Sears, Alan. (2000). "Education for a Lean World." In *Restructuring and Resistance: Canadian Public Policy in an Age of Global Capitalism*, ed. Mike Burke, Colin Mooers, and John Shields, 146–58. Halifax: Fernwood Publishing.

Selden, Sally. (1997). *The Promise of Representative Bureaucracy: Diversity and Responsiveness in a Government Agency*. Armonk, NY: ME Sharpe.

Shields, John, and Mitchell B. Evans. (1998). *Shrinking the State: Globalization and Public Administration Reform*. Halifax: Fernwood Publishing.

Simard, Carolle. (1991). "Visible Minorities and the Canadian Political System." In *Ethno-Cultural Groups and Visible Minorities in Canadian Politics: The Question of Access*, 161–261. Research Studies, vol. 7, ed. Kathy Megyery, Royal Commission on Electoral Reform and Party Financing and Canada Communications Group. Toronto: Dundurn Press.

Simeon, Richard, and Ian Robinson. (1990). *State, Society, and the Development of Canadian Federalism*. Toronto: University of Toronto Press.

Smith, Miriam. (2010). "Federalism and LGBT Rights in the US and Canada: A Comparative Policy Analysis." In *Federalism, Feminism and Multilevel Governance*, ed. Melissa Haussman et al., 97–110. Burlington, VT: Ashgate.

Smith, Miriam. (2008). "Introduction: Theories of Group and Movement Organizing." In *Group Politics and Social Movements in Canada*, ed. Miriam Smith, 15–32. Peterborough, Toronto: Broadview Press and University of Toronto Press.

Smith, M. (1999). *Lesbian and Gay Rights in Canada : Social Movements and Equality-Seeking, 1971–1995*. Toronto: University of Toronto Press.

Sossin, Lorne. (1999). "Democratic Administration." In *Handbook of Public Administration in Canada*, ed. D. Dunn. Toronto: Oxford University Press.

Sossin, Lorne. (1993). "The Politics of Discretion: Toward a Critical Theory of Public Administration." *Canadian Public Administration* 36 (3): 364–91.

Stivers, Camilla. (1993). *Gender Images in Public Administration: Legitimacy and the Administrative State*. Newbury Park, CA: Sage Publications, Inc.

Taylor, Verta, and Leila J Rupp. (2008). "Preface." In *Women's Movements: Flourishing or in Abeyance?*, ed. Sandra Grey and Marian Sawer, xii–xvi. New York: Routledge.

Teghtsoonian, Katherine. (2004). "Disparate Fates in Challenging Times: Women's Policy Agencies under Governments of the Right in Aotearoa/New Zealand and British Columbia." Paper presented at the Canadian Political Science Association, 3–5 June. Winnipeg, Manitoba.

Teghtsoonian, Katherine. (2000). "Gendering Policy Analysis in the Government of British Columbia: Strategies, Possibilities and Constraints." *Studies in Political Economy* 62 (Spring): 105–27.

Tobin, Ann. (1990). "Lesbianism and the Labour Party: The GLC Experience." *Feminist Review* 34 (Spring): 56–66.

Tremblay, Manon, and Linda Trimble. (2003). "Women and Electoral Politics in Canada: A Survey of the Literature." In *Women and Electoral Politics in Canada*, ed. Manon Tremblay and Linda Trimble, 1–20. Don Mills: Oxford University Press.

Trickey, Jean. (1997). "The Racist Face of 'Common Sense.'" In *Open for Business, Closed to People: Mike Harris' Ontario*, ed. Diana S. Ralph, André Régimbald, and Nérée St-Amand, 113–21. Halifax: Fernwood Publishing.

United Nations. United Nations Development Fund for Women (UNIFEM). (2000). *Progress of the World's Women 2000: UNIFEM Biennial Report*. Coordinated by Diane Elson.

Vickers, Jill. (2011). "Gendering Federalism: Institutions of Decentralization and Power Sharing." In *Gender, Politics and Institutions: Towards a Feminist Institutionalism*, ed. Mona Lena Krook and Fiona Mackay, 129–46. Basingstoke: Palgrave Macmillan.

Vickers, Jill. (1997a). *Reinventing Political Science: A Feminist Approach*. Halifax: Fernwood Publishing.

Vickers, Jill. (1997b). "Toward a Feminist Understanding of Representation." In *In the Presence of Women: Representation in Canadian Governments*, ed. Jane Arscott and Linda Trimble, 20–46. Toronto: Harcourt and Brace.

Vickers, Jill. (1994). "Why *Should* Women Care about Federalism?" In *Canada: The State of the Federation*, ed. J. Hiebert, 135–51. Kingston: Queen's School of Public Policy.

Vickers, Jill, Pauline Rankin, and Christine Appelle. (1993). *Politics as if Women Mattered: A Political Analysis of the National Action Committee on the Status of Women*. Toronto: University of Toronto Press.

Vosko, Leah F. (2000). *Temporary Work: The Gendered Rise of a Precarious Employment Relationship*. Toronto: University of Toronto Press.

Vosko, Leah F. (1996). "*Irregular* Workers, *New* Involuntary Social Exiles: Women and U.I. Reform." In *Remaking Canadian Social Policy: Social Security in the Late 1990s*, ed. Jane Pulkingham and Gordon Ternowetsky, 256–72. Halifax: Fernwood Publishing.

Wainwright, Hilary. (2003). *Reclaim the State: Experiments in Popular Democracy*. London: Verso.

Wainwright, Hilary. (2002). "Participatory Democracy." Oakham House, Ryerson University, 17 October.

Wainwright, Hilary. (1993). "A New Kind of Knowledge for a New Kind of State." In *A Different Kind of State? Popular Power and Democratic Administration*, ed. Gregory Albo, David Langille, and Leo Panitch, 112–21. Toronto: Oxford University Press.

Walby, Sylvia. (2004). "The European Union and Gender Equality: Emergent Varieties of Gender Regime." *Social Politics* 11 (1): 4–29.

Waring, Marilyn. (2000a). *Counterspin with Avi Lewis*. CBC Newsworld, 16 March.

Waring, Marilyn. (2000b). "Sex, Lies and Global Economics." OISE, Toronto. 13 March.

Warskett, Rosemary. (2000). "Feminism's Challenge to Unions in the North: Possibilities and Contradictions." In *Socialist Register 2001: Working Classes, Global Realities*, ed. Leo Panitch and Colin Leys, 329–42. Halifax: Fernwood Press.

Watson, Sophie. (1992). "Femocratic Feminisms." In *Gender and Bureaucracy*, ed. Mike Savage and Anne Witz, 186–206. Oxford: Blackwell Publishers.

Waylen, Georgina. (2011). "Gendered Institutionalist Analysis: Understanding Democratic Transitions." In *Gender, Politics and Institutions: Towards a Feminist Institutionalism*, ed. Mona Lena Krook and Fiona Mackay, 147–62. Basingstoke: Palgrave Macmillan.

Waylen, Georgina. (2009). "What Can Historical Institutionalism Offer Feminist Institutionalists?" *Politics and Gender* 5 (2): 245–53.

Weber, Max. (1999). *Essays in Economic Sociology*, ed. Richard Swedberg. Princeton: Princeton University Press.

Weber, Max. (1997). *The Theory of Social and Economic Organization*. New York: The Free Press.

Weber, Max. (1994). "Bureaucracy." In *Critical Studies in Organization and Bureaucracy*, 2nd ed., ed. Frank Fischer and Carmen Sirianni, 4–19. Philadelphia: Temple University Press.

Weinroth, Michelle. (1997). "Deficitism and Neo-Conservatism in Ontario." In *Open for Business, Closed to People: Mike Harris' Ontario*, ed. Diana S. Ralph, André Régimbald, and Nérée St-Amand, 54–67. Halifax: Fernwood Publishing.

White, Julie. (1993). *Sisters & Solidarity: Women and Unions in Canada*. Toronto: Thompson Educational Publishing Inc.

White, Linda A. (1997). "Do Women Need a National Government? Portents and Prospects for Social Policy in a Decentralized Federation." *Atlantis: Critical Studies in Gender, Culture & Social Justice* 22 (1): 82–96.

Wilson, Seymour V., and Willard A. Mullins. (1978). "Representative Bureaucracy: Linguistic/Ethnic Aspects in Canadian Public Policy." *Canadian Public Administration* 21 (4): 513–38.

Wise, Lois R. (2003). "Representative Bureaucracy." In *International Handbook of Public Administration*, ed. B. Guy Peters and Jon Pierre, 343–53. Thousand Oaks, CA: Sage.

Wolf, Diane L., ed. (1996). *Feminist Dilemmas in Fieldwork*. Boulder: Westview Press.

Wood, Ellen Meiksins. (1995). "The Separation of the 'Economic' and the 'Political' in Capitalism." In *Democracy against Capitalism*, 19–48. Cambridge: Cambridge University Press.

Wyckoff-Wheeler, Donna. (n.d.). "From *Feminism* to *Women's and Gender Studies*."

Yalnizyan, Armine. (1993). "From the DEW Line: The Experience of Canadian Garment Workers." In *Women Challenging Unions: Feminism, Democracy and Militancy*, ed. Linda Briskin and Patricia McDermott, 284–303. Toronto: University of Toronto Press.

Yeates, Nicola. (1999). "Social Politics and Policy in an Era of Globalization: Critical Reflections." *Social Policy and Administration* 33 (4): 372–93.

Yeatman, Anna. (1990). "Dilemmas for Femocracy." In *Bureaucrats, Technocrats, Femocrats: Essays on the Contemporary Australian State*, 80–97. Sydney: Allen and Unwin.

Young, Lisa. (2000). *Feminists and Party Politics*. Vancouver: UBC Press.

Index

Abella, Rosalie, 78

Aboriginal peoples, 4, 51, 64, 73, 88, 89, 91, 96, 112, 126, 156, 160, 203

Aboriginal women, 51, 75, 88, 89, 109, 112, 113, 135, 152, 192, 220n20, 226n43, 227n56, 228n75

abortion, 126

accessibility: childcare, 241n23; disability, 112, 113, 211

accountability: bureaucratic, 9, 187; to citizens, 143–4, 170, 198, 199, 200, 205; of femocrats, 60, 144, 188, 197, 188, 199, 202, 207; ministerial responsibility, 63, 67, 85, 197, 199; New Public Management, 164, 165, 166; public reporting, 88

A Commitment to Training and Employment for Women (ACTEW), 110, 111, 119, 153, 180, 227nn53 & 54, 228n81

Adamson, Nancy, et al., 205, 207, 216

Advisor on Race Relations, 143. *See also* accountability

Advisory Committee on Gender Equality (Indian and Northern Affairs Canada), 75

Advisory Council on the Status of Women: Canada, 75, 207 (*see also* CACSW); New Brunswick, 76, 91; Nova Scotia, 76; Ontario, 76, 91, 106, 171, 192, 223n22 (*see also* Advisory Council on Women's Issues); PEI, 76; Saskatchewan, 76

Advisory Council on Women's Issues: Alberta, 76, 91; Ontario, 76, 91, 106, 171, 192, 223n22; Yukon, 91. *See also* Advisory Council on the Status of Women

advocacy: Australia, 39; and childcare, 221n10, 229n88; and bureaucracy, 39, 66, 69, 72, 76, 104, 230n111; and femocratic administration, 197–200, 212; organizations, 33, 96, 158–9, 212; and OWD, 108, 110, 111, 112, 130–41, 144, 156–9, 205, 224n1, 234nn38 & 44

affirmative action, 127. *See also* Employment Equity

agency: in feminist institutionalism, 25, 26, 28, 29–36, 219n4; in feminist political economy, 38–57, 74; and femocrats, 107, 124, 131, 141, 195, 208

Agócs, Carol, 8, 64, 96, 203, 204, 221n3
Agriculture and Agri-Food Canada Gender Analysis and Policy, 75
Alberta, 76, 91, 127, 128, 129, 159, 167, 168, 193; Advisory Council on Women's Issues, 76, 91; Women's Bureau, 76; Women's Secretariat, 76, 127
Albo, Greg, 13, 71, 79, 98, 150, 162, 167, 189, 197, 199, 201, 205, 214, 235n56, 241n21
Alboim, Naomi, 108, 110, 207
Allen, Judith, 23
Andrew, Caroline, 191
Andrew, Joan, 108, 195
anti-feminism, 210, 223n19
Anti-racism Secretariat, 98, 112, 125
anti-racism strategy, 112
Arbour, Louise, 175
Armstrong, Pat, 18, 23, 50, 181
Arscott, Jane, 103
Assembly of First Nations (AFN), 88
assistant deputy minister (ADM), 16, 17, 108, 110, 122, 126, 130, 135, 138, 153, 155, 170, 195
Attorney General (Ontario), 108, 125, 126
Aucoin, Peter, 67, 79, 80, 81, 83, 84, 85, 86, 98, 147, 154, 160, 161, 164, 190, 222n15
Australia: federalism, 31; femocrats, 6, 102, 121, 166, 218n8; New Public Management, 98, 166; Office for the Status of Women, 102; Office of Women's Affairs (Australia), 102; Prime Minister and Cabinet Department, 121; Women's Bureau, 102, 218n8; Women's Coordinator, 102; Women's Electoral Lobby, 102;

women's movement, 74. See also advocacy

Bacchi, Carol, 219n3
Bakan, Abigail, 95, 96, 97, 180, 182, 187, 222n9, 223n23
Bakker, Isabella, 4, 82, 214, 222n14, 242n34
Bannerji, Himani, 50
Barrett, Michèle, 220n21
Bashevkin, Sylvia, 58
Beijing Conference, 111
best interests of the child doctrine, 53
Bezanson, Kate, 45, 46, 71
bilingualism, 71, 77, 211, 222n8
Bliss case, 11
Boyd, Marion, 17, 108, 116, 121, 123, 124, 125, 128, 137, 138, 139, 151, 156, 159, 169, 171, 224n10, 225n10, 235n49, 237n107, 238n120
Bradford, Neil, 168, 227n54, 236n85
Brand, Dionne, 42, 50, 59, 200, 210, 221n27
Brennan, Deborah, 31, 33, 219n10
British Columbia (BC), 4, 128; Ministry of Women's Equality, 76, 91, 228n75, 234n38, 236n75, 238nn108 & 114
Brock, Kathy, 35, 39
Brodie, Janine, 5, 82, 94, 144, 241n31
Brown, Wendy, 30
buffer effect, 82. See also hidden costs of adjustment
bureaucracy: Australia, 6, 13, 16, 18, 31, 39, 43–4, 63, 69, 70, 92, 93, 98, 102, 121, 121, 130, 147, 166, 187, 194, 206, 217n2, 218nn8 & 9, 221n28, 232n2; and capitalism, 58, 64–6, 70–2, 85; democratization of, 16, 21, 45, 94, 100–4, 141–5,

186–216; neoliberal restructuring of, 9, 20, 21, 79–94, 97, 98, 104, 146–85, 189–92, 223n24, 232nn2 & 13, 236n85, 240n22; Ontario, 105–88, 192–4, 197, 200, 203, 205, 207–8, 209, 232n2, 238n110, 240n19; representative, 8, 44, 73–4, 77–8, 95, 101, 131, 189, 202–4, 221n5, 222n9; Weberian, 4, 8, 11, 25, 63–78, 94, 95, 97, 104, 106, 120–45, 158, 186, 223n17, 240n21; and women, 7, 9, 13, 15, 18, 19, 21, 43, 45, 55, 58, 63, 105–216, 223n22, 232nn2 & 13, 233nn18, 19, & 31. *See also* accountability; advocacy

Bureau of Women's Health and Gender Analysis, 222n7

Burke, Mike, 5, 217n5

Burt, Sandra, 67, 106, 197, 225n10, 227n52

Burstyn, Varda, 219n12

Business Ownership for Women Program, 227n52

Business and Professional Women's Association, 169

business plan, 85, 157, 158, 164–6, 174, 232, 236nn75 & 85

Byrne, Lesley Hyland, 225

Bystydzienski, Jill, 60, 221

cabinet, 4, 17, 58, 63, 64, 89, 90, 92, 108, 112, 114, 119, 121, 122, 123, 128, 132, 133, 134, 144, 147, 148, 155, 160, 190, 195, 199, 225n10, 233n37, 234n47

Cameron, Barbara, 19, 31, 47, 49, 89, 92, 209, 220n14

Canadian Advisory Council on the Status of Women (CACSW), 75, 207

Canadian Charter of Rights and Freedoms, 39, 206, 210

Canadian Council on Social Development (CCSD), 83, 88

Canadian Human Rights Commission, 96

Canadian International Development Agency (CIDA), 75, 193

Canadian Jobs Strategy, 228

Canadian Labour Congress (CLC), 152

Canadian Union of Public Employees (CUPE), 88

Canadian Women's March Committee, 212

capitalism, 6, 10, 19, 32, 41, 50, 64–6, 68–9, 241n29

Carr, Glenna, 110, 122, 138

Carty, Linda, 42, 50, 59, 200, 210, 221n27

C.D. Howe Institute, 81, 222n12

census, 84, 96

central advocacy agency, 108, 156. *See also* advocacy

central agency, 108, 120, 124, 156

centralization: of federalism, 33; of power, 98, 147, 190, 199

Centre for Management Development, 85

Change Agent program, 115, 118

Chappell, Louise, 18, 24, 25, 28, 29, 30, 31, 33, 34, 36, 39, 50, 69, 166

charitable status, 158, 159

childcare: cuts to, 147, 180, 181; and democracy, 209, 212, 215, 229n88, 240n21; and federalism, 33, 36, 128, 209, 219n10, 229n88; and public reporting, 88; and women's equality, 106, 114, 115, 116, 120, 138, 179, 180. *See also* Ontario Coalition for Better Child Care (OCBCC)

child poverty, 180

chilly climate, 70, 221n4
Cho, Sumi, 53
Chouinard, Vera, 112, 211
Chrétien, Jean, 90, 212
citizen engagement/participation, 88,
    90, 101, 112, 130, 144, 168, 170, 191,
    196–216
citizenship, 3, 9, 11, 27, 35, 36, 46, 56,
    74, 87, 88, 95, 118, 209, 211, 213
Citizenship and Immigration
    Canada, 75, 96
class, 6, 8, 12, 18, 19, 29, 37, 47, 49,
    50, 51, 52, 53, 54, 58, 59, 64, 65, 67,
    68, 70, 71, 73, 79, 81, 136, 137–9,
    171, 181, 213, 215, 231n131,
    241n32
Coalition for Fair Working Condi-
    tions for Homeworkers, 119
Coalition of Visible Minority Women,
    192
Cohen, Marjorie Griffin, 5, 93, 207
Collier, Cheryl, 218n12, 219n10
colonialism, 37, 41, 48, 50, 55
Comack, Elizabeth, 10
Common Sense Revolution, 147, 149
Community Grants Program, 118
compartmentalization, 9, 20, 62, 63–7,
    98, 100, 104, 120, 121, 124–30, 141.
    See also bureaucracy
Confederation of Canada, 31, 50
Congress of Aboriginal Peoples
    (CAP), 88
Connell, R.W., 16, 41, 55, 56, 60
Connelly, Patricia, 18, 23, 51, 83, 84,
    87, 181
consciousness-raising groups, 191
Conseil du statut de la femme (CSF),
    76, 121, 207
constitution, 9, 31, 32, 44, 48, 50, 56,
    89, 94, 106, 192

consultation, 91, 106, 110, 111, 112,
    116, 138, 139, 140, 168–71, 199, 208,
    209, 211, 223n22, 227n54, 236n85
contracting out, 5, 80, 83, 85, 122
Convention on the Elimination of All
    Forms of Discrimination Against
    Women (CEDAW), 193, 210
co-optation, 7, 43, 99, 142, 144, 191,
    210
core funding, 111, 117, 212, 221n27,
    236n87
Cossman, Brenda, 10, 42, 46, 158,
    217n5, 220n22
Coulter, Kendra, 149, 171, 177, 181
Court Challenges Program, 241n28
Crenshaw, Kimberlé, 53, 220nn15
    & 17
critical disability studies, 50
Cross Cultural Communication
    Centre, 117
Cunningham, Dianne, 17, 151, 164,
    166, 182–3, 232n10, 234n37, 236n84,
    237n93, 238n108, 239nn131 & 132

D'Agostino, Maria, 4
Davis, Bill, 106, 107, 116, 130, 178
Days of Action, 168
debt, 6, 79, 147
decentralization: and democracy
    191; of federalism, 36, 48, 49, 86–7,
    190, 223n16 (see also re-scaling);
    of power 6, 9, 85–6, 98, 189, 190,
    222n10
de-gendering, 69, 180, 181, 230n109,
    235n60
deficit, 79, 181
democracy: 3, 4, 6, 10, 15, 20, 21, 23,
    35, 54, 57, 60, 61, 63, 74, 90, 94, 97,
    99, 100, 101–2, 104, 158, 189, 192,
    208, 211–16, 230n109, 241n29; and

gender 9, 12–14, 16, 20, 49, 57–8, 59,
  63, 88, 97–8, 101, 104, 105–6, 147,
  150, 171, 184–5, 189, 192–3, 204,
  208, 211–12, 215, 241nn28 & 29; liberal, 10, 61, 78, 171; procedural, 8,
  10, 11–12, 14, 56, 59, 73, 87, 88, 103,
  107–14, 144, 147, 150–72, 191, 196,
  201, 239n6; representative, 9, 44, 60,
  63, 74, 92, 101–2, 215; substantive
  10, 11–12, 14, 56, 59, 73, 87, 88, 103,
  107, 114–44, 147, 150, 172–84, 190,
  196, 198, 201, 213, 239n6
democratic administration, 4–6, 7, 13,
  15, 16, 20, 21, 60, 102, 104, 142–4,
  186–7, 189, 204–16, 218n6, 241n31
deputy minister, 83, 108, 123, 126,
  157, 161, 234n42
deregulation, 5, 80, 92, 93, 148, 149
disability, 4, 45, 50, 66–7, 112 13,
  118–19, 133, 135, 151, 180, 203–4,
  211, 215, 228nn75 & 81
Disability Secretariat (BC), 228n75
Disabled Women's Network
  (DAWN), 118, 139, 211
discourse, 3, 7, 18, 25, 27, 42, 46, 47,
  48, 56, 78, 83, 91, 92, 94, 98, 100,
  157, 160, 165, 167, 180, 181, 183,
  189, 190, 202
discourse analysis, 37, 219n3
discursive institutionalism, 25, 219n3
Diversity, Equality and Access to Justice Division, 75. See also Diversity
  and Gender Equality Office; Office
  of the Senior Advisor on Gender
  Equality
Diversity and Gender Equality Office, 75. See also Office of the Senior
  Advisor on Gender Equality;
  Diversity, Equality and Access to
  Justice Division

Dobrowolsky, Alexandra, 7, 44, 100,
  102, 206, 218n11
downsizing, 5, 8, 20, 36, 48, 62, 79,
  82–4, 89, 98, 104, 146, 147, 184, 190,
  222n10
Driscoll, Amanda, 23, 29, 219n2
Dua, Enakshi, 52, 220n20
dual earner model, 52

Earles, Kimberly, 240n16
early childhood development (ECD),
  88
econocrat, 92
economic rationalism, 92, 93, 98, 99,
  149. See also fiscal conservatism
Edwards, Merideth, 69, 70
Eisenstein, Hester, 7, 41, 43, 59, 60, 70,
  92, 93, 102, 206, 207, 217n2, 218n10,
  221n28
electoral politics, 4, 9, 34, 57, 60,
  101–3, 183, 187, 211, 218n9, 224n29,
  240n16
electoral reform, 6, 60, 94, 101, 199,
  211, 218n7, 240n16
employment equity: An Act to
  Repeal Job Quotas and to Restore
  Merit-based Employment Practices in Ontario, 95–6; Canada,
  58, 75, 77, 78, 84, 96, 203, 222n9,
  240n18; Employment Equity Act
  (Canada), 78, 96; Employment
  Equity Act (Ontario), 78; Employment Equity Commission, 117, 181;
  Employment Equity Network, 117;
  Employment Equity Tribunal, 78;
  Office of the Employment Equity
  Commission, 117; Ontario, 81, 84,
  95–6, 111, 115–17, 120, 124, 138,
  158, 168, 180, 181–3, 187, 203, 223
  n23, 227n48, 238n110, 240n18

Employment Insurance (EI), 11, 45, 193, 220n13. *See also* Unemployment Insurance (UI)

entrepreneurialism, 84, 85, 128, 129, 147, 172, 173–6, 183, 227n52, 238n108. *See also* self-employment

Equal Pay Coalition, 116. *See also* pay equity

Esping-Andersen, Gøsta, 15, 56

Evans, Bryan Mitchell, 81, 84, 86, 92, 94, 145, 215, 218n4, 223n24, 234n43, 241n31

Evans, Patricia, 196

Expenditure Management System (EMS), 85

Expenditure Review Committee (ERC), 85

expertise, 4, 32, 58, 63, 67–74, 97, 99, 100, 130–41, 154, 158, 161, 165, 197–8, 201, 204, 224n25, 225n10

Fair Tax Commission, 115

Farm Women's Bureau, 75

Farmers Home Administration's Rural Housing Loans program (US), 196

Federal Plan for Gender Equality, 193

Federal-Provincial-Territorial (FPT) meetings, 126–30, 154–5, 179, 208–9, 229n86, 233n31. *See also* abortion; childcare

federalism: and accountability, 88, 89, 192, 208–9, 229n88; and coordination, 126–30, 228n81, 232n18; executive federalism, 88, 191–2, 208–9, 240n22; and feminist institutionalism, 31–3, 34–6, 40, 47, 90, 229n88; and gender, 16, 19, 49–50, 88, 126–30, 190, 192, 194, 208–9, 232n18, 239n6; and political

economy, 19, 40, 47–50, 192, 239n6. *See also* childcare; forum shopping; FPT meetings

feminism, 4, 7, 8–9, 23–36, 37–54, 54–61, 63–104, 105–45, 147–85, 186–216, 221nn27 & 4, 223n19, 224n10, 231n150, 239n131, 241nn29 & 31; liberal, 37, 109, 152; post-colonial/anti-racist, 8, 37, 43, 50–2, 53–4, 59, 114, 152, 220n20, 241n32; post-structuralist, 36, 37, 43; queer, 36, 50, 52–4; radical, 30, 41, 63; socialist, 8, 30, 37, 41, 43, 45. *See also* federalism; feminist bureaucratic restructuring; feminist economics; feminist institutionalism; feminist methodology; feminist political economy; feminist political science; femocratic administration; gender democracy; intersectionality; state feminism

feminist bureaucratic restructuring, 21, 94, 189–202, 216. *See also* feminism; state feminism

feminist economics, 82, 93

feminist institutionalism (FI), 18–19, 23–36, 38–9, 54–61, 113, 219nn2, 3, 4, & 7

Feminist Institutionalist International Network (FIIN), 24

feminist methodology, 16–17

feminist political economy (FPE), 18–19, 24, 37–61, 65, 71–2, 74, 80, 82, 115, 234n47, 241n32

feminist political science, 18, 23, 24, 26, 27, 30, 36, 38, 54, 56, 100, 103, 220n24

feminization of poverty, 81, 115, 128, 138

femocrat. *See* state feminism

femocratic administration, 3–9, 10, 13, 14, 15, 19, 21, 24, 40, 61, 87, 104, 106, 141, 185, 186–216, 217n2, 218n6, 241n29. *See also* advocacy

Ferguson, Kathy, 30, 31, 41, 44, 63, 64, 202, 219n5

Ferguson, Susan, 216

Findlay, Sue, 7, 12, 13, 44–5, 57–8, 61, 58, 61, 64, 66–7, 69, 70, 70–1, 143, 170, 190, 195, 196, 204, 205, 221n4, 224n27, 231nn134 & 150

fiscal conservatism, 149. *See also* economic rationalism

Fordism, 66

Forum for Women in Democracy (Uganda), 193

forum shopping, 35, 36, 90, 153, 191

Foucault, Michel, 41

francophone women, 113, 119

Francis, Mayann, 153, 223n21

Franzway, Suzanne, et al., 63, 65, 218n10

Fraser Institute, 223n24

free trade, 5, 6, 93, 115, 137, 140, 210, 241n27

Fry, Hedy, 234n37

Fudge, Judy, 10, 42, 46, 158, 217n5, 231n134

Gabriel, Christina, 66, 125, 192, 220n19

Gaebler, Ted, 81, 85, 94, 222n15

Geller-Schwartz, Linda, 69, 93, 206, 241n27

Gender Analysis and Policy Directorate, 221n6

gender-based analysis (GBA), 99, 121–3, 155, 193

Gender-Based Analysis Unit (Citizenship and Immigration Canada), 75

gender-blindness, 36, 41. *See also* gender insensitivity

gender budgeting, 8, 60, 99, 102, 193, 215, 218n8

gender democracy. *See* democracy

Gender Equality Division (Canadian International Development Agency), 75

Gender Equality Initiative (Justice Canada), 75

gender framing, 183–4

gender insensitivity, 27, 69, 93, 155, 180, 190, 230n109. *See also* gender-blindness

gender order, 16, 37, 46, 49, 50–2, 55–7, 59, 82, 86

gender regime, 9, 10, 13, 15–16, 19–20, 24, 54–61, 62, 63, 65, 67, 74, 78, 79, 82, 84, 86, 94, 95, 141–4, 186–216; New Public Management, 14, 15, 20, 62, 79–94, 95–104, 105–6, 146–85, 186; Weberian, 14, 20, 62–79, 95–104, 105–45, 156, 186

ghettoization, 110, 175, 192, 194

Gindin, Sam, 6

globalization, 16, 36, 41, 48, 49, 62, 78, 86–8, 97, 105, 186, 192, 214, 217nn3 & 4

Goodine, Laura A., 4

Grace, Joan, 28, 31, 33, 40, 47

Graefe, Peter, 19, 29, 37, 39–40, 43, 44, 46, 218n17, 220n14

Gray, Gwendolyn, 33

Greater London Council (GLC), 66, 201, 207, 210

Grey, Sandra, 36, 159, 191, 204

Haddow, Rodney, 222n54

Handler, Joel, 205

Harder, Lois, 127, 129, 159, 167

Harper, Stephen, 96, 241nn25 & 28
Harris, Mike, 14, 15, 20, 89, 95, 96,
    114, 146–85, 193, 205, 227n57,
    235nn47 & 55, 236n83
Human Resources and Development
    Canada (HRDC), 193
Haussman, Melissa, 48, 49
heterosexism, 50, 52–3, 215
hidden costs of adjustment, 82. See
    also buffer effect
hierarchy, 4, 8, 20, 42, 62, 63–7, 72, 97,
    98, 104, 106, 120–4, 136, 141, 188,
    189, 190, 227n60
Hirst, Paul, 217n3
historical institutionalism, 25–7, 28,
    38, 39, 219n1
homophobia, 70
housing, 51, 52, 120, 122, 123, 147,
    166, 180, 181, 183, 190, 196
hub and spoke model, 97, 191
Human Rights, Humanitarian Affairs
    and International Women's Equal-
    ity section (Foreign Affairs and
    International Trade), 76
Hutchinson, Janet R., 4

ideas (in policy), 16, 18, 24, 25, 27, 31,
    39, 64, 71, 72, 104, 183, 184
identities, 12, 41, 46, 61, 67, 71, 72, 74,
    97, 103, 192, 211
immigrant women, 109, 111, 118, 123,
    137, 152, 169, 173, 181, 207, 209,
    215, 233n18
Increased Ministerial Authority and
    Accountability (IMAA), 85
individualism, 5, 25, 67, 79, 80, 81, 95,
    96, 147, 173, 175–8, 184, 185, 189,
    238n110
Information Technology Training for
    Women (ITTW), 178

inside/outside ties, 8, 27, 29, 43–4, 55,
    59, 60, 62, 97, 102, 104, 109, 130–41,
    143–4, 158, 168–72, 196, 197–201,
    203, 204–16, 237n91
institutionalism. See neo-
    institutionalism
institutionalization of power rela-
    tions, 7, 41, 54, 55, 144, 187, 188
interests, 24, 25, 26, 27, 30, 33, 39, 40,
    41, 42, 44, 51, 55, 59, 61, 67, 68, 71,
    72, 73, 74, 98, 99, 103, 132, 133,
    137, 149, 154, 171, 196, 199, 204,
    209, 211
INTERCEDE, 119
Interdepartmental Action Committee
    on People with Disabilities, 66
International Ladies Garment Worker
    Union (ILGWU), 119
International Women's Year, 129
Interministerial Consultation on Im-
    migrant Women, 111
Inter-Ministerial Council on Women's
    Economic Status, 119
intersectionality, 8, 37, 38, 50–4, 61,
    66–7, 97–8, 111–14, 125–6, 135–9,
    192, 211, 238n110
Inuit Tapiriit Kanatami (ITK), 88
Inwood, Gregory, 86, 87, 88, 209
Irving, Helen, 50

Jenson, Jane, 159, 220n23
Jobs for the Future, 178
Johns, Helen, 151
Jung, Kyungja, 191

Kantola, Johanna, 15, 48–9, 113–14,
    150, 205, 232n2
Kaplan, Gisela, 7, 92
Kenny, Meryl, 24, 26–7, 28, 38, 39, 40,
    53, 56, 219nn2 & 6

Kernaghan, Kenneth, 73, 77, 221n5, 222n8
Keynesian Welfare State (KWS), 15, 51, 52, 55, 97, 105, 106
Kitchen, Brigitte, 180
Klassen, Tom, 119, 223n16, 227n54
knowledge production, 9, 32, 44, 46, 69–71, 81, 92–3, 97–9, 161, 184, 188, 191, 197, 201–2
Kobayashi, Audrey, 78, 95–6, 180, 182, 187, 222n9, 223n23
Koshan, Jennifer, 51, 220nn15, 17, & 20
Krook, Mona Lena, 23, 24, 27, 29, 32, 36, 54, 55, 219n2
Kulawik, Theresa, 25, 38

labour law, 45, 119
labour market policy, 14, 15, 17, 77–8, 95–7, 114–20, 147, 172–85, 222n16, 233n18. See also employment equity; pay equity
labour movement, 134, 168
labour unions, 6, 57, 77, 82, 100, 110, 118, 138, 168, 181, 187, 193, 214, 227n45, 231n134
Langille, David, 13, 240n15
Lankin, Frances, 108
law, 10–11, 42, 45, 52–3, 56, 68, 114, 115, 116, 119, 147, 157, 158, 175, 187, 234n47
law-and-order approach, 157, 237n107, 241n28
Law Commission of Canada, 241n28
Language Instruction for Newcomers to Canada (LINC), 209
Leading Girls, Building Communities Awards, 177
Leading Women, Building Communities Awards, 177

Levi, Margaret, 69, 70
Levine, Helisse, 4
Lewis, Stephen, 143, 144
liberal democracy, 10, 61, 78, 171
Liberal party, 14, 15, 17, 90, 106, 107, 108, 111, 116, 130, 131, 149, 160, 166, 170, 171, 177, 178, 180, 181, 182, 183, 185, 188, 195, 212, 224n6, 233n23, 234n47, 236n75, 238n108
liberalism, 5, 10, 34, 37, 41, 56, 57, 61, 67, 70, 71, 73, 78, 94, 101, 106, 109, 149, 152, 171, 217n4, 219n6. See also neoliberalism
Lipsky, Michael, 196, 200
Little, Brian R., 4,
Little, Margaret, 189
logic of appropriateness, 31, 32, 41
Lorenzin, Elizabeth, 106, 197, 225n10, 227n52
Lovenduski, Joni, 24, 27, 39, 183, 219n4; —, et al., 49, 103, 183, 196
Luxton, Meg, 37, 45, 46, 71, 214n35

MacDonald, Martha, 84
Mackay, Fiona, 24, 27, 29, 32, 36, 38, 40, 53, 54, 55, 56, 113, 219nn2 & 4; —, et al., 27, 31
MacKinnon, Catharine, 30, 31, 219n6
Mackintosh, Maureen, 207, 241n24
Macpherson, C.B., 10–11
Maddison, Sarah, 191
Magnusson, Warren, 215
Mahon, Rianne, 7, 44, 57–8, 64, 71–3, 86, 120, 192, 195, 198, 220n10, 221n23, 240n6; —, et al., 36, 47, 49, 221n23
Maillé, Chantal, 44, 102
male breadwinner model, 51, 52, 53, 65, 220n21
Maley, Terry, 11, 70

Malloy, Jonathan, 7, 18, 106, 122, 123,
   130, 134, 136, 138, 140, 142, 143,
   151, 157, 163, 173, 188–9, 219n15,
   223n22, 224n4, 231n9, 233n21,
   237n91, 240n14
managerialism, 8, 79, 84–94, 95, 104,
   146, 150, 156–68, 222n10
Manitoba, 76, 127, 128; Women's
   Advisory Council, 76; Women's
   Directorate, 76; Women's Ministry,
   76. See also Minister Responsible
   for the Status of Women
Mann, Hollie S., 4
marketization, 48, 79–99, 146–72,
   222nn10 & 11, 223n
Maroney, Heather Jon, 37
Martin, Paul, 212
Marxism, 32, 220n15
Mayor's Committee on Community
   and Race Relations (Toronto), 66
Mazur, Amy G., 7, 103
McBride, Stephen, 5, 217n4
McCall, Leslie, 53
McGuinty, Dalton, 177
McIntosh, Mary, 51
McIvor, Heather, 58
McKeen, Wendy, 149
McNally, David, 217n3
Meech Lake Accord, 88, 210
Mental Health and Addictions
   Strategy, 181, 183
merit hiring, 63, 75–8, 95, 221nn1 & 5,
   222nn8 & 9
merit pay, 85
methodological nationalism, 47
Métis National Council (MNC), 88
Millbank, Jenni, 52–3, 220nn16 & 18
Minister of Women's Equality (BC),
   76, 234n38

Minister Responsible for the Status of
   Women: Canada, 75, 90; Manitoba,
   76; New Brunswick, 76; Newfound-
   land and Labrador, 76; Northwest
   Territories, 76; Quebec, 76
Minister Responsible for the Status of
   Women Council (Nunavut), 76
Minister Responsible for Women's
   Issues (Ontario), 76, 107, 121, 127,
   128, 152, 156, 224nn3 & 6, 228n77
ministerial responsibility. See
   accountability
Ministerial Task Force on Program
   Review, 85
Ministry of Agriculture and Food
   (Ontario), 133
Ministry of Citizenship and Culture
   (Ontario), 112, 152. See also Min-
   istry of Citizenship, Culture and
   Recreation
Ministry of Citizenship, Culture and
   Recreation, 151. See also Ministry of
   Citizenship and Culture
Ministry of Community Services
   (BC), 91
Ministry of Community and Social
   Services (COMSOC) (Ontario), 108,
   125, 128, 195, 225n24
Ministry of Finance: Australia, 92;
   Canada, 64, 72, 92, 198; Ontario,
   167
Ministry of Health: Australia, 218n8;
   Canada, 75, 193; Ontario, 126,
   225n24
Ministry of Justice: Canada, 75; On-
   tario, 108, 125, 126, 128, 237n107
Ministry of Labour: Australia, 102;
   Canada, 72–3, 75, 206; Ontario, 107,
   110, 116, 125, 135; Saskatchewan, 91

Ministry of Northern Development and Mines (Ontario), 133
Ministry of the Environment (Ontario), 133, 230n111
Ministry of Women's Affairs (New Zealand), 93
Ministry of Women's Equality (BC), 76
minority government, 106, 107, 114, 116, 212, 224n1, 228n81
mobility, 36
Mohanty, Chandra, 54
Mooers, Colin, 5, 217n5
Mouffe, Chantal, 202
Mullins, Willard A., 73–4, 221nn1 & 5
Mulroney, Brian, 83, 85, 212, 223n24, 234n43
Multiculturalism Strategy and Race Relations Policy (Ontario), 112
multilevel governance. See federalism and multiscaler analysis
multiscaler analysis, 31, 37, 38, 47–50, 54, 61, 62, 71, 75–7, 85, 87–8, 89–91, 97, 98, 99, 147, 191, 192, 240n6
multi-skilling, 162
municipalities, 7, 40, 49, 66, 78, 87, 115, 119, 133, 147, 190, 201

National Action Committee on the Status of Women (NAC), 101, 152, 206, 210–12, 219n8, 221n27, 241nn25 & 27
National Anti-Poverty Organization (NAPO), 88
National Child Benefit Supplement, 177
Native Women's Association of Canada (NWAC), 89
neoconservatism, 159, 217n5, 224n25

neo-institutionalism, 18, 24–7, 28, 29, 30, 32, 33–5, 38, 40, 49, 53, 54, 219n7. See also feminist institutionalism
neoliberalism, 4, 5, 6, 8, 9, 11, 13, 14, 15, 20, 21, 34, 36, 44, 47, 51, 52, 55, 57, 58, 62, 69, 78, 79–94, 95, 99, 104, 105, 114, 144, 146–85, 186, 187, 189, 190, 191, 192, 205, 215, 232n2, 235n70, 238n109, 241n31. See also New Public Management
neutrality, 4, 9, 20, 31, 42, 58, 62, 63, 67–74, 75, 95, 97–8, 100, 104, 105, 120, 130–41, 143, 156–8, 161–2, 188, 196–201, 221nn1 & 5. See also advocacy
New Brunswick: Advisory Council, 76, 91; Minister Responsible for the Status of Women, 76; Women's Directorate, 76, 91; Women's Equality Branch, 91; Women's Issues Branch, 76
New Democratic Party (NDP), 14, 15, 17, 106, 107, 108, 111–13, 116, 117, 119, 120, 121–2, 125–6, 130, 132, 135–6, 142, 151, 152, 159, 160, 187–8, 197, 224n4, 225n10, 227nn52 & 54, 230n118, 231n134, 236n75, 238n108, 239n131
Newfoundland and Labrador, 128; Minister Responsible for the Status of Women, 76; Provincial Advisory Council, 76; Women's Policy Unit, 76
New Left, 81
Newman, Jacquetta, 103
New Public Management (NPM), 9–10, 13, 14, 15, 19, 20, 36, 57, 62, 78, 79–94, 95–105, 114, 145, 146–85,

186, 188, 190, 198, 205, 233n20, 235nn47 & 56
New Right, 81, 93, 167
non-governmental organizations (NGOs), 23, 111, 169, 187, 193
non-traditional occupations, 114, 115, 118–19, 172–80, 227n52, 238n114
Northwest Territories (NWT), 76, 128; Minister Responsible for the Status of Women, 76; Special Advisor to the Minister Responsible for the Status of Women, 76; Status of Women Council, 76; Women's Directorate, 76, 91
Nova Scotia: Advisory Council on the Status of Women, 76
Nunavut, 76; Minister Responsible for Status of Women Council, 76; Qulliit Nunavut Status of Women Council, 76

Office of the Coordinator for the Status of Women in the Privy Council Office, 75
Office of Equal Opportunities for Women, 77–8
Office for People with Disabilities (OPD), 125
Office of the Senior Advisor on Aboriginal Women's Issues and Gender Equality (Indian and Northern Affairs Canada), 75
Office of the Senior Advisor on Gender Equality (Justice Canada), 75. See also Diversity, Equality and Access to Justice Division; Diversity and Gender Equality Office
Older Women's Network (OWN), 239

Omnibus Bill (Savings and Restructuring Bill, Ontario), 148, 168
O'Neil, Maureen, 64, 223n19
Ontario, 127
Ontario Child Benefit, 183
Ontario Coalition for Better Child Care (OCBCC), 120
Ontario Council on the Status of Women, 76. See also Advisory Council on Women's Issues (Ontario)
Ontario Native Affairs Secretariat (ONAS), 126
Ontario Public Service (OPS), 17, 107, 109, 110, 114, 134, 164, 186, 188, 194, 240n19
Ontario Skills Development Strategy, 114
Ontario Training and Adjustment Board (OTAB), 119, 168, 181, 227n54
Ontario Women's Action on Training Coalition, 209
Ontario Women's Directorate (OWD), 14, 16, 17, 20, 42, 44, 55, 66–7, 70, 76, 89–90, 91, 104, 105–45, 146–85, 186, 187, 188, 190, 192, 194, 196, 197, 199, 205, 208, 216, 223n22, 224n2, 225n24, 226n34, 231n138, 232nn2, 10, & 13, 233nn23, 31, & 37, 238n120; budget, 107, 120, 121, 150, 152–3, 164, 232n10; and compartmentalization, 20, 63, 66–7, 98, 100, 104, 117, 120, 121, 124–30, 141, 154–5, 192, 233n31, 235n49, 236n83; creation of, 106–7, 120; and diversity, 42, 66–7, 98, 111–14, 117, 119, 123, 125–6, 135–40, 142–4, 152, 156, 180, 192, 200, 209, 230n125, 238n110; and feminism,

108, 109–11, 114, 124, 130–5, 137–9,
143–4, 151–2, 161–2, 224n10,
239n131; labour market policy, 17,
70, 95, 114–20, 152, 155, 172–84,
227n52, 238n110; mandate, 14, 66,
106–8, 109, 111, 113, 116, 120, 124,
130–41, 142–3, 151, 153–66, 179,
223n22, 224n2, 225n24, 226n34,
232n13, 233n37; marginalization,
44, 110, 112, 120–30, 141, 150–85,
188, 194–5, 197, 232n13, 237n91;
and New Public Management
regime, 20, 55, 89–90, 95–6, 98, 104,
114, 145, 146–85, 188, 198, 232n13,
233n20, 237nn91 & 107, 238n110;
relationship with community, 17,
18, 55, 109–14, 117–18, 119, 130–41,
143–4, 153–4, 156, 168–73, 176,
196–7, 199, 205, 207–9, 223n22,
225n10, 236n87; staffing, 17, 107,
109–10, 112–13, 120, 134–8, 142–3,
152–3, 162–3; structure, 14–15,
17, 107–10, 112, 120–1, 123, 150–2,
156–7, 194–6, 223n22, 224n2,
230n125, 234n42; and Weberian
regime, 20, 55, 66–7, 78, 96, 104,
105–45, 157, 188. See also advocacy;
neutrality; state feminism
Open Doors, 114, 178
Osborne, David, 80, 81, 85, 94, 222n15
Our Fair Share campaign, 212, 221n27
outcomes-based measurement, 85,
149, 163, 165–7, 236n75. See also
managerialism; performance
measurement
Outshoorn, Joyce, 15, 48–9, 113, 114,
150, 205, 232n2

Panitch, Leo, 6, 13, 189, 200, 205, 208,
213, 215, 241n30 .

parental leave, 115, 226n45
Parliamentary Joint Committee on
the Improvement of the Quality of
Life and Status of Women (South
Africa), 193
parliamentary system, 67, 94, 131.
See also accountability (ministerial
responsibility)
Parliamentary Women's Caucus
(Uganda), 193
participatory budget, 99
participatory democracy, 4, 8–9,
11–12, 14, 20, 44–5, 58–61, 71, 76,
89, 92, 99, 101–4, 112, 122, 130, 144,
167–8, 170, 191, 193, 194, 196, 197,
199–201, 204, 208, 210–16, 241n29.
See also democratic administration;
femocratic administration; gender
democracy
Partners for Change, 169, 183, 237n93
patchwork, 50. See also childcare
path dependency, 26, 28, 40
patriarchy, 31, 41, 43, 50, 51, 56, 142,
215, 216, 220n20, 242n33
Pay Equity, 70, 107, 108, 115, 116–17,
120, 125, 137–8, 147, 175, 181–2,
183, 188, 206, 220n13, 231n134,
238n120
pension reform, 114–15, 127, 128, 138
performance measurement. See
accountability; outcomes-based
measurement; managerialism; and
New Public Management
Peters, Guy, 80, 191, 222n10, 223n24,
234n43
Peterson, David, 14, 106, 116, 130,
132, 135, 160, 234n48
Philipps, Lisa, 158, 234n47
Phillips, Anne, 12, 58, 101, 103, 191,
213, 239n5, 241n29

Phillips, Susan, 4, 60, 159, 201, 211
Pierre, Jon, 79, 145, 222nn10 & 11, 223n24, 231n154, 234n43
pluralism, 32, 39, 67
political economy, 18, 19, 30, 37, 38, 39, 43, 47, 49, 54, 94, 198. *See also* feminist political economy
political opportunity structure (POS), 34, 48, 89
political parties, 15, 36, 44, 48, 58, 68, 73, 100, 106, 110, 201, 205, 211
politicization of public service, 70, 81, 86, 98, 158, 190, 223n24, 234n46
politics-administration dichotomy, 68. *See also* advocacy; neutrality
Pollit, Christopher, 86
Porter, Ann, 18, 40, 46, 52, 55, 141, 206, 218n11, 220n20, 221n2
Porto Alegre, Brazil, 191, 215
post-colonialism, 37, 43, 50, 220n15. *See also* feminism
post-structuralism, 37, 41, 43, 219n3, 220n15. *See also* feminism
Poulantzas, Nicos, 41, 43, 71
poverty, 3, 81, 88, 115, 128, 138, 166, 168, 170, 177, 178, 180, 181, 183. *See also* feminization of poverty
Poverty and Human Rights Project (PHRP), 88
precarious employment, 3, 84, 117, 124, 181, 183, 203, 214
Prince Edward Island (PEI): Advisory Council on the Status of Women, 76; Women's Secretariat, 76
privatization, 5, 8, 15, 20, 42, 62, 79–82, 83, 84, 86, 93, 104, 146, 147, 158, 165, 184, 190, 222n10, 234n47. *See also* neoliberalism; New Public Management; re-privatization
Privy Council Office (PCO), 75, 195

procedural democracy. *See* democracy
procedural representation / descriptive representation, 9, 73, 75, 88, 100, 103, 204
production, 5, 16, 19, 32, 45, 46, 52, 53, 57, 58, 59, 64, 65, 66, 68, 115. *See also* social reproduction
Progressive Conservative (PC) party / Tories, 14, 15, 17, 89, 107, 114, 117, 145, 147, 149, 150–1, 152, 153, 154, 155, 156, 159, 160, 166, 168, 169, 170, 171, 172, 173, 175, 176, 178, 179, 180, 181, 182, 183, 188, 210, 223n19, 227nn48, 50, & 52, 233nn18 & 20, 235n60, 236n84, 237n107, 238nn108 & 110, 239n131, 241n27. *See also* neoliberalism; New Public Management
project-based funding, 90, 218n8
Pross, Paul, 198, 240n15
public choice theory, 80, 99
public education, 106, 112, 115, 177, 206
public/private divide, 31, 50, 51, 52, 58, 64, 65, 100, 241n29. *See also* sexual division of labour; social reproduction; unpaid labour
public-private partnerships, 79, 88, 149, 165, 236n85
Public Service Commission of Canada, 77
Public Service Reform Act, 83
Public Service 2000 (PS 2000), 83, 85
Public Services Employment Act, 77

Quebec, 4, 44, 101, 121, 126, 128, 190, 194, 219n10; Conseil du statut de la femme, 76, 121, 207, 208; Ministère responsable de la Condition de la

femme, 76; Secretariat à la condition feminine, 76
queer theory, 36, 50, 53. *See also* feminism; intersectionality

Race Relations Directorate (RRD), 66,
98, 112, 192
racialization, 3, 4, 6, 50–4, 173. *See also*
anti-racist strategy; intersectionality; racism; women of colour
racism, 50, 52, 66, 98, 101, 112, 113,
125, 136, 137, 138, 211, 238n110. *See
also* feminism (post-colonial/anti-
racist); intersectionality; racialization; women of colour
Rae, Bob, 14, 106, 108, 122, 130, 144, 155
Randall, Melanie, 55, 56, 59
Rankin, Pauline, 7, 15, 55, 69, 87, 89,
91, 98–9, 108, 126, 130, 150, 194,
194, 199–200, 209, 225n25
rational choice, 25, 36, 47, 219n2. *See
also* neo-institutionalism; public
choice
rationalization, 89, 91, 221n1. *See
also* managerialism; New Public
Management
Reagan, Ronald, 223n24
REAL Women, 210. *See also*
anti-feminism
Rebick, Judy, 6, 60, 190, 210, 218n7
Red Tape Secretariat, 148–9
representation. *See* democracy; procedural representation; state feminism; substantive representation
representative bureaucracy. *See*
bureaucracy
re-privatization, 82, 158, 190, 234n47.
See also privatization
re-scaling, 86, 87, 88, 192. *See also* decentralization; multiscaler analysis

Research Network on Gender Politics
and the State (RNGS), 196
Resource Mobilization Theory, 48
Roach, Kiké, 8, 210
Roadmap to Prosperity, 236n86
Robinson, Ian, 19, 220n14
Rönnblom, Malin, 219n3
Rowat, Donald C., 221n5
Royal Commission on Bilingualism
and Biculturalism, 77
Royal Commission on Equality in
Employment, 78
Royal Commission on the Status of
Women (RCSW), 74
Rupp, Leila J., 12

Sainsbury, Diane, 16, 220n25
Saskatchewan, 128; Advisory Council
on the Status of Women, 76; Status
of Women, 91; Women's Secre-
tariat, 76, 91
Sauer, Birgit, 48, 49, 150, 218n13
Savings and Restructuring Bill, 148.
See also Omnibus Bill
Savoie, Donald, 83, 86, 223n24,
234n43
Sawer, Marian, 6, 27, 31, 34, 35, 36,
63, 92, 93, 99, 159, 191, 204, 218nn8
& 10
scientific management, 86, 98, 221n1.
See also gender regime (Weberian)
Scott, Ian, 108
Scott, Katherine, 82, 182, 239n124
Sears, Alan, 178
Sector Partnership Fund, 168
Sekhon, Joti, 60, 221n27
Selden, Sally, 196
self-employment, 84, 85, 128, 129, 147,
172, 173–6, 183, 227n52, 238n108.
See also entrepreneurialism

sex segregation, 3, 83, 117, 118, 119, 122, 175–6, 220n13

sexual division of labour, 8, 45–7, 48, 52–3, 58–9, 64–5, 82, 87, 115, 120, 173, 179–84, 191–2, 213–15, 218n14, 241n33. *See also* public/private divide; social reproduction; unpaid work

sexual harassment, 70, 118, 178, 217n1

sexual orientation, 8, 12, 35, 51, 52–3, 67, 79, 215. *See also* feminism (queer); intersectionality; queer theory

Shields, John, 5, 81, 84, 85, 86, 92, 94, 145, 215, 217nn4 & 5, 223n24, 234n43, 241n31

Simard, Carolle, 211

Simeon, Richard, 19, 220n14

Skocpol, Theda, 28

Smith, Miriam, 25, 29, 32, 35

social assistance, 4, 41, 66, 79, 81, 115, 120, 132, 137, 147, 158, 168, 177, 180, 189, 190, 220n13, 237n94, 238n120. *See also* "spouse in the house"

Social Contract, 224n4

social control, 46, 215

social democracy, 9, 14, 15, 56, 145, 201

social reproduction, 19, 31–2, 37, 38, 45–7, 49, 52, 53, 54, 57, 58–9, 61, 64–5, 71, 82, 87, 115, 158, 184, 213, 214, 215, 234n47. *See also* public/private divide; sexual division of labour; unpaid labour; work-family balance

social rights, 86, 209. *See also* citizenship

Social Union Framework Agreement (SUFA), 88, 208–9

sociological institutionalism, 25. *See also* neo-institutionalism

Sossin, Lorne, 13, 68, 81, 189, 200, 240n17

"special interest" groups, 7, 71–2, 95, 98, 99, 158, 160, 168, 170, 197, 224n25

"spouse in the house," 137, 220n13, 237n94, 238n120. *See also* social assistance

state feminism, 6–8, 9, 12–15, 16, 18, 19–21, 24, 31–2, 48–50, 57, 59, 60, 69–70, 89–94, 97–104, 105–45, 147–85, 185–216, 217n2, 218nn8, 9, & 13, 223n17. *See also* femocrats

state funding, 210–12, 221n27

state-market-family nexus, 41, 46, 47, 58. *See also* feminist political economy

Status of Women Canada (SWC), 44, 70, 75, 90, 135, 152, 214, 218n8, 223n25, 241nn26 & 28

Stetson, Dorothy, 7, 103

Stivers, Camilla, 4, 13, 65, 66, 69, 71, 74, 143, 196–7, 201, 216, 217n1

structural inequality, 30, 36, 37, 38–45, 53–4, 56, 61, 65, 115, 124, 147, 176, 185

subsidiarity principle, 34

substantive democracy. *See* democracy

substantive representation, 9, 73, 75, 88, 100, 103, 150, 196, 198, 204

Sutherland, Sharon, 64, 223n19

Swarbrick, Anne, 108, 228n77

systemic discrimination, 30, 54, 74, 78, 95, 96, 173, 180, 181, 193, 223n23, 238n110

Taylor, Verta, 12

Taylorism, 66

technocratic approaches, 98–9
Teghtsoonian, Katherine, 93, 211,
    234n38, 236n75, 238n108
Thatcher, Margaret, 79, 147, 223n24
think tank, 81, 223n24
third sector. *See* voluntary sector
Thompson, Grahame, 217n3
Tobin, Ann, 66
Total Quality Management (TQM),
    85, 86
Training, 17, 77, 112, 114, 115, 117–19,
    123, 125, 126, 127, 128, 135, 140,
    147, 151, 176, 178, 181, 182, 209,
    222n16, 223n16, 227n53, 238nn108,
    114, & 122; Training Access Fund,
    114. *See also* A Commitment to
    Training and Employment for
    Women (ACTEW); Ontario Train-
    ing and Adjustment Board (OTAB)
Tremblay, Manon, 103
Trickey, Jean, 238n110
Trimble, Linda, 103

Unemployment Insurance (UI), 11,
    45, 193, 220n13. *See also* Employ-
    ment Insurance
unequal structure of representation,
    7, 58, 195. *See also* Findlay, Sue;
    institutionalization of power rela-
    tions; Mahon, Rianne
unitary system, 33
United Nations Development Fund
    for Women (UNIFEM), 193
United Nations Experts Advisory
    Group on National Machineries, 89
United Nations Platform for Action,
    192–3
unpaid work, 3, 8, 45–6, 52, 82,
    87, 115, 173, 213–14, 222n14.
    See also public/private divide;

sexual division of labour; social
    reproduction
Urban Alliance on Race Relations,
    117

Vickers, Jill, 27, 28, 31, 34, 35, 36, 39,
    69, 89, 91, 98–9, 100, 126, 130, 194,
    199, 200, 202, 203, 204, 209, 211
Victorian Order of Nurses (VON), 84
violence against women, 4, 14, 17,
    42, 51, 93, 102, 110, 111, 114, 116,
    121, 123, 125, 129, 134, 138, 151,
    164, 165, 172, 177, 179, 180, 181,
    194, 205, 218n12, 224n10, 235n60,
    237n107
visible minority women. *See* women
    of colour
voluntary sector, 46, 66, 80, 81, 82, 87,
    88, 151, 158, 178, 190, 214, 219n11,
    234n47, 239n4
Voluntary Sector Forum, 88

wage gap, 3, 84, 116, 128, 166, 173
Wainwright, Hilary, 69, 101, 196, 201,
    240n21, 241n31
Walby, Sylvia, 57, 218n14
Waring, Marilyn, 214, 242n34
Waylen, Georgina, 25, 28, 29, 38, 39
Weber, Max, 12, 63, 65, 66, 68, 69,
    70–1, 132, 136
Weberian regime. *See* bureaucracy
    (Weberian); gender regime
Weinroth, Michelle, 148, 149
Wekerle, Gerda R., 196
Welch, Robert, 128, 224n3
Weldon, Laurel, 211
welfare regime, 15–16, 33, 55–7, 58.
    See also gender regime
welfare state, 15–16, 31, 33, 46, 51,
    52, 55–6, 81, 82, 86–7, 97, 105, 106,

145, 171. *See also* Keynesian Welfare
  State (KWS)
Westminster system, 67
White, Graham, 33
White, Linda, 87, 103, 209
Wilcox, Krista D., 99
Wilson, Mavis, 132
Wilson, Seymour V., 73, 221nn1 & 5
Wolfe, Judy, 17, 125, 131, 136, 139,
  140, 151, 154, 165, 167, 182, 183,
  226n45, 227n54, 231n134, 237n107,
  239n132
women of colour, 3, 42, 50–4, 59, 66,
  75, 81, 89, 98–9, 106, 109, 111–14,
  117–18, 123, 125, 133, 135, 137–8,
  143, 151–2, 173, 180, 181, 192, 196,
  200, 203–4, 207, 209, 211, 218n8,
  220n20, 228nn75 & 81, 233n18,
  238n114. *See also* feminism (post-
  colonial/anti-racist); racism;
  racialization
Women Crown Employees Office,
  107
Women in Skilled Trades (WIST), 166
Women in Skilled Trades and Information Technology Training, 176
Women's Bureau: Canada, 70, 75, 206,
  221n6; Ontario, 107
women's centres, 110, 111, 165, 168
women's economic independence,
  14, 45, 47, 114, 120, 125, 138, 155,
  157, 172, 177, 179, 180
Women's Health Bureau (Health
  Canada), 75
Women's Issues and Gender Equality
  Directorate (WIGE), 75

women's movement, 7, 9, 12, 13,
  15, 17, 18, 34, 35, 40, 44, 48–9, 50,
  59, 60, 69, 73, 74, 87–8, 91, 94, 97,
  99–101, 103–4, 106, 109, 110, 113,
  130, 131, 133–5, 139, 140–1, 142,
  144, 150, 157, 161, 171, 182, 186,
  188–91, 195, 196–7, 199, 205, 206–7,
  208, 210, 212–13, 219n8, 240n13;
  Australia, 44, 74, 102, 194, 206;
  Quebec, 44, 101, 207
women's policy machinery / structures
  of representation, 6–7, 14, 15, 20,
  44–5, 48–9, 57, 59, 66, 69–78, 89–91,
  95, 98, 102–3, 106–14, 121–2, 124–45,
  146–72, 184, 194–6, 205, 208, 211,
  217n2, 223nn20, 22, & 25, 224nn3 &
  6, 228n75, 232n2, 233n37, 234n38,
  241nn26 & 28. *See also* Ontario
  Women's Directorate; state feminism
Women's Program (Canada), 75,
  77, 90, 91, 159, 190, 206, 211, 212,
  230n119, 241n26
Wood, Ellen, 241n29
work-family balance, 47, 59, 115,
  218n8, 226n44. *See also* sexual division of labour; social reproduction;
  unpaid work
working time, 213, 215
World Bank, 48, 99
World March of Women, 221n27
Wyckoff-Wheeler, Donna, 12

Young, Lisa, 34, 219nn8 & 9
Yukon: Advisory Council on Wom-
  en's Issues, 91; Women's Directorate, 76, 91, 223